The
VELVET
UNDERGROUND
Companion

The VELVET UNDERGROUND *Companion*

Four Decades of Commentary

Edited by
ALBIN ŻAK

OMNIBUS PRESS
LONDON • NEW YORK • SYDNEY

ISBN: 0.7119.6719.9
Order No: OP 48026

Printed in the United States of America

Exclusive Distributors
Book Sales Limited,
8/9 Frith Street,
London W1V 5TZ, UK.

To the Music Trade Only:
Music Sales Limited,
8/9 Frith Street,
London W1V 5TZ, UK.

A catalogue for this book is available from the British Library.

Visit Omnibus Press at http://www.musicsales.co.uk

This paper meets the requirements of ANSI/NISO Z39.48-1992 (Permanence of Paper).

for Richard Kassel,
composer, scholar, and Velvet Underground fan

Contents

Acknowledgments

This book has been mostly a lonely undertaking—researching, tracking down material, and editing. Still, it would never have come about without the help of several people. Thanks are due first of all to Joseph Darby for steering me to Richard Carlin at Schirmer, who instantly took an enthusiastic interest in the project. He and the rest of the folks at Schirmer have been unfailingly helpful.

Richard Kostelanetz generously offered initial guidance in the permission quest racket. Richard Kassel brought some overlooked items to my attention (as is his habit) and generally led the cheering. Most of all, however, I would like to thank all of the contributors for lending their talents and passion to the project, for, in the end, they are responsible for the book's success. Of these, I should single out M.C. Kostek and Ignacio Julià for their generous and honorable assistance.

Preface

"They were the stark, elusive balloon that burst upon an inflated scene, injecting that scene with a radiance that connected poetry, the avant-garde and rock & roll. They were a band of opposites, shooting freely from pole to pole, without apology, with dissonant beauty, trampling the flowers of peacemakers, treading the blond depths, black in a white world, white in a black world. They opened wounds worth opening, with brutal innocence, without apology, cutting across the grain, gritty, urbanic. And in their search for the kingdom, for laughter, for salvation, they explored the darkest areas of the psyche."

—*Patti Smith*

This book owes its existence first of all to the fans of the Velvet Underground. An old cliché has it that though there were relatively few of those during the band's existence, they all went on to start bands of their own. That would help to explain the unlikely, yet profound and continuing influence the Velvets have had on rock during the last three decades. In this scenario, they are the inspirational source whose seeds were carried far and wide by devoted acolytes. But this version of the story gives too much credit to the band and too little to the fans. The Velvets were less a source than a symbol and a mirror. For those to whom the band meant so much, it represented confirmation of a deeply held, yet perhaps unarticulated belief in rock itself: that this music—so bound up with the workings of industrial capitalism, pimply teenage fantasies, and absurd celebrity poseurs—could yet be a revelation of truth, a way of knowing and understanding, a way of getting through. The belief that rock was above all a path of possibility already existed when the Velvets came along. Their fans believed in rock and roll with all their hearts, or at least wanted to. They were waiting, perhaps unconsciously, for a band that would embody and reflect upon them the light of their own faith. And whether they had any idea what that would mean, they recognized it when they heard it.

Philip Milstein, for one, knew when he heard *The Velvet Underground and Nico* for the first time that he would "never see things quite the same way again." In 1977, he and M.C. Kostek started the Velvet Underground Appreciation Society and the fanzine *What Goes On,* in whose pages many of the pieces in this collection first appeared. Against many odds, economic and otherwise, *What Goes On* continues to come out once every five or six years, a labor of love carried on by Kostek (perhaps the world's greatest Velvet Underground scholar) with the help and goodwill of various contributors. Paul Williams and Lester Bangs were among the earliest published proselytizers for the band. Williams takes obvious pleasure in spreading the news of this music that "has a revelation to offer in almost every area!" Bangs wrote about the band and its members often over the years, but he expressed the depth of his commitment most succinctly when he wrote, "I would suck Lou Reed's cock, because I would also kiss the feet of them that drafted the Magna Carta." Liberation has many forms.

It is said that the power of faith is fueled by the fires of passion. And the Velvets' fans were as certain of the revealed truth they had discovered as they were few in number. Once they glimpsed the "sea of electric possibilities in Rock And Roll," as Kostek had in his first Velvet encounter in 1968, they began to testify to the fact that rock and roll, in the right hands, could in fact save one's very soul. In the words of Spanish rock journalist Ignacio Julià, "We, the Velvet Underground fanatics, are a very serious bunch." It is their seriousness that has sustained the band's memory by proudly displaying the Velvet Underground influence, circulating and collecting the bootlegs, tracking down and collecting oral histories from band members, and over time building what has become the legend and myth of the Velvet Underground.

Many bands have been influential. Many bands have failed to attain popularity in their time. Rarely in rock, however, are these two conditions combined and never to the degree seen with the Velvets. When the band was inducted into the Rock and Roll Hall of Fame in 1986, John Cale said it showed that "(record) sales are not the be-all and end-all. Inspiration and artistic freedom are the cornerstones of rock and roll." Because it was not a commercial success, the Velvet Underground represents a cultural nexus whose significance is yet to be fully grasped. As the most influential unpopular pop band in history, the Velvets embodied a new kind of artistic reality, one that merged the ultraromantic ideology and challenging noises of avant-garde modernism with the attitudes and rhythms of pop culture.

The Velvets operated in the ragged seam between "high" and "low" art that opened up in the 1960s and has grown increasingly irritating (to some) and fascinating (to others) ever since. Their work posed fundamental aesthetic questions that have been taken up again and again by succeeding generations of artists (e.g., the Stooges, Patti Smith, Jonathan Richman, Joy Division, R.E.M., Nirvana) and have become central to cultural debates in general. For those who view pop music as primarily a disposable commodity whose value is measured in sales units, the case of the Velvets is especially problematic. Their records were utter failures as commodities, yet have become extremely successful as . . . artworks. Their commercial failure dictated that the records be made for next to nothing, but even this did not diminish their artistic success. Their sonic rawness has added to their aura of authenticity, increasing their symbolic, and ultimately mythic, power. As Kostek puts it, "The Velvets existed to tell, not to sell."

The influences of Delmore Schwartz, Hubert Selby Jr., LaMonte Young, and Andy Warhol were part of the bedrock of the Velvets. So was rock and roll. Although pop-as-art debates—usually centered around the Beatles or Bob Dylan—were already common in 1965, when the Velvet Underground was officially formed, it was still unclear how broad a range of expressive possibility this music for teenagers could legitimately offer or how much artistic exploration it could sustain. The Velvets proved that rock could be stripped of its status as a popular music almost altogether and enter upon new paths of possibility that stretched the music's context and frame, yet still resonate with the spirits of Elvis Presley, Fats Domino, and Johnny Ace.

The story of the Velvet Underground has been told many times, but in this collection there are two very personal versions of the story, told from the points of view of the band members themselves. The Maureen Tucker interview, conducted over a period of ten years beginning in 1980, is as straightforward as her drumming, or her singing on "Afterhours," revealing just how deep and pure are her love for this music and her appreciation for the opportunity to have played with the Velvets. Sterling Morrison's recollections, upon which Ignacio Julià's *Feedback: The Legend of the Velvet Underground* is based, are those of a wise and articulate soul who left the trappings of the rock world in 1971 after the band dissolved. As Julià puts it, "Sterling's memories of that time are of a life rich in music, fun, and young vitality. For him, it is the experience itself, and not the results, that are important." Indeed, Morrison's recollections and comments have a reasoned detachment to them, an unhyped, real-life tone that consistently resists any misty nostalgia.

Cale and Lou Reed have been somewhat more reticent about the band, clearly enjoying their association with a rock legend, yet wary of detracting from their own post–Velvet Underground careers. The band was larger than its parts, and neither of these two former Velvet Underground members, whatever fine work they have produced since the band's breakup, would wish to compete with a thing that has passed into the realm of myth. Nor would Lennon or McCartney wish to compete with the Beatles, or Robbie Robertson with The Band. Like all great bands, the Velvet Underground represents a confluence of time, place, personalities, and art. The band is a symbol and a mirror, and it's come to mean more than any of its members could have envisioned.

In the summer of 1970, new mother Maureen Tucker went to see her band play at Max's Kansas City. "I didn't hate it," she recalled later, "but it wasn't the Velvets. To me, there were only two Velvets there, Lou and Sterling. And it didn't work. It was a nice, tight little band. But it wasn't the Velvets." In the midst of that series of gigs at Max's, Reed left the band and returned to his parents' home in Long Island. Cale had been booted two years and albums previously. The Velvet Underground was finished as a band. But as the focal point of a cult of rock and roll true believers, it was just getting started. Keepers of the flame continued to emerge from their encounters with Velvet Underground records with great tales to tell—personal tales of faith, salvation, beauty, and power. Together, they gradually built the Velvet Underground we know today.

Inasmuch as artworks come to life as they are encountered and experienced, the space between the work and the listener is where the life force resides, fed by a two-way exchange of energy. The Velvet Underground's fans have continued to expand and deepen that space. In the process, they continually renew and extend the value of the works, and their acts of conscious engagement and appreciation serve to enrich the culture in which we live. Some of their stories are in this book.

PART ONE

The
Exploding
Plastic
Inevitable

GRACE GLUECK
SYNDROMES POP AT DELMONICO'S (1966)

Before Andy Warhol "produced" the Velvets' first album, he enlisted them to supply the music for his *Exploding Plastic Inevitable,* a multimedia event that also included film, dance, and various conceptual stunts. Grace Glueck's and Linda LaMarre's contemporary newspaper accounts represent fairly common reactions to the *EPI.*

Andy Warhol and His Gang Meet the Psychiatrist

The New York Society for Clinical Psychiatry survived an invasion last night by Andy Warhol, Edie Sedgwick and a new rock 'n' roll group called "The Velvet Underground."

"The Chic Mystique of Andy Warhol," described by an associate of the painter as "a kind of community action-underground-look-at-your-self-film project," was billed as the evening's entertainment for the psychiatry society's 43d annual dinner at Delmonico's Hotel. And until the very last minute, neither group quite believed the other would show up.

But sure enough, as the black-tied psychiatrists and their formally gowned wives began to trickle into Delmonico's lobby at 6:30, there was Andy, and in evening get-up, too—sunglasses, black tie, dinner jacket and corduroy work pants. And right there with him were some of his "factory" hands—Gerard Malanga, poet; Dannie Williams, cameraman, and the "factory" foreman, Billy Lunich.

3

The "factory," as any Warhol buff knows, is the big, silver-lined loft where he and his coterie make their underground films and help mass-produce Andy's art.

What "The Chic Mystique" was nobody really explained. The Warhol part of the program included a showing of his underground films as background for cocktail conversation and, at dinner, a concert by the rock 'n' roll group. And Warhol and his cameramen moved among the gathering with hand-held cameras, using the psychiatrists as the cast of a forthcoming Warhol movie.

The psychiatrists who turned out in droves for the dinner, were there to be entertained—but also, in a way, to study Andy. "Creativity and the artist have always held a fascination for the serious student of human behavior," said Dr. Robert Campbell, the program chairman. "And we're fascinated by the mass communications activities of Warhol and his group."

Delmonico's elegant white-and-gold Colonnade and Grand Ballroom had probably never seen such a swinging scene. Edie Sedgwick, the "superstar" of Warhol's movies, was on full blast—chewing gum and sipping a martini.

There was John Cale, leader of "The Velvet Underground," in a black suit with rhinestones on the collar. There was Nico, identified by Warhol as "a famous fashion model and now a singer," in a white slack suit with long blond hair. And there were all those psychiatrists, away from their couches but not really mingling, not letting their hair down at all.

"I suppose you could call this gathering a spontaneous eruption of the id," said Dr. Alfred Lilienthal. "Warhol's message is one of super-reality," said another, "a repetition of the concrete quite akin to the L.S.D. experience." "Why are they exposing us to these nuts?" a third asked. "But don't quote me."

Dr. Arthur Zitrin, director of psychiatry at Bellevue Hospital, was slightly worried. "We've had everyone appear at these annual dinners, from Paul Tillich to Warhol," he said. "I'm program chairman for next year. How the hell are we going to follow this act?"

The act really came into its own about midway though the dinner (roast beef with stringbeans and small potatoes), when "The Velvet Underground," swung into action. The high-decibel sound, aptly described by Dr. Campbell as "a short-lived torture of cacophony," was a combination of rock 'n' roll and Egyptian belly-dance music.

The evening ended with a short talk by Jonas Mekas, film director and critic. But long before that, guests had begun to stream out. The reaction of the early departees was fairly unanimous. "Put it down as decadent

Dada," said one. "It was ridiculous, outrageous, painful," said Dr. Harry Weinstock. "Everything that's new doesn't necessarily have meaning. It seemed like a whole prison ward had escaped."

"You want to do something for mental health?" asked another psychiatrist. "Kill the story."

LINDA LAMARRE

MOTHER'S MOD LAMENT:
"NOT THE WEDDING WE HAD PLANNED" (1966)

Holy matrimony was replaced by unholy pandemonium in what was billed as a wedding yesterday at the State Fairgrounds Coliseum.

It was marriage in the Mod Tradition. The country's first. And let's hope it's not what's happening, baby.

Wearing a white minigown, eight inches over her knees and white, thigh-high boots, Randy Rossi, 18, became the bride of clothing salesman Gary Norris, 25, amid a melange of simultaneous "happenings."

Andy Warhol, of soup can painting fame and the "father of Pop art," arrived from New York to give away the bride. With him came his rock 'n' roll group, the Velvet Underground, vocalist Nico, and the Exploding Plastic Inevitable, Warhol's gaudy lighting effects.

Some 4,500 shaggy-haired wedding guests swarmed the arena for the prenuptial rituals. Electronic devices screamed, guitars and drums throbbed and a fiddle added to the din as purple and orange lights splashed dots and squares across the stage.

"Hey, we're really witnessing something, it's history, history!" a young girl shouted.

Huddled on the sidelines were the bride's parents, Mr. and Mrs. John Rossi, of Mt. Clemens, the bridegroom's mother, Mrs. Thelma Norris, of Taylor, his sister and brother-in-law, the Robert Wionceks, of Dearborn.

"It's not the kind of wedding we had planned for our daughter," Mrs. Rossi said, as eerie screeches emitted from the stage.

"He's old enough to know his own mind," Mrs. Norris added, while Nico, clad in lavender pantsuit, cupped the mike in both hands and began moaning some song.

After an eternity of noise, a black Rolls-Royce with the bridal couple slowly backed into the arena. The pair wisely chose to stay inside the car a few moments.

Warhol's psychedelic sounds, which seek to create the same illusion as mind-expanding drugs, succeeded.

Gerard [Malanga], the whip dancer, slithered and spun across the darkened stage. Another member of the cast hopped atop a wrecked DeSoto, bashing it with a sledge hammer.

Paint Paper Dress

"If I take to love, will I find you gone," groaned Nico. Warhol ascended the platform, paint bucket and catsup bottles in hand. Contents of both containers were carefully applied to a girl wearing a white paper dress throughout the proceedings.

The bride smiled as she marched up the platform steps. The bridegroom wore a gray checked, Beatle-type suit, black boots, green and white flowered tie. He looked sober.

The couple volunteered for the Mod wedding, which concluded the three-day Carnaby Street Fun Festival. Their reward, a free honeymoon in New York and screen test with Warhol.

After giving away the bride Warhol sat serenely upon a box of tomato soup, autographing cans. A color film of Nico's face flickered on and off the back curtains as she read a few appropriate, but indistinguishable sentences from a yellow book.

A Wedding Gift

Another member of the cast paraded with a five-foot Baby Ruth candy bar balloon, Warhol's gift to the newlyweds.

Judge David L. Golden, of Highland Park, conducted the ceremony to pulsating rhythms from drums and guitars. "You may kiss the bride," he concluded. Vigorous applause followed.

It was over. But things were still happening. The 4,500 skinny, young bodies swayed toward the stage, toward cake, catsup and soup cans.

M.C. KOSTEK
BEGINNING TO SEE THE DARK (1978)

Outside the circuslike atmosphere of the *EPI*, the focus was on the music, which struck some as the ultimate rock and roll truth. Here are three very big VU fans—M.C. Kostek and Philip Milstein, founders of *What Goes On,* and Paul Williams, the originator of *Crawdaddy!*—testifying to their experiences of the band's epiphanic power.

"This next song's called 'Heroin.'" The thin figure dressed in black on stage looks nervously around. "It's not, uh, for or against it. It's just about it." The two South Deerfield, Mass. cops at the side entrances are momentarily distracted from their evening's boredom (the only relief provided by teen drunks and gate-sneakers). Now this weird-o with black leather jacket and sunglasses is talking to them about heroin. The cops gaze up blearily as the Velvet Underground begins the slow walk of "Hair-row-in."

March, 1968. I am 16, and consequently walking down the halls of Greenfield High School to driver education class. Neatly tacked to the Things To Do bulletin board is this great poster, with the photo from the back of the *White Light/White Heat* album, advertising an upcoming concert with admission prices of "$2.75; Chicks 50c off." A striking black and white invitation to see the Velvet Underground at the Woodrose Ballroom, in nearby South Deerfield. Now I don't know what to make of this, so I fold up the poster and sit and ponder the mysteries of the Velvets while watching those screwing highway safety films. All I knew of the Velvets was they had an album with a banana and Andy Warhol's name on it. The few things I'd read said they were dirty, evil, mean and nasty. And quite appealing. But the Woodrose Ballroom was a carpeted old roller rink slung amidst Connecticut Valley tobacco fields. Why were these guys playing South Deerfield? (Time and the devil later revealed that by 1969 the Velvets were happy to find somewhere that would let them play, and South Deerfield was a convenient stop-off between Boston and NYC.)

I was intrigued. The month previous I had gone to my first big rock show (not counting intense sessions with local groups like Purple Grass in high school hops in the basements), a posh girls school in Northfield. That had been to see Steve Katz, late of the Blues Project and what he was up to. That was fun (they [Blood, Sweat and Tears] sang some songs about odd things like a spinning wheel smiling faces, and a piece of his heart), and I wanted more. The Who, Mothers of Invention and the Amboy Dukes were pushing the Monkees further back in my small record assortment. So I was ready and willing for some weird hot rock to blast me out. I had no idea what I was in for.

"This song's been banned in San Francisco. Hope you like it." That small guy in the shades and leather turned out to be Lou Reed, and he didn't say much all night. Half of what he did say was about this or that song being banned (such as that one up there for "White Light/White Heat") or maimed. The whole bizarre situation had been highlighted by some *dumb* local band opening with *lame-o* versions of "You Keep Me Hanging On" (V. Fudge style), and then these strange figures walked through the crowd to the stage, to unleash this . . . roar. So imagine you're a kid, and you're at your second concert ever, and you're sitting in 1969 with whatever there is of the small farming town area hippie slick of kids. These people with nasty clothes get on stage and BANNNGGO! Such noise! This guy who sings funny is waving a guitar, another's hunched over the keyboards unearthing some mighty *odd* sounds, another's hunched over the bass, and the drummer, who looks like a woman, is playing with big mallets (the kind that kick the bass drum on regular kits), the better to bang her bass drum turned on its side as a snare with.

For the first screech, I'm transfixed. The songs, about waiting, love, call my name, all fly by in a vicious torrent. During the break, we dare each other to go chat with them. It's tempting, but they're too forbidding, and we try to relax.

A few buzzheads dance near the front of the stage, but the rest of the few hundred hipsters sit immobile on the floor, trying to deal with this howl. It gets late, and the "leader" says they're going to do this story-song. He kicks out this riff, and while things before were intense, they are now erupting; they slowly build, and begin to fly. The singer's yelling something about "she's sucking on my ding-dong", and they kick into a harder, faster wail. The singer's hand is a blur, stroking and making this twelve-string shudder and scream; the bass player's got another guitar, and is ripping up on that; the organist is leaning, slapping the keys, and is also stroking demonic sounds from an electric violin. And the drummer—not only has she stood all night, but she's pounded steadily with those big mallets all the while, raising one up over her head for the big BAMP-BAMP-BAMP. Steady, I'm not quite sure how long this went on. It seemed a half-hour—but time, space, driver's ed meant nothing. I was gone. No drink or drugs, I was flattened by the raw power. It rocked—but it was so twisted. Pete Townshend says rocknroll is when you stand up and forget where you are—OK, these strange people were playing the loudest, crudest music I'd ever heard—or enough of. They were making lots of "mistakes", but they were obviously much more interested in getting up there and ripping it out. The roar increased, then built until I could hardly stand it. My heart felt like an alligator (years before fear and loathing) and they swept and glided back down.

I couldn't stand it. I ran out they next day and paid my $3.49 for *White Light/White Heat*. I figured the 17 minute "Sister Ray" *had* to be that incredible heap of noise they played. It was, but I recall even now the disappointment on hearing it the first time. The studio version still lives in my top ten all time tracks, but doesn't compare with the gush that had sent my brain to Jupiter the evening before. I'd give nine years off my next few lives for a tape of that night. Take the ending of the studio "Sister Ray"—the last four minutes or so—start from there, go faster, crank it UP and take off faster and harder.

The Velvet Underground played in S. Deerfield and Springfield, Mass. several times before they entered the void. It was hard for me to get around to see them. Once I had promised my friends that for the cost of a ride I would take them to a king devil guitar freakout supreme. We got there in time to see them do a long, pensive, halting almost acoustic "Sister Ray."

So it's a klassic—kid in high school gets bent by N.Y.C. gutter band. I've been to a few hundred concerts since and that night in the roller rink remains special—the first, and one of the greatest openings of the sea of electric possibilities in "Rock And Roll" I'll ever get.

PHILIP MILSTEIN

NOTES FROM THE VELVET UNDERGROUND (1983)

I grew up in the suburbs, Bergen County, New Jersey, an area which might as well be Long Island. The members of the Velvet Underground were mostly from Long Island, but they all wound up in New York City.

The suburbs are for people who want to suck out the life juices of the city by day and spit them back out in the safety of their tract homes by night. The only way to consistently find true beauty is to constantly seek it out among ugliness. Living in the ugly city is one of the best ways to do that, and the Velvet Underground consequently lived in the city. Ironically, the book they took their name from is about wife-swapping in the suburbs. The Velvet Underground, the band, took the name, but they couldn't take the suburbs.

Velvet Underground. One needn't even hear "Venus in Furs" to envision the scenes depicted therein. Underground . . . dungeon, chains, stockades, whips, furs, sensuous velvets. Beauty in the ugliness, velvet in the underground.

I am now 25 years old. Thus, I was only 13 when the Velvet Underground, for all intents and purposes, came apart. It took me another five years after that to first hear their noise. At age 13 I wasn't aware of much music, least of all the Velvet Underground. I wish I'd had the Velvet Underground with me in high school. I could have held my head up so much higher. Anyone could have called me anything and it wouldn't have bothered me, because I had the Velvet Underground, and thus I *knew*. I envy those high school kids who do have the Velvets. They're luckier than the rest of us.

I remember my parents driving me through New York City. Lower Manhattan. 17th Street and Park Avenue South. Union Square. Seeing the sign marking Max's Kansas City. Consciously, I did not know what that sign meant, but I do indeed recall connecting that sign with the words "Velvet Underground." Something must have seeped unwittingly into the back of my young mind, something from the New York media. It must have been that legendary summer, 1970, 13 years old, when the Velvet Underground triumphantly returned to New York City, slaying the ugly beast nightly upstairs at Max's. The memory, for me, is just a vague blur, but I do recall seeing that sign and thinking "Velvet Underground," not knowing what either meant.

Three years later, or thereabout. High school library, diligently and excitedly reading Lillian Roxon's *Rock Encyclopedia*. I was struck by the mysteriousness and reverence of her words about the Velvets. Those words got me very curious, but I did manage to knock that curiosity back into the recesses of my brain.

I also remember weekly bike rides to the local record shop. Never with enough money to buy anything, always just looking. I'd flip through their skimpy import bin, and week after week that third Velvet Underground album would still be there, carefully wrapped in one of those plastic import bags. Connected that album with Lillian Roxon, maybe also with Max's Kansas City. That cover added fuel to the already smoldering flame of curiosity growing within me. Underground . . . Velvet Underground, photograph looks like it was taken in a basement somewhere, just one little light bulb but that's enough, everything else in shadow. No liner notes, few credits. Dark as the images evoked by Roxon, mysterious, scary, seductive as Velvet. But once again to the back of my mind.

Late 1975. They'd been gone for five years. I'm a college freshman in Massachusetts. Finally free of my parents' record-buying restrictions, and determined to buy one a week (a habit which later grew to one a day). First week *Rod Stewart's Greatest Hits*. Next week hunting around for something new, something different from the Beatles/Stones/Beach Boys/Elton John axis I'd theretofore known. Pick up this odd green two-record set, *1969 Live* . . . the Velvet Underground, some more mystery. This silly cover, little information again, "Special Price—Contains 103 Minutes Of Music." A good deal. Ah-hah, there it is! That moment, that pivotal moment when you decide to purchase your first Velvet Underground record, sound unheard. There is no turning back.

Took it home, expecting to hear all those wild and weird sounds Roxon described, all that bleakness the cover of the third album seemed to indicate. I put it on. Get this rhythm, this rhythm guitar, this swirling mass of sound. Circular swirls, curlieques, moving around itself but all the while also moving forward rapidly, like a hurricane or a tornado. It's not very "weird," not at all what I'd expected, but it is urgent and exciting. My life wasn't quite changed, but I did want to hear more.

Next came a budget compilation album, the one on Pride with the extinct-looking swan creatures on the cover. Yeah, finally there's that weirdness I'd been looking for: that death-coaxing/death-defying ebb and flow of "Heroin"; the pure incendiary *volume* of "Sister Ray," the apocalypse in my dormitory room; the frightening water torture of "All Tomorrow's Parties"; the story-song, "Lady Godiva's Operation." And then I discovered the other side of this Velvet Underground, the soft white underbelly of the nasty monster . . . "Femme Fatale," "Sunday Morning." That's the difference between wrong and right.

I'm glad the Velvet Underground hit me before most of the other stuff did. Until that time, Top 40 was pretty much all I'd known musically, but as soon as I heard the Velvet Underground I figured there was a whole lot more where they came from. It was now late 1975. Patti Smith's *Horses* (produced by ex-Velvet John Cale) had just been released, the first new wave album. At the same time as I was picking up on the grandfathers of the new wave I was also picking up on its mother. In just a few months the new wave would erupt in a frenzied burst of activity, and I was lucky enough to be able to sit right on top of the volcano. But the Velvet Underground were first in real time, and I'm glad they were first for me as well, if only by a very short while.

If there were 40 minutes in my life that I'd like to have back again, I'd have to choose the first time I heard the banana album. I can't really remember my reaction. I'd already heard a lot of those songs from my budget compilation, but was not yet very familar with them. I knew them just well enough to know that I loved them, and that I didn't have to get *too* intensely involved with them just yet because I could sense that these records would be sticking with me for a long long time. I knew that there was a depth here that I'd probably still be picking apart years hence (and, indeed, still am). I could feel that this was one group I was not going to outgrow, like I was then outgrowing Elton John. Not many people outgrow the Velvet Underground.

I cannot recall my initial impression of the banana album, but I knew that from that point on things would be a little different. I'd be a little more jaded, and yet in a strange way a little more innocent as well, a little more insightful, a little more curious, a little harder—hard with that veneer that one needs to survive in the city; although I wouldn't need that veneer to survive this Massachusetts college life I knew it'd be a good thing to help me get by in any real world. I'd never see things quite the same way again—I don't really know if there's any greater compliment that can be paid to art.

With the Velvet Underground now fully transfused into my blood stream, I don't see how I can ever again go back to the suburbs.

PAUL WILLIAMS

I'M BEGINNING TO SEE THE LIGHT (1969)

Everybody loves the Velvets' new lp! I am surprised, I am delighted! I mean—my friends who hear the album ask to hear it again, they walk around singing it, they talk about it during dinner. They buy copies themselves if they have phonographs. They drop by to hear it otherwise. *The Velvet Underground*, their third album, on MGM, is currently competing for attention with Dylan's spanking new love-gift—and holding its own! It's my own favorite album since *Forever Changes*. And I haven't had so much luck in turning people onto a record since *The Doors*. That came out in winter 1967, concurrent with an album called *The Velvet Underground & Nico*. I was an eager propagandist for that first Doors lp in those days, and somehow never paid much attention to the one or two Velvet evangelists afoot. Almost two years later, last fall, I began to open my ears. "Let me tell you people what I've found."

"I met myself in a dream, and I just want to tell ya everything was all right." I think the Velvets are speaking to the insides of our minds today, as the Band did last summer, the Beatles the summer before that, the Stones even earlier on in our lives. "No kinds of love are better than others." *The Velvet Underground* is one of those few albums that allow us to suspect great music is being created in our time. On the inner sleeve of my copy of *Nashville Skyline*, I read some fascinating propaganda for the medium Dylan's message is impressed upon (the word "tape" was never once mentioned in the spiel, but I surmise some threat is felt) and came upon this shocking reminder: long-playing records are this year twenty-one years old, mere children by this world's standards. 1948, same year as Stevie Winwood, Israel, and me! Why is all this barely mature stuff taken so seriously?

. . .

Lying on a bed. *Do Androids Dream of Electric Sheep?* The Velvets now world's finest. Better than the Stones. Dylan alone remains. But is Phil Dick really the Herman Melville of this century? What do I mean when I say that? Why do I so want it to be true?

Group experience. Why can't I read and listen alone?

I must tell you. I must tell you. The Velvets are the greatest. Phil Dick will have more impact on the consciousness of this century than William Faulkner, Norman Mailer or Kurt Vonnegut, Jr. Perhaps that statement is only true at this moment. Perhaps this moment no longer exists.

Judy I want you. Which is more important—the book, the record, the girl? If she were here I would know the answer.

. . .

We just listen to the Velvet album over and over. Sometimes "Some Kinda Love" is the track that most amazes me, the way it rolls and barks, so sweet, so sensitive. Reminding me always of a formal French lovesong & the blues of John Lee Hooker. Earlier I was amazed that one song could resemble such apparently diverse stuff; now I am so busy being amazed by Lou Reed's voice, the depth of humanity it encloses and breathes, and by his words, and by the guitar, bass, drums singing along, I am so thoroughly and immediately astonished by everything I hear in this song, now, every time I listen, that I no longer can focus on resemblances. I can only absorb, opening every receptor in my nervous system in my effort to feel this incredible moment more fully. One word for this music is "sensual."

Another word is "human." Not just the words, which really do speak directly to our human situation, but the music, especially the performances: there is something so real, so immediate and personal, in the movement of these songs, the touch of fingers to guitar strings, the extension of energy through a drumstick so that it is strike and touch both, an intimate, human action, you can feel this in the music as it touches you, strikes you, awakening in you a knowledge of the texture and movement of being alive. Bass notes like pulse beats, spoken words like the sensory explosion of opening my eyes.

"Got my eyes wide open"—the Velvets have always been in touch with the world. Now they are making that world, the real one, palatable, not by sugar-coating but by being gentle. The penetrating. Magic on the level of the Beatles, stark and subtle awareness on some higher level still, the Velvets have finally made an album we can all listen to; they have found a way to be even more honest. They have brought the whole world—not just the harmless parts—closer, and without scaring anyone. Now, *that's* revolution! We're set free.

. . .

It's frustrating. This essay feels like it's done, and yet there's so much more I want to say. About the Velvet album: how it moves, stopping and starting, the break in "Candy Says" ("if I could walk way from *me*") which is simply the best example I can think of of how beautiful motion can be, the breakthrough in "The Murder Mystery" (the listener is set up, the repetition of the word "structures" becomes increasingly ominous, both streams call for attention more and more in their quiet ways, until you're completely split and suddenly realize that the piano is a part of both streams and something else, at which point, with the aid of the word "perverse" and a sense of timing that is evidence of genius, you break through, three streams become a thousand, the song wanders to an ending and you are left on a higher plane—and ready to hear "Afterhours"), the way everyone identifies with "Jesus," the way everyone walks around singing "Afterhours" and plays it again when the album's over. I want to get into a rap on subject matter, how "Some Kinda Love" is about the worthiness of casual affairs ("Situations arise/Because of the weather/And no kinds of love/Are better than others") and "Pale Blue Eyes" is about more than adultery, maybe the significance of adultery's *texture*. I want to declare that "I'm beginning to see the light" is the best line I've heard in months, and the song is better, and the "How does it feel to be loved" ending is almost more than I can hold in . . . which is fine, because the next song is "I'm Set Free" ("I've been set free, and/I've been bound"), in which the growth cycle of release leading to greater need leading to grander release, etc. is not merely described but created, expressed, performed. And followed by "That's the Story of My Life," another perfect transition: ". . . that's the difference between wrong and right. But Billy said, both those words are dead . . ." (It is incredible how this album talks about almost everything that is worth talking about these days, and has a revelation to offer in almost every area! And the music, the music. . . . But I guess that's what it means to be completely in harmony with the moment.) I want to discuss so many things, all those wonderful lines in "The Murder Mystery" and what they do to your head as they seep, one by one, into consciousness—I would like to analyze every line of "Afterhours" and of course Maureen's magnificent vocal as a study of the nature of perfection in this century—I would like to play this album with you about a hundred times and share more every time. . . .

TIM BRADSTOCK

VELVET UNDERGROUND APPRECIATION SOCIETY, PEKING LANGUAGES INSTITUTE CHAPTER (1983)

"How the Velvet Underground got me through the night" is an oft-told tale. This version, however, is notable not only for its unusual setting but also for the accompanying Chinese vodka and Albanian cigarettes.

Peking is about the unlikeliest place you'd expect to find afficionados of the Velvet Underground, or hear their music. That was where I found myself in October, 1974, as an exchange student, starting a year of language study at the Peking Languages Institute to be followed by a year of Chinese history at Peking University.

Those were different times, Jim. China was then in the middle of a massive campaign to criticize Confucius and many saw the possibility of a return to the extremes of the Cultural Revolution when all things western had been deemed bourgeois, decadent and only worthy of being swept onto "history's garbage heap." Western society was typically characterized as being on the verge of collapse and rock music, or "yao-bai yin-yueh" as it was called in Chinese, was regarded as the undesirable by-product of a sick society.

It was with this situation in mind that I decided to make the most of my last couple of weeks at home before going to China by cramming two years worth of listening to you-know-who while I could. Bringing their records into the country seemed just a little uncool, given the political and

The Exploding Plastic Inevitable
15

cultural climate prevailing at the time. I had visions of scenes in a back room at Customs, having just arrived in China: "Uh, this song, well, it's about the virtues of patience, he's waiting patiently for his friend and uh, he's sick and dirty more dead than alive but still likes to be, uh, generous which is why he's got 26 dollars in his hand . . ." So with a heavy heart on the day before my departure I entrusted all my VU/Reed/Cale/Nico records to my brother's care with instructions that he guard them with his life while I was away: "especially *The Marble Index,* man; that's practically irreplaceable."

My second day at the Peking Languages Institute I was sitting in the cafeteria with a group of fellow students and everyone was comparing notes on the farewell parties they'd had in their respective countries just before coming to China. When I mentioned how I'd gotten as wasted as possible and spent the evening playing every Velvets album I had, loud cheers sounded and I discovered there were two other people, both from Britain, who'd done the same thing. Immediately we fell into a discussion on the relative merits of various Velvets albums and from that point on the "fan club" was established.

Better yet, one of the British had even brought in a couple of cassettes of VU albums, plus a cassette player. It appeared that the Chinese, while officially maintaining their attitude of disapproval, had not been so strict about the importation of Western music as I'd expected. Apparently they felt that what foreigners did *among themselves* did not really matter. With the first and third Velvets albums as a nucleus we began building up a collection from there, our next acquisition being a cassette of *Berlin.* Someone in one of the embassies in Peking had unwittingly bought it during a trip to Hong Kong, played it once and shuddered, offering it to me to keep when I asked if I could borrow it. Other records followed, but always on cassette as there were problems with bringing stereo systems into the country.

So that fall, for the first time in history, no doubt, the Velvets' music was being played in China. Mostly we only played their stuff when we were by ourselves, on weekends, when most of the Chinese students and staff were away with their families. There was little else to do on a Saturday night in Peking in those days. We were eight miles from downtown (or two hours by bus, if you prefer) which in any case closed up pretty much at about eight o'clock. No movie theatres, no rock concerts, no bars; you had to make your own entertainment. A group of us would always congregate then in one of the cell-like dormitory rooms on the top floor of Block Eight (for males, principally those from western countries), on Saturday and party until the wee hours.

The weekend ritual always began with a trip to the local liquor store for Chinese and Russian vodka—at around a buck and a half a bottle—plus a few packs of Albanian cigarettes. There was other music we played as well, but in our circle, which was comprised of mostly British, Canadians, and Scandinavians, the Velvets' music always occupied center stage. Those who socialized with us and who had never heard the Velvets' music before soon became pretty familiar with it. Quite a lot of converts were made. Soon people were passing the tapes around and some whose native language was not English were asking for the lyrics of certain songs to be written down for them.

Weird scenarios drift into the mind even now: of a tiny smoke-filled room at the top of this almost deserted gigantic stone building, tape machine blaring and the whole company, bleary-eyed, screaming along when a familiar refrain came along: "I am tired, I am weary, I could sleep for a thousand years . . ."

Once in a while the occasional Chinese would drift in. Early risers, they usually visited early enough in the evening so that we still had our heads reasonably together when they came. Sometimes we'd ask what they thought of the music. Though they never said anything particularly negative about it the most frequent response was that they couldn't make any sense of it. The only other comments I remember the music eliciting from the Chinese who heard it was that "Sunday Morning" sounded pleasant and soothing to one, and from someone else who noted that the viola in the climax of "Heroin" sounded remarkably like a Chinese stringed instrument from the outer regions of China, near Mongolia. The lyrics I always kept rather quiet about, or faked in the manner described earlier. Luckily none of the Chinese knew enough English—or street talk—to suspect anything, or they might have had that extra Cultural Revolution after all.

WAYNE McGUIRE
THE BOSTON SOUND (1968)

For Wayne McGuire, who sent this unsolicited, passionately opinionated stream of consciousness review of *White Light/White Heat* to *Crawdaddy!* in 1968, the Velvets were the only rock artists who exemplified the austere ideals of 1960s jazz modernism. He places them alongside the late John Coltrane, Albert Ayler, and Cecil Taylor as artists for whom the stakes and consequences of music making are high indeed. The "new music isn't about notes and pretty structures," he writes. "It's about spirit, energy, presence and nervous systems." Over the years, the band members themselves have characterized their music in much the same way.

One must marvel at the presumption of the Doors: Break On Through To The Other Side? Hardly, they are firmly ensconced over here. For to break on through to the other side is a difficult thing to be sure. Probably the only rock group to ever make it through is the Velvet Underground, sons of metallic Burroughs and leather Genet, on "Sister Ray" from *White Light/ White Heat*. For to break on through to the other side one must squeeze through that tiny pin hole which connects this dimension of human energies with the jet stream of superhuman energies. Of course, a few American musicians have broken through to that ionosphere, most notably John Coltrane and Pharoah Sanders on *Meditations*. But whereas Coltrane and his disciples are the culmination of New Black Music, the Velvet Underground are prophets of a new age, of breakthrough on an electronic:intermedia:total scale. But enough of this pseudo-review style for:

Now is the time for distortions to burn. I have, with a heavy heart, silently watched while spiritual dwarves multilated all that was sacred. But now my resignation has ended and with flaming sword in hand I will clear away those ugly growths which parade as insightful musical criticism.

Probably the most blatant injustice perpetrated by the media on the contemporary music scene has been the virtual black-out on coverage of the Velvet Underground. There have been a few timid stabs at descriptive praise in *Crawdaddy*, *Vibrations* and *Jazz & Pop*, but on the whole reviewers, when confronted with a phenomenon which doesn't conform to any easy slot of reference, choose to turn out reams of material on synthetic groups which have gained mass acceptance. So the Velvet Underground, which is musically and mentally at least two years ahead of its time, goes unrecognized while the Doors, a group which artificially pretends to the chaotic nonentity of which the Velvet Underground are masters, receive torrents of publicity. But eventually, as always, the truth must out and in time the artificial husk will disintegrate and drop away revealing the Velvet Underground firmly at center where they've been all along.

This is a review of the Velvet Underground, this is a review of the end of the world, this is a review of the Antichrist and Christ, this is a review of Life and Death, this is a review of tomorrow and of ever and ever.

But first you must come up/down/into here where the air is so heavy/thin but oh so intoxicating. Or as C. S. Lewis once described an important facet of Burroughsian feedback in *That Hideous Strength*:

Suddenly, like a thing that leaped to him across infinite distances with the speed of light, desire (salt, black, ravenous, unanswerable desire) took him by the throat. The merest hint will convey to those who have felt it the quality of the emotion which now shook him, like a dog shaking a rat; for others, no description will perhaps avail. Many writers speak of it in terms of lust: a description admirably illuminating from within, totally misleading from without. It has nothing to do with the body. But it is in two respects like lust as lust shows itself to be in the deepest and darkest vault of its labyrinthine house. For like lust, it disenchants the whole universe. Everything else that Mark had ever felt—love, hunger, ambition, lust itself—appeared to have been mere milk and water, toys for children, not worth one throb of the nerves. The infinite attraction of this dark thing sucked all other passions into itself: the rest of the world appeared blenched, etiolated, insipid, a world of white marriages and white masses. . . . These creatures of which Frost had spoken—and he did not doubt that they were locally present with him in the cell—breathed death on the human race and on all joy. Not despite this but because of this, the terrible gravitation sucked and tugged and fascinated him towards them. Never before had he known the fruitful strength of the movement opposite to Nature which now had him in its grip; the impulse to reverse all reluctances and to draw every circle anti-clockwise. The meaning of certain pictures, of Frost's talk about "objectivity," of the things done by witches in old times, became clear to him. The image of Wither's face rose to his memory: and this time he did not merely loathe it. He noted, with shuddering satisfaction, the signs it bore of a shared experience between them. Wither also knew. Wither understood. . . .

Warhol also knew. Warhol understood. . . . Yet surely this must be an oversimplification, no? After all, C. S. Lewis was merely an apologist for a dying Christianity, no?

But why was Bob Zimmerman scared shitless of Warhol? Why did Zimmerman fear that Warhol wanted to destroy him? It wasn't merely a case of country boy meets the big city. 'Cause something's happening, Bob, and . . . ? But enough of this petty sneering criticism. It would be better to ask why has Bob Zimmerman turned moralist, perhaps even Christian fundamentalist, on *John Wesley Harding*? Do you remember before the accident when his lyrics were becoming increasingly schizophrenic, when he cried out in horror that he thought he might be becoming "evil"? And the accident itself must have presented an exceedingly intense vision of nonbeing. So then came Christian conversion? I doubt it. For in case you haven't heard there is a fantastic war now being waged and our greatest human spirits are either standing or falling in battle. Most of you out there are still engaged in your petty pursuits unaware that the roof is about to cave in but wait, I hear a message from the battlefield: "BULLETIN . . . BULLETIN . . . BULLETIN . . . I-uh-would like to-uh-report a case of circuit overload and-um-many cases-uh-of creeping mindless idiotism . . . signed A. Warhol."

Yes, so Bob Zimmerman decided to withdraw from the heat of battle for awhile (too much of nothing), it was getting pretty nightmarish there, and when a *Life* reviewer asserts that Dylan has pulled the plug out on modern music one must reply wha? For Dylan is no longer at the vital core and has abdicated his right to significant action or dialogue. He has come full swing from humanism (the protest songs) to "nihilism" (the schizophrenic surrealistic songs) back to humanism (the songs with a moral), a more sophisticated humanism than before, but humanism none-the-less. In the arts today, Tolkien alone has the Christian perspective honestly, lucidly and poetically wrapped up.

I have before me the February *Crawdaddy* with a pretentious review by Paul Williams on the Beach Boys, the Rolling Stones and the Jefferson Airplane. The review is a bubble which begs to be pricked, but why bother. I remember you guys from high school, remember? I tried to play Coltrane's "Impressions" for you, a heavy piece of music engaged in significant dialogue created by a noble spirit who was risking all on the battlefield but you were too busy listening to the Beatles and the Stones and into adolescent masturbation (I can't get no satisfaction; you call this slop a rebellion?), and now you've learned some musical terms and have taken some speed for insight and are busy fueling the Beatles-Airplane-Doors syndrome or are into ever-so-tired black blues riffs via Cream, Butterfield, Bloomfield, Canned Heat or Traffic. Christ, don't you realize that you are engaged in creating and perpetuating New American Muzak? For instance, Charles Lloyd is New American Muzak (may God grant Frank Kofsky patience who has seen Pharoah Sanders verge on transformation into pure spiritual energy). But the time is coming when you'll be forced to discard your illusions for as the Buddha once moaned in the throes of a Dionysian ecstasy: "Intermedia will be the spiritual microcosm of the world, the tool of a spiritual and political revolution in the West, a manifestation of man's next evolutionary leap in consciousness." Which in translation means: "Ah, to be a media freak plugged into the collective unconscious of the country and ride the electric tidal wave of human history." Which further translated simply means: "Intermedia will be the collective consciousness of the Aquarian Age."

But I digress. Put quite simply, the Velvet Underground is the most vital and significant group in the world today. They are at the fiery center of the twentieth century dilemma, as was Nietzsche. For Nietzsche foresaw that moment in the future when the spiritual citadels of the Judaeo-Christian West would crumble silently to dust. And at that moment our poor human souls will be rent with a pain greater than the heat of a hundred hydrogen bombs. Of course some have anticipated this pain. (For instance, Johnny Jones described to me this dream: It is 1982. John Lennon, master of the Western world, is sitting in the control booth while the yellow barbarians attack the walled western citadel. Lennon, seemingly in control of the situation because of his dynamism and mastery of technology, pokes at some of the myriad of buttons which face him on the control panel causing powerful psychedelic tranquilizers to be shot at the enemy. But still the barbarians charge. Beads of sweat break out on Lennon's brow. He pushes more buttons sending superpowered thought control image barrages at the enemy. But still the barbarians charge and with an inhuman intensity smash through the tired walls. A horrendous shriek pierces the deaf skies as Western Man has his eyeballs gashed out and his body cut up in a slow tortuous death. But goodness, I wouldn't want to invoke the yellow peril threat!) Nietzsche himself fell in battle without compromise as did Van Gogh, Rimbaud, Artaud and maybe Joyce and Beckett. (In our own time those two oracles, Burroughs and Warhol, are still standing. And, of course, Mel.) Many turn to the East but those with integrity know the dilemma facing them to be dimensionally greater than that solution (it being no accident that Hesse wrote *Steppenwolf* after *Siddhartha*.) Others explore their Western roots for surcease and again the passionately honest know the roots to be severed and the apparent solution irrelevant to the dilemma (since the Renaissance and Enlightenment were a cashing-in of the assets of our Medieval legacy and now there's nothing left, we're bankrupt). Put in a nutshell, the real question is: how can we control and humanize an increasingly uncontrollable and proliferating technology, an overpoweringly dehumanizing technology, when the value foundation for that attempted humanization is rapidly disintegrating and when the attempt by humans to control such power (who would be the master programmer?) would most certainly be corrupting in the extreme? And if you don't have a solid answer to that question you might as well shut up. Of course, if you're a child of the post-nihilistic era, a part of the emerging crystalline-like growth of humanity, in short, a Crystal Person, faceless and rootless, the question will not have presented itself to your mind, it will appear meaningless. But your ionic solution is now being prepared and when the master seed is dropped you will become the first unwitting victims. Planet Earth, which quakes and trembles, is bathed in a strange light, a demon light electric. All creation groans and strains towards its next evolutionary growth. Or as Confucious recently muttered: "Within the next ten years will be sought and found within Intermedia the Cosmic Haiku, the Apocalyptic Orgasm, which will reverberate throughout planet earth and trigger group mental telepathy." And all this time you probably thought the Velvet Underground was talking about drugs, homosexuality and sadomasochism. Look a bit closer.

But you are probably too occupied delving into the subtleties of *Sgt. Pepper* due to an astigmatism of the mind, a lack of perspective. It is true that the Beatles feel vibrations from the fiery center, but they are weak vibrations manifested in an elegant cynicism seeking escape in a watered down Eastern mysticism. Musically, this piddling spiritual odyssey has resulted in a bag of pretty musical tricks produced primarily by George Martin drawing on superficial characteristics of electronic and Indian music. Jonas Mekas' criticism of USCO, the New York-based mixed media cooperative, is quite applicable to the Beatles:

The USCO show . . .is a search for religious, mystical experience. Whereas in the case of the Plastic Inevitables [the Velvet Underground] the desire for the mystical experience is unconscious, the USCO is going after it in a more conscious way. They have arrived somewhere, and gained a certain peace, certain insights, and now they are beginning to meditate. Nevertheless, often I get the impression that the mystical meditative mood of many of my friends that I meet in psychedelic circles is really not the beginning of the new age or cosmic consciousness, but the sunset peace of the Age of the Fish, of the Christian era—the sunset mediation. At the Plastic Inevitables, however, the dance floor and the stage are charged with the electricity of a dramatic break just before the dawn. If at USCO's show I feel surrounded by the tradition, by the past, by the remnants of the oriental religions—at the Plastic Inevitables it is all Here and Now and the Future.

Spiritually the Velvet Underground's only equivalent is Mel Lyman. It is interesting to note the similar reactions both forces produce in people: uncomprehending indifference, vaguely comprehending hostility and comprehending submission. The first group doesn't have the barest inkling of what's happening since they're dead to the world; the second group feel their small ego base threatened (like the character after the last V.U. performance who, his face distraught and angry, spit out: "They stink!" in much the same way Mel receives letters from pipsqueaks telling him how he's screwed up); the third group understand that the V.U. and Mel are merely vessels through which greater forces are working and they listen attentively.

But what I really want to talk about is the Velvet Underground's music. Essential to that music is drone. Not the pencil-thick drone of Indian music which emanates from spirits and nervous systems which think they've found it and probably have within their limited structure of things, but a drone which is as broad as a house, a drone which is produced by New World Citizen nervous systems plunging into the Cosmic Whirl. The drone has two levels, high-pitched and low-pitched (corresponding to the drones of the central nervous and the circulatory systems), which are produced by two very heavy nervous systems belonging to Lou Reed and John Cale respectively. The drone is not always heard but rather felt as pure essence and perpetual presence.

The constant feedback is produced *by* those nervous systems and projected *through* the amps which have been made perfect human extensions; it is organic and comes from the inner recesses of their souls; and their souls are connected to mother earth, their energy is generated from the core of planet earth up through their feet to their heads through their hands and amps to create a wall of sound which is a beautifully intricate and richly textured abstract-expressionist motion picture. The feedback at peak moments is a suspended mystical ecstasy in which spirit is transformed into a negative mirror of itself, in which streams of energy travel into and out of spirit simultaneously at the speed of light. The only other musician to approach such a profound conception of feedback was Jimi Hendrix on *Are You Experienced?* But, as can be heard on *Axis: Bold As Love,* he didn't have enough energy to maintain that powerful conception; and by concentration on such superficial musical aspects as melody and harmonic progression has degenerated to the level of a second-rate jazz musician a la Roland Kirk or Yusef Lateef.

And in case you haven't heard, the new music isn't about notes and pretty structures. It's about spirit, energy, presence and nervous systems. Why is John Cale the heaviest bass player in the country today? Because his nervous system is an aristocrat among nervous systems, because of the deep dark electricity he is able to convey through his bass and viola. And why is Maureen Tucker the perfect drummmer for the V.U.? Because of her spirituality and nervous system. No other drummer in the world could play the archetypal 1234 with such perfection, with a weight that verges on religious ritual (not necessarily a Black Mass). And it is that ritualistic quality which is a mainstay of the Underground's powerful stylistic unity, a stylistic element which is immediately recognizable from the initial bar as the driving pulse of a machine-like organism (just listen to one bar of "The Gift"). In essence, she's playing Elvin Jones to Lou Reed's Coltrane or Sonny Murray to Reed's Albert Ayler.

It is no accident that the Velvet Underground was an organic element in Andy Warhol's Exploding Plastic Inevitable. The now defunct Inevitable remains as the strongest and most developed example of intermedia art. Although productions such as Al Rubin's Third World Raspberry have since achieved greater technical dexterity on a visual plane, no one has yet managed to communicate a guiding spirit through the complex form as well as Warhol and the Underground. Again Mekas: "The Inevitable remains the most dramatic expression of the contemporary generation—the place where its needs and desperations are most dramatically split open."

That the Velvet Underground is now the only true intermedia group in the country has been brought out clearly by their appearances at the Boston Tea Party. While all other groups (i.e. Country Joe and the Fish at the Tea Party, the Doors at the Crosstown Bus, the Grateful Dead at the Psychedelic Supermarket, etc.) do their music thing while the "light show" (what an inane phrase) does its thing and never the twain shall meet, the V.U. brings about an organic fusion of image, light and sound. They bring about this fusion by 1) their high energy level, 2) their intense conscious awareness of image and light: "I've got my eyes wide open" attempts to gobble up the light/image flow organism through peripheral vision, 3) their sophisticated use of film projections (for instance, one night while playing "Venus in Furs," Lou Reed focused his vision on a film of his face rhythmically zooming in and out, thus establishing a spiraling feedback connection through himself, the music and light/image flow).

In the beginning I said in so many words that "Sister Ray" made a breakthrough in the grey room. The piece stands as the supreme accomplishment of the rock revolution and a reproach to the musically inorganic patchworks of *Sgt. Pepper* (an underlying motif does not make an album musically organic), *Their Satanic Majesties Request* and even the Mothers' (bless their hearts) *We're Only in it for the Money*. I know of only five recorded tracks of contemporary American music to match it: "India" and "Impressions" from *Impressions* by John Coltrane, "Bells" from *Bells* by Albert Ayler, "D Trad, That's What" from *Live at the Cafe Montmartre* by Cecil Taylor, and "The Father and the Son and the Holy

Ghost" from *Meditations* by Coltrane and Pharoah Sanders (along with hundreds of aborted attempts, Love's "Revelation" being one gross miscarriage among many). "Sister Ray" is much like "Impressions" in that it is a sustained exercise in emotional stamina and modal in the deepest sense: mode as spiritual motif, mode as infinite musical universe. As for organic unity—although the piece shifts gears at least 12 times during the 17 minutes, you will be hard presssed to find any clearly demarcated transition points, each section flows and blends so beautifully into the next.

Devote special attention to Lou Reed's verbal techniques on this track. He molds and bends and stretches and diffracts words and phrases to create effectively complex rhythmic cross-currents in a manner unprecedented in rock. Also notice how Sterling Morrison perfectly performs his usual function by filling in the middle ground between Lou and John Cale.

"Sister Ray" surpasses "Impressions" in its profound textural structure, which is provided by the organ work of John Cale. Cale's architectural conception is remarkably subtle and broad—it is reminiscent of Cecil Taylor's orchestral approach on piano but more effective because of its electronic austerity (fusion and transcendence of Taylor and Stockhausen). Cale is in fact building an awesome granite castle of tonal clusters around Lou, Sterling and Maureen—such an amazing place to live in. And the tidal wave organ drones which inundate the last sections of the piece beginning with the air raid drum explosion—this is the jet stream of superhuman energies, this is the discovered dimension after breakthrough. And remember, "Sister Ray" is not about shooting meth, fellatio or murder. Rather, it is describing the greatest cosmic upheaval in the history of man and you are living in the midst of it. (And I'm not referring to those minor disturbances, the Vietnam War and the racial crisis, inconsequential in the Aquarian Age which will witness the quiet disappearance of all political systems, including communism and capitalist democracy, and its replacement by a universal electronic theocracy.)

"I Heard Her Call My Name" is also a remarkable track simply because it contains the most advanced lead guitar work I think you're going to be able to hear for at least a year or two. I'm talking about Lou Reed's excitingly unpredictable but precisely deliberate phrasing and the tense taut line he walks breathtakingly verging on diffraction of tonality. Compare it to the relative blandness of Hendrix's or Clapton's lines and I think you'll see what I mean. This track also contains one of the most pregnant and highly charged moments I've ever heard in music: a split-second pause of silence after the second "my mind's split open" foreshadowing the following feedback explosion.

The track "White Light/White Heat" best illustrates my earlier contention that John Cale is the heaviest bass player in the country today. While listening to the track on a portable stereo phonograph with the speakers held to each side of the head, notice how profoundly deep and resonant each bass note feels. Most bass players play two-dimensional notes, but John plays three-dimensional granite slabs (it's a question of intonation and density, not volume; it's like the difference between Rauschenberg's two-dimensional Coke bottles and Warhol's three-dimensional Campbell soup cans) which reveal an absolute mastery of his instruments and a penetrating awareness of the most minute details of his music. His body and mind are in perfect tune to the bass range which accounts for his ability to project a bass drone even when playing a simple bass line (a sensibility which was perhaps developed during his stay with LaMonte Young's Theater of Eternal Music). I pointed out this particular quality to LeRoi Jones and he remarked: "So deep, so satisfying. Especially the way it goes thud thud."

Under closer scrutiny, the apparent simplicity of the bass line takes on subtle dimensions. For instance, notice during sections of "White Light/White Heat" how John just barely holds back the beat, subtly altering the rhythmic infrastructure to create a weird tension. This same razor-sharp sensibility was also apparent in the opening of "European Son" on the first album. Notice there how Lou, when entering after John's solo bass opening, slightly but so meaningfully tightens the rhythmic infrastructure.

As for the rest of the album, I'll let you get into it yourself. Forget about hearing it on the radio because even most underground jocks have their heads up their asses. So buy a copy. In a few years it will be recognized as a landmark in the growth of the universal music which is now emerging. But more importantly, hear the V.U. in person. It is absolutely necessary, if you are going to get their complete message, to feel the full visceral impact. And you don't have to worry about getting a watered-down version from the album because the V.U. finds it unnecessary to rely on studio gimmickry.

* * *

As I read back I realize now that I've told you only 50% of the story. For the Velvet Underground possesses more than electronic mastery of that hideous strength and "Sister Ray" (which has been described as "Cakewalk for Frankensteinian Metal Monster") reveals only a part of their nature. They are also creators of a folk music in the deepest sense. Particularly in his latest pieces which are as yet unrecorded ("I'm Waiting for the Man" and "Heroin" have already achieved a certain status as folk classics), Lou Reed is fast becoming an incisive lyricist, creating a folk mythology of New York City and our generation which rings deep and true through the pap of fumbling unfocused artificial surrealistic imagery and facile pseudo-mystical-morality lessons produced by most new groups. They are lyrics which breathe of real life, not empty conjecture, and reveal a very human and loving side, an almost Wagnerian sentimentality (in spite of the crude remark made by one wiseacre regarding John Cale's beautifully mournful viola work on "The Story of My Life": "Even the unjustly persecuted and seemingly insensitive mighty Hulk has feelings, can shed an occasional tear.") The V.U. may well inherit the throne vacated by Dylan as the primary myth-makers of our generation. But that is a subject for a book which no doubt someone will write this summer.

* * *

There has been much nonsense spoken and written recently about the existence or nonexistence and nature of a Boston Sound. It should be quite clear by now that the Boston Sound is the Velvet Underground and Mel Lyman. It is irrelevant that the Velvet Underground first received significant exposure in their home city New York with Andy Warhol's Exploding Plastic Inevitable. It was in Boston, through record sales and Boston Tea Party performances, that they began to find some acceptance and meaningful response (like getting their equipment stolen). It is irrelevant that Mel Lyman's present instrument is *Avatar* and film, not music. What is relevant is that these two voices best express the character and spirit of the forces at work in Boston, home of the first American Revolution. It is a character and spirit which in the near future will make Boston the center of the second American Revolution, a revolution of the spirit. It is a spirit which reveals its sturdy health and moral purity by rejecting, in the name of truth, false resolutions: the Christian cop-out, the Eastern cop-out, the African cop-out and the Humanist cop-out. The powerful energies which first emerged on the West Coast are finding their focus and direction here. Like Mel Lyman, the Velvet Underground have made their "Declaration of Creation" and translated it into sound.

PART TWO

Beginning
to See
the Light

JIM CONDON
ANGUS MACLISE AND THE ORIGIN OF
THE VELVET UNDERGROUND (1983)

Along with Cale, drummer Angus MacLise brought the avant-garde sensibilities associated with LaMonte Young's Theatre of Eternal Music to the Velvets' early band rehearsals (pre–Maureen Tucker). He also contributed a multicultural rhythmic approach, mixing influences he had picked up in his Eastern travels. Though he left the group when it appeared that they might be in danger of actually making money (seventy-five dollars split four ways), his influence lingered in the Velvets' unconventional approach to rock drumming.

Angus MacLise, a founding member and percussionist of the Velvet Underground, died of malnutrition in June 1979 in Kathmandu, Nepal.

One friend described the circumstances of his death as "closing walls of karma, consumption and intestinal malady intensified or brought on by junk. He is said to have ripped out the feeding tubes from nose and arm in last days . . ."

Angus graduated from Forest Hills (Queens, New York) High School in 1956 and went on to study geology at New York University where he was a member of the track team. It was during this period that he evolved his unique hand drumming style, while playing with jazz groups on the Catskill Mountain "borscht belt." "When Angus played the bongos, it was just like poetry," his friend Piero Heliczer recalled.

31

After a brief stint in the Army, Angus joined Piero and Piero's first wife, Olivia, in Paris where they founded The Dead Language Press to publish their own poetry, as well as early works by beat poet Gregory Corso. Angus published two books of poetry before traveling to Greece and India. Upon his return to New York in the early 1960's, Angus and Piero rented the top floor of a house on Avenue C, and resumed their collaborations with Angus publishing his third book, a calendar entitled *Year.* According to Piero, "By giving each day its proper name Mister MacLise has rendered an invaluable service to all those who found the system of setting down a month and number despicable."

In 1961, Angus began to perform with the LaMonte Young Trio (which later became known as the Theatre of Eternal Music), formed by the American avante-garde composer LaMonte Young for the performance of his own music. Its membership at various times included John Cale, Tony Conrad, Terry Riley and an early assistant to Andy Warhol named Billy Linich (aka Billy Name).

While the group was rehearsing in Angus' apartment, Young met Marian Zazeela, an artist living on the floor below, who later became his collaborator and wife. "It sounds corny, but we really never left each other after that day in '62," Marian recalled. "Later LaMonte and I became very close to Angus and really lived by his calendar."

When Marian moved in with LaMonte Young, her apartment was taken over by Tony Conrad, who described the group at the time: "It was not a popular group. In fact, I think that a number of the people involved sort of felt a sense of mission and quest almost because of the fact that so little of interest was going on elsewhere within the music scene. Around that point it was becoming clear to a number of us that the thing to do was not to write directions as a composer, but to perform and to focus on the design of the activity in a way which returned to the source of that activity. Angus came in immediately at that point—where the performance was beginning to become apparent again. There was a lot of listening to Oriental music in there for a while, not just Indian, but also other types of sounds that were exploratory in a sense of different legendary mentalities, and this was Angus' particular interest."

One of the more unique features of Young's music is his use of sustained tones for extended durations relying on the establishment of a drone and the placing of harmonically-related frequencies (overtones) around this drone. Cale, who played in the Theatre of Eternal Music while completing his Bernstein Fellowship, said that the performances of the group "consisted of holding one chord for 45 minutes. It was a form of sense deprivation for all concerned." Cale played a viola that had been modified with a flat bridge so that three strings could be played simultaneously with equal intensity. Tony Conrad would play double-stops on a violin reinforced with a resonating string while Young and Zazeela would produce other tones vocally. Young's concerts are sometimes given in conjunction with projections of calligraphic light art by Marian Zazeela.

Through Young, Angus became involved in the Fluxus group of experimental composers, filmmakers, artists and poets based in New York. Members of this group included Walter DeMaria, Henry Flynt, Young, Conrad and Yoko Ono, with whom Angus collaborated for her piece *Music for Dance*.

Throughout the period Angus lived on Ludlow Street, he worked with a number of remarkable individuals. From 1963 through 1966, Angus composed and performed instrumental music for John Vacarro's Theatre of the Ridiculous, a theatre company responsible for such plays as *Whores of Babylon* and *Hot Turds in Hell* and featured early acting performances by Jackie Curtis (c.f. "Walk on the Wild Side" on *Take No Prisoners*). In 1964 he played the soundtrack for Ron Rice's last film *Chumlum* on the cymbalum, an exotic stringed instrument that Tony Conrad discovered in a Rumanian-Jewish music shop on the East Side. Angus made a number of tapes with Piero, Cale and Conrad when they all lived in the same building on Ludlow. When Tony Conrad vacated the apartment he was sharing with Cale, Lou Reed moved in and introduced Cale to Sterling Morrison.

With Angus, these three friends formed a group that played around the Lower East Side during 1965, under such names as the Warlocks and the Falling Spikes.

Angus' and Piero's influence on the group's direction at this point is incalculable. They introduced the group to the world of underground filmmakers and they began to accompany film screenings and theatrical events, first for Piero's films, and later for those of Kenneth Anger (*Scorpio Rising*) and Barbara Rubin's *Christmas on Earth* which eventually led to the meeting with Warhol.

Sterling Morrison described their relationship with the group in *Little Caesar* #9: "Angus was the most rabidly artistic of us all . . . Angus, however, was not a filmmaker. But his friend Piero Heliczer both inspired and shared his visions . . . Piero was a filmmaker . . . It wasn't long before I met him, learning what the underground film scene was about . . . I was eager to work with him, and the things we did changed the direction of my life."

Cale, Reed, Morrison and MacLise performed in two mixed-media "ritual happenings" that Angus and Piero organized for the Film-Maker's Cinematheque on Lafayette [Street]. Entitled respectively "The Launching of the Dreamweapon" and "The Rites of the Dreamweapon," these pieces were examples of "expanded cinemas," combining movies and slide projections with poetry, live action, and music. Piero also played tapes of the group at other screenings of his films. It was Angus who named the group The Velvet Underground, from a paperback Tony Conrad had found in a Times Square subway station bookshop. This was shortly before Piero arranged for them to appear in a CBS News feature on underground film. Heliczer played saxophone on this performance and used the sound portion for his film *Venus in Furs,* which featured Lou, John, Angus and Barbara Rubin in acting roles.

Angus, however, was an erratic individual. Morrison said that Angus once played one half-hour after the band had left the stage to make up for having been a half hour late for that performance.

"Angus was a true beauty," Sterling remarked. "He thought Keith Moon was too controlled as a drummer."

His interests were too diverse for him to become a rock and roll star, and he believed in art for art's sake, feeling that art and money were mutually exclusive. When Angus decided not to show up for a gig that the Velvets were playing in the West Village, Lou fired him on the spot. Eventually he was replaced by Maureen Tucker.

Angus continued to work with LaMonte Young and his group. By 1968, Young had added Terry Riley on vocals because "a third voice offers a less-sustained pitch than John Cale could produce with a three-string drone," Young explained. "With two male voices I can produce certain timbral blends impossible with one male and one female voice. Similarly, Tony Conrad on the violin didn't have as much to relate to when John Cale was gone."

Lou did recruit Angus as a temporary replacement when Reed was in the hospital with hepatitis and Nico was in Ibiza. The Exploding Plastic Inevitable was playing at Poor Richard's, a club on Sedgwick St. in the Old Town section of Chicago, in summer, 1966. Reed called on Angus, but made it clear that the arrangement was only on a temporary basis until Lou could resume his duties. Angus took over on drums while Maureen switched to bass. Gerard Malanga assisted with the percussion and Cale became the leader of the group for a week. Sterling later said that with the odd lineup they rehearsed for this series of shows more intensely than ever. One of these shows was filmed by Ron Nameth for his film *Exploding Plastic Inevitable.*

Some of Angus' poetry appeared in a literary anthology entitled *Intransit: The Andy Warhol Gerard Malanga Monster Issue,* which was published in 1968. He also guest edited an issue of *Aspen* magazine in 1970 that featured a flexi-disc on which he and Hetty played, on a piece entitled "Joyous Lake."

Among the many performances that Angus conceived was a free-form improvisation piece entitled *Brain Damage in Oklahoma City*. It played at the Cinematheque, then on Wooster Street in Manhattan, featuring Angus playing the barrel-conga, Angus' wife Hetty on tamboura, Tony Conrad on limp-string drone, poet Jackson MacLow on recorder and voice, and the composer Henry Flynt on tonnette (song flute) and voice. Flynt described his impression of Angus' style:

> When he would play his simplest style, then you could hear the complexities and the tricks he was doing. You had to make him play very simply in order to hear how clever his drumming was.
>
> It's curious about Angus—I don't know if he was following a definite system, although he travelled a lot in North Africa and the East. I don't know how much training he'd had, but he was doing syncopations where he knew exactly what he was doing. If he had been interested in such things, he could probably have written it out.
>
> Angus was doing something that would be like Indian drumming except that he was not following that particular system. Indian drumming very clearly had a regular beat which is being sub-divided and Angus either would not use a regular beat or else would do so much syncopation that it would get lost. You did not hear a regular, underlying beat in what he was playing.

Angus, Hetty and their son Ossian flew to the Sri Aurobindu Ashram in Pondicherry, India with filmmaker Sheldon Rochlin in 1971. A year and a half later, Angus moved to Nepal, where he spent most of the remainder of his life. He soon began publishing books of poetry and a literary magazine *Tingpa* through his own Dreamweapon Press.

He also renewed his acquaintance with Ira Cohen, a poet and photographer who was living there at the time. Cohen is most widely known for his work on the album *The Twelve Dreams Of Doctor Sardonicus* by Spirit as well as covers for books by the Olympia Press. Angus and Hetty provided the soundtrack for Cohen's film *Invasion of the Thunderbolt Pagoda*, a film that Cohen described as "a spiritual voyage through the unconscious by way of alchemical dream exorcism and celestial rebirth."

Angus was a life-long student of the occult, a qabalist interested in Aleister Crowley. Shortly before his death Angus was scripting a film version of Crowley's book *Diary of a Drug Fiend*.

Angus spent most of the last year of his life in New York, providing a soundtrack for Sheldon Rochlin's *Hymn to the Mystic Fire,* an experimental diary film shot in India and New York. This was Angus' last major work before returning to Swayambunath, a small village outside of Kathmandu. His drug habit and declining health led to his hospitalization at the Shantih Bhawan hospital in Kathmandu, where he died on June 21, 1979, the last solstice of the seventies.

JIM CONDON

THREE INTERVIEWS: TONY CONRAD, HENRY FLYNT, TERRY RILEY (1983)

Terry Riley Interview

"I met Angus when he was playing hand-drums in LaMonte Young's Theatre of Eternal Music. Angus had already left the group when I was there, but he used to come over and just visit. At the time Angus was playing in The Velvet Underground. They were definitely originals. They brought a lot of the feeling from LaMonte's group via John Cale and Angus. That kind of long drone extended type riffs definitely came from the Theatre of Eternal Music. Just the general feeling, the general droning qualities, especially when Cale was playing.

"Cale and I had played together in LaMonte's group and we had been getting together a lot on our own. We were both signed to Columbia Records at one point, so John McClure, who was our producer, asked us to do a record together. We originally thought that Angus might play on it, but I think at the time we did the recording (*Church of Anthrax*), Angus wasn't around. But John, Angus and I had done sessions together before that album. Angus and I used to play together, and we made quite a few tapes.

"Angus was a very intuitive drummer. He could play an amazing amount and complexities of different kinds of licks. He was a great poet and mystic, so he listened a lot to the inner sound, the inside. He was very unique and original. He was influenced a lot by his travels, by the dervishes and the people that he met in his travels."

Henry Flynt Interview

Henry Flynt, an experimental composer with the Fluxus group, allegedly coined the term "concept art."—J.C.

"I played with Angus a number of times. I think I played violin in all cases. It was free-form music. There was one time when I was trying to compose some sort of quasi-Indian music for unaccompanied violin and I tried to play with him and have him be the drummer. It was rather funny. We were unable to get it to work. One reason was that I wanted him to play very simply. He told me that in order for it to be interesting to him, he had to play the much more complicated style. At that point it became so complicated that I couldn't appreciate what he was doing. It was on some kind of authentic hand-drum, probably Middle-Eastern or North African. That's what he usually played.

"LaMonte Young, when he moved to New York lived on Bank Street, 119 Bank Street. Angus hung out there a lot. They played together a lot, even in that apartment. It didn't really have an ethnic sound to me, it was more like playing improvised European music, sort of in the period of Debussy. LaMonte Young and Terry Jennings were both kind of like that. They'd come out of the jazz background, but they'd sort of gone one step beyond Jimmy Giuffre in kind of eliminating all of the black influences and kind of doing a very fast, more European scale.

"Angus was playing with Terry Riley when Riley was living on Grand St. Riley was playing saxophone. The interaction between the drums and saxophone sounded like it was very ring-modulated, just the acoustic interaction between the instruments—just the way they were playing very fast in the relationship between the horn and the drums. All of these fellows took their jazz background in a direction where the black feeling dropped out of their music completely. It sounded to me like something that you could very well notate as much as the Debussy clarinet pieces. It was very fast, very proficient playing.

"But at the *Brain Damage* thing around 1970, everyone was in effect making noise, and Angus got involved in a lot of situations like that. He didn't really care if the other musicians were proficient or they were just getting sound out of their instruments. He was always very enthusiastic about the violin playing that I did for him at the Cinemateque.

"I performed very briefly with the Velvet Underground. I just substituted for John Cale for four performances in 1966. I took a couple of long lessons from Lou Reed. What he actually taught me was the basics of rock. A little rock, a little blues. They had Nico and Gerard Malanga. He was dancing in this S&M act that they had with the Velvet Underground.

"I'm surprised that Angus was ever involved with the Velvets at all because they started as the Primitives. It started in Tony Conrad's apartment on Ludlow St. As a matter of fact, that's where I met Lou Reed, and Cale spent a lot of time there, too. Reed's apartment was over on the East

Broadway area of the Lower East Side. I happen to know because they abandoned the apartment and left the door unlocked with a lot of tapes just lying around.

"They just called me up. I think it was Sterling. He called me up at 4 a.m. and said that Cale was out and they needed me to substitute for him. I came in and Reed taught me their pieces. In about five minutes he taught me their whole repertoire because basically he just wanted me to be in the right key. That was about all that he was interested in. At one point I kind of got in a fight with him on stage because I was playing a very hillbilly-influenced style on the violin and that upset him very much. He wanted a very sophisticated sound, he didn't want rural references in what was supposed to be this very decadent S&M image that they were projecting. I only played in New York, only at the Dom, or whatever you call that Polish place that later became the Electric Circus. Playing in those things was strange. They would play for an hour at a time and sometimes I had the feeling that I was in hell. After you began to play for 45 minutes in this thing, everything began to get blurry. Sometimes I wasn't even aware of the relationship between what I was doing and what was coming out of the speakers."

Tony Conrad Interview

Until now, very little has been known for certain about the Primitives. About all that most of us knew about the group was that they had been formed to showcase "The Ostrich," a single about a dance step that Lou Reed wrote and recorded after reading in a fashion column that ostrich feathers were big that season. "Sneaky Pete" was the flip side.

"I decided to make up a dance, so I said, 'You put your head on the floor and have somebody step on it,' Lou explained, 'It was years ahead of its time.'"

Tony Conrad, a member of the Primitives, vividly recalled the events leading to the formation of the group, as well as Lou's first meeting with John Cale:

"When John and I were living on Ludlow Street, Piero Heliczer lived next door and Angus MacLise lived down the hall. Piero's working methods were less systematic than most people on this planet, and I liked that. Piero had sublet his apartment to a guy named David Gelber. Gelber hung out with some young ladies who came from Brooklyn and from Queens and he said, 'Hey, you gotta go to these people's party because they say they're gonna turn you into a rocknroll star.' This girl liked John (Cale) and me because we had long hair and she thought that we looked sort of like Beatles or something.

"So we thought this was hysterical, and these women were very like Woolworth's and very twerpy and the scene was unbelievable. So we actually went to their party up on the East Side somewhere. At the party there were these hyper-sleazy types from Brooklyn and Long Island City, people from Pickwick Records, who approached us and asked if we wanted to promote a record. Very limited information, but we thought yeah, that we were secretly rocknroll types anyway, and that we would like to do it.

"We had a meeting with Pickwick in their warehouse and recording studio. The studio was a cement basement type room with an old Ampex tape machine in it. They played Cale and I this single, "The Ostrich." We lined up Walter DeMaria to join us on this whole escapade. The idea was, what had happened is that the person we later came to know as Lou Reed and these other guys had gotten together and stuffed down a lot of pills and so forth and went nuts in the studio. They recorded it all in one night or something, they recorded and mixed down this cut and decided that they'd release it. But some of the guys were 'executive material,' so they were not going to go out on the road. They had to have stand-ins to go out for them. Once we agreed to this, they tried to sign us up for a seven-year contract—the sleazy assholes.

"We refused to sign these contracts, but in the meantime we actually went through a lot of negotiations and went back over there and met Lou and then we started going out on these promotion gigs. They would come around to pick John and I up in a station wagon. On the way to the gigs they would pass out the guitars like, 'Hey, maybe I'll play bass this time.' The song was very easy as they explained it to us because all the strings were tuned to one note, which blew our minds. We couldn't believe that they were doing this crap just like in a sort of strange ethnically Brooklyn style, tuning their instruments to one note, which is what we were doing too (in Young's group), so it was very bizarre. In fact we were tuning to two notes and they were tuning to only one.

"We were trying to break this record in the Lehigh Valley area like Reading and up and down there and we played a couple of high school gigs. We played on the same bill as Shirley Ellis ("The Name Game") and we did some interviews. We did one interview at station WREW in Reading. They'd say, 'Here they are from New York with their new hit single, "The Ostrich," THE PRIMITIVES!' Everybody would scream and we would try to play our guitars which we didn't know how to play.

"So that's how we met Lou. John was really impressed with Lou because he was very struck by Lou's ability to improvise rocknroll. He was stunned by the fact that Lou could just open his mouth and make rocknroll happen instantly. After a while, the record wasn't going to break, nothing happened. We used to play the two numbers, "The Ostrich" and "Sneaky Pete," which was the flip. It was really terrible. So then after this was all sort of run down, we went out about half a dozen times or so, and then I left the apartment. Lou and John remained in touch, and they started thinking about Lou getting out of Brooklyn, which was a great idea because he was living at home very uncomfortably. Lou at this point was eager to get something happening, so that when I left, John invited him to come over and stay where I had been staying."

JIM CONDON

THE PERILS OF NICO (1983)

> Nico's presence around (she was never *in*) the Velvet Underground was Andy Warhol's inspiration. He enjoyed putting together unlikely chemical combinations and observing the unpredictable results. Nico's surreal cabaret style added to the overall outsider-bohemian image of the band, and though she only appeared on the first album, her association with the Velvets is indelible.

My enthusiasm for Nico's music was never shared by any of my friends. They found her music depressing. I've been an avid follower of hers since discovering The Velvets, via *Transformer*. Naturally, I jumped at the chance to do the interview, which Nico would only allow in person. We met in New York, December 13, 1980, at a bar near the Chelsea Hotel. She more closely resembled the cover photograph of *June 1 1974* than any of the more recent pictures I've seen. She was dressed in her own inimitable style, clad in black boots, a black Moroccan shawl, and the same scarf she wore in the liner photos of the Neuronium album. She seemed to be in good spirits, despite a bad cold. We proceeded to Ferdinand's, a Spanish restaurant nearby. It was here the bulk of the interview was conducted, while we were treated royally by our bartender Willie.

J.C.: Is "Henry Hudson" going to be on the new album?

Nico: Of course. What do you think? Would you like an argument?

Are you putting "You're Lost Little Girl" on it?

(laughs) What makes you think that?

You said you were thinking of recording it with Robbie Kreiger.

When did I say that? Three years ago?

Yes. You said that you had seven or eight songs written for the album.

Oh no. I have 13 exactly—my lucky number. Today is the 13th that you're here—right on the spot! I'm not quite here—you understand? I mean I really want to give you a good interview. I don't want to just babble.

Feel free. Do you have a contract for this album?

It's right in there, yes. (Gestures toward a manilla envelope lying on a table.) It's not signed yet.

Do you know who will be producing?

Officially, Adrian Barber, but it will be me mainly. I have some good ideas about doing it. I'm very well oriented. I mean I'm really into everything, and I'm mainly into jazz. Not from the very beginning because I grew up with opera. I guess a combination of what I'm doing.

Do you still listen to medieval baroque?

Not at all. I like guitar players. Guitarists like Larry Coryell.

Did you see Bowie in The Elephant Man?

No, it was too difficult to get in. I don't want to pay 20 bucks to get in there. I mean in Paris I always had free tickets very easily, but over here I don't know, he protects himself too well I guess.

Are you using Lutz Ulbricht on this album?

He's not here. I would use him, but it depends on how big the budget is. I really would like Christian Vander from Magma . . . Have you ever had a Planter's Punch? I prefer the Myer's rum best. I am a rum fanatic.

Who is the person with you on the cover of Desertshore?

Oh, that is Ari. (Her son.)

(Nico did not know that her albums were cut-outs. She didn't really know what one was so I showed her my copy of The Marble Index that had a hole punched through it. Several people in the bar offered to buy it.)

That's funny, he wants to buy the album. If everybody walked around with my albums everybody would try to buy them. And I never get a peanut out of it. On my own albums I have not had royalties at all. Like Joe Boyd's pretense that Desertshore sold 3000 copies. That's the best joke. I learned that last night.

Have you seen Joe Boyd?

My manager tells me this.

How long have you known Anita Pallenberg?

Since we were first hanging out in London with the Rolling Stones. She was a real nasty person. She would do anything to upset her girlfriends. I don't know her anymore.

Have you seen her since Le Berceau de Cristal?

I wasn't with her. I was in Rome and Barcelona when he was shooting that sequence. I was working in Barcelona, writing songs for this album. It is already two years—a year-and-a-half ago that I got out of this con-tract finally after four painful years.

The Island contract?

It was Isle Of Man. Some guy that used to handle me in the beginning with Andrew Oldham. I did the "Ready Steady Go" show in London when I did a single with Andrew Oldham. Did you ever hear that? (C. nods.) You did? "I'm Not Sayin'"? What a terrible song!

Is Un Ange Passe in color?

Un Ange Passe? But I only had a small role in that. I am not even sure, maybe I'm wrong, because I made so many movies with him that I can't remember which ones I'm in.

Did Ash Ra Tempel release the soundtrack they composed for Le Berceau de Cristal?

Yes, that's one of my life stories. It's a version, one of the versions.

Which one of your songs was used in Le Lit de la Vierge?

Le Lit de la Vierge? It was "The Falconer."

Were you ever in The Living Theatre?

No, I studied with Lee Strassberg.

Have your films ever been shown in festivals?

Yes, at the New York festival one time, but I guess it wasn't advertised well enough.

Have you considered working with anyone else in films?

No, I don't think anybody is near as good as Garrel.

Do you have a favorite movie?

The Sea Wolf by Jack London.

(Nico was not aware that some of the Velvet Underground albums are out of print in America.)

They are? How come?

I presume because no one here was buying them.

Then how come Lou Reed has such a big house and how does he manage to live like this?

I'm really not in a position to answer that question. (Nico and I have a short conversation about my trip to New York.)

Do you drive?

I drive like the devil.

Andy wrote about the time you drove him up to Ann Arbor in his book . . .

(laughs) Oh my god. He was the only one who wasn't scared. He just couldn't care less. He figured that if I could take charge of 15 people on the bus, I have to be a good driver not to land in a ditch or something.

Lou Reed has written songs based on life at the Factory. Did you get any inspiration or material from it?

I wrote "The Falconer" for Andy. Do you remember "Innocent And Vain" from the last one? That is partially about the "Wanted Series." He painted a "Wanted Series"—men in profile and men facing you. That's when you get caught in jail . . . I think that's the most interesting series he's ever done, to be quite honest.

Do you like his new work?

We are not friendly enough that I should say that. I mean, if I were a materialist, I would say that he owes me a lot of money.

How did you meet Andy?

I really met Andy and the whole group in Paris . . . He is too much of a businessman to be a true artist.

Did you think that Andy's new book is accurate?

I've read a passage, maybe. (Nico starts to apply makeup from a small compact.) Oh my goodness—I look absolutely terrifying . . . He is too much of a businessman. Now he is getting his own TV show.

What's the name of it?

"Andy Warhol's Show." It has the same lettering as InterView magazine.

Do you remember anything about a half-hour segment of Four Stars called "Nico-Katrina"?

A half-hour? It was 28 hours long.

This was only one part of it.

I know, but I never acted with her together. She acted separately.

Were you ever managed by Danny Fields?

No, he was my friend. I hardly see him anymore ever.

Did you meet Iggy through Danny Fields?

Yes.

You first went to Spain with your mother when you were 15?

Yes, to Ibiza.

How is your mother?

She has gone away. It is already some time ago, 11 years ago.

Did she influence you by introducing you to opera?

She didn't. The music did by itself.

Did your parents have any effect on your career?

Well, my father was an archeologist, so he might have influenced me in that sense.

Were you brought up as a Lutheran or a Catholic?

I was baptized a Catholic and I was brought up as a very strict Protestant.

You said that your music is intentionally pagan.

Well, it tries to be, I hope.

Do you consider yourself a pagan?

Sometimes. But there is a little bit of everything in everyone. It's just got to come out.

Have you ever used tarot cards?

No, that is one thing I cannot stand. I just don't like tarot cards. I mean, I like the four of swords. That's about all.

Are you familiar with Aleister Crowley?

Yes, but not that much. I think Houdini was a great man.

Have you seen Lou Reed recently?

No, I don't hang out in gay bars like he does.

But he's married now. Do you think that's just a ruse?

He likes to manipulate women. You know, like program them. I guess that's why he got married. He wanted to do that with me.

He wanted to manipulate you when you were in The Velvets?

He told me so. Like, computerize me.

Would you say that he was the leader of the group?

He always will be . . . Wee-ly! Por favor! (We pause to order Margueritas.)

What happened at your concert at Rheims?

I was just thinking about that this morning. It was on December the 13th. It was in a cathedral, and there were 6000 people there. I can't believe that it was only six years ago.

I read that they called in the local bishop to perform purification rites after the concert.

You know how small town people are. It needed to be resanctified. People were dropping works on the floor. People in the audience were shooting up. I didn't know it until afterwards, until I read it. It was so cold in that place. They had to do something to keep themselves warm. Two thousand people were standing outside, they couldn't all get in. It was so cold, they had to do something. Artificial heat.

Did you like Sabotage Live?

Yes, really. He really comes across like a miner. He wants to be a miner. He is in Wales right now visiting his parents. His father is totally deaf and his mother is totally mute—can't talk. Isn't that strange?

I would suppose that would make a person somewhat withdrawn. Is Cale a withdrawn person?

Oh, not at all. He is very authoritarian. He likes to always point his finger at you. He likes to give orders.

Are your songs used without Cale's arrangements in La Cicatrice Interieure?

Except for "Evening Of Light," yes. "Evening Of Light" is the original.

Did John play harpsichord on that?

No, it was me. It was a little spinet that somebody stole for me.

Do you play instruments other than keyboards?

No. I would play the trumpet. I can make sounds on brass instruments, but it just doesn't suit a woman these days.

Do you still use your harmonica?

Yes, what else should I use? That's the only instrument that I have left. It's been busted up on the airplane.

Do you have a favorite out of your four albums?

I like all three of them. I don't like Chelsea Girls. I think it's a flop. I got so depressed when I heard the results of that album.

Do you read music?

I refuse to. I play by memory.

When did you make Evening Of Light?

1968. I didn't totally agree with the way it's edited. I liked the version before better.

Who edited it?

François de Menil. Who else? It was his attempt at being a movie director. He also made a full-length feature that cost him a fortune.

Doesn't he have a fortune?

Yes, but he likes to deny it.

There was another guy in the film from Ann Arbor.

Oh, him. I can't remember his name. We used to go up there to sing at the university. We stayed at this woman's house who had two sons. It was a child of movie makers.

So you knew Iggy before he was a recording star?

Oh, yes. But I told everybody that he would be a big star and I took him to the Factory to see Andy and they all laughed at me, they were kind of teasing me for bringing him around. This little kid with a runny nose.

What did Andy think of him?

He thought he was a cute little thing. He didn't think much of him, I don't think.

When was the last time you saw him?

In Paris, last time. (Apparently not wishing to go into the subject any further . . . Iggy's side of the story is detailed in Nick Kent's interview in NME and Creem from around the time of New Values.)

When did you meet Bob Dylan?

In Paris, when he was 20. I met him through a friend.

Did he play the piano on "I'll Keep It With Mine"?

He sent me the acetate because he had promised me a song for my singing, but it never went on a single, it just went on Chelsea Girls . . . There is something about your eyes that reminds me of Dylan at that same age.

I've never been told that. What was he like when you knew him?

He was on junk.

I thought he was known to be on speed at that time. Maybe it was a little later.

You mean when he broke his neck? That's very easily possible. I wouldn't know about that. I was in Spain then.

What do you think of Dylan's Christianity?

I think he's a little late to all of a sudden be writing about Christianity 11 or 12 years later. I mean if this is the promised land, I've just been crucified the past two weeks. It really hurts. I'm not kidding. I wouldn't look the way I look.

You look better than photographs of you from CBGBs.

That was last year, yes? Which one? You mean the one in Wet magazine? That horrible picture where I look like Mama Cass?

Do you listen to Arabian music?

First Spanish, because that's more important. It's so hard to sing. Weely! Por favor! (More drinks and shrimps in green sauce. Nico selects Spanish music for the jukebox.)

Did you ever meet John Lennon?

Yes. He was a wise guy. It (his assassination) had to happen sooner or later. It will happen to me too . . . (Referring to the music on the jukebox:) He used to be my favorite flamenco singer when I first went to Spain. I am going to get myself a fantastic flamenco dancer's suit. Not for women, but for men.

Are you going to wear a rose in your teeth?

No, that is for women. I am talking about the men flamencos. They are so beautiful, the way it is designed.

Did you ever write any songs with Jim Morrison?

He told me I should write songs for him and that he should write songs for me. One of them on the very first one—"Frozen Warnings." "Frozen Warnings" is about a hermit crossing the borderline . . . He was so much ashamed of his Christianity. He was a Jesus freak for a while. It was during the "Purple Haze" era. Were you already born then?

Yes, I was born in 1960.

You're only two years older than my son. I never knew I could write songs until I met Jim Morrison. He told me I should do this. He showed me how to do it, too.

When was the last time you saw him?

I knew him four or five years before he went to Paris. He only came to Paris because he had fallen off of a roof and he hurt his lungs. He couldn't sing anymore. He was always coughing up blood. He was always climbing around the edge of the roof. It had to happen.

Do you think Brian Jones had a death wish?

Not at all. He was totally separate. Why Brian?

Some people have described him as being very self-destructive.

But a true artist must self-destruct.

Do you think that you're going to.

I think I'm already doing it. Don't you?

That's not for me to judge. I'd like to say that I don't see that happening.

Can't you tell by the way I live? It is a continual battle, a drama, being
a stranger to myself. I don't have any references to know who I really
am. I mean everyday.

I don't think anyone ever really knows.

I mean to be really always in exile. I'm a total stranger to myself.
Except sometimes when I get reminded.

LESTER BANGS
NICO: *THE MARBLE INDEX* (1983)

According to biographer Richard Witt, Nico blamed the tepid
reception for *Chelsea Girl* on "the flute," a metaphor for Tom
Wilson's overall production. She then enlisted John Cale to orches-
trate the songs for *The Marble Index,* which she thought of as her
"first real record." Cale had been dismissed from the Velvet
Underground and was "looking for a profession." He agreed to
write the arrangements provided that he could also produce the
album. On the strength of his work for Nico, he went on to produce the Stooges and, as he recalls, "never looked back."

This article was originally written in 1978, for Diana Clapton's brief-lived
but much-missed *New Wave Rock* magazine. It was laid out and ready to
go, then aced out at the last second by coverage of the Nancy Spungen

murder, after which the magazine folded. Although it may seem a bit dated in places, I think the piece holds up, especially inasmuch as A) the album is timeless, and B) it is now available again, as an import item. I would like to thank Diana again for having the editorial soul to make such an assignment in the first place.—L.B.

In the autumn of 1968 an album came out which changed my life. Apparently it is still changing it, and has had similar impact on others, because the editor of this magazine not only asked me to write this article, but has been calling, cajoling, nearly threatening in her attempts to have me get it in. This from the editor of a national commercial magazine, over an article about a ten-year-old, out-of-print record which most people haven't heard and wouldn't want to if they knew what was in it.

So I guess my editor and I are smitten. But the quality of the smiting is more than just peculiar; this article was assigned and written for fear as much as love, or the love of fear. In his poetically definitive book on the Andy Warhol universe of the 1960's, *Stargazer*, Stephen Koch, in trying to come to some understanding for himself as much as his readers of Warhol, resorted to a quote from Baudelaire: "Half in love with easeful death." Then, just to drive home the point he was making about the intimacy between narcissism and Warholvian deathly otherness, he wrote: "*Half* in love. Exactly."

Anyone more than half in love with death would have to be a monster, of course, perhaps a Gilles de Rais, Idi Amin, Adolf Hitler. But there are some who would inflict the rarefied atrocities of Gilles de Rais, Idi Amin's bludgeoning nullification of all humanity, and the howling yet systemized totalitarian lockstep of Hitler—all upon themselves and no other. Sometimes, for performing such stupefying acts against their own persons, such basically pathetic people become culture heroes. In such a climate, the relationship between the artist (for that is what the people who I'm talking about are, through there are plenty of private citizens torturing and snuffing themselves in the same way) and his or her audience must be exceedingly odd.

Lou Reed went on the radio here in New York the other night to play some of his favorite records by other people and take calls from listeners. One kid called in and said, "That girl who died in 'Street Hassle,' was that someone you knew?" "Why?" said Lou. "Well," said the kid, "I mean did that really happen, did somebody really die in real life?"

"Would that make it a better song?" asked Lou Reed.

Now it's very easy to just write that kid off as an asshole, until you start to ask yourself just why you would want to listen, all the time, to a song about someone dying from an overdose of heroin. You might then begin to wonder if you are not the junkie, a junkie for the glimpses of the pit, half in love with easeful death at best—at worst an asshole vicariously getting off on other people's pain and calling it cute decadence.

The only trouble is that there is so much beauty mixed in with the ugliness. So what we have is a simultaneously transcendent and twisted work of art by a creative force whose vision has been itself twisted by circumstance, but because of that, and because the intertwining of beauty and horror runs so deep, the creator perversely keeps pursuing an admixture of his basest and purest elements. And if you are the type of person who likes being around such art as a regular thing then you are going to end up a little twisted too, if you weren't in the first place.

In which case you will have a minor problem which you will never be able to share with most people. A minor problem and a minor jewel. A jewel with facets of disease running all through it. You can turn it any way you like, look at it any light or from any angle, but you can only escape being . . . sullied? by the grace of what amounts to the soft hand of death by turning your back entirely.

And that too would be unfair, in a sense, to both yourself and the artist. Because in raising the base or crippled or tormented or mutilated to such a level, the artist has it seems done something at once noble and rather evil. In loving it you too become culpable, and then will try to seduce others, secretly hoping the whole world might one day come to wear your stigmata. Hence this article which is about *The Marble Index*, an LP by a German woman who calls herself Nico, with arrangements by John Cale. Like Lou Reed, both of them used to be in the Velvet Underground, though neither has ever attained anything close to the media attention and record-rack popularity Lou Reed may or may not be enjoying. There are reasons for that, of course: whether he's creating good art like *Street Hassle*, or crap like *Rock And Roll Heart*, Lou Reed seems to be an idea of the negative which most people can accept, or even find funny.

I think *The Marble Index* is the greatest piece of "avant-garde classical" "serious" music of the last half of the 20th century so far. The other night I played it for my new girlfriend, and she pronounced it "depressing." That doesn't particularly alienate me from her, because it's not like the only alternative for her was Peter Frampton, but more especially because her reaction was perfectly reasonable and even, in being negative, perhaps ultimately correct. Great art has always confirmed human values, but what are we to do when the most that our greatest works of art can affirm is that the creator fears he or she may be slowly, but surely, losing humanity entirely, along with the rest of mankind?

I don't know if I would classify it as oppressive or depressing, but I do know that *The Marble Index* scares the shit out of me. But what scares me even more is what most people seem to want instead. Every time I see some kid with concentration camp cropped hair maybe tinted green with maybe a garbage bag over his or her genuinely pathetic belittled frame, I want to puke and maybe even cry a little at the same time. Because so much of this punk rubbish is based on the stupidest apprehension and declamation of how proud one can be that "We don't *feel!*" when they didn't even realize the horror and irony Johnny Rotten spat into that particular phrase. When *The Marble Index* was released lots of record buyers wanted some vainglorious apocalypse and now most of them want either to be mommied Frampton-style and told that everything is okay snookums, or they want to be bludgeoned into a kind of terminal insensibility that they mistake for freedom from the contradictions in their lives and surroundings which are eating them alive, or they want to be told that it's all just a bunch of shit and the best is as good as the worst. But it just ain't so, and they know it in their guts, so they resort in desperation to something like Elvis Costello, who, when he last played a big hall in New York and mouthed that cheap line about how he doesn't wanna be your lover / "I just wanna be your victim," the audience actually fucking *cheered,* as if there never was anything alive between the hand-in-glove poles of happyhappy and what is finally merely banally disgusting meanspiritedness.

Maybe this would make more sense to you if I told you that I want to run so far from presuming to define or even describe this record because I love it so passionately that I'm terrified of what that might say about me. There are not cheap thrills on *The Marble Index,* no commercials for sadomasochism, bisexuality or hard drugs dashed off for a ravenous but vicarious audience—rather, it stares for a relatively short time that might just seem eternity to you into the heart of darkness, eyes wide-open, unflinching, and gives its own heart to what it finds there, and then tells you how that feels, letting you draw your own value judgments.

I played *The Marble Index* for a woman I loved about a year ago. She had never heard about Nico, never heard of John Cale, never really heard the Velvet Underground except in the context of this whole humorous but basically jive media game I set up with Lou Reed for a while. She listened to the whole thing in a state of mesmerism bordering on shock, then said of Cale, "He built a cathedral for a woman in hell, didn't he?" I called her up again today when I was fucked up about this article and she said, having still only heard it that one time, that she thought Nico was lost in her own blackness. I said, "But there's a pearl in there." I could hear her shudder over the phone, and suddenly she started talking very fast, and this is what she said as I madly pecked at my typewriter struggling to keep up: "Her whole body can glisten, she's just like a seed, the original seed of intercourse, her whole body can shine like the sun hits the water with sprays of light, and yet she's chosen to *de*-create from the surface to decreate again and again until the only message is 'I'm the life force itself, I'm the will to live,' a human embryo without hope of maturity, just sending signals. SHE'S IN THE WOMB, and what you call the pearl is just the pearl inside Mama's belly, the pulsebeat. She's accomplished decreation: 'Let me be behind everything human, oh god, the fact to catch a star in your eye or touch another human being, to feel another human being, to touch another universe is nothing, is just a frozen borderline'—that there is no nexus, just retreat, until the frozen borderline, until all you feel is the white light of survival and the abyss is the ocean around her. It's one teeny star, one microstar in the macrocosm of her body, and it's all she's chosen to have, she's obliterated them all, stamped them out. She is a black hole in space with one point left. And then this is what she says: 'It's empty, it's black, it's alone, it's a whirlpool, an eddy, it's nothing,' but it's not nothing, it's HER that's nothing. And that's why she could mutilate an insect, because that little wasp or grasshopper had more life than she ever could at all. She wants to mutilate it too because it's another act of negation, because it snuffs more light out of her star. She's like Beckett's play *Breath*, she's trying to find the last breath so she can negate breath, love, anything. A soft look would kill her."

She's quite a rock critic, that old girlfriend of mine—sometimes she scares me even more than Nico. But then, I'm scared of everybody—I'm scared of *you*. My girlfriend's eloquence was one reason I loved her almost from first sight, but not why I had to get halfway to the other side of the geographical world to be able to write a song that said how much I loved her. It was because of something obviously awry in me, perhaps healing, at least now confronting itself, which is one way to perhaps not rot. There's a ghost born every second, and if you let the ghosts take your guts by sheer force of numbers you haven't got a chance though probably no one has a right to judge you either. (Besides which, the ghosts are probably as scared of you as you are of them.) Nico is so possessed by ghosts she seems like one, but there is rather the clear confrontation of the knowledge that she had to get that awfully far away from human socialization to be able to write so nakedly of her love for damn near anyone, and simultaneously and so crucially the impossibility of that love ever bearing fruit, not because we were born sterile but directly the opposite, that we come and grow ever fiercer into such pain that we would sooner eat the shards of a smashed cathedral than risk one more possibility of the physical, psychic and emotional annihilations that love between two humans can cause, not even just cause but generate totally as a logical act of nature in its ripest bloom. Strange fruit, as it were. But only strange to those who would deny the true nature of their own flesh and spirit out of fear, which reminds me somehow that if you seek this album out you should know that this is a Catholic girl singing these songs, and perhaps her ultimate message to me was that the most paralyzing fear is no sin, not even the flight from the feared object/event/truth/confrontation/*who cares what*—that only sin is denial, you who would not only turn your eyes away from what you fear as I sometimes must turn my ears away from this album, but would then add injury to what may or may not be insult by asserting that it does not exist.

But is she only asking us to let the full perception of the fear flood our hearts, or leading us on to embrace the death she seeks? I don't know. What I do know is that when I first set out to write this article I got very high—I was so stupid I thought I'd just let the drugs ease my way into Nico's domain of ghosts, then trot back and write down what I'd found there. But when I went and picked up the album, her face on the cover, in a picture I've seen a thousand times, seemed to be staring directly at, *into* me with a malevolence so calm it was inhuman. It was like holding a snake in your hands and having it look you right in the eye. I put the album down and walked away, but when I looked back I saw those two eyes, following me around the room. Let me add that drugs have not ordinarily affected me in this way, at least since the Sixties. I finally got up the nerve to put the album on after that experience, but found it almost unbearable to listen to. Not that it wasn't beautiful, rapturous in fact, but that its beauty was so deathly and its rapture out of such agony. It's putting lead weights in my heart because I don't want to listen to it right now (and of course the lead weights are not *The Marble Index* but its reflection into me of my unknown fears and pangs), but I have to get some notes and lyrics for this article, so you all be sure to run right out and buy it, okay kids? Except you can't, because it's not even available on import anymore. I can just imagine the demonstration in front of Jem Records or Elektra demanding its reissue: everyone in black robes and hoods, carrying torches with cold fire and a casket containing the wax effigy of a giant insect. But enough evasion; I'm going to go subject myself to this damn thing once more. And I certainly hope you bastards appreciate the passion behind this pointless self-torture.

RICHARD MORTIFOGLIO

THE VELVET UNDERGROUND AND NICO (1979)

In the next two essays, Richard Mortifoglio assesses the Velvets' first two albums from the perspective of the late seventies–early eighties, or after the rise of the vital New York punk/new wave scene that seems unimaginable without the Velvets (see for example, Clinton Heylin's *From the Velvets to the Voidoids: A Pre-Punk History for a Post-Punk World*).

"Decadence" has been synonymous with The Velvet Underground since their beginnings as the main attraction in Andy Warhol's sixties roadshow, The Exploding Plastic Inevitable.

Just a look through the blurbs from their reviews (conveniently reprinted on the inner sleeve of their first album) shows how fast they were typecast; Richard Goldstein's pronouncing The Velvets a "marriage between Bob Dylan and the Marquise de Sade" was more than typical. There were more than a few references to post-Weimar Berlin with Nico filling in as Der Blau Engel. What with Gerard Malanga's whip dances and The Velvets' sinister stage presence—they all wore shades; Lou Reed claimed it was because of the lights. As for the black leather, the strobes bounced nicely off it—this instant labeling wasn't unjustified. But it had little to do with the band The Velvets would ultimately evolve into. And despite or because of the initial notoriety, it did them great harm.

They never did quite live down the tag of "Andy Warhol's band" (whatever that was supposed to mean; it would be hard to imagine a more unmusical person than Andy Warhol). Still, Lou Reed has only praise for his former patron (even though it has been recent habit with him to savage every one in sight). Warhol's use of banal, consumer imagery in his paintings, the "acting out" and role-switching of his stable of performers, his nihilistic, cool voyeurism—all these seeped into Lou's method, or confirmed tendencies already there. Yet although The Velvets were certainly not bereft of irony or humor, irony was *the* major Warholian mode; quite simply, Warhol was camp and The Velvets weren't (though *White Light/White Heat* had its campy moments). But while Warhol himself was too personally austere to be called decadent (an austerity Lou Reed is too quick to admire in others—witness his deference to the "ice-man" Bowie in the early '70's), his lapsed Catholic scene was. And The Velvets were central figures in it.

Still, one aspect of The Exploding Plastic Inevitable that is generally overlooked is that they were the first multi-media shows, forerunners of Pablo light shows at the Fillmore. More than most rock performers, Lou Reed has always been interested in purely formal possibilities; he has much of the "pure" artist in him, despite periods of cynical hackwork. (The binaural recording procedures used on *Street Hassle* and subsequent releases is merely a current instance of Reed's longstanding technological fascinations.) One problem of interpretation with The Velvets and Lou Reed, in particular, is mistaking mere experimental strains for permanent features. And to add to the confusion, The Velvets never repeated themselves. Each album reveals a very different band than the preceding one, even if, paradoxically they managed to project a rather consistent image. (Lou Reed has continued this paradox throughout his erratic solo career.)

As for "experimental strains," their first album, *The Velvet Underground And Nico,* is notable for its "as if" songs. "Heroin," "I'm Waiting For The Man," and "Venus And Furs" were merely examples of Lou Reed flexing his literary style and considerable powers of identification ("I am a Camera cum Junkie"). But it was three songs more than any others that scared away potential listeners (though the first album did quite well compared to the others). It reached the point where Reed would refuse to perform "Heroin" at the last Velvets' gigs at Max's, summer of 1970. Much like the matter-of-fact treatment The Doors gave their grand guignol pop (though unlike Lou Reed, Jim Morrison was romantic, hence "decadent"), The Velvets played this sensational material rather straight. (It was only in Reed's Alice Cooper ripoff *Rock & Roll Animal* period that he began to "Taiwan on" during "Heroin.") "Venus In Furs" is especially interesting in this light since S & M is chic now. The whips 'n' chains atmosphere called up by John Cale's viola drones cut by slashes and Maureen Tucker's slave-master time keeping on kettle drum and tambourine is among the Velvets' most musically satisfying; any current S & M song would be a pose or drone for sniggers.

Warhol is all over this album. He did the famous banana peel on the cover which, lifted, revealed a pinkish (though apparently the first few were green), slightly obscene banana. He is also listed as producer, presumably because he paid the initial studio costs. He probably also sat there and watched, as was his wont. The irony of this is that "Sunday Morning," overproduced by professional A & R man Tom Wilson, sounds shoddier than any other cut on the album. Which says something for the Warholian aesthetic of letting things be. *White Light/White Heat* would sound even worse. There is no well-produced Velvets album (part of their charm, I would say). Even *Loaded* is over-produced and edited badly.

But despite the primitive sound, *The Velvet Underground And Nico* is probably the strongest debut ever made by a rock band. It is no exaggeration to say that every song is a small masterpiece. The degree of craft on display here is even more impressive since there was no precedent for this kind of international "art rock" and songwriting. Dylan was the nearest comparison, which Goldstein dutifully noted. Though The Velvets could be vaguely called "folk rock," unlike Dylan their music was purged of most blues and R & B strains. This was extremely rarified rock and roll, very "white," much like Buddy Holly's abstracted rock and roll lyricism with only the essential riffs and rhythms remaining.

Reed's lyrics revealed an unusually firm command of schooled English, too. This is where the comparison with Dylan really breaks down since Dylan's whitmanesque "grocery lists," his effusive wordplay, were the models for the burgeoning singer-songwriter movement at this time. I've always felt that Reed's unique combination of plain talk and elegant late medieval imagery suggested T.S. Eliot as an influence. And indeed, Lou's schooltime mentor, Delmore Schwartz (who Lou dedicated "European Son" to) was a world authority on Eliot. Reed himself has expressed amazement that Eliot could write the masterful "Love Song Of J. Alfred Prufrock" at age 25. All this points to a classical severity in Lou Reed's makeup that should counteract the charges of "decadent." Though the imagery on the first album is richer here than any subsequent Velvets album, Reed still avoided any over-reliance on metaphor or stream-of-consciousness techniques. "Black Angel's Death Song" is an exception and this itself is a deft tour-de-force. In fact, the dizzying avalanche of words here helps to underscore the understated language on the rest of the album.

This incongruous mixture of urban speech framed by medieval conceits had its musical parallel in the early Velvets blend of rock and roll flash supported by Eurogothic folk melodies. This was because of John Cale, primarily. With his "classical" training and his mad-hatter Dada sensibility, he broadened the Velvets' musical base, lent it a vividness and romantic feel it certainly would have lacked with only Lou Reed's "minimalism" to draw from. Cale is so dominant on this album that there are few classic rock beats at all. (*White Light/White Heat* would right the balance.) Only "I'm Waiting For The Man" and "There She Goes Again" qualify as straight rock and roll, with "Run Run Run" and "European Son" running distant seconds. And since Maureen Tucker didn't use a conventional drum set till much later, her kettle drumming only stressed the rhythmic novelty.

One paradox embodied by the early Velvets was the contrast between the ballad tone of their first album and the sonic blast of their stage show, which by all accounts was background music for a malign psychedelic three-ring circus. The only connections are the white noise jam at the end of "European Son" (with Lou Reed and Sterling Morrison trading off frantic rhythms in archetypal Velvet style) and Reed's occasional guitar solos—high strung, near tuneless assaults, for the most part (ostrich guitar).

An exhilirating feature of the Velvets' music is the tension between this dissonance and a pure melodic quality that reaches its peak in the back-up vocals. "Run Run Run" chugs along in crackling Bo Diddley style till the chorus, where Maureen's voice lights up the atonal field like illumination rounds. These vocals generally lend the songs unexpected dimensions whenever they enter. "There She Goes Again," which plays off some of Reed's most forceful singing with the running "there she goes," is the fullest sounding performance on the record. And when Reed goes it alone, Cale's instrumental work, such as his viola drones on "Heroin," "Venus In Furs" and "Black Angel's Death Song" as well as his percussive piano attacks on "All Tomorrow's Parties" and "I'm Waiting For The Man," color what otherwise would be a dark landscape. (Lou Reed's tendency toward "black" or blank music can be seen on *Berlin* or *Street Hassle* and of course *White Light/White Heat*, which is unrelieved by any melodic values whatsoever, though it is the Velvets' most musically ambitious album.)

The album's few pure rock and roll moments are stunning, though prefiguring the virtuoso rock and roll the Velvets would be famous for by the time of *Loaded*. Throughout "I'm Waiting For The Man," they play what John Piccarella identifies as "forced rhythm," a beat that stressed all accents equally, a feature of punk rock that he credits the Velvets with innovating. The end of "Waiting For The Man" features frantic piano-thumping that turns dissonant at the last minute just as a fluid bass line (Cale or Morrison) unexpectedly starts to climb the ropes of the song, one of the finest moments in all of rock and roll. This kind of dynamic bass playing opens up "European Son" and gives the album's closing lines a special urgency, as Lou Reed sings, "Your clowns bid you goodbye." The intro to "There She Goes Again" is stolen from Marvin Gaye's "Hitchhike," but the rock and roll highlight is a condensed guitar solo whose staccato riffing kicks off just in time for Reed's trademark stammering vocal at the end.

Lou Reed once claimed that the first three Velvets albums are a narrative trilogy with identifiable characters and continuing plot. While this must be taken with a grain of salt it is also convenient to take him at his word. If there is a "story" on the first album, it is the narrator's attempt to navigate the obstacles of rejection and loneliness as he pursues love in the city. "Watch out! The world's behind. There's always someone around you who will call," from "Sunday Morning," the album's opening song, indicates the lyrical paranoia that permeates the whole record. Nico's appearance as "chanteuse" on three songs is perfect in the context because of her snow-queen image. While they are sung in the third person, her performances on "Femme Fatale" and "All Tomorrow's Parties" suggest a willful '60's vamp who succeeds in fucking over Lou's protagonist. But this sketch is too neat and downbeat to describe the real effect of the Velvets' songs.

While every Velvet Underground song is about some kind of loneliness, there is also great joy in the Velvets' music, a proud, noble quality that has made their appeal almost universal. This is the joy of overcoming pain, of "coming through," of transcendence—whether through drugs, psychological adjustment or, most important, small Joycean epiphanies, a new, purely secular, religious feeling. The current of salvation in the Velvets' work is very strong. This has to do with the texture of the music, the light-in-the-night method, as well as any explicit themes in the lyrics themselves. Lou Reed was probably the first artist to see the healing qualities of pure rock and roll. He finally wrote a song about it, "Rock And Roll," at the height of his powers just before *Loaded*. And this religious side of the Velvets would reach an apex on their masterpiece, the "third album," whose meditative depth makes it a personal favorite.

The Velvet Underground And Nico is a sensational album, in both the good and bad senses. While its evil aspect is ultimately cartoonish, its overall effect is very "real"—the beginning of the Velvets' urban naturalism. And while the cast of characters is a little too exotic for any strong identification, the major character is the city itself. The Velvets' novel achievement was to create a myth of city life that both rang true, unlike romantic street poetics from Laura Nyro through Springsteen, and charged each small detail of one's urban (or suburban) existence with adventure. This was implicit in rock and roll since Chuck Berry but the

Velvet Underground made it all quite explicit. And with the notable exception of The Dolls, it's taken almost a decade for someone else to celebrate city life with the same fervor and artistry.

RICHARD MORTIFOGLIO

WHITE LIGHT/WHITE HEAT (1983)

Elvis Costello, that master of prolific sameness, recently observed you have 20 years for your first record, about six months to cough up the second one. It's natural to use the second time around as a chance to refine the initial burst of inspiration. (We're talking about good bands here.) So it's logical that the end product turns out either a slick repeat or a really mature advance which doesn't alter the original premise. Records such as *Funhouse, Too Much Too Soon, The Rolling Stones Now*, yes, *This Year's Model* are all superior versions of their predecessors. As usual, the Velvet Underground were an exception. With *White Light/White Heat*, they abandoned the relatively structured "folk-rock" characterizing their debut and, instead, focused on the most dissonant, distended, improvisatory aspects of their sound. *White Light/White Heat* is the most resolutely anti-melodic rock ever recorded before punk, a truly "black" record, from the color of the cover to the last crackling electronic burp closing "Sister Ray," that monster opus which summarizes the album's high anarchy and takes 17 minutes to end it.

I've always wondered what the Velvets actually sounded like during the Exploding Plastic Inevitable roadshows. As far as I know, there are no bootlegs *[this was written shortly before the emergence of the 1966 boot—Ed]* and though there does exist a Warhol/Morrisey film from this period, no one I know has seen it. Judging from the reviews, however, one can make a safe guess that the Velvets played something like *White Light/White Heat* from the very start. Which is strange. Again, here is a band whose recorded work stresses strong material, edgy lyricism, audible literate lyrics and their stage show disregards these virtues all for an (anti-) psychedelic, amorphous, pounding blur. Strange but prophetic in the end. This move is the first in a straight line of turnarounds, identity shifts, radical experimentation that characterized the Velvets', and especially Lou Reed's, career as a whole.

This first major move is perhaps the most important. It is the key to understanding why the Velvet Underground is the most *artistically* influential rock and roll band ever. Simply put, rock and roll is a rigid form and is best served by sticking within its limits. So the Velvets' ability to extend that form, to open up various aesthetic stances within the music, while always playing and sounding "classic," was uncanny and prescient. In the past five years, we have witnessed the full-blown results of the Velvets' original explorations. Talking Heads' cerebral funk, DNA's slyly chaotic action-sound, Pere Ubu's big industrial beat, Television's strained lyricism, Suicide's stiff streetwaves; all can be traced to the Velvet Underground as primary ground, first cause, spiritual source.

What were the Velvets up to on *White Light/White Heat*? Why has it lasted as an influence? It's an extreme record and this very extremity marks it for the kind of failed brilliance most "experiments" suffer in time. And there have been weirder pop records before and since. *Trout Mask Replica, Song Cycle, Anthem Of The Sun, Sgt. Pepper* et al are clear redefinitions of popular music. But *White Light/White Heat* is in a class alone. Instead of obviously importing other genres into the rock form—i.e., freaky blues, "classical" arrangements, music-hall pastiches, bluegrass counterpoint—the Velvets expanded rock and roll by stripping it down to its essential element: the beat, the electric pulse of the whole rock and roll feeling. They then made this explicit by heating that element up to an excruciating level and sustaining it for a whole set. *White Light/White Heat* is the paradigm of rock and roll energy. Only the Stooges, early Modern Lovers, Sex Pistols, and Clash even approached it and none of these possessed what has to be called the Velvets' high spiritual intelligence—their self-consciousness and ability to work it through like practitioners of high art.

They did this on *White Light/White Heat* as a working band. Consequently, individual discussions about Lou Reed's persona, songwriting, singing, while important, have to be soft-pedaled in equal attention to the contributions of the other members. It is here that Maureen Tucker's Bo Diddley tom-tom drumming is elevated from an eccentric textural "touch" into a leading voice in a frenetic four-way conversation. Remember, this record concerns the uses of the beat and, on climactic cuts like "I Heard Her Call My Name" and "Sister Ray," Moe Tucker's masterful negotiation of the most torturous rhythmic changes saves the album from a descent into arty chaos. Her drumming flies on these cuts, reminiscent of the superb Andrew Cyrille, who followed Cecil Taylor's flash-lightning piano work through convoluted, treacherous by-paths and swung anyway.

All God's chillun' got rhythm. Jonathan Richman once said he thoroughly "studied" *White Light/White Heat* and concluded that Sterling

Morrison was the greatest of all rhythm guitarists. This is a tricky insight because *White Light* is perhaps the most badly recorded rock album ever. (Part of its charm, Lou Reed claimed.) So it's hard to separate the instruments in the opaque muddle that's left. One can always tell Morrison apart from Reed on the basis of their shared lead work though, especially on "Sister Ray." Reed's is the classic nervous style, deliberately out-of-tune, abrasive, askew, fuzztoned, while Morrison prefers the more cleanly sketched blues riffing. Melodically, he was a much more conventional rocker than Reed. (This was put to good use when the Velvets returned to a more traditional rock and roll; the straight lead guitar on *Loaded* and *1969* is mostly Morrison's.) But it was also Morrison who developed the broken-down syncopated guitar strumming that defined the Velvets' rave-ups as early as "European Son" on the "banana" record. Since John Cale's bass-work rarely provides a steady backbeat—very often, there's no bass at all—it fell to Morrison to ground this band in some order of a rocking chordal cushion. Like Moe Tucker, Morrison manages to bring some semblance of roots to the most freestyle jams. In the process, he made the Yardbirds' machinegun rhythm over in his own personal signature. This audacious exploitation of the psychedelic style applies to the others as well, as we shall see.

As for John Cale, the free-for-all atmosphere of *White Light* allows him a perfect opportunity to indulge his autodestruct musico-saboteur instincts. Cale always brings a little of Europe wherever he goes. On the first album, he brought the viola, gypsy melodies, percussive "Appassionata" piano, and an overall feeling of gloomy, gothic lyricism. On *White Light,* he travels with a suitcase full of Dada, that established tradition of well-heeled nihilism that delights in smashing pianos and other icons. Rock-wise, this translates into bass-playing that functions as lead instruments, violently executed in a manner neither Jack Cassady nor Phil Lesh ever approached. On "I Heard Her Call My Name," Cale stops and starts with no particular regard for the upward propulsion Morrison and Tucker generate. "White Light/White Heat" itself closes with a noisy tag that finds the bass sputtering in a repetitious loop that negates the whorehouse cakewalk that holds the track together.

So much for the trashing of rock and roll bass-playing. Cale's greatest moments are reserved for his organ work on "Sister Ray." Since "Sister Ray" is musically little more than an atonal drone, Cale's sustained rococo fugal counterpoint provides this epic with the small color it possesses. Cale begins with a controlled chordal block-building, carefully filling the track, layering the sound till midway he reaches a screaming apex and abruptly stops short and leaves Reed and co. a clean slate to mark up with a steady Eastern buzz-drone that chases its tail till the repetitions lose any sense of resolution and just fly out into the black hole of climax after climax. These progressions are so inspired that, by the time of the closing verse, Cale's steely intervals and inversions have pushed the band to the outer limits of rock and roll musicianship. Not for nothing did this man play in godfather minimalist LaMonte Young's Theatre of Eternal Music. On "Sister Ray," Cale led the keynote psychedelic organ of the Seeds and ? and the Mysterians to lengths they never dreamed of.

Cale also contributes two lead vocals to this record. The seedy elegance (Sandy Pearlman calls him "oily") of his Welsh accent adds some extra sinister quality to Lou Reed's black humor short, short story, "The Gift." Likewise, after some nicely-phrased poetic turns, "Lady Godiva's Operation" changes into a nightmare straight out of a Burrough's cut-up. Lou Reed always gave away vocals to the other members when he felt his own delivery couldn't match his lyrics. And since *White Light/White Heat* features some of his most bizarre songwriting, Cale's Frankensteinian aspects are all the more called for. In every way, the concept is as much Cale's as it is Reed's.

It was on the debut that Lou Reed introduced his "ostrich" guitar, a jagged, deliberately dissonant lead style that considerably harshened the overall lyrical tone of that record. On *White Light* this coloring effect determines the sound of the whole band. Like Morrison, Reed was basically a rhythm guitarist who occasionally doubled on lead. And though his lead work lacks Morrison's rootsy facility, it is undeniably original. The earlier reference to Cecil Taylor is apt, for Reed himself stated he wanted to produce a rock and roll analogous to the "free jazz" of Ornette and Taylor.

Actually, what Reed's guitar-work most resembles is the sour rhythmic fill-ins that a blues-rocker like John Lee Hooker specialized in. (Hooker himself sounded as if he could never quite get his guitar in tune.) *White Light/White Heat* is nothing less than a violently strung-out urban blues. The jam set-ups of "Sister Ray" and "The Gift" give Reed ample room to stretch out and display his peculiarly dessicated chops. "I Heard Her Call My Name" features the most astounding trash lead work ever recorded, a chaotic zig-zag that threateningly teeters over the edge of atonal breakdown. As with Morrison and Cale, Reed brought the psychedelic amateursitar style to the nether regions.

Reed's singing is also bluesier than before. With honky tonk piano in tow, he glides through "White Light/White Heat" in a giggly, black-face voice, sounding like he's getting goosed by Cale's bass-neck. His masterfully sustained vocals on "Sister Ray" run from Chuck Berry to Pran Din Panth in five lengthy movements. Even the album's most conventionally "pretty" song, "Here She Comes Now," ends with one of Reed's funkier vocal effects, the stutter that he first introduced on the debut's "There She Goes Again." And again, on "I Heard Her Call My Name," Reed matches his wrenching guitar-playing with a manic vocal display, kept barely in check by the clear back-up singing. It is the "Light" to Reed's overheated performance.

I've dwelled mostly on the musical aspects of *White Light/White Heat* since I believe it eventually opened up the formal possibilities within rock and roll without the obvious device of importing other genres and gimmicks. It's somewhat an instrumental record and it's "pure." Not that the blues and the psychedelic open-endedness don't constitute influences. Only that these styles are never copied directly; they act as stylistic shadings, the blues for some street-raunch gutsiness and the Eastern drone for its "space." In fact, the Velvets' use of these two most popular sixties genres was a brilliantly original recasting of what was merely derivative in most other bands. "Sister Ray," in particular, stands square in the tradition of the long cut so popular at the time. "Inna Gadda Da Vida," "Time Has Come Today" by the Chambers Brothers, "When The Music's Over," "East-West" by the Butterfield Blues Band all reflected the general mood of mind-expansion prevalent at the time. They also have dated badly and "Sister Ray" hasn't. Why?

It's a cliche that the Velvets were anomalies in the counterculture. This is partly true but not as much as some anti-hippie punks would have it. The Velvets were definitely a sixties phenomenon; they enjoyed the same cultural freedoms the Jefferson Airplane did and made full use of them. You're never innovative in a vacuum and the sixties were a time for innovation. The fact that Lou Reed was more interested in real life than most of his contemporaries is another matter. Much is made of the Velvets being ahead of their time but, in the context of the late sixties, they were a throwback to the New York art-bohemia of a few years back, the world of pop art, Warhol, Jack Smith's *Flaming Creatures,* underground films, Happenings, etc. The Velvets were cultural modernist aesthetes in an old-fashioned sense while the hippie psychedelic mentality was an ahistorical, provincial reaction to urban life and its attendant evils. In fact, the Velvets were a striking example of that "evil" to many. (Witness their disastrous show with the Mothers at Fillmore West, Rolling Stones' refusal to feature them, the whole ultra-hype concerning their alleged "decadence.") The mentions of smack and S&M on the debut were nice, though sensational-istic, undercuttings of the hippie attitude. (So was playing Buddy Holly riffs, for that matter, straight rock and roll being another "evil.") But its use of psychedelic free-space made *White Light/White Heat* an especially audacious challenge to the prevailing utopianism of the sixties mind-set. The counter-culture allowed the Velvets to rip off the freedom they needed to do what they did but their vision was solely their own.

What was that vision? At the time, it seemed to be guided by drugs. While the Grateful Dead were the ultimate acid band and the hedonist Stones' drug of choice was cocaine, *White Light/White Heat* explored the highs and burned-out lows of speed. This is no mere interpretation. The songs' lyrics literally mention drug-taking and it's clear, from the record's high panicky quality, that drug isn't heroin. "Heroin" itself was basically a literal exercise which asked, "What's it like to be a junkie?" On *White Light,* Lou Reed is writing out of a more urgent personal situation. Reed understood that drug-taking was a 20th century equivalent of a religious experience. "White Light/White Heat" makes speeding out to be a metaphor of mystic illumination. The key line in "Sister Ray," "I'm searching for my mainline," serves as a sign-post in the quest for the knowledge that is Sister Ray's and Sister Ray's alone. As with Stencil's in Pynchon's *V,* it is ultimately a paranoid quest but, then, speed is one pre-lude to paranoia.

The whole lyric content of *White Light* is either macabre or fearful. "The Gift" finds its protagonist being unknowingly stabbed in the head by his girlfriend under the most sick-comic circumstances. "Lady Godiva's Operation" ends with a sex-change operation gone haywire. The whole of side two is an exercise in excessive excitability. "I Heard Her Call My Name" magnifies the feeling of being noticed by *that* woman to absurd proportions. And the narrator in "Sister Ray" is made more and more des-perate by the watchful eye of Sister Ray, his godhead, master, source of insight and illumination. A similar scenario occurs in Steely Dan's "Doctor Wu." But that song is more concerned with love and the ultimately futile resistance to it. "Sister Ray"'s street-story is ultimately about those moments when everything is absolutely *clear,* when one can be protected by what one knows.

It is on the third Velvet Underground album that Lou Reed will resolve these problems of drugs and insight, love and religion in a less extreme manner. But *White Light/White Heat* stands as an exceedingly strong statement of what it means to "search." In that way, it is very much of its time and the fact that it has lasted proves again that the Velvets were right on target. The extremes of playing, singing, songwriting on this record are all the more remarkable because they are all so solid, so "right." That was the Velvets' gift to us, the chance to be outside and right in life all at once. There was much more to come.

PAUL WILLIAMS
FOGGY NOTION (1993)

In Paul Williams's list of the 100 greatest rock singles, the Velvets are represented by "Foggy Notion," "the great Velvets AM radio world saturation essence of rock and roll pure statement of existence hit single that never was."

Alternate universe time. In some other reality just under the surface of this one, the Velvet Underground were bigger than the Beatles, and "Foggy Notion," despite its six-minute-and-twenty-second length, was #1 for eleven weeks in the fall of 1969. In this reality, however, the Velvets never scratched the top 100 on either side of the pond, despite being the quintessential (and, in the long term, perhaps the most influential) rock and roll band of their era. It's true "Sweet Jane," a rock classic if ever there was one, was released as a 45 at some point in the U.K., but no one noticed and it's not a song I think of as a single, its identity rests somewhere else. "Foggy Notion" on the other hand I first encountered as a slice of seven-inch vinyl, a 45-rpm bootleg issued (reputedly with the tacit cooperation of Lou Reed) in New York City in 1976. To me it's the great Velvets AM radio world saturation essence of rock and roll pure statement of existence hit single that never was. I think they should set up the planet's last record-playing phonograph in the Smithsonian with a copy of "Foggy Notion" on it playing over and over and over through tinny speakers till the turntable rusts or the record wears flat or the barbarians storm the city and destroy all traces of our once-great civilization.

Until then, we dance.

Leaving aside the vaguely sadomasochistic lyrics (no no you don't understand they're just hitting her to make sure she doesn't overdose), this song is sheer white riff. White because unlike most of the other rhythms in rock and roll, this nervous double-time repeating drum figure, and the amazing guitar bursts that dance alongside it, don't seem to have

The Velvet Underground Companion
68

roots in any black American musical traditions I'm aware of. There is some kinship perhaps to Coltrane in his more frenetic moments, but no obvious predecessor. Maureen Tucker on drums, Sterling Morrison on rhythm guitar, and Lou Reed on lead guitar and vocals have in fact created something new under the sun (Doug Yule on bass contributes significantly to the gestalt of this track, but the others were working on the riff years before he showed up), and punk rock and speed metal are probably just the first of many musical genres that will draw from this well in years to come.

It's so simple. "Discoveries of great moment in mathematics and other disciplines," says G. Spencer Brown, "once they are discovered, are seen to be extremely simple and obvious, and make everybody, including their discoverer, appear foolish for not having discovered them before." Maureen is standing in the middle with her mallets, beating out this insistent boom-boom-snap! rhythm over and over with incredible speed and steadiness—a fraction early on the snap! I think this is the trick that drives the engine, makes the blood boil in musicians' and listeners' veins. Behind her (aurally) is the bass, supporting the beat at times but also free to solo around, jazz-fashion, commenting on and exploring and deepening the mystery before returning to home base. The two guitars stand on either side of the drum riff, which is really a drum/rhythm guitar riff, Sterling riding the drumbeat with his "broken-down syncopated guitar strumming" (thanks Richard Mortifoglio), Lou presumably responsible for the more lyrical lead guitar excursions, except that when you listen carefully both guitars are playing rhythm much of the time, and either one seems capable of taking off in unexpected "lead" lines, explorations of the narrow but infinite free space dead ahead, the corridor between the hood of the engine and the horizon (rushing closer at every moment, though you know we're never going to get there).

And that's all. Drums in the middle, guitars all around, speed in a straight line (with broken fingerings, creating nervous insistent inventive polyrhythms) from here to the event horizon. And every now and then (according to very rigorous song structure imperceptible to us as we race along with the runners) this music of the spheres is interrupted by astonishing timeless vocal passages, Lou Reed so present, so totally outside of time, laughing, standing still like the hummingbird, doing calisthenics with his voice while the music rushes ever forward. "Well, I've got a foggy notion. All right . . ." And then back to the infinite. "Do it again." "All right." "Do it again." Welcome to the new world. "I've got a foggy notion . . ."

First release: "White Heat" bootleg single, 1976; recorded May 6, 1969.

VELVET UNDERGROUND (1978)

Originally a contribution to *Stranded: Rock and Roll for a Desert Island*—a collection of essays in which critics responded to the question, "What rock and roll album would you take to a desert island?"—Ellen Willis's piece remains one of the most insightful commentaries on the nature of the Velvets' brand of punk aesthetics and its relation to the punk ideologies of the seventies.

I'll Let You Be in My Dream

A change of fantasy: I have just won the first annual Keith Moon Memorial Essay Contest. (This year's subject was "Is Ecstasy Dead?") The prize is a fallout shelter in the bowels of Manhattan, reachable only through a secret entrance in CBGB's basement. It is fully stocked: on entering the contest I was asked to specify my choice of drugs (LSD), junk food (Milky Way), T-shirt ("Eat the Rich"), book (*Parade's End*), movie (*The Wizard of Oz*),[1] rock-and-roll single ("Anarchy in the U.K."), and rock-and-roll album. The album is *Velvet Underground,* an anthology culled from the Velvets' first three L.P.s. (My specially ordered version of this collection is slightly different from the original; for "Afterhours," a song I've never liked much, it substitutes "Pale Blue Eyes," one of my favorites.) The songs on *Velvet Underground* are all about sin and salvation. As luck would have it, I am inspecting my winnings at the very moment that a massive earthquake destroys a secret biological warfare laboratory inside the Indian Point nuclear power plant, contaminating New York City with a virulent, radioactive form of legionnaire's disease. It seems that I will be contemplating sin and salvation for a long time to come.

I Love the Sound of Breaking Glass

In New York City in the middle sixties the Velvet Underground's lead singer, guitarist, and *auteur,* Lou Reed, made a fateful connection between two seemingly disparate ideas—the rock-and-roller as self-conscious aesthete and the rock-and-roller as self-conscious punk. (Though the word "punk" was not used generically until the early seventies, when critics began applying it to unregenerate rock-and-rollers with an aggressively lower-class style, the concept goes all the way back to Elvis.) The Velvets broke up in 1970, but the aesthete-punk connection was carried on, mainly in New York and England, by Velvets-influenced performers like Mott the Hoople, David Bowie (in his All the Young Dudes rather than his Ziggy Stardust mode), Roxy Music and its offshoots, the New York Dolls and the lesser protopunk bands that played Manhattan's Mercer Arts Center before it (literally) collapsed, the antipunk Modern Lovers, the archpunk Iggy Stooge/Pop. By 1977 the same duality had surfaced in new ways, with new force, under new conditions, to become the basis of rock-and-roll's new wave.

There are important differences, both temperamental and musical, that divide today's punks and punkoids from the Velvets and other precursors and from each other; American punk (still centered in New York) and its British counterpart are not only different but in a sense opposed. Yet all this music belongs to a coherent genre, implicitly defined by the tension between the term "punk" and the more inclusive "new wave," with its arty connotations. If the Velvets invented this genre, it was clearly anticipated by the Who: Pete Townshend, after all, is something of an aesthete, and Roger Daltrey something of a punk. It was not surprising that the impulse to make music that united formal elegance and defiant crudity should arise among working-class Englishmen and take shape among New York bohemians; each environment was, in its own way, highly structured and ridden with conflict. And as a vehicle for that impulse, rock-and-roll had unique advantages: it was defiantly crude, yet for those who were tuned in to it it was also a musical, verbal, and emotional language rich in formal possibilities.

The Who, the Velvets, and the new wave bands have all shared this conception of rock-and-roll; their basic aesthetic assumptions have little to do with what is popularly known as "art rock." The notion of rock-as-art inspired by Dylan's conversion to the electric guitar—the idea of making rock-and-roll more musically and lyrically complex, of combining elements of jazz, folk, classical, and avant-garde music with a rock beat, of creating "rock opera" and "rock poetry"—was from the rock-and-roll fan's perspective a dubious one. At best it stimulated a vital and imaginative eclecticism that spread the values of rock-and-roll even as it diffused and diluted them. At worst it rationalized a form of cultural upward mobility, concerned with achieving the appearance and pretensions of art rather than the reality—the point being to "improve" rock-and-roll by making it palatable to the upper middle class. Either way, it submerged rock-and-roll in something more amorphous and high-toned called rock. But from the early sixties (Phil Spector was the first major example) there was a countertradition in rock-and-roll that had much more in common with "high" art—in particular avant-garde art—than the ballyhooed art-rock syntheses: it involved more or less consciously using the basic formal canons of rock-and-roll as material (much as the pop artists used mass art in general) and refining, elaborating, playing off that material to produce what might be called rock-and-roll art. While art rock was implicitly based on the claim that rock-and-roll was or could be as worthy as more established art forms, rock-and-roll art came out of an obsessive commitment to the language of rock-and-roll and an equally obsessive disdain for those who rejected that language or wanted it watered down, made easier. In the sixties the best rock often worked both ways: the special virtue of sixties culture was its capacity for blurring boundaries, transcending contradictions, pulling off everything at once. But in the seventies the two tendencies have increasingly polarized: while art rock has fulfilled its most philistine possibilities in kitsch like Yes (or, for that matter, Meat Loaf), the new wave has inherited the countertradition, which is both less popular and more conscious of itself *as* a tradition than it was a decade ago.

The Velvets straddled the categories. They were nothing if not eclectic: their music and sensibility suggested influences as diverse as Bob Dylan and Andy Warhol, Peter Townshend and John Cage; they experimented with demented feedback and isolated, pure notes and noise for noise's sake; they were partial to sweet, almost folk-like melodies; they played the electric viola on Desolation Row. But they were basically rock-and-roll artists, building their songs on a beat that was sometimes implied rather than heard, on simple, tough, pithy lyrics about their hard-edged urban demimonde, on rock-and-roll's oldest metaphor for modern city life—anarchic energy contained by a tight, repetitive structure. Some of the Velvets' best songs—"Heroin," especially—redefined how rock-and-roll was supposed to sound. Others—"I'm Waiting for the Man," "White Light/White Heat," "Beginning to See the Light," "Rock & Roll"—used basic rock-and-roll patterns to redefine how the music was supposed to feel.

The Velvets were the first important rock-and-roll artists who had no real chance of attracting a mass audience. This was paradoxical. Rock-and-roll was a mass art, whose direct, immediate appeal to basic emotions subverted class and educational distinctions and whose formal canons all embodied the perception that mass art was not only possible but satisfying in new and liberating ways. Insofar as it incorporates the elite, formalist values of the avant-garde, the very idea of rock-and-roll art rests on a contradiction. Its greatest exponents—the Beatles, the Stones, and (especially) the Who—undercut the contradiction by making the surface of their music deceptively casual, then demolished it by reaching millions of kids. But the Velvets' music was too overtly intellectual, stylized, and distanced to be commercial. Like pop art, which was very much a part of the Velvets' world, it was antiart art made by antielite elitists. Lou Reed's aesthete-punk persona, which had its obvious precedent in the avant-garde tradition of artist-as-criminal-as-outlaw, was also paradoxical in the context of rock-and-roll. The prototypical rock-and-roll punk was the (usually white) working-class kid hanging out on the corner with his (it was usually his) pals; by middle-class and/or adult standards he might be a fuck-off, a hell-raiser, even a delinquent, but he was not really sinister or criminal. Reed's punk was closer to that bohemian (and usually black) hero, the hipster: he wore shades, took hard drugs, engaged in various forms of polymorphous perversity; he didn't just hang out on the corner, he lived out on the street, and he was a loner.

As white exploitation of black music, rock-and-roll has always had its built-in ironies, and as the music went further from its origins, the ironies got more acute. Where, say, Mick Jagger's irony was about a white middle-class English bohemian's (and later a rich rock star's) identification with and distance from his music's black American roots, his working-class image, and his teen-age audience, Lou Reed's irony made a further leap. It was not only about a white middle-class Jewish bohemian's identification with and distance from black hipsters (an ambiguity neatly defined when Reed-as-junkie, waiting for his man on a Harlem street corner, is challenged, "Hey white boy! Whatchou doin' uptown?") but about his use of a mass art form to express his aesthetic and social alienation from just about everyone. And one of the forms that alienation took pointed to yet another irony. While the original, primal impulse of rock-and-roll was to celebrate the body, which meant affirming sexual and material pleasure, Reed's temperament was not only cerebral but ascetic. There was nothing resembling lustiness in the Velvets' music, let alone any hippie notions about the joys of sexual liberation. Reed did not celebrate the sadomasochism of "Venus in Furs" any more than the celebrated heroin; he only acknowledged the attraction of what he saw as flowers of evil. Nor did he share his generation's enthusiasm for hedonistic consumption—to Reed the flash of the affluent sixties was fool's gold. Like Andy Warhol and the other pop artists he responded to the aesthetic potency of mass cultural styles; like Warhol he was fascinated by decadence—that is, style without meaning or moral content; but he was unmoved by that aspect of the pop mentality, and of rock-and-roll, that got off on the American dream. In a sense, the self-conscious formalism of his music—

the quality that made the Velvets uncommercial—was an attempt to purify rock-and-roll, to purge it of all those associations with material goodies and erotic good times.

Though it's probable that only the anything-goes atmosphere of the sixties could have inspired a group like the Velvets, their music was prophetic of a leaner, meaner time. They were from—and of—hard-headed, suspicious New York, not utopian, good-vibes California. For all Lou Reed's admiration of Bob Dylan, he had none of Dylan's faith in the liberating possibilities of the edge—what he had taken from *Highway 61 Revisited* and *Blonde on Blonde* was the sound of the edge fraying. Like his punk inheritors, he saw the world as a hostile place and did not expect it to change. In rejecting the optimistic consensus of the sixties, he prefigured the punks' attack on the smug consensus of the seventies; his thoroughgoing iconoclasm anticipated the punks' contempt for all authority— including the aesthetic and moral authority of rock-and-roll itself.

Throughout this decade rock-and-roll has been struggling to reclaim its identity as a music of cultural opposition, not only distinct from but antagonistic to its own cultural conglomerate, rock. The chief accomplishment of the punks has been to make that antagonism explicit and public in a way that is clearly contemporary—that is, has nothing to do with "reviving" anything except the spirit of opposition itself. What is new in rock-and-roll—what is uncomfortable and abrasive and demanding—is the extent to which it insists on a defensive stance; the authentic late seventies note is nothing so much as cranky. Though the British punk movement was in some respects a classic revolt of youth—a class-conscious revolt, at that—its self-mocking nihilism is a classic crank attitude, while the American new wave makes up in alienated smart-assism for what it lacks in shit-smearing belligerence. The power and vitality of the crank posture are attested to by the way it makes less discordant sensibilities sound corny, even to those of us who might prefer to feel otherwise. Bruce Springsteen may still pull off a credible mélange of fifties teen-age-street-kid insurgency, sixties apocalyptic romance, and early/mid-seventies angst, but he is an anomaly; so is Graham Parker, whose stubborn and convincing faith in traditional rock-and-roll values recalls John Fogerty's. Patti Smith, on the other hand, is a transitional figure, half cranky messiah, half messianic crank. The rock-and-rollers who exemplify the current aesthetic do so with wide variations in intensity, from Johnny Rotten (maniacal crank) to Elvis Costello (passionate crank) to Nick Lowe or Talking Heads (cerebral cranks) to the Ramones (cranks of convenience). (The Clash, one convolution ahead, is boldly anti- or post-crank—the first eighties band?) The obvious core of their crankiness is their consciousness of themselves as a dissident minority, but it's more complicated than that. Real, undiluted rock-n-roll is almost by definition the province of a dissident minority (larger at some times than at others); it achieved its cultural hegemony in the sixties only by becoming rock— by absorbing competing cultural values and in turn being absorbed, making a new rebellion necessary. What is different now is that for the first time in the music's twenty-five-year history, rock-and-rollers seem to accept their minority status as given and even to revel in it. Which poses an enormous contradiction, for real rock-and-roll almost by definition aspires to convert the world.

In some ways the crankiness of current rock-and-rollers resembles the disaffection of an earlier era of bohemians and avant-gardists convinced they had a vision the public was too intractably stupid and complacent to comprehend. But because the vision of rock-and-roll is inherently populist, the punks can't take themselves seriously as alienated artists; their crankiness is leavened with irony. At the same time, having given up on the world, they can't really take themselves seriously as rock-and-rollers, either. They are not only antiart artists but antipeople populists—the English punks, especially, seem to abhor not only the queen, America, rich rock stars, and the uncomprehending public but humanity itself. The punks' working-class-cum-lumpen style is implicitly political; it suggests collective opposition and therefore communal affirmation. But it is affirmation of a peculiarly limited and joyless sort. For the new wave's minimalist conception of rock-and-roll tends to exclude not only sensual pleasure but the entire range of positive human emotions, leaving only what is hard and violent, or hard and distanced, or both: if the punks made sex an obscenity, they make love an embarrassment.

In reducing rock-and-roll to its harshest essentials, the new wave took Lou Reed's aesthete-punk conceit to a place he never intended. For the Velvets the aesthete-punk stance was a way of surviving in a world that was out to kill you; the point was not to glorify the punk, or even to say fuck you to the world, but to be honest about the strategies people adopt in a desperate situation. The Velvets were not nihilists but moralists. In their universe nihilism regularly appears as a vivid but unholy temptation, love and its attendant vulnerability as scary and poignant imperatives. Though Lou Reed rejected optimism, he was enough of his time to crave transcendence. And finally—as "Rock & Roll" makes explicit—the Velvets' use of a mass art form was a metaphor for transcendence, for connection, for resistance to solipsism and despair. Which is also what it is for the punks; whether they admit it or not, that is what *their* irony is about. It may be sheer coincidence, but it was in the wake of the new wave that Reed recorded "Street Hassle," a three-part, eleven-minute antinihilist anthem that is by far the most compelling piece of work he has done in his post-Velvets solo career. In it he represents nihilism as double damnation: loss of faith that love is possible, compounded by denial that it matters. "That's just a lie," he mutters at the beginning of part three. "That's why she tells her friends. 'Cause the real song—the real song she won't even admit to herself."

The Real Song, or I'll Be Your Mirror

If the Velvets suggested continuity between art and violence, order and chaos, they posed a radical split between body and spirit. In this way too they were closer to the Who than to any other contemporaries. Like the Velvets the Who were fundamentally ascetic; they too saw the world as hostile—particularly the world as organized by the British class system. Their defiance was cruder than the Velvets', their early music as hard and violent as any to come out of the new wave. But they were not cranks; they were determined to convert the world, and Townshend's guitar-smashing expressed his need to break through to his audience as well as his contempt for authority, including the authority of rock-and-roll itself. That need to connect also took another form: even before Townshend discovered Meher Baba, the Who's music had a side that could only be called religious. If it seemed, at first, surprising that the same band could produce music as uncompromising in its bitterness as "Substitute" and as miraculously transcendent as the "You are forgiven!" chorus of "A Quick One," it was no contradiction; on the contrary, it was precisely Townshend's sense of the harshness of life, the implacability of the world, that generated his spiritual hunger.

The same can be said of Lou Reed, except that "spiritual hunger" seems too self-important a phrase to apply to him; the Velvets' brand of spirituality has little in common with the Who's grand bursts of mystical ecstasy or Townshend's self-conscious preoccupation with the quest for enlightenment. It's impossible to imagine Lou Reed taking up with a guru, though he might well write a savagely funny (and maybe chillingly serious) song about one. The aesthete-punk and his fellow demimondaines are not seeking enlightenment, though they stumble on it from time to time; like most of us they are pilgrims in spite of themselves. For Townshend moral sensitivity is a path to spiritual awareness; for Reed awareness and the lack—or refusal—of it have an intrinsically moral dimension. While he is not averse to using the metaphors of illusion and enlightenment—sometimes to brilliant effect, as in "Beginning to See the Light" and "I'll Be Your Mirror"—they are less central to his theology than the concepts of sin and grace, damnation and salvation. Some of his songs ("Heroin," "Jesus," "Pale Blue Eyes") explicitly invoke that Judeo-Christian language; many more imply it.

But "theology" too is an unfairly pretentious word. The Velvets do not deal in abstractions but in states of mind. Their songs are about the feelings the vocabulary of religion was invented to describe—profound and unspeakable feelings of despair, disgust, isolation, confusion, guilt, longing, relief, peace, clarity, freedom, love—and about the ways we (and they) habitually bury those feelings, deny them, sentimentalize them, mock them, inspect them from a safe, sophisticated distance in order to get along in the hostile, corrupt world. For the Velvets the roots of sin are in this ingrained resistance to facing our deepest, most painful, and most sacred emotions; the essence of grace is the comprehension that our sophistication is a sham, that our deepest, most painful, most sacred desire is to recover a childlike innocence we have never, in our heart of hearts, really lost. And the essence of love is sharing that redemptive truth: on the Velvets' first album, which is dominated by images of decadence and death, suddenly, out of nowhere, comes Nico's artless voice singing, "I'll be your mirror/ . . . The light on your door to show that you're home."

For a sophisticated rock-and-roll band with a sophisticated audience this vision is, to say the least, risky. The idea of childlike innocence is such an invitation to bathos that making it credible seems scarcely less difficult than getting the camel of the gospels through the needle's eye. And the Velvets' alienation is also problematic: it's one thing for working-class English kids to decide life is shit, but how bad can things be for Lou Reed? Yet the Velvets bring it off—make us believe/admit that the psychic wounds we inflict on each other are real and terrible, that to scoff at innocence is to indulge in a desperate lie—because they never succumb to self-pity. Life may be a brutal struggle, sin inevitable, innocence elusive and transient, grace a gift, not a reward ("Some people work very hard/But still they never get it right," Lou Reed observes in "Beginning to See the Light"); nevertheless we are responsible for who and what we become. Reed does not attempt to resolve this familiar spiritual paradox, nor does he regard it as unfair. His basic religious assumption (like Baudelaire's) is that like it or not we inhabit a moral universe, that we have free will, that we must choose between good and evil, and that our choices matter absolutely. If we are rarely strong enough to make the right choices, if we can never count on the moments of illumination that make them possible, still it is spiritual death to give up the effort.

That the Velvets are hardly innocents, that they maintain their aesthetic and emotional distance even when describing—and evoking—utter spiritual nakedness, does not undercut what they are saying; if anything, it does the opposite. The Velvets compel belief in part because, given its context, what they are saying is so bold: not only do they implicitly criticize their own aesthetic stance—they risk undermining it altogether, ending up with sincere but embarrassingly banal home truths. The risk is real because the Velvets do not use irony as a net, a way of evading responsibility by keeping everyone guessing about what they really mean. On the contrary, their irony functions as a metaphor for the spiritual paradox, affirming that the need to face one's nakedness and the impulse to cover it up are equally real, equally human. If the Velvets' distancing is self-protective (hence in their terms damning), it is also revelatory (hence redeeming); it makes clear that the feelings being protected are so unbearably intense that if not controlled and contained they would overwhelm both the Velvets and their audience. The Velvets' real song is how hard it is to admit, even to themselves.

That song in its many variations is the substance of *Velvet Underground*. This album can be conceived of—nonlinearly; the cuts are not at all in the right order—as the aesthete-punk's *Pilgrim's Progress,* in four movements ("Sha la la, man, whyn't you just slip away?" I can hear Lou Reed say to that.)

One: Worldly Seduction and Betrayal. "Sunday Morning," a song about vague and ominous anxiety, sums up the emotional tone of this movement: "Watch out, the world's behind you." "Here She Comes Now" and "Femme Fatale," two songs about beautiful but unfeeling women (in the unlovable tradition of pop—not to mention religious— misogyny, Lou Reed's women are usually demonic or angelic icons, not people), sum up its philosophy: "Aah, it looks so good/Aah, but she's made out of wood." These songs underscore the point by juxtaposing simple, sweet, catchy melodies with bitter lyrics sung in flat, almost affectless voices (in "Sunday Morning," Reed's voice takes on a breathiness that suggests suppressed panic). "White Light/White Heat," a song about shooting speed, starts out by coming as close as any Velvets song does to expressing the euphoria of sheer physical energy; by the end of the trip the music has turned into bludgeoning, deadening noise, the words into a semiarticulate mumble.

Two: The Sin of Despair. "Heroin" is the Velvets' masterpiece—seven minutes of excruciating spiritual extremity. No other work of art I know about has made the junkie's experience so powerful, so horrible, so appealing; listening to "Heroin" I feel simultaneously impelled to somehow save this man and to reach for the needle. The song is built around the tension between the rush and the nod—expressed musically by an accelerating beat giving way to slow, solemn chords that sound like a bell tolling; metaphorically by the addict's vision of smack as a path to transcendence and freedom, alternating with his stark recognition that what it really offers is the numbness of death, that his embrace of the drug ("It's my wife and it's my life") is a total, willful rejection of the corrupt world, other people, feeling. In the beginning he likens shooting up to a spiritual journey: he's gonna try for the Kingdom; when he's rushing on his run he feels like Jesus' son. At the end, with a blasphemous defiance that belies his words, he avows, "Thank your God that I'm not aware/And thank God that I just don't care!" The whole song seems to rush outward and then close in on itself, on the moment of truth when the junkie knowingly and deliberately chooses death over life—chooses damnation. It is the clarity of his consciousness that gives the sin its enormity. Yet the clarity also offers a glimmer of redemption. In the very act of choosing numbness the singer admits the depths of his pain and bitterness, his longing for something better; he is aware of every nuance of his rejection of awareness; he sings a magnificently heartfelt song about how he doesn't care. (A decade later, Johnny Rotten will do the same thing in an entirely different way.) A clear, sustained note runs through the song like a bright thread; it fades out or is drowned out by chaotic, painful distortion and feedback, then comes through again, like the still small voice of the soul. Reed ends each verse with the refrain, "And I guess that I just don't know." His fate is not settled yet.

Three: Paradise Sought, Glimpsed, Recollected. This movement consists of four songs about world-weary sophistication and the yearning for innocence. "Candy Says" defines the problem: "I've come to hate my body and all that it requires in this world/ . . . I'd like to know completely what others so discreetly talk about." "Jesus" is a prayer: "Help me in my weakness, for I've fallen out of grace." In "I'm Set Free" the singer has his illumination, but even as he tries to tell about it, to pin it down, it slips away: "I saw my head laughing, rolling on the ground/And now I'm set free to find a new illusion." In "Pale Blue Eyes" the world has gotten in the way of the singer's transcendent love: "If I could make the world as pure and strange as what I see/I'd put you in the mirror I put in front of me."

Musically these songs are of a piece. They are all gentle, reflective. They all make use of the tension between flat, detached voices and sweet melodies. They all have limpid guitar lines that carry the basic emotion, which is bittersweet: it is consoling to know that innocence is possible, inexpressibly painful that it always seems just out of reach. In "Pale Blue Eyes" a tambourine keeps the beat, or rather is slightly off where the beat ought to be, while a spectacular guitar takes over completely, rolling in on wave after wave of pure feeling.

Four: Salvation and Its Pitfalls. "Beginning to See the Light" is the mirror held up to "Heroin." I've always been convinced that it's about an acid trip, perhaps because I first really heard it during one and found it utterly appropriate. Perhaps also because both the song and the acid made me think of a description of a peyote high by a beat writer named Jack Green: "a group of us, on peyote, had little to share with a group on marijuana the marijuana smokers were discussing questions of the utmost profundity and we were sticking our fingers in our navels & giggling." In "Beginning to See the Light" enlightenment (or salvation) is getting out from under the burden of self-seriousness, of egotism, of imagining that one's sufferings fill the universe; childlike innocence means being able to play. There is no lovelier moment in rock-and-roll than when Lou Reed laughs and sings, with amazement, joy, gratitude, "I just wanta tell you, *everything* is all right!"

But "Beginning to See the Light" is also wickedly ironic. Toward the end, carried away by euphoria, Reed cries, "There are problems in these times/But ooh, none of them are mine!" Suddenly we are through the mirror, back to the manifesto of "Heroin": "I just don't care!" Enlightenment has begotten spiritual pride, a sin that like its inverted form, nihilism, cuts the sinner off from the rest of the human race. Especially from those people who, you know, work very hard but never get it right. Finally we are left with yet another version of the spiritual paradox: to experience grace is to be conscious of it; to be conscious of it is to lose it.

Coda: I'd Love to Turn You On

Like all geniuses, Lou Reed is unpredictable. In "Street Hassle" he does as good a job as anyone of showing what was always missing in his and the Velvets' vision. As the song begins, a woman (or transvestite?) in a bar is buying a night with a sexy young boy. This sort of encounter is supposed to be squalid; it turns out to be transcendent. Reed's account of the odd couple's lovemaking is as tender as it is erotic: "And then sha la la la la he entered her slowly and showed her where he was coming from/And then sha la la la la he made love to her gently, it was like she'd never ever come." Of course, in part two he almost takes it all back by linking sex with death. Still.

What it comes down to for me—as a Velvets fan, a lover of rock-and-roll, a New Yorker, an aesthete, a punk, a sinner, a sometime seeker of enlightenment (and love) (and sex)—is this: I believe that we are all, openly or secretly, struggling against one or another kind of nihilism. I believe that body and spirit are not really separate, though it often seems that way. I believe that redemption is never impossible and always equivocal. But I guess that I just don't know.

Notes

1. On second thought, I'd rather have *Gone With the Wind*, or maybe *The Harder They Come.*

Sister Ray

SYLVIA'S HUSBAND (1987)

Donna Gaines takes a critical look at Lou Reed's songwriting from the perspective of one who thinks deeply about social relationships. A sociologist by training, she takes her work personally in this piece, placing herself right in the middle, filtering theory through her own lived experience. She traces the path of her engagement with Reed's work over the years—beginning with the Velvets—with an eye and an ear to the nuances of the human dynamics involved, particularly those that animate attractions and repulsions between friends and lovers, individuals and society.

This is a story about Lou Reed. But it has very little to do with Reed or his wife, Sylvia Morales. Lou Reed remains unrevealed, just like any other mass-mediated icon. Madonna, for example—is she really Tom Ward's "capitalist slut," or is she Barry Walters's "prosex feminist," or Vince Aletti's "prokie"? We don't know and some of us don't care. So I'm not concerned with deconstructing Mr. Reed's oeuvre, in finding its telos, or in figuring out if he fucked us over by "selling out." I don't care whether Lou Reed is a legend, or a has-been grasping at maximum video revenue. What does it matter if he prefers Hondas to Harleys or if he's just putting us on? These are his problems, not mine. I'm not even one of his many obsessive fans. Some of my best friends are, though, and they've already warned me to watch what I say about Him.

First there was the Bible, then Marx, and then there was rock 'n' roll. When things get ugly I guess I *should* invoke the psalms or Marcuse or de

Beauvoir. I should be calling on them to help me understand living in the world. I mean, how else can we explain the everyday excrement where animals endure Auschwitz for human vanity and progress, where the only hold on life that teenagers feel they have left is suicide (ending it) or pro-creation (starting it). And then there are the betrayals: friends die too young, lovers who turn out to be assholes, people we believe in who stick it to us. In the minutes that lie between the hurt, anger, and confusion and finding the guts to call a friend, what do I do? You got it—I stick my head inside my speakers.

But Lou Reed was never my patron saint. The thing that stood between me and mass murder was always a buzz-saw guitar. Thanks to Jimi Hendrix, somebody's life was saved by rock 'n' roll, but not mine. As a general rule I'd rather dish it out than take it—but please, don't play an album like *Berlin* around me on a bad day. My mother was a band vocal-ist who sang beautiful, sad songs like "Tenderly" and "Solitude." But she was a widow in mourning. My favorite lullaby was "Summertime." It still makes me cry. I feel helpless and hopeless until I can get angry—if daddy is not "standing by," well, I want to know who is responsible. I want blood and I need noise.

Unfortunately, Lou Reed isn't loud enough to make my ears bleed. But the biggest strain in my relationship with him is that he's always seemed too smooth, too distant, too hard, too "male." Almost every obsessive female Reed fan think he's sexy, and has desires and fantasies about him. Not me. My great dark man has a big nose, high cheekbones, droopy eye-lids, and pops a rooster in the center of his crown. He's raw, loose, slop-py, and unprofessional: Johnny Thunders. But I'm not interested in having sexual fantasies about Thunderella, or Keith Richards, or even Chuck Berry. Look, it's not that simple.

Consciously, Lou Reed doesn't interest me that much. The only reason I think about him is because my friends constantly annoy me about him. (They are compelled to give me tapes of his newest albums and periodi-cally force me to go see him live. In turn they must go with me to see Thunders, and if I am really pissed, I even make them sit through one of his annoying acoustic sets. We aren't *totally* retro, we do like to see all the new, now bands. But I'm not talking about music here, this is religion.) Unconsciously, I think I've internalized Lou Reed more than anyone else. Like everyone else I loved the Velvets. And at least one song on every solo album has broken off some of the ice around my heart. In the gut level moment of anger, pain, hatred, horror, passion, or despair it's Lou I turn to. He says all the creepy things I can't put into words. Often I'll say something wise to myself. Then I'll realize it's a Lou Reed proverb I've picked up off my turntable. I'm talking, but it's his voice.

It's now twenty years after the Velvets' first album, and people get fixated at different phases of Reed's career. Some know him only from "Heroin." Other people remember the Rock 'n' Roll Animal boy. But my Lou Reed is the wretch who found salvation, the one who became whole. Lou Reed After Sylvia.

Some people are offended by Reed's "misogyny"—his cold mistrust of women or his glass-menagerie treatment of them. At the very least, women have been problematic in Reed's work. This never bothered me, since I felt the same way about men. Reed as faggot junkie was another peacock, just like all the young dudes of that era. This "pop transvestism" revolutionized nothing much in the world of genital politics but it was fun. Anyway, the brutal feelings of fear, rage, and disgust that Reed expressed never seemed gender specific to me. Whether the loved one is the other or the same sex, the roles of power and submission don't really change. There is always a struggle, always some permutation of ecstasy, trust, pain, and confusion.

From the beginning I could handle Reed's surface anger and strut, but stayed happily immune to his ever-present vulnerability. In his earlier albums there were some possibilities for getting close. But there was always a buffer zone, some escape valve that protected him from us, and us from him. For example, the bitterness and cold resolve of his "universal truth" that the dead "bitch" in "Street Hassle" will "never fuck again" is quickly betrayed by a pathetic whine that "love is gone." Here, the whiner just slips away, sha la la la, so easy to forget.

A year later, in 1979, Reed gives us the song of songs. "The Bells" is the "Kol Nidre" of rock 'n' roll. The wedding march of the mutant bride down the aisle of some bizarro-world Brooklyn catering hall. Rococo-bop. Ave Maria, baby. Here we are as usual, waiting for something: the Messiah, the man, the beloved, the "show of shows." Meantime, we get *King Crimson Live at the Yiddish Theater*. In nine minutes and eighteen seconds we have the good old wavering flame of truth, a flicker of hope for our redemption. But it's just a good drunken cry. Reed's shaky goat voice is shrouded in so much pissy schmaltz, we can laugh it off and sneak quietly out the back door.

In *Growing Up in Public*, the moth flies dangerously close to the flame. First Lou has to drag us through the mud of the human condition in "How Do You Speak to an Angel?" It's getting pretty hot, but we are not at all prepared. Our clothes are off, but we leave our shades on. We're playing it safe again in "So Alone," we're on for one last hustle.

And then the sop goes and gets married on Valentine's Day!

Two years later, in 1982, he came out with *The Blue Mask*. For no apparent reason, my friend bought it for me. I listened to "Heavenly Arms." *This is very creepy,* I thought. *This is too pure. The goat voice is steady and he sounds like he means it. No apology, no bravado, and no gimmicks?* I waited for the punch line, but it never came.

I wondered, is Lou Reed serious—all this talk about women on the album, "only a woman can love a man"? Why? Because *they're* so disgusting and *we're* so degraded that we'll put up with them? Or is it because women are angels of mercy, not human beings? Or because only we *really* know how to give love? Even worse, was Reed just like all the other boys in the glitter bands of the seventies now asserting an orthodox heterosexuality to advance the career in Reagan's homophobe eighties? So, he "loves women"? Was he reading Ashley Montagu? Was he for real or what? Was this born-again feminism a knee-jerk reaction or a true-blue confession? In the title song, he was really baiting me—"take the Blue Mask down from my face and look me in the eye." Fuck off!

This was too much. I was confused. After the years of fancy approach-avoidance footwork, how could I trust him not to laugh at me for believing that this time he really meant it? What *was* Lou Reed's angle anyway? And what would a man be able to tell me, a woman, about emotions? How dare he intrude on female turf, to try and teach me something about feelings? No way could icy Lou be this open. Was salvation finally to be found in romantic, hetero love—the premier ideological weapon of the patriarchy? No way would I fall into that trap, and how could *he,* of all people, buy into it? He was supposed to be so smart. What about God, the movies, revolution, the purge (writing), alcohol, and noise—those more trusted saviors? Where did this leave me? I had to consult the panel of experts, among them some of my best friends.

* * *

My best friend Anthony says that Lou Reed is someone to grow old with. Reed is an organic intellectual of New York. Every region has a few, and sometimes these mentors reach out to people in other places. Anthony was brought up in rural Northwest Florida, about thirty miles south of the Alabama border. He was raised a Christian, a member of the Popular Head Free Will Baptist Church. He claims that he *was* an atheist, but now he "believes in Lou Reed." Anthony's mother has "never traveled north of the Mason-Dixon line, and has no intention of doing so." She does not like Yankees, but every Christmas she sends me Tupperware. In high school, Anthony overdosed from recreational Thorazine. The next week he was voted president of the school's honor society. He tells me that if it were not for Lou Reed, he would have done himself in long ago. Like many people, Anthony is a lonely genius. He was hard to get close to at first. But once we became friends, he was the kindest and most giving of all.

Anthony got involved with Lou through the mail. The album came rural delivery. Sometime in the early seventies he picked up a fanzine at a local convenience store. Some distributor from New York was advertising an album that looked "ultrahip." Anthony ordered it and embraced Lou after hearing this, the Velvet Underground's third album. Anthony admits that a skinny middle-class Jewish boy from a suburb of New York is not a likely sage for 315-pound biker from Bonifay, Florida. Anthony's obsessions should have included Lynyrd Skynyrd, Hank Williams, Jr., or Molly Hatchet. He could care less if he ever meets Lou Reed. Some people have a friend in Jesus, Anthony has one in Lou. Anthony has at least five copies of everything ever issued by or about Lou Reed. This includes legitimate and bootleg albums and tapes, books, interviews, and videos, although he does not own a VCR. He has an inventory written to computer disk, consisting of five pages of text in need of chronic updating. So far Anthony has three elaborate tattoos inspired by Lou Reed, and inscribed for eternity with Reed titles—"Berlin," "Venus in Furs," and "Rock & Roll Heart."

* * *

The 10 Best Proverbs of Lou Reed as Told to Me by Anthony

1. "But remember the princess who lived on the hill who loved you even though she knew you were wrong"—"Coney Island Baby," *Coney Island Baby* (1976)
2. "The first thing you learn is that you always have to wait"—"I'm Waiting for My Man," *The Velvet Underground and Nico* (1967)
3. "I ain't no dog tied to a parked car"—"New Sensations," *New Sensations* (1984)
4. "It's either the best or it's the worst, and since I don't have to choose I guess I won't"—"Street Hassle," *Street Hassle* (1978)
5. "Some like wine and some like hops but what I really love is my Scotch"—"The Power of Positive Drinking," *Growing Up in Public* (1980)
6. "Things are never good, things go from bad to weird"—"Underneath the Bottle," *The Blue Mask* (1982)
7. "How do you think it feels when all you can say is if only"—"How Do You Think It Feels?" *Berlin* (1973)

8. "Between thought and expression lies a lifetime"—"Some Kinda Love," *The Velvet Underground* (1969)
9. "I dreamed that I was young and smart and it was not a waste. I dreamed that there was a point to life and to the human race"—"The Day John Kennedy Died," *The Blue Mask* (1982)
10. "And I guess that I just don't know"—"Heroin," *The Velvet Underground and Nico* (1967)

* * *

Anthony's idea of a blissful New Year's Eve is to sit alone in the woods of his Florida plantation, with a bottle of Johnnie Walker Black and a tape of *Berlin*. He finds this cathartic. Anthony admits that his relationship with Lou Reed is a little psychotic. It even drove him to violate me by dragging me to a poetry reading by Lou Reed and Jim Carroll, at the West Side YMCA a few years back. I hate poetry. Anthony never refers to Lou Reed as Lou or as Reed. Only as Lou Reed. He owns about eighty-six black T-shirts, many of which are Reed memorabilia, some of them in triplicate. This obsessive collecting behavior spilled over into my life when he bought me seven copies of *L.A.M.F.*, the Heartbreakers' classic album. *L.A.M.F.* has my favorite Thunders back-room pleasure hymn, "Pirate Love." Once, when I got Anthony the "Berlin" tattoo for his birthday, I almost got drunk enough to get "Pirate Love" tattooed on my forearm. But I didn't—I still hope to be buried in a Jewish cemetery, in Israel.

Anthony admires Ellen Willis, since she shares his obsession with Lou Reed. When he taught sociology at Big Science University out on Eastern Long Island, Willis's book *Beginning to See the Light* was required reading for his course. He perpetrated several abuses against the youth of America in the name of Lou Reed, like making the kids listen to *Metal Machine Music*. They were also expected to write a critique of Diana Clapton's book on Reed, drawing on sociological theories of deviance. Anthony got very good teacher evaluations, one from the vice-provost of undergraduate studies himself.

Anthony does respect that Thunders is my guiding light—the principle behind my haircut and everything else that really matters—but he is a true believer. He sincerely wants to help me develop my relationship with Lou Reed. Since Ellen Willis is a feminist, Anthony figures he can use her arguments to spread Lou's word to me. In her essay about the Velvets, Willis says that listening to "Heroin" she feels "simultaneously impelled" to save Lou from the needle *and* to take it herself. Anthony twists this around to argue that men mainly identify with Lou, whereas women want to save him. I think about this. I hate heroin as much as poetry, so yeah, maybe I wouldn't identify with Lou. But the idea of saving some man, even my beloved St. John of the gutter guitar, does not move me. In rock 'n' roll's hetero discourse of romantic love, women save men. For the man, Love is Salvation. For the woman, it's just another burden to bear. The idea of symbiosis is appealing, and some men do save women, but a chemically dependent lover of any sex is just a pain in the ass. No way. Johnny Thunders puts out hard chord in a blues field—just the thing I need to feel better. Transcendence for the moment. There's no feminist theory generated in his brilliant dick-for-brains lyrics. But that's okay, I'm just using him, I don't want to marry him.

After "Heavenly Arms" Anthony and I began using the name of Lou Reed's wife Sylvia metaphorically, to signify the most committed form of nurture. "Sylvia" was the one who would always love you, believe in you, tell you how great you were. The lover as one big pep talk. Again, this is a concept and probably has nothing much to do with Ms. Morales and her husband. If one of our friends was depressed, Anthony would say I should call him and "be Sylvia." Forget Yoko, she had an ego of her own. "Sylvia" represented the purest form of unconditional positive regard.

Anthony's reading of Willis on Reed was convincing until I got a phone call from California. My friend Vicki said she was coming to New York for a few days. I asked her how things were going between her and Lou. Vicki comes from Brighton Beach, and her father is an accountant, just like Lou's, she says. Brighton is right next to Coney Island. And so when Lou sings "Coney Island Baby" she knows he wrote it for her, even if it is dedicated to Rachel. In the summer of 1970 Vicki and I hitchhiked into New York City to see the Velvet Underground at Max's. It was the first time either of us saw Lou. I think I was a hippie then, since I remember wearing a cotton, Indian print tablecloth that I had made into a dress. I had gotten the tablecloth from Babs's father, who owned a schlock store in Brooklyn. Babs had moved to New York City and opened a boutique with a guy named Richard. Richard was an artist, and he was gorgeous. He wore antique clothes and old ladies' orthopedic shoes and streaked his long brown hair with blue and red vegetable dyes. They lived on Second Avenue with Holly Woodlawn and *Warhol* was the word. Babs was glitter and dressed very hot and vampy. Vicki and I didn't know what the fuck, but that night at Max's we were sure that Lou was singing to us. Babs is now retired and living in Florida with her three children. Vicki went on to the wild life, then marriage, divorce, and now a brilliant career in microchip.

Vicki says that Lou is still the great love of her life, and thinks he's really sexy. She'd love to "fuck his brains out" and "could give a shit about saving him." Vicki is about ten years younger than Lou Reed, and believes that Reed makes an impressive adult role model. For Anthony, Lou Reed is the men's liberation movement. He helps Anthony to allow and understand feelings like "the violent rage that turns inward." He "knows" he will never be "like most people," or ever "be happy." Lou understands why, so it's all right. I feel that way, too, a lot, but I just blame it on monopoly capitalism. Unfortunately this insight isn't much help to the atomized, in those moments of pain when we all feel so alone.

* * *

Two years ago Anthony drove out to Freeport, Long Island, to find a certain high school. He walked across the football field trying to understand Lou's relationship with the coach he did it for in "Coney Island Baby." Anthony didn't care if this was the same high school football field where the real Lou Reed and his coach had a moment or if it all happened in Coney Island near Vicki's house or off the back of Lou Reed's eyelids one night. We've never seen god except in pictures. People have always needed something to believe in. The rock 'n' roll sage is there for us, the message is inscribed in vinyl, to guide us in sickness and in health.

Now, I'm real tough and Anthony's groovy. Lou is a reptile. He's cold and hard and distant, he's so "male." Lou Reed has always played both sides of the fence: too cool, and too deep. Reed the trickster explores the things we won't 'fess up to. Then, just when it gets scary, he lets us off the hook. Except sometimes he makes us sweat and that's good for us, and for him. I remember hanging out at Max's back then, with Babs and Vicki; everyone is trying to be so cool that nobody will make eye contact. People are high and sneer at anyone they aren't cruising. By 1987 we are mature, even bored, thinking about alienation. We have our lovely lives. We're beyond these questions. But Lou Reed knows better, like the way he cautions the pained and frustrated to "spit it out" on *Mistrial*.

There are political explanations for the personal things that Lou Reed has articulated all these years. We know all the reasons why we protect and pretend the self, and about how order is served by "self-control." We're wise to how we get burned in the name of the things we hold sacred. Lou Reed's naked embrace of "Sylvia" in "Heavenly Arms" was the most subversive move he's made so far. And whatever the hell he "really" had in mind, I don't know. And where he's gone from there, I don't care.

'Cause when I heard that, I could deny the possibilities he held out. And though this embarrassed me, it made a few of my friends very happy.

JEFF SCHWARTZ

"SISTER RAY": SOME PLEASURES OF A MUSICAL TEXT (1996)

Jeff Schwartz deconstructs "Sister Ray" using some of the critical strategies of the "new musicology." His essay belongs in the still small, yet growing, category of rock criticism that treats the music with as much critical thought as has previously been directed at lyrics, imagery, and socio/political context.

In this paper, I am opposing the current overwhelming preeminence of lyric analysis in popular music studies. Instead, inspired by Barthes' *The Pleasure of the Text,* I offer a series of readings of "Sister Ray," showing how the theme of transgression of gender, self, and body structures every aspect of the text. I am not arguing for unity as an aesthetic standard, on which every musical text should be judged. After all, many of the most interesting popular songs, from "Teen Angel" to Sonic Youth, derive their power from conflicts among what is signified by the harmony, rhythm, lyrics, melody, recording technique, vocal stance, etc. Elvis Costello's first album *My Aim is True* is a great example of this; the complete banality of the music is a perfect foil for the viciousness of Elvis' lyrics and attitude. However, the thematic unity of "Sister Ray" makes it a good example to demonstrate my approach. A longer analysis of dialogic relationships between words and music will wait for another time.

"Sister Ray" is from the Velvet Underground's second album *White Light/White Heat.* Ellen Willis, who is (to my knowledge) the only other academic to write on the Velvet Underground, claims that the band's work is dominated by the themes of sin and salvation. However, she reaches this conclusion based on a reading of the band's first *three* records, mainly the third. This third record (self-titled) was a major change of direction. First, keyboardist-bassist-viola player John Cale, who was the only member of the group without a background in or commitment to popular music, being instead a formally trained avant-garde classical composer, was forced out of the group. Without Cale's experimental background and multi-instrumental skills, the Velvet Underground became a much more conventional-sounding band. There was also a more mundane and material cause for the band's sonic transformation on the third album: the group's collection of effects boxes was stolen immediately before the recording of this record (Heylin 1993: 29).

"Sister Ray" is also a significant item in the Velvet Underground's *oeuvre* because it is the closest thing in their officially released work to the music they improvised live for Andy Warhol's *Exploding Plastic Inevitable* happenings and screenings of his films. Judging from descriptions of the Velvet Underground's early live shows, "Sister Ray" is the most accurate representation (short of bootlegs) of what the band sounded like in person for the first 2 or 3 years.

Anecdotes

Here are Lou Reed's and Sterling Morrison's accounts of the recording process:

Reed:

"Sister Ray" was done as a joke—no, not as a joke, but it has eight characters in it and this guy gets killed and nobody does anything. It was built around this story that I wrote about this scene of total debauchery and decay. I like to think of Sister Ray as a transvestite smack dealer. The situation is a bunch of drag queens taking some sailors home with them, shooting up on smack and having this orgy when the police appear. When it came to putting the music to it, it had to be spontaneous. The jam came about right there in the studio. We didn't use splices or anything. I had been listening to a lot of Cecil Taylor and Ornette Coleman and wanted to get something like that with a rock and roll feeling. When we did "Sister Ray," we turned up to ten flat out, leakage all over the place. That's it. They asked us what we were going to do. We said "We're going to start." They said "Who's playing bass?" We said "There is no bass." They asked us when it ends. We didn't know. When it ends, that's when it ends. (Bockris and Malanga 93–94, Doggett 55).

Sterling Morrison:

We didn't want to lay down separate tracks, we wanted to do it studio live with a simultaneous voice, but the problem was that the current state of studio art wouldn't let us do it. There was fantastic leakage because everyone was playing so loud and we had so much electronic junk with us in the studio—all these fuzzers and compressors. Gary Kellgren the engineer, who is ultra-competent, told us repeatedly, "You can't do it—all the needles are on red." And we reacted as we always reacted: "Look, we don't know what goes on in there and we don't want to hear about it. Just do the best you can." And so the album is all fuzzy, there's all that white noise.

No producer could override our taste. We'd do a whole lot of takes, and then there would be a big brawl over which one to use. Of course, everyone would opt for the take where they sounded best. It was a tremendous hassle, so on "Sister Ray," which we knew was going to be a major effort, we stared at each other and said, "This is going to be one take. So whatever you want to do, you better do it now." And that explains what's going on in the mix. Everyone's trying to do what he wants to every second, and no one backs off. (Thompson 35)

Harmony

According to the published sheet music for "Sister Ray" (Reed 1991b: 118–120), the entire song consists of three chords: G, F, and C.

Curiously, this is also the principal chord progression of Madonna's song "Express Yourself." Melanie Morton, in the only musicological essay in Cathy Schwichtenberg's *The Madonna Collection,* discusses "Express Yourself," and finds in its harmonic and melodic organization elements that subvert the phallic narrative assumptions of standard Western harmony (226–229).

Here is a brief summary and paraphrase of Morton's analysis, expanded to include "Sister Ray": Although G is obviously the tonal center of these songs, the F chord cannot be explained in the key of G except as the subdominant of the subdominant (the IV chord of C, the IV of the tonic G), too arcane a relation to make sense of such a crucial element of the song's structure. This chord progression contains nothing that can function as a dominant chord or indicates an appropriate major scale. Furthermore, Madonna's vocal melody includes notes that imply a variety of scales, but the connection of these melody notes with the underlying harmony never coalesces into the logic of Western tonality. Instead, that logic, whose phallic, teleological underpinnings have been exposed at great length by Susan McClary, is maintained at a distance, an object for Madonna's play, instead of her master.

Lou Reed is a much less tonal singer than Madonna, and I have not tried to transcribe his vocal melodies, but I think it's safe to say that his work equals hers in terms of funky harmonic and melodic play. I use the word "funky" here, not to be cute, but to open an area in which Morton may be criticized.

The G-F-C chord progression is difficult to explain only from the perspective of European tonal music. In rock (and other African-American inspired musics such as blues and country), it is a very common progression. Current rock musicologists (writing mainly in musician oriented magazines such as *Guitar Player, Bass Player, Guitar World,* etc.) are fond of modal analysis, and G-F-C is clearly a progression derived from the mixolydian mode. However, both Madonna and the Velvet Underground do not simply draw their melodic material from the G mixolydian scale, but combine it with the G blues pentatonic scale. The Velvet Underground go even further outside, with long segments of freely atonal soloing and straight-out noise.

Morton claims that Madonna's subversion of harmonic logic is a form of feminist deconstruction, but this is severely weakened if "Express Yourself" is considered in the context of specifically popular music practices. The Who's "Magic Bus" and Van Morrison's "Gloria" are just two of the many rock songs that use melodies of ambiguous scalar origin over the I-VII-IV progression. The sentiments of these songs can hardly be described as feminist (unless maybe if Patti Smith is singing them).

"Sister Ray," on the other hand, pushes the limits of tonality much farther. The chord progression I've been discussing, actually only appears for the first minute or two of the song, and then only in Lou Reed's guitar part. Even at the start, Morrison and Cale are playing figures that imply different, though related harmonies, which appear to mesh consistently with the underlying chord progression. The only real sources of tension are from Sterling Morrison's guitar fills, where his use of the G blues pentatonic scale clashes with the chords Reed and Cale are playing (although even these dissonances are common rock sounds: adding the fourth, lowered seventh, or lowered third to a major chord) and from Cale's not playing the F chord with Reed, staying on the G instead. When Cale does this, the resulting formation cannot be accurately described using existing nomenclature; it is neither of the extended chords generated by the combination of the two, G9sus or F6/9#11, which imply jazz chords that belong in a Steely Dan or Stevie Wonder song, nor is it a sound-effect, like Stravinsky and Bartók's use of polytonality. The languages of Western tonality, modernist experimentation, modality, and jazz are all inadequate for the analysis of rock.

Much like the theme of a jazz song, these opening figures are soon discarded anyway. Considering the various riffs used in the course of the piece, and their relationship to the opening figure, perhaps the best way to describe the harmonic structure of "Sister Ray" is to steal a phrase from guitarist John Scofield and say it's in "G whatever." This is more than a joke. Lou Reed, like Scofield, has listened a lot to Ornette Coleman and often dropped his name during, and when discussing, the early Velvet Underground period (Bockris and Malanga 93; Doggett 18, 25; Heylin 1993: 22). The major revolutionary contribution Coleman made in the early '60s was to omit chord progressions and song form from most of his compositions, leaving only a tonal center, which can be moved by the musicians following the flow of the improvisation (Litweiler 62–63 and throughout; Schuller 80–85). This describes "Sister Ray," except that the tonal center stays fixed. Even when Reed, Morrison, and Cale are producing noise (feedback from the guitars, tone clusters on the organ), it is heard with the center of G, because it has been established as a drone, through extreme repetition. This is the influence of LaMonte Young. John Cale described his pre-Velvet Underground project with Young as "The concept of the group was to sustain notes for two hours at a time." (Bockris and Malanga 13).

The use of the G drone creates a limit and, as Foucault says in his essay on Bataille, transgression requires a limit. Only because this G has been repeated and repeated can Lou Reed have the pleasure of syncopating an F chord over several barlines (8:49) or Sterling Morrison that of hammering away at an out-of-tune tritone (8:57) (this, of course, later becomes the favorite move of Sonic Youth). Besides straining at the limits of harmonic explanation, the musicians are also in constant friction with even the minimal boundary they have set for themselves. Likely, it only exists in order to produce this friction.

Despite my criticism of Morton previously, I do believe that McClary's ideas about the gendered nature of harmony as a system of musical narrativity can be productively applied to popular music, "Sister Ray" in particular.

The most controversial chapter of McClary's book *Feminine Endings* is her discussion of contemporary composer Janika Vandervelde (112–131). She identifies Vandervelde's use of a rhythmically insistent but harmonically ambiguous academic minimalism as a way of representing female embodiment and pleasure. In Vandervelde's *Genesis II*, the piece McClary analyzes, the piano plays in this style, while the violin and cello forcefully enact the teleological gestures of Romanticism. McClary sees the conflict in this piece as a perfect example of the convergence of sexual politics and harmonic logic.

The music to "Sister Ray" reflects this same conflict between an interest in repetition and ambiguity, culturally coded as feminine, and one in violence and linear narrative, coded masculine. The important difference between *Genesis II* and "Sister Ray" is that, unlike the clear division of the ensemble in Vandervelde's composition, on the Velvet Underground record, the instruments are all frantically simultaneously signifying in both directions. The music mirrors the transvestites who populate its lyrics.

Instrumentation

Lou Reed, in one of his accounts of the recording of "Sister Ray" included above, emphasizes that no one is playing bass (Bockris and Malanga 93). Not only does the absence of a bassist decenter the harmony, since outlining it is traditionally the bass's role, it also enables a greater mobility of instrumental roles. There is no bass—there is no base. The guitar and organ both are common lead and accompaniment instruments in rock and, as my transcriptions have shown, the types of figures used blur these roles.

Sterling Morrison takes the first guitar solo (0:47). His guitar can be distinguished from Reed's by its twangier, less distorted sound; he is using a Fender Stratocaster, while Reed is playing a heavily customized Gretsch Country Gentleman (Fricke 48, 51). This first solo is the only one that really functions as a feature for a single musician and it gives the impression that Reed and Cale are being generous to him, since as soon as it ends, they turn up and nearly drown him out for most of the rest of the song. This solo is strongly reminiscent of "Louie Louie" in timbre and tonality; Morrison stays in typical blues pentatonic rock territory.

The many instrumental breaks that follow are quite different. Cale or Reed will start an improvisation, and the other will enter after a couple of bars. The instrumentals then alternate between simultaneous melodic playing by Cale and Reed or exchanges of percussive chords and noises. This is another example of the influence of avant-garde jazz, particularly Ornette Coleman's album *Free Jazz* and John Coltrane's *Ascension*. Both of these are LP length improvisations. In the Coleman piece, each horn player is featured in a solo, during which the other horns are free to interject commentary and engage in dialogue with the soloist and each other. The Coltrane LP is similar, but each horn solos with only the rhythm section. After each of the individual performances, the entire ensemble reconvenes, as if collectively discussing what was just played. Cale's and Reed's playing on "Sister Ray" differs from that on these albums however, because there is no overall plan and because they lack the harmonic ingenuity of the jazz players. Reed always begins his solos in the blues pentatonic, while Cale uses the mixolydian. Both quickly move outside of these bounds, but their improvisations are quite different from those on *Ascension,* which has a modal basis (though the players are not obliged to follow it strictly), and *Free Jazz,* which has no apparent harmonic outline for the improvisations.

Reed's vocal, rather than being the privileged, featured lead, functions simply as another instrument in the mix. When he is singing, the other players, especially Cale, get in his space just as violently as they do when he is playing a guitar lead. This is especially apparent at the start of the fourth section of the first iteration of the lyrics (6:35), where the instrumental jam continues, without changing intensity, despite Reed's vocal entrance.

Up to this point, I have said nothing about Maureen "Moe" Tucker, the Velvet Underground's drummer. Moe is not a full participant in the collective improvisation for most of "Sister Ray." Instead, she keeps to a strict time keeping function.

However, Tucker's performance embodies what Richard Middleton, Dave Laing, and Jon Stratton have identified as the musical equivalent of Freud's death drive, a kind of musical entropy, in her dramatic moves from a four unit beat (one and *two* and three and *four* and) to a two unit beat (one *and* two *and* three *and* four *and*) to a one unit beat (*one and two and three and four and*), which they call the monad (Stratton 50; Middleton 235–7, 265; Laing 85–86). As the beat increases in intensity, it decreases in information content, until the one unit beat is indistinguishable from stasis, while it at the same time represents the most frenetic activity.

Furthermore, there is a crucial two and a half minute segment, long after the three boys have exhausted their repertoire of thrashing gestures, where Tucker triggers what is the true climax of "Sister Ray." Fourteen minutes, twelve seconds into the track, after Reed has finished his second iteration of the lyrics, Moe abandons the simple beats she has been playing and begins floating freely around her kit. Sterling Morrison, coming to the forefront for the first time since his solo in the first minute of the song, takes over the time keeping role with his guitar. Here, there is a profound experience of decenteredness since the listener has become so accustomed to Moe's steady beat. In this last extended improvisation, the last thing that has been assumed as a source of stability dissolves.

In the lyrics of "Sister Ray," three means of transgressing the body's boundaries are featured: queer sex, I.V. drug use, and murder. Above all, it is a profound violation of the idea of masculinity for the male body to become penetrated, whether this penetration is by a cock, a needle, or a bullet (Simpson 69, 84, 132, 134–141, 160–161, for example). While it is clear that someone, usually referred to as "she" is performing fellatio on another character or the narrator in the scene being described, in the third section of the first iteration of the lyrics, Reed sings "Oh no man, I haven't got the time-time/Too busy sucking on a ding-dong," suggesting that the narrator himself may also enjoy giving, as well as getting. This, of course, is purged from the published lyrics, though the reference to the narrator's being sucked remains (Reed 1991b: 121).

Martin Chalmers, in his essay "Heroin, the Needle, and the Politics of the Body," gives an excellent account of the bodily transgressions associated with I.V. drug use. Not only is the surface of the body literally violated, but the ideal of the body as "a healthy, working machine, ready for labour and the conspicuous consumption of consumer leisure-time" is also punctured by the illogically defiant use of the body for self-destructive pleasure (151, 153). Body play in all its forms, he writes, has been always associated with women and (male) homosexuals (152).

The song's complete lyrics are repeated two and a half times and, with each successive repetition, Reed's enunciation becomes more and more distorted. He stutters, repeats words, interjects other comments and vocal sounds, and melismatically stretches phrases. This play with language as sound is a violation of the communicative function of words, emphasizing instead the bodily pleasure of speech (Stratton 50–51). This is another production of pleasure at the mouth, a liminal area of the body.

The fact that the same story is told more than once in "Sister Ray," by the repetition of the lyrics, undermines the ability of the lyric narrative to structure the song, since the patterns of tension, development, climax, and resolution in the story do not have a determinative relation to the form of the music.

Also, as with the drive to the rhythmic monad in Maureen Tucker's drumming, repetition is the manifestation of the death drive in art.

Recording

The LP *White Light/White Heat*, which includes "Sister Ray," is often considered one of the worst recorded albums in music history. As Reed's and Morrison's accounts of the recording sessions described, the fidelity of the tapes and the balance of the mix are quite poor, because of the band's abuse of the studio equipment. However, rather than flaws in the work, which should be ignored in order to hear the music, like the hiss on early blues recordings, for example, the "bad" sonics of *White Light/White Heat,* especially on "Sister Ray," are another example of the theme of transgression.

The 1995 remastered version, on the Velvet Underground's *Peel Slowly and See* box set is startling. While the technical skill involved in cleaning up the tapes is obviously admirable and (especially as a part time musicologist) it is great to be able to hear the guitars and organ separately and distinctly, the remastering is questionable. Regardless of the intentions of the Velvets and their producer and engineer, the noise and distortion of the original version of *White Light/White Heat* have become part of the standard text of the album. Presently, the original version is available on the CD version of the album and I recommend it as a supplement to the box set (as well as the third album and *Loaded,* both of which appear in substantially remixed form on *Peel Slowly and See.* See Kostek 57–63, 171–178 for more on variant mixes and edits).

In multitrack recording, each instrumental and vocal part occupies a narrow segment of the surface of the magnetic tape. Think of these as separate, parallel lanes, or tracks. Since the information is physically divided, one track can be changed or replaced, without affecting the others. This is how Prince, for example, played all the instruments on his early records. When a signal that is too loud is recorded on one track, its representation requires more space than is available in that track, and it infringes on the neighboring ones, distorting them and making it impossible to balance the levels of the different tracks, since they are in each other's space. The language recording engineers use to describe this phenomenon shows its transgressive, bodily nature: if a track is too hot, it will bleed onto other tracks.

Leakage is another result of excessive recording volumes. When recording more than one instrument simultaneously to different tracks, engineers use a separate microphone for each. If the music is too loud however, it will leak into other microphones, again preventing proper mixing, since there will be traces of the drums on the vocal track, the bass on the drum track, etc.

Also, the recording tape can physically only handle a certain overall signal level. Most better home tape decks have a recording level control to prevent the distortion that results from exceeding the capacity of the medium. Experiment with this at home, or at your rich friend's home; you can't break anything—I don't think.

All three of these audio "don'ts" are in evidence on "Sister Ray." The instrumental tracks are too hot, leaking and bleeding over one another's boundaries, until it becomes difficult to separate one from another. Furthermore, the whole recording, the body of the text, is too hot, captured in a permanent state of over-excitation.

Sexuality

We all know better than to place the text in an essential relation to its author, whether the source for this is the New Critical intentional fallacy, the poststructuralist death of the author, or Dave Laing's theorization of external and internal modes of address in popular song (87–91). All the same, Lou Reed's sexuality has been at the center of most attempts to make sense of his work and besides, inquiring minds want to know. *I* want to know.

Peter Doggett's *Lou Reed: Growing up in Public* is the only full length biography of Reed in English.[1] Briefly, Doggett, following interviews Reed has given, tells how Reed's desire for men led his parents to have him given electro-shock treatments when he was seventeen (an event which forms the basis of the song "Kill your Sons" (18). Later, when he was in college at Syracuse, Reed dated both men and women, but formed no satisfying relationships, emotionally or sexually (23). No information is given on his sex life during the Velvet Underground period.[2]

Reed has married twice, but both marriages took place at the periods in his career when he most involved in exploring gay life. His first marriage, to a woman named Betty, came in 1973, when he was spending a lot of time with David Bowie, working on the album *Transformer* (84) his most blatantly gay themed record. This marriage dissolved during the recording of the *Berlin* LP, a case of life imitating art, or vice versa (87). From 1976 to 1978, Reed lived with Rachel, a (male) transvestite (95–99). Doggett claims that this was the most serious relationship Reed had had to this point (114). At the fadeout of "Coney Island Baby," probably Reed's best love song, Reed says "I'd like to send this one out to Lou and Rachel and all the kids out at PS 192—man I swear I'd give the whole thing up for you." (101). In 1979, Reed gave a series of interviews in which he spoke explicitly about his homosexuality, and lived in an apartment on Christopher Street, in the center of New York's gay community. However, shortly after this, he met Sylvia Morales at a S/M club in Greenwich Village, and they married on Valentine's Day 1980 (115, 121–122).

Since Doggett's book was published, Reed has apparently left Sylvia and is now involved with Laurie Anderson (Lemon 104).[3]

I have rehearsed all of this gossip not simply out of the voyeurism of a fan, but to get to a point where I can address two recent issues dealing with Reed's work.

First, John Gill, in his new book *Queer Noises: Male and Female Homosexuality in Twentieth Century Music,* in a chapter called "Dire Straights: Ziggy, Iggy, Marc, Lou," accuses Reed, along with David Bowie, Iggy Pop, Brian Eno, and Marc Bolan, of cynically exploiting gay identities for publicity (106–113). However, Gill mentions Reed only in his subtitle, and devotes the entire essay to Bowie. Furthermore, elsewhere in his book, Gill is eager to claim Miles Davis as a "queer saint" based on unsubstantiated rumors (65), yet it is clear from Davis' own autobiography that he was no saint, especially in his treatment of the women in his life, and it is odd that Gill is so willing to discard the "dire straights" and at the same time canonize Miles.

Second, and more important, starting in 1989 with the release of Reed's *New York* LP, there have been a series of moves to establish Reed as a Serious Rock Artist, to place him in a group with, for example, Bob Dylan and Neil Young. The book of poems and lyrics *Between Thought and Expression,* the boxed set of the same title, and the *Words and Music* sheet music anthology are all attempts to sum up Reed's work and argue for its importance. However, each of these, by omission and editing, is also an attempt to heterosexualize Reed and his work (Doggett 175). "Sister Ray" does not appear on the box set or in the poems and lyrics book. Allegedly, a live version from Reed's first solo tour was considered for the box set and eliminated by Reed (Heylin 1994: 407–408). Though it is included in the songbook, it too has been straightened out. Not only, as I previously mentioned, have the lyrics been changed to clarify who is sucking whom, but the decision to represent the ambiguous music of "Sister Ray" as nice tidy triads is also a way to restrict its signification, to force it into reasonable limits.

These events can lead towards a critique of the idea of "classic rock" based on feminist and queer concerns. Charles Shaar Murray, Greg Tate, and Nelson George have all written on the racism of the AOR radio format but, during a recent unscientific skimming of the radio available on a drive from Toledo to Detroit, I found that classic rock stations' ads consistently positioned themselves between feminine Top 40 and weak male "alternative" on one side, and ethnically other rap and dance music on the other.

The case of the Velvet Underground's exclusion from the classic rock format suggests the importance of musicology and an anti-essentialist position to this critique. Elton John works as a counter-example. No matter how many times John comes out, people will still be requesting "Your Song" at weddings.

Endnotes

1. Two important sources have appeared since the first version of this essay: McNeil and McCain and Bockris 1994. Neither contradicts Doggett in any significant way. Their additions to the public record of Reed's personal life are included as footnotes to my summary of Doggett.

2. Reed had an affair with Nico in 1965 and 1966 (Bockris 1994: 106–108; McNeil and McCain 8–10) and was involved with Warhol's assistant (and *White Light/White Heat* cover model) Billy Name (né Linich). Bockris makes much of this second relationship, arguing that Reed's simultaneous relationships with his college sweetheart Shelly Albin and Name inspired most of the lyrics on the third album (Bockris 1994: 165–166, 169–170). McNeil and McCain, on the other hand, quote Name downplaying his relationship with Reed, describing it in utilitarian sexual terms: "There was no rapture or romance involved. It was just about getting your rocks off at the moment . . ." (14–15).

3. Bockris confirms all Doggett's work and gives more information on the breakup of Reed's marriage to Sylvia and his relationship with Laurie Anderson (1994: 401–418).

Works Cited

Bockris, Victor. *Transformer: The Lou Reed Story.* New York: Simon and Schuster, 1994.

Bockris, Victor and Gerard Malanga. *Up-tight: The Velvet Underground Story.* New York: Quill, 1983.

Bowman, Rob. Liner notes to Lou Reed, *Between Thought and Expression.* New York: RCA, 1991.

Chalmers, Martin. "Heroin, the Needle and the Politics of the Body" in McRobbie, *Zoot Suits and Second-Hand Dresses,* 150–155.

Davis, Miles and Quincy Troupe. *Miles: The Autobiography.* New York: Simon and Schuster, 1989.

Doggett, Peter. *Lou Reed: Growing Up in Public*. New York: Omnibus Press, 1992.

Foucault, Michel. "A Preface to Transgression" in *Language, Counter-Memory, and Practice*. Ithaca, NY: Cornell University Press, 1977, 29–52.

Fricke, David. Liner notes to The Velvet Underground, *Peel Slowly and See*. New York: Polygram, 1995.

George, Nelson. *The Death of Rhythm and Blues*. New York: Plume, 1988.

Gill, John. *Queer Noises: Male and Female Homosexuality in Twentieth-Century Music*. Minneapolis: University of Minnesota Press, 1995.

Heylin, Clinton. *Bootleg: The Secret History of the Other Recording Industry*. New York: St. Martin's Press, 1994.

———. *From the Velvets to the Voidoids: A Pre-Punk History for a Post-Punk World*. New York: Penguin, 1993.

Kostek, M.C. *The Velvet Underground Handbook*. London: Black Spring Press, 1992.

Laing, David. "The Grain of Punk: An Analysis of the Lyrics" in McRobbie, *Zoot Suits and Second-Hand Dresses*, 74–101.

Lemon, Brendan. "Laurie Anderson," *The New Yorker*, April 10, 1995, 104–105.

Litweiler, John. *Ornette Coleman: A Harmolodic Life*. New York: Da Capo, 1992.

McClary, Susan. *Feminine Endings: Music, Gender, and Sexuality*. Minneapolis: University of Minnesota Press, 1991.

McNeil, Legs and Gillian McCain. *Please Kill Me: The Uncensored Oral History of Punk*. New York: Grove Press, 1996.

McRobbie, Angela, ed. *Zoot Suits and Second-Hand Dresses: An Anthology of Fashion and Music*. Boston: Unwin-Hyman, 1988.

Middleton, Richard. "'Play It Again Sam': Some Notes on the Productivity of Repetition in Popular Music," *Popular Music* 3 (1983).

Morton, Melanie. "Don't Go for Second Sex, Baby!" in Schwichtenberg, *The Madonna Connection*, 213–235.

Murray, Charles Shaar. *Crosstown Traffic: Jimi Hendrix and the Rock 'n' Roll Revolution*. New York: St. Martin's Press, 1989.

Reed, Lou (1991a). *Between Thought and Expression: Selected Lyrics of Lou Reed*. New York: Hyperion, 1991.

——— (1991b). *Words and Music*. Secaucus, NJ: Warner Bros., 1991.

Schuller, Gunther. *Musings: The Musical Worlds of Gunther Schuller*. New York: Oxford University Press, 1986.

Schwichtenberg, Cathy, ed. *The Madonna Connection: Representational Politics, Subcultural Identities, and Cultural Theory*. Boulder: Westview, 1993.

Simpson, Mark. *Male Impersonators: Men Performing Masculinity*. New York: Routledge, 1994.

Stratton, Jon. "Beyond Art: Postmodernism and the Case of Popular Music," *Theory, Culture, and Society* 6 (1989).

Tate, Greg. *Flyboy in the Buttermilk: Essays on Contemporary America*. New York: Simon and Schuster, 1992.

Thompson, Dave. *Beyond the Velvet Underground*. New York: Omnibus Press, 1989.

Willis, Ellen. "Velvet Underground" in *Beginning to See the Light: Sex, Hope, and Rock-and-Roll*. Hanover, NH: Wesleyan University Press, 1992, 110–124.

DAVID FRICKE

LOU REED: THE *ROLLING STONE* INTERVIEW (1989)

Lou Reed has spent most of his career as a solo artist, and he handles the mythical stature of the Velvets carefully, cautioning in this interview that we should not "get too lost in the mystique of the Velvet Underground." Still, his time with the Velvets set the tone for all subsequent expectations of his fans and critics alike, and thinking about his solo work without connecting it to its apparent historical roots is especially difficult. Rolling Stone senior editor David Fricke is himself a historian and the author of the essay included with The Velvet Underground: Peel Slowly and See. With a deft touch, Fricke elicits some illuminating comments from Reed about the band that laid the groundwork for his solo career.

The heckling starts in the middle of the very first song. Above the steely guitar strains of "Romeo Had Juliette," the gritty ode to love under siege that sets the stage and the tone for Lou Reed's urban-apocalypse suite *New York,* some bozo up in the balcony of the Orpheum Theater in Boston keeps yelling, "This sucks! Play some rock & roll!" The bozo wants hits; Reed couldn't care less. He is opening his two-hour-plus show tonight by presenting *New York* in a manner befitting its urgent content and narrative structure, as a complete song cycle, all fourteen songs in order, from start to finish.

The bozo nearly ruins "Halloween Parade," a bittersweet hymn for the bodies and souls lost to AIDS, with his yapping. At which point, Reed, never one to suffer fools gladly or otherwise, stops the show, takes dead aim and fires.

"This *is* rock & roll. It's *my* rock & roll," Reed snaps with acidic relish. "If you don't like my rock & roll, why don't ya just split? Get a refund, motherfucker." Upstairs, silence. The bozo is history.

Nobody humbles a heckler better than Lou Reed. Of course, nobody does Lou Reed better than Lou Reed. He said so himself in 1978 on the aptly titled live album *Take No Prisoners:* "I do Lou Reed better than anybody." A decade before that, he set the standard for literate streetwise verse, dark lyric humor, white avant-noise and primal rock & roll throb with the Velvet Underground, arguably *the* most influential American band of rock's last quarter century.

Reed's disciples and descendants range in age, genre and temperament from David Bowie, Ric Ocasek and Chrissie Hynde to U2, Sonic Youth and R.E.M. Reed remains, however, unbeatable at his own game. He is also at the height of his powers. *New York* is his best album since the harrowing 1982 document of love and obsession *The Blue Mask;* it is also the closest he has truly come to recapturing the Velvets' rarefied magic on record since their demise. On *New York* he dramatizes the physical and moral rotting of the Big Apple with the same corrosive wit, whiplash language and poker-faced humanity with which he depicted drug addiction in "Heroin," errant sexual behavior in "Walk on the Wild Side" and, in the epic "Street Hassle," the fragility of hope and love among the ruins.

Tonight at the Orpheum, part of a spring tour that includes a sellout week on Broadway, Reed animates the album's characters and crises with the slow-boil indignation of his unmistakable deadpan singing and the vibrant guitar cross-talk between himself and Mike Rathke, which recalls the heady primitivism of Reed's six-string dialogues with Sterling Morrison in the Velvets. "Dime Store Mystery," Reed's farewell to his friend and the Velvets' original manager and mentor, Andy Warhol, is a deliberate, dynamic evocation of the group's singular style of dissonant, and poignant, art song—the ominous serrated bowing of electric standup bassist Rob Wasserman, à la John Cale; Robert Medici's ghost-dance drumming, à la Maureen Tucker; Reed's own fireball guitar distortion; the howling feedback coda. At forty-seven, an age when many of his contemporaries are just rehearsing for retirement, Lou Reed remains true to the sonic extremes and uncompromised vision of the Velvet Underground.

"I did what I always do," Reed says of the songs, sound and sentiment of *New York* between swigs of Perrier and drags on a cigarette before sound check. "The only change has been—and I know it sounds clichéd—

but if you practice something over and over and over and over, you're supposed to get better at it."

The fans agree. *New York* is Reed's highest-charting album since the mid-Seventies heyday of *Transformer* (which spawned his only Top Ten single, "Walk on the Wild Side"), *Rock n Roll Animal* and *Sally Can't Dance*. There have been a few near misses in the interim, like the user-friendly power rock of 1984's *New Sensations,* but Reed insists his interest in mainstream pop success is less than zero. "I've become completely well adjusted to being a cult figure," he says.

What does bug him is the continuing furor, twenty-two years after the release of the first Velvet Underground album, over his style of writing and choice of subjects. To the young Lou Reed, fresh out of Syracuse University—where he divided his time between creative-writing courses, poetry studies with Delmore Schwartz and a series of campus bar bands—frank discussions of sex, drugs and ravaged romance were no big deal in serious literature. If pop music was indeed art (a major mid-Sixties premise), scoring these discussions to electric guitars and tribal drums was the most logical thing in the world.

"I never in a million years thought people would be outraged by what I was doing," Reed says. "You could go to your neighborhood bookstore and get any of that." Except Reed's version of the Great American Novel, now more than twenty-five albums in length, has the weight of keen personal observation and, during a particularly colorful period in the Seventies, autobiographical truth. (Today his worst vice is smoking—"the next thing to go," he vows.)

With *New York* in the Top Fifty, the tour drawing rapturous audiences and anticipation high for the November première of *Songs for 'Drella*—Reed and John Cale's dramatic and moving requiem for Andy Warhol (recently debuted as a work-in-progress in New York)—Reed sat down with ROLLING STONE for in-depth conversations in Boston and Washington, D.C., combined here with a session that took place earlier this year in New York. With his round-rimmed glasses giving him a slightly professorial air, he talked of his songwriting; his love of Fifties rhythm & blues; the spiritual and artistic influence of Andy Warhol; the music and mystique of the Velvet Underground; the making, and the message, of *New York.*

"It's interesting when you've been around as long as I have to see these things come around," Reed remarked near the end. "It's like, do you want to be serious? About your own life? And if you don't want to be serious, there's party records, and that's a lot of fun. But I'm interested in something else. I'm not saying it's better than all the rest. It's just different. "I have a few more words at my disposal. And I can't ignore that."

When you recently inducted Dion into the Rock and Roll Hall of Fame, you reminisced in your speech about studying geometry at home on Long Island in the Fifties while grooving to R&B vocal groups like the Paragons, the Diablos and the Jesters on the radio. Most people do not associate you or your records with that kind of vintage street-corner soul.

Well, they might not equate me, either, with someone trying to figure out solid geometry. But listen to the end of "Halloween Parade." Jeffrey [Lesser], the engineer, did that great high falsetto. All my background vocal parts are based on that kind of music.

Like "And the colored girls go do da-do da-do" in "Walk on the Wild Side"?

Sure, all of it. I had my first record out when I was fourteen [the Jades' "Leave Her for Me," in 1957], doing those kinds of songs. Now listen to "There Is No Time" [on *New York*]. If you get past the sonic blast, "There Is No Time" is just a very hyped version of *that*.

Where was the R&B in the songs and sound of the Velvet Underground?

It was always in the band somewhere. There were two sides of the coin for me. That kind of music—R&B, doo-wop, rockabilly. And then Ornette Coleman and Don Cherry, Archie Shepp, stuff like that. When I was in college, I had a jazz radio show. I called it *Excursion on a Wobbly Rail*, after a Cecil Taylor song. I used to run around the Village following Ornette Coleman wherever he played. There was his song "Lonely Woman," Charlie Haden's bass on that [*he hums the riff*]. Extraordinary.

At the same time there was this other song, one of my all-time favorites, called "Outcast," by Eddie and Ernie. Like pre-Sam and Dave. Just killed me. I used to play it for the Velvet Underground and say, "Listen to this bass part, it's astonishing."

There is that little guitar quote from Marvin Gaye's "Hitch Hike" in "There She Goes Again," on 'The Velvet Underground and Nico.'

A nice little introductory thing, right? The thing is, we actually had a rule in the band for a while. If anybody played a blues lick, they would be fined. Of course, we didn't have any money to fine anybody with. But that was because there were so many of these blues bands around, all copping on that. And while I really liked the stuff for singing, I can't sing that. I had to find my own way. So all the arranging and stuff, those R&B kind of parts might be in the back of the mind, but it came out white. I meant what I said about Dion at the induction ceremony. There was a white guy singing that way, very obviously from New York. And I was impressed by that.

How did Andy Warhol actually "produce" the first Velvet Underground album?

By keeping people away from us, because they thought he was producing it. They didn't sign us because of us. We were signed because of Andy. And he took all the flak. We said, "He's the producer," and he just sat there.

Was he merely a benign presence?

We just did what we do, and he would say, "Oh, that was great." "Oh, you should leave it that way." "Oh, no, that's wonderful." I'd been around studios before, writing and recording these cutout-bin kind of records, trendy songs that sell for ninety-nine cents. But Andy absorbed all the flak. Then MGM said they wanted to bring in a real producer, Tom Wilson. So that's how you got "Sunday Morning," with all those overdubs—the viola in the back, Nico chanting. But he couldn't undo what had already been done.

Were any of the songs on the first Velvets album written during your previous tenure writing quickie hits to order at Pickwick Records?

Some of them. "Heroin." I don't remember the other ones, but I know I had "Heroin" down.

Didn't you feel a bit schizophrenic, writing trendy, prefab pop songs such as "The Ostrich" and "Cycle Annie" by day and then something like "Heroin" by night?

But Andy was doing commercial art, then he was doing his other art. He supported the show [the Exploding Plastic Inevitable] with his commercial art. Where do they think we got the money to put it on? We didn't have inheritances or something. We were broke. Then Andy would to a *TV Guide* cover or something.

So I didn't see that as schizophrenic at all. I just had a job as a songwriter. I mean, a real hack job. They'd come in and give us a subject, and we'd write. Which I still kind of like to this day. I really love it if someone comes in and says they want a song, they give me a subject. And it's even better if they tell me what kind of attitude they want. I can divorce myself from it completely. Andy used to say he really liked it when people corrected his commercial art because he had no feelings about it one way or the other. He didn't feel anything, and since they did, they must be right.

Would Andy give you subjects to write about?

Sure. He said, "Why don't you write a song called 'Vicious'?" And I said, "Well, Andy, what kind of vicious?" "Oh, you know, vicious like I hit you with a flower." And I wrote it down, literally. Because I kept a notebook in those days. I used it for poetry, things people said. Just like in "Last Great American Whale" [on *New York*]—"Stick a fork in their ass, and turn them over, they're done." I first heard it in the Midwest; I heard John Mellencamp say it. I'd never heard the expression before. He said, "Stick a fork in my ass, turn me over, I'm done." I wrote that one down and changed it a little.

But I was doing that around the Factory. I went back and wrote a song, "Vicious/You hit me with a flower/You do it every hour/Oh baby you're so vicious." Then people would come up and say, "What do you mean by that?" I didn't want to say, "Well, ask Andy."

Or he said, "Oh, you should write a song, so-and-so is such a *femme fatale*. Write a song for her. Go write a song called 'Femme Fatale.'" No other reason than that. Or "Sister Ray"—when we were making the second record, he said, "Now you gotta make sure that you do the 'sucking on my ding-dong' song." "Okay, Andy." He was a lot of fun, he really was.

He was perceived more as an instigator, a kind of puppeteer.

He was this catalyst, always putting jarring elements together. Which was something I wasn't always so happy about. So when he put Nico in, we said, "Hmmm." Because Andy said, "Oh, you've gotta have a chanteuse." I said, "Oh, Andy, give us a break." There we are, doing six sets a night at this terrible tourist trap in the Village, the audience was attacking people over the music.

Warhol and the Velvets parted ways in 1967. Did he lose interest in the band?

No. Andy passes through things, but so do we. He sat down and had a talk with me. "You gotta decide what you want to do. Do you want to keep just playing museums from now on and the art festivals? Or do you want to start moving into other areas? Lou, don't you think you should think about it?" So I thought about it, and I fired him. Because I thought that was one of the things to do if we were going to move away from that.

What was Andy's reaction to that?

He was furious. I'd never seen Andy angry, but I did that day. He was really mad. Called me a rat. That was the worst thing he could think of.

How do you look back on the Velvets now? Do you think, after only five years and four albums, that the band left behind a lot of unfinished business?

John [Cale] says that it broke up before we'd accomplished what we should have accomplished. I think he's right in a way. My records are my version of it. John's records are his version of it. The drumming of Maureen Tucker is something that can't be replaced by anyone. And then, of course, *Loaded* didn't have Maureen on it, and that's a lot of people's favorite Velvet Underground record. So we can't get too lost in the mystique of the Velvet Underground.

Yet that mystique is more pervasive now than it ever was before. Where do you hear the influence of the Velvet Underground today?

I hear things that sometimes make me think, "Oh, that sounds like Velvets." Or, "That sounds like me," or Maureen. It's rare to hear it all together. Then on the other hand, the Velvet Underground could do a lot of things a lot of ways. They could be very dissonant, very pretty. And they were all two-, three-chord songs. My albums are all two-, three-chord songs. I know for a young band, if they need some material, my stuff is kind of good for them, because it doesn't have a lot of chords. It's all right there. Maybe that's why people like it, because it is so simple.

After leaving the Velvet Underground in 1970, you worked for your father for a while.

As a typist. He had this company, he was like president of it. He really wanted me to be in the family business. But that was a real impossibility. But when I left the Velvet Underground, I just packed up. I'd had it. So I was a typist for two years. My mother always told me in high school, "You should take typing. It gives you something to fall back on." She was right.

There is an old Lou Reed press bio issued by RCA that has handwritten comments by you. And for that period immediately following the Velvets, you put down "exile and great pondering." Pondering what?

What the next move I was going to make was. Did I want to do it myself? Did I want to have a band? Did I just want to do songwriting, not even get onstage? I'm the last person in the world I'd have thought should be on a stage. Some people really like having a spotlight on them. I don't. What I like is the song and performing it. Doing it for people—who like it.

I want out of the rock & roll thing. I really do. It's a little late now. But I don't enjoy that end of it. Yet there I am, up onstage, performing my stuff. Certainly part of the reason originally was because no one else would. And I still think that to some extent. I do me really well.

With the success of "Walk on the Wild Side" and the subsequent renewed interest in the Velvets, you became best known as the man who dared to put great social taboos in song—drug addiction, sexual deviance. . . .

It was only taboo on records. Let's keep that in mind. Movies, plays, books, it's all in there. You read Ginsberg, you read Burroughs, you read Hubert Selby, Jr. If you want to have this stuff taken on a level that's worth considering, you can't compare yourself to the other stuff that's on record. You start looking at Brecht and Weill.

Did you feel pressured, though, to keep writing so-called Lou Reed songs?

For a while, I felt a little self-impelled to write Lou Reed kind of songs. I should have understood that a Lou Reed song was anything I wanted to write about.

But during the Seventies you didn't just write about extremes in art and lifestyle. You also lived them.

Real-life zigzagging. Yeah, why not? It's taken me a while. Maybe I'm a late bloomer. Put it this way. I'm not harsh on myself for any of that. If anything, I have an understanding and sympathy for the situation. What I'm devoted to now is never letting those situations happen ever again. I would just walk away.

In 1989, how do you relate to that Lou Reed?

I don't look back on it. I wrote a record about it, though. I wrote a song, "Growing up in public/With your pants down." That's what I thought of the whole thing. And that said all that I had to say about that. Most of the major mistakes were in public, and I put them on record to boot. Lots of novelists have put it in their books. Norman Mailer's got his *Advertisements for Myself.*

It's quite remarkable that considering your colorful history and notable lack of hits, you can still get your "advertisements" put out on record by a major label.

Weird, isn't it? I don't know why people give me record deals. I think it's because they at least break even, and I think they're making a few bucks while they're at it. I'm a cult figure, but I sell some records.

What about that memorable instance in 1979 when, during a show at the Bottom Line, in New York, you pointed out your record-company president, Clive Davis, in the audience and demanded, "Where's the money, Clive"?

I was drunk, and I've always regretted that I did that. On the other hand, I was mad because there were supposed to be some promotional displays in the city, and I thought I was being jerked around. I responded in a way that I'm not particularly proud of. But that's the way I was then. You pushed me, I pushed back. Or I waited until I could do to you what I thought you did to me. I don't think Clive was trying to do anything to me. But I was frustrated, so I took it out on him, and I've always regretted that I did that.

On the other hand, that's Lou! [*Laughs.*]

What would you say is the most common misconception about you?

Oh, I don't know. I would have to hear them.

For instance, that you're difficult.

I'll tell ya, I'm a genuinely nice guy. I really am. A real nice guy. But I think I'm temperamental. And I'm talking about me, today. I think I have a pretty good handle on it. But sometimes temperamental can be misconstrued as being difficult.

For instance, I don't like being interviewed. Why would anyone want to be interviewed? Anybody in [his] right mind? Why would you, if the position was reversed, want to sit here and have me ask questions about you? "What was it like, this failure you had when you were twenty-two, David?" Who needs it, unless you're an egotist and you really like talking about yourself? And I don't. Because I know myself. I think I'm a nice guy.

I've certainly been really difficult in the past, in a lot of ways, or extremely temperamental. But that's because I was beset, and I didn't have it together. It's a different story now. Of course, I'm older. upposedly when you get older, you get something from all of it before, or you drop dead and that's the end of it. I think I know about certain things better than other people. And I'll fight for it. And I don't think that's being difficult, I mean, it sounds tacky, but it's like being true to your vision.

How did you feel when "Dirty Blvd." [from 'New York'] was released as a single to radio with the words "piss" ["Give me your tired your poor I'll piss on 'em/That's what the Statue of Bigotry says"] and "suck" ["The TV Whores are calling the Cops out for a Suck"] blipped out? It was no big deal in 1972 to hear "Walk on the Wild Side" on AM radio complete with the line "even when she was giving head."

I did the blipping on "Dirty Blvd." I didn't want the promo people to feel defeated before they ever went in. I was with [mastering engineering] Bob Ludwig—Bob and I go back a long time, all the way to *Metal Machine Music*—and Bob said to me, "If you think they're gonna have a problem with this, why don't you just give 'em a choice, so promo guys don't have to go out and bang their heads against the wall? Just put a guitar there instead of the words." So I asked the company, "Would that make life easier for you?"

"Oh, are you kidding? We didn't want to bring it up."

Doesn't it bother you that you of all people would have opted for such a compromise?

It would bother me if the other version didn't exist. I thought the song was representative of the album, and I wanted to make it easier for everybody. I didn't want to get into a battle about those two words. I've been around way too long. I've made my point. People understand where I'm coming from.

'New York' is certainly quintessential Reed. The city and its citizens have been grist for your mill since the dawn of the Velvets.

Well, Faulkner had the South, Joyce had Dublin. I've got New York—and its environs. It's just a big city. The reason I don't think the album's inhibited by topicality is because I travel around a lot. I talk to people, and it's just the same old stories over there. Different name, same situation.

But there is a difference in perspective. There's anger and urgency in these songs. Whereas in your Velvets songs, you were more of an observer, an emotional journalist.

I don't know if there's any anger in there.

Urgency?

That's different from anger.

But there is a feeling of an eye for an eye, being up against the wall, in songs like "There Is No Time," "Busloads of Faith" and "Hold On."

It's interesting, from a writing point of view, the techniques I used. The sequence is important. Because every time you're hit with a song, you've been hit with a few others before it. There have been these other things whispered in your ear, setting you up for what that song's going to talk about. In "Romeo Had Juliette," you have the two teens. You have "Halloween Parade," people dying of AIDS, then Pedro in the welfare hotel in "Dirty Blvd." Then you have these two people who are *fighting* ["Endless Cycle"] and what if they had a kid.

Then it's into the ecology ["Last Great American Whale"], and suddenly you've got a guy talking about "Gee, maybe I oughta have a kid" ["Beginning of a Great Adventure"]. But while he's talking about that, you've loaded up with five other ones. What has been happening to the kids? What is happening to the land?

In recent years you've performed at benefit concerts, appeared on "Sun City" and toured on behalf of Amnesty International. Did those experiences in any way inspire or influence the attitude and subject matter of 'New York'?

There's a lot of things to write about. I could write about the table, who sat at the table, what the table means to me. It's a great old antique table, look at that spot over there. There's a lot of things you can write about. But this is what came out. Plus, I've been privately talking about these things with a lot of people, about what *is* going on. And as a writer, that really drew my attention, today, now. It's perfectly possible I'll put out a party record next. But in my own way, I think this is a party record. Just not the kind you're used to. It's not a pop record. I don't even think I'm part of rock & roll anymore. There's a niche that's "Lou Reed music." And that's over *there.*

Let's talk about some of your contemporaries. Bob Dylan, for example. He hung out with Warhol at the Factory quite a bit in the mid-Sixties and was at the time, like you, busy transforming rock & roll songwriting.

I always go out and get the latest Dylan album. Bob Dylan can turn a phrase, man. Like his last album [*Down in the Groove*], his choice of songs. "Going ninety miles an hour down a dead-end street"—I'd give anything if I could have written that. Or that other one, "Rank Strangers to Me." The key word there is *rank*.

I can really listen to something like that. The rest of it is all pop. I have zero interest in it. But Dylan continuously knocks me out. "Brownsville Girl," the thing he did with Sam Shepard, he said, "Even the SWAT teams around here are getting pretty corrupt." I was on the floor. I have that same reaction to some of my own stuff. And the only other person I can think of who does that for me is Dylan.

What about John Lennon? Like you, he wrote frankly in his songs about his life and lifestyle.

He wrote a song called "Mother" that I thought was a really good song. "Jealous Guy." I liked his stuff away from the Beatles. Just my own taste. But the kind of phrasing that knocks me out is Dylan's. For language, Dylan kills me to this day.

Bruce Springsteen.

I like him in concert. He's a great live performer. What I really like is the little skits with Clarence and everything, these great spoken introductions.

How did he come to recite those lines on "Street Hassle"?

Because if I'd done them, they'd have come out funny. And when he did it, it sounded real. He was at the same studio, the Record Plant. It wasn't making it with me doing it. So the engineer said, "Why don't you ask Bruce to do it? He could really do that." So we asked Bruce to do it, and he rewrote it a little.

The ending of his passage is a clever takeoff on "Born to Run"—"There are tramps like us/Who were born to pay." Was that his contribution?

No, that was mine. It had been written with him in mind, but he wasn't there. I was just playing off the title.

As someone who was part of the Warhol celebrity circus at its height, what do you think of the "celebutante" party scene in New York now?

I'm not familiar with it. I don't go to clubs, I don't go to concerts. See, after being with Andy, if I never went to another one of those things, it would be too soon. And I still feel that way. I don't go to the China Club, I don't go to M.K., I don't go to the Tunnel. I get cards from all these places, but I don't go. Not interested. I'm kind of dull, huh?

Is there any pop music out there now that interests you at all?

I haven't heard enough. I don't listen to the radio. I don't know what's out there. I know my wife, Sylvia, is really mad about the Waterboys. So we listen a lot to the Waterboys. But of course, I'm really interested in the lyrics. There are few and far between, someone who can really do that.

After you got out of college, did you ever seriously pursue writing—that is, poetry or prose, as opposed to songwriting?

I won a poetry award. While I was at the Factory, Gerard Malanga [a Warhol associate and Velvets biographer] submitted one of my poems to a little magazine. I was getting published in these little magazines. Eugene McCarthy gave me the award, something like "one of the five best new poets in a small literary magazine." I was actually mad at Gerard for submitting it, because I hated the poem. I didn't care if someone else thought it was good. I knew it was terrible. I thought my song lyric was way better than that particular poem.

You've always contended that your records are your version of the Great American Novel.

Yeah, when you play it all in a row. If you have the patience to follow it.

Do you think your "novel" would have made it as poetry or prose, rather than rock & roll?

It wouldn't have had a drum. It wouldn't have had guitars. So you wouldn't have gotten that physicality from it. That's kind of what I like about it.

Ironically, given the country's increasingly conservative disposition, your work seems more drastic, more potent, than it did ten, fifteen, even twenty years ago.

I think the cover-up of Kennedy's assassination, then the pardoning of Nixon finished it for a lot of people. They said, "Well, we didn't know it was bullshit before. We certainly know it's bullshit now. So fuck it. Every man for himself." No one gives a shit. They know they're getting fucked. No time to take care of anything else.

But 'New York' is very much your way of saying you do give a shit.

It is. It's also about the use of language. That's why I say maybe we shouldn't think of me making rock & roll records. I'm in this for the long haul. I feel I've just started to get a grip on it, what I can do with it, what I want to do with it. And who I'd like to take with me when I do it.

It's really easy, in a sense, because the people who like it will go with me. And the people who don't will say I'm full of shit. And more power to them. They don't want me, and I'm not interested in them, either. That's okay. [*Smiles*] I have no problem with that.

PHILIP MILSTEIN, M.C. KOSTEK, AND KATHERINE MESSER
THE MAUREEN TUCKER INTERVIEW (1980–90)

The Maureen Tucker interview from *What Goes On* #4 is an extended affair conducted by seven interviewers over the space of ten years (1980–90). This excerpt is the result of Tucker's conversations with M.C. Kostek, Phil Milstein, and Kate Messer.

Philip (Phil) Milstein: *What are your earliest memories of the band? What they sounded like, what those times were like.*

Maureen (Moe) Tucker: Well, I can remember when I first went to John's apartment to hear them. They played a couple of songs. I think I was gonna be the drummer at that point, and that's why I went. And really, I don't remember if I went because Sterl said, "Why don't you come and hear these guys." I was very impressed when I first heard the songs, the few that I did hear at first. I remember when they played "Heroin" I was really impressed. My brother had been telling me about Lou for a while, because he had known him a few years before that. And he was impressed also. And you could just tell that this was different.

The Velvet Underground: 1965, 1966

M.C. Kostek: *Did you ever have any formal music training at all?*

Moe: I took clarinet when I was in fourth grade or fifth grade. That's all. I played drums in a three-piece band called The Intruders. We played once or twice on Long Island, doing Chuck Berry songs. At [a] club where we played, the drummer of the band was shot by a ricochet bullet the night after we played.

Phil: *Did Sterling play music before he joined the band?*

Moe: Yeah, he started playing guitar when he was about eighteen, I think.

M.C.: *How was Lou as a guitar player when it started?*

Moe: Maybe he is now, but then he wasn't technically as nimble, as "finger-wise" as Sterling. Of course, he knew the instrument, and could do a lot of tricks with the feedback and all that Sterling couldn't do.

Phil: *Was Lou trying to improvise some Sun Ra, Cecil Taylor at this time into the rock and roll format?*

Moe: I don't know.

M.C.: *On the first album it says, "Lou Reed: Ostrich Guitar."*

Moe: That was this guitar, a Gretsch, semi-hollow body, old, green. Lou had taken the frets off of it. And it really had this odd sound. Fantastic sound. Of course you couldn't use it for many songs, but for what he wanted it was tremendous. And it got stolen shortly thereafter. Along with his record collection. He had a record collection, oh, he must have been collecting singles since he was twelve. Songs, groups you never heard of, for the most part. He used to live with Sterling and a couple of other guys in the city, in this real slum-type area. It was the "great sneaker robbery," we called it, because there were actually sneaker prints on his bed [laughter]. But they came and took his guitar, and all of his records. Oh, it was heartbreaking. Some of those records, there isn't a copy left in the world. But they were tremendous. I loved them, because we both liked the same music, and once in a while we would have sort of a party, and he would say, "Listen to this!" He'd be half-drunk, and I'd be half-drunk, and so would everybody, and he would put it on, and I'd say, "Yaaaaa! Who is it?" and he'd say, "The Goofballs," or whoever. He must have had two or three hundred records, anyway.

M.C.: Do you remember how you and the band felt about rock music at the time? The Beatlemania stuff that was going on, the Kinks?

Moe: We enjoyed it, we liked it.

M.C.: How did you feel in relationship to all that?

Moe: We loved the Who. John had gone to England and come back with an EP of the Who. We had never heard them before, and he was raving. We heard that and really loved that. And we liked the Kinks, and the Stones, of course, we loved them. I did. They all liked them. I was a little crazier. The Beatles they liked a lot, and I was a big Beatle fan. We enjoyed their music, and I don't think we felt competitive if that's what you mean.

M.C.: I mean did you feel that you were the same sort of thing? Did you feel, "They're a band, we're a band, sometime we might tour together," something like that.

Moe: No, I never thought that kind of thing would happen. That we would ever get famous, or that Mick Jagger would ever listen to a record with me on it . . . Whoo! That still blows my mind.

Phil: That Brian Epstein might consider managing the band?

Moe: Yeah, those things didn't occur to me.

Phil: When you first started with the Velvet Underground, did the band consider itself a full-time, professional rock group?

Moe: No. In fact the first job I did with them was just for fun. I didn't expect to be with them after that.

Phil: Did the band members have day jobs then?

Moe: I did. They didn't. Sterling was still going to school. I don't know what the hell Lou and John were doing. I know they weren't working actual nine-to-five day jobs.

Phil: How often did you rehearse?

Moe: I don't think we ever did. I think the first time when we rehearsed when I actually had drums was the afternoon of that first job, in New Jersey. So I wasn't that sure of the songs, plus everything was breaking, so [laughter] we never rehearsed, it was weird. When we had to do an album, we'd rent a little rehearsal hall, and we'd go in for a few hours, a few days. But usually, when we recorded, we had been playing the songs live for months and months, so we really didn't have to rehearse. When Lou would have a new song or two, we'd go wherever we were playing at the time, in the afternoon, and learn the song a couple of times, and fool around with it until we were ready to play it. But we never said, "Rehearsal twice a week." We never did that.

Phil: How did the band go about working out their songs?

Moe: They would play it for a little bit before I'd bother trying, 'cause they were still trying to get it together. And when they were pretty sure of their ideas, I'd play with them for a while, and think about what I wanted to do. Then we'd play it and play it and play it.

M.C.: How did you ever find out the words?

Moe: I would find them out by playing it live. A lot of the songs I couldn't sing to you [laughter]. We'd just fool with it until we got a comfortable arrangement.

Phil: *Was the sound as wild as on that first record? Wilder?*

Moe: About the same.

Phil: *So the structure of the songs, and the atmosphere of the musicians playing together, that was more or less the same as when the record appeared?*

Moe: Yeah, I think so.

Phil: *What were the goals of the band in the beginning? Where did you want to take your music, take the band?*

Moe: I don't know. When we were starting out, like any group that is just starting out playing here and there, you don't think you're really good and "We're going to make a million dollars." You just go along as it comes, you know? You get another job in a better place, a few people start to like you, you get a little picture in the paper, it's nice. But you don't think, "Okay, this is the beginning." It just sort of rolls along.

Phil: *The first gig was the Summit High [New Jersey] job. You said you played three songs. How long after that was the Bizarre gig?*

Moe: It was instantly, two days later, or something. In fact, the guy who got us into the New Jersey thing had a hand in getting the Bizarre job for us.

Phil: *Alan Aronowitz?*

Moe: Yeah, right.

Phil: *So that lasted only a few days at the Bizarre?*

Moe: I think less than one week.

Phil: *Did the residency at the Café Bizarre start you thinking about being in a band?*

Moe: Not in my mind. I didn't think that would happen. But as soon as Andy came on the scene, there were actually prospects of being in a working band.

Phil: Did that bring about any changes in the band's music or attitude?

Moe: Nothing I noticed. I got serious about it, and changed my hours at my day job so I'd run in the door at 11 in the morning, and fly out the door at four in the afternoon, because I had to go to the Dom every night. I took it seriously, and they did too, of course. I don't know if anybody expected to be together for a long time. I guess we hoped to. I don't think any of us thought, "Let's play this this way, then we'll have a hit and be rich." None of us thought really in terms of money. It was fun, enjoyment.

Phil: What sort of effect did playing in a band have on the way you were living at the time?

Moe: None really. I was still living at home. I wasn't making any money so I couldn't really move anywhere. I guess it did change my attitudes a lot, in a way I can't explain. I can't explain it myself. I know I changed a lot. I really loved it.

Phil: How long was it before you quit working at your day job?

Moe: About six months. Maybe not that long.

Phil: What about now, how do you look back at that early period?

Moe: Well it was really exciting, interesting. A nice way to live. Tiring sometimes, maddening sometimes. But basically, I miss it a lot.

Phil: I wanted to ask you about a couple of recordings from those early days. One of them was in this book, called the Index Book, and it has a lot of pictures of the Factory, and from the Phillip Johnson estate party. A lot from that session and few others of the band, and all the Warhol people. It has all sorts of little pop-outs: as you turned the pages, little things pop up, and balloons, and little games, and spinners, and there was a record in there, with a picture of Lou on the record. And when you play it, it's from a party. You can hear the banana album playing in the background, and it's Lou, and Nico, and a few other people paging through the book, talking about the book that the record came in.

Moe: I haven't heard it in so long.

M.C.: Well, Nico talks, for the most part. It doesn't sound like you or Sterling are on there. Do you remember who's actually on there talking?

Moe: I know I've heard it, and I could pick out who it was, but now I don't remember. No, it's not me, and I'm pretty sure Sterling is not on there. But from having heard it, it was Lou and . . . now I don't remember. It was probably one of those afternoons when Lou would just stroll over there, and they were fooling around. Bridgid [Polk], it might be. Bridgid might be on there.

Phil: Have you heard "Noise," which was recorded for the East Village Other album? It's hard to tell what that's all about, 'cause on one side part of it is a radio report of the marriage of Lucy Johnson [laughter]. And behind it is the band playing this song called "Noise." It's hard to pick out the song because it's pretty low in the mix.

Moe: I don't think I've heard that.

Phil: What about that "Loop" record, which was in that Aspen magazine.

Moe: No, no, I don't know what the hell that was.

Phil: You weren't on any of those?

Moe: No.

Produced by Andy Warhol

Phil: When did Andy approach you?

Moe: Andy came down, maybe the third night that we were playing there.

Phil: So, shortly before leaving the Bizarre, did he instantly say, "I want you people to play with me?"

Moe: Yeah.

Phil: Right that night? And did you instantly decide to do it?

Moe: I did. Yeah, I think we all did.

Phil: So, shortly after there you went and started paying at the Factory?

Moe: The Factory was just his studio, and we'd play there once in a while, just for fun really. Not as a formal thing. We got The Dom together shortly after we were with Andy. We played around first, we'd go to art shows, and then we got The Dom maybe six months after we were first with Andy. We played there for a month every night. I'd work during the day, rush into the city and play 'til two in the morning, and then zoom back home. So that was fun, and it also provided us a tremendous place to get it together. Then we went to California.

Phil: When did you go to California?

Moe: It was in '66. It was just after the Dom. We played a month at the Dom, and we got this offer to go play at the Trip and Fillmore, so we said we'd do that. The idea was that we were supposed to keep the lease to the Dom while we were gone, 'cause that was nice, it was fun. Besides, it was building up a nice crowd, too. At first there wouldn't be many people, but then it got to the point where there was a lot of people there every night. So, it was a nice way to do it. And, of course, by the time we got back from California, some bastard had gypped us out of the lease, so we lost that.

Phil: Sterling put a conspiracy theory to that.

Moe: There was, but I don't remember the names.

Phil: No, he suggested that the people who suggested you go to California were the same ones who all along had the idea of stealing the lease.

Moe: Yeah, that was his theory then. It sounds probable because it was at that point a going concern. It was a place to go.

M.C.: Was this all Andy paying for the tour and everything?

Moe: With us; the money we all earned together in doing these shows.

M.C.: There was no record company or anything like that?

Moe: No.

Phil: What sort of effect did Andy have on the band? Did he impose any musical changes?

Moe: No, not at all.

Phil: Did he make any suggestions, or did any of the people that were around at the time?

Moe: No, no.

Phil: He left you alone and let you play?

Moe: Yeah, he just loved everything we did.

M.C.: What did you think about Andy's work at that time?

Moe: I thought it was a little wacky. I had heard of him before, of course, before we met him, and I was very impressed to meet him. And I really liked him a lot. We had a nice sort of rapport, and I thought it was very funny, his stuff. Not funny—"ha-ha," but funny that people would pay what they did for it. And it was sort of a joke to him, at the time, anyway. He'd set up his silk-screening, and Gerard and some guys from the Factory would do all the silkscreens of the cow, or whatever he was doing at the time. And Andy had a big stamp with his name on it, and he'd stamp that on and that was it. He'd sell them for fifteen hundred dollars, or whatever.

M.C.: Have you seen anything he's done recently? [1980]

Moe: No, no.

M.C.: You might be interested in one of his books. That philosophy one that came out two years ago.

Moe: I have that. Is that what it's called, *The Philosophy of Andy Warhol?* Yeah, I bought that. It has a Campbell's soup can? I bought that for old times sake.

M.C.: *Did you read any of that?*

Moe: No [laughs].

Phil: *I heard a story about you typing his novel.*

Moe: [Laughter.] That one, *A*?

Phil: *Yeah.*

Moe: Oh. That was funny. I typed that up for him. I wouldn't type any dirty words in it [laughter].

Phil: *Why was that?*

Moe: It was unnecessary, you know. Really, I just felt, "Come on," and I didn't want to be part of it.

M.C.: *So that was artistic censorship, not prudery.*

Moe: No, it was probably prudery. I left spaces where he could fill them in, but I [laughter] wouldn't type them. I'd be sitting there typing away, and have a tape recorder, and listen to some and type it. And he'd come over and sit on the desk, and he'd say, "Oh Moe, but you have to put those words in," and I'd say, "No, no, no, I'll leave the room, and you can go back" [laughter]. Also, a lot of the film stuff I had nothing to do with. A lot of it I refused to do, because it was so dirty and ridiculous. I just said, "I'll go home." So a lot of it I just didn't bother with. I remember one film where, and I don't even know what it is called, they were tying me up, with these little sunglasses on, and Gerard was dancing.

M.C.: *Do you remember any other films like that, where you were acting and not playing?*

Moe: No, that's the only one. Aside from when they'd take films of us when we were practicing. That was a good deal though, by the way. He'd give me five dollars a day, or something. Plus, I was allowed to sign for anything to eat at Max's Kansas City, which was right up the street from me. And that was heaven, because I'd go in and spend the whole night. First I'd eat, and then I'd spend six hours drinking beer with a friend. "Hey, just sign Andy's name." So that was a nice deal.

Phil: How did the whole Exploding Plastic Inevitable show come about?

Moe: That was Andy's idea in the first place, when he was looking for a band. That's what he wanted to have, a multimedia show, as they say.

Phil: What was one of those like?

Moe: Tremendous. That's another thing I really regret, not having a film of those days. Especially because now, you talk about it, and it doesn't seem like that much, but this was what, fifteen years ago, and it was unheard of. There'd be lights of course. It wasn't just one guy with a light, it was programmed. Nothing fancy at all—a guy on a spotlight, turning it on and off, other people running other banks of lights. But they knew the songs, these guys, and they knew the mood of the songs, and they had the same sort of ideas that we had. So they would play to the songs. And there'd be films being shown behind us, on a great big screen, not a little home projector. And dancers—we'd have Gerard Malanga, and Mary Woronov, and they were good dancers.

Phil: Rock dancing?

Moe: No. No. Just dancing. I don't know what you'd call it. Improvising, I guess. But they were both good dancers, and got very funny at a point. The audience didn't notice it, but we did, having seen it all the time. It was a really good show, it was a tremendous idea, and must have been really something to come in and see that fifteen years ago.

Phil: What were some of the reactions like?

Moe: Well, older people, of course, at first they were kind of horrified. Kids, younger people, would be kind of freaked out and really, really enjoy the whole thing. Once we played in a place in Chicago [Poor Richard's], when Lou wasn't able to come—he was sick—and Andy didn't want to come, so we had a girl, Ingrid Superstar, pretending she was Andy. She had real blonde, platinum hair. She had a leather jacket, and she came off playing him for two weeks. Everybody thought she was Andy [laughter]. I played the bass, and Angus came back and played drums, like tabla drums, Indian drums. Sitting on the floor. We built up a tremendous audience there. It was a small place, probably held two hundred, and when we first went we were supposed to be there, I think, for a week. We were held over for another one. And we really got a nice following there.

Phil: When would that be, early '66?

Moe: Maybe later. I know it was summer, so it was probably '66.

Phil: When did you first go out with Andy's show?

Moe: That would be probably either April or May of 1966.

The Velvet Underground & Nico

Phil: How did the first album come about?

Moe: Well, we just talked about it with Andy, and everybody thought it would be a good idea to put out an album, since the show did nicely, and we were building up a name also, by being with his show. So we thought, "What the hell."

M.C.: This was on your own, your own money?

Moe: Andy's and ours, yeah, paid for the studio time. Then, whoever, I don't know who, took it around to try and get a company to buy it. It might have been [Steve] Sesnick, in fact.

Phil: What was Andy's role as producer? He's credited—

Moe: No, [chuckles] we just said, "Let's let Andy be the producer." I don't think he was even there, or he was there for a few hours. Actually, I suppose the engineer was the producer, when you come right down to it. What we lacked, I think, is that we didn't have a really experienced person there to say, "Well, let's try this now," or, "Let's overdub . . . ," and give us ideas. They're supposed to give you ideas, too. We had us, and our songs, and that's how we played them. We pretty much just put them down. We did very little re-arranging, if any. We had a piano at our disposal, so we added some piano parts, which we didn't have onstage, because there's only four people. We didn't do any musical overdubbing—well, a solo you might overdub, because it's easier to do it later. But we basically just played the songs straight, and then Lou would put the vocals on. A couple of them, "Heroin," of course, he sang at the same time. In fact, possibly all of them he sang at the same time. You know, we just put it all down at once. But we didn't know what the hell—I didn't, anyway, and from what came out, I assume no one else knew what the hell we were doing. I don't remember the engineer, at all, on the first one. I don't remember anyone sitting in the booth. I know there had to be someone there. But we were paying for it, and there was no one there to tell us what to do, so we just did what we wanted to. We didn't have time, of course, to do anything really over. Just trying to do this stupid song I'm trying to do now [for her at-home solo production, *Playin' Possum*—*Ed.*], it's incredible how many times I think, "Well, now I'll try this, now I'll try that." And if you can't do this in a studio, with a group, this is the result.

Phil: What did the band think of the album?

Moe: We were pleased with it. I was pleased because it was really exciting to have a record out. I was just so excited to have a record in the store, that I could go up the street to my local Levittown store and find my record. I was thrilled! I was now very excited about the production. Back then, it didn't bother me as much as it does now, but the boys, they were, for some zany reason. I don't know, maybe they thought, "Well, this is the best we can do with the time given, so we'll take it," but I hate it. "Heroin" is a mess. We had done the album in eight hours in the studio, and the producer was . . . Andy [laughter]. So we didn't know what the hell we were doing, and he certainly didn't, as you can hear from the record. And then when MGM bought it, and agreed to put it out, they gave us three hours in California in the studio to fix it, to fix ten songs. And you can't do anything in three hours. We did "Heroin" over, and, I'm pretty sure, "Waiting for the Man," and maybe two others, which I don't remember now. But so quickly, and with no time to say, "Well, let's do this" or "Let's do that." We just didn't have the time. "Heroin" drives me nuts. That's such a good song, I remember getting chills whenever we played it, and to listen to it on the album, it's really depressing. Especially to think of someone who listens to that, and never heard us play live. And they think that that's "Heroin," and they say, "What's the big deal?" It's a pile of garbage on the record. Because on that one, for instance, the guys plugged straight into the board. They didn't have their amps up loud in the studio, so of course I couldn't hear anything. Anything. And when we got to the part where you speed up, you gotta speed up together, or it's not really right. And it just became this mountain of drum noise in front of me. I couldn't hear shit. I couldn't see Lou, to watch his mouth to see where he was in the song. And I just stopped. I was saying, "This is no good, this isn't gonna work, we need phones or something." So I stopped, and being a little wacky, they just kept going, and that's the one we took [laughter]. And it's infuriating, because [to M.C.] you've seen us live, that's a bitch, that song. I consider that our greatest triumph. Lou's greatest triumph too, maybe, songwriting-wise.

Phil: Have you heard any of his later versions of it, from any of his solo live albums?

Moe: No. I heard him do it when I saw him at the Palladium. I can't remember how he did it, to tell you the truth. I think he did it with an acoustic, but I'm not sure.

M.C.: Who put in the noise in the middle part of "European Son"?

Moe: Which noise? That first part you mean . . .

M.C.: It's a crash . . .

Moe: Oh, that's funny. That's a chair being scraped across the room by Cale, at which point he stops in front of Lou, who drops a glass, or a bottle, whatever it was. I think that's great, 'cause it's in time and everything.

Phil: It sounds amazing. That becomes a major part of the song.

Moe: Yeah, that was a nice touch. I like that.

M.C.: *That happened then, that day?*

Moe: That was funny. The engineer, my God, he's saying, "What are you doing?" [laughter]. But it was like you said, it was tremendous, because it is in time, and the music starts right up. I don't know how we timed it like that. It was done separately, of course, but I don't know how we got it timed like that. But, I love that.

M.C.: *"European Son" is credited to everyone on here. How did that come about?*

Moe: Because that was just different every time. There was no structure, we just did it.

Phil: *"Sunday Morning" on here is produced by Tom Wilson. Was that at a different time? It's very different from the rest of the album.*

Moe: Yes, that was in New York, I think. I can't imagine why we went in and did that one. I think we had in mind for that to be a single. We did have Tom do that.

Phil: *Was that after the contract?*

Moe: With MGM, you mean?

Phil: *Yeah, he was an MGM staff producer. What did you and the band think of that song?*

Moe: I was very happy with it.

M.C.: *Do you like these blurbs they have in, these little quotes?*

Moe: Yeah. In fact I love the picture they have of me. Everybody got the chance to pick their own picture but me. I was working, and couldn't go into the city that morning, and Paul Morrisey picked that out. And I thought, "Oh my God, what did he pick?" 'cause his taste is a little different than mine. And when I saw it I was really relieved.

M.C.: *Who put together the whole first album package?*

Moe: Andy and us, I guess. I'm sure it wasn't the record company.

M.C.: *Was it a conscious decision to leave the titles out?*

Moe: What do you mean?

M.C.: *There's no song titles on the outside cover. I remember being about fifteen, and going to the record store, and thinking, "Boy, I wonder what this is . . . Andy Warhol . . .boy." But it was very expensive for those days—$3.98, a dollar more than other records. Too much for my budget. I would just look at it and wonder what it was. I knew it must be something weird [laughter]. Knowing about Andy's films Empire, and Sleep, I thought it might even be an album of party noises.*

Moe: That was just the way we wanted it, as I recall. We didn't want to clutter it up with writing on the back.

Phil: *The songs that Nico was given on the album, were they already written before she came in, or were they written specifically for her?*

Moe: No, they were already written.

Phil: *Did she ever sing any other songs besides those on the album?*

Moe: Yeah.

Phil: *Really! What else did Nico sing?*

Moe: We used to do one called "Melody Laughter." We never recorded it. It was a very odd, long, improvised song. I was the only one who stayed doing the same thing. Everybody else did what they wanted. And she would just sort of, moan, throughout it [laughter]. I thought it was atrocious, but it was different. There were a few songs we played that we didn't put on this album, and I think she sang more than that. Maybe two more songs. She got to the point where she wanted to sing "Heroin." And that was when I said, "Wait a minute . . . come on." I think the ones that she sang were perfect. They really fit her, or she fit them, whatever. Especially "All Tomorrows Parties." I like that a lot.

Phil: When and how did Nico leave the band?

Moe: You're asking the wrong person. I really don't remember.

Phil: Do you know if she lasted the whole run of the Exploding Plastic Inevitable?

Moe: Yeah, I'm pretty sure. But I don't think she was with us after that.

Phil: So, as far as you can remember, she went when it went.

Moe: I think so.

Phil: How long did the Exploding Plastic Inevitable last?

Moe: A year and a half.

Phil: Was it an ongoing thing, or sporadic?

Moe: Pretty ongoing, we were busy with that. We played quite a bit.

Phil: What brought about the end of that show?

Moe: I guess Andy got bored with it, and we wanted to make records, and be a group. I don't think either he or us ever entered into it as a five-year proposition. It was something fun to do, and sounded like a good thing to do. And as we got into it, it became more fun and more interesting, but then he had other interests and so did we. So we parted all the best of friends.

Phil: Was there a lapse after that, before you started playing again?

Moe: No, no . . .

Phil: Or did you get gigs as the Velvet Underground immediately there-after?

Moe: Yeah, we did. I don't remember where or how. I believe we had Sesnick at that point.

Phil: *How did he come into the picture?*

Moe: Sesnick was in California when we were at the Dom. And Andy knew him somehow, and had been telling him to poke around there and look for a band, because he had this idea for a show. Sesnick claims it was his idea, but who knows? So anyway, when Andy found us, he called him and said, "I have a band," and Sesnick set up jobs in California.

Phil: *How did he become the official manager?*

Moe: After he heard us and decided he had something, he started thinking more about just being our manager. He sort of made sure he kept in touch with us, so that when we did want to have a manger, he'd be there. It came to a point at Philip Johnson's estate, at the party there, as a matter of fact. That may have been the last Andy job we did together. But anyway, that night we were discussing getting a manager. There was another guy who wanted to be our manager.

Phil: *Who was that, do you remember?*

Moe: No, I don't remember at all, but, I hate to say it, and I hope Steve doesn't read this, we might have been better with him, simply because he wouldn't have been our friend. But we wanted Sesnick because he was more of our type of person. This other guy was too "businessy," you know?

The Velvet Underground Live

Phil: *Would you say that having Andy's name with the Exploding Plastic Inevitable, that whole show, did a lot at the beginning of the band's career?*

Moe: Oh, yeah.

Phil: *Gave them a big push?*

Moe: Yeah. Not a push as much as exposure. Although most of the places we played were for older art people who really weren't interested in us, we were seen at least. And then we'd play at a college or something, and they would see and hear us. And also, it wasn't just playing locally, we were in Boston, Los Angeles, Cleveland, and all different places. So we got a good, widespread footing.

Phil: What was the effect when the Exploding Plastic Inevitable broke up, and Andy's name wasn't associated with the band, at least not officially? Was there a certain loss of some of the audience that was coming along with Andy? Did it take a while to build up your own audience again, or was there a strong overlap?

Moe: There wasn't a strong overlap. It took a while to build up an audience of our own. The biggest effect, I guess, was that we had a little harder time finding jobs, for a little while. As soon as the guy saw we were bringing in people, then, of course, we'd be welcome back, and he'd want us back. But for a little while it was harder to get jobs. At first when we were with Andy, we played places like art shows. They really wanted him and his shows. They weren't asking for us at first. And they would get hit by this insanity we'd bring. It was funny, we'd decide how good we'd been that night by, honestly, how many people left. We played one place in Philadelphia at a . . . YMJA?—a Jewish YMCA.

Phil: YMHA.

Moe: We played at one of those, at some art show, and I'm telling you, it was funny, we used to laugh! I'd be beating the shit out of those drums, and I'd look up and see—Urgh!—it was, like, 50-year-olds, people who came to see a soup can, and this is what they got. And Gerard [Malanga] swooping around in his bikini with the American flag. We actually got attacked a couple of times. Out in the hinterlands, in Ohio, oh my God, one time we had a bus that broke down. And there was us, and Andy, and about eight or nine freaks. Nice people, part of the show. And our bus broke down at this little crossroads, at this little town, right at a gas station. As soon as the owner saw the occupants, he told us we had to get off his land. This wasn't a minibus, it was a real bus, forty feet long. So how the hell are we gonna move this thing off of his land? The next thing we know, we're surrounded by state troopers, all peering in the front window, going, "What the hell is this?" Anyway, it developed into this incredible hassle. One of the townsfolk volunteered to drive to Detroit or someplace to get this part for the bus. We were told to leave the county by noon the next day. That was early for us, so we all had to get up and run to Howard Johnson's to eat. All this is simply because the boys had long hair. And it wasn't that long. In Chicago one time, John got punched as he was walking down the street, simply because his hair was long. A guy just came by and "Boom!" . . . Lotta wacky people out there. But later, it became nice when we developed our own following. It's impossible to explain to someone, unless you've done it yourself, how nice it is to be on stage playing music, acting, whatever you are into, and have the people who are watching really enjoy it.

Phil: How does that differ from the days when you measured your success by how many people left?

Moe: We enjoyed those days, because we enjoyed the music. So if we thought we were good, that's all we worried about. Those people back then were too old for it. It's different when younger kids come to see you, and they really like it. I used to get pissed off, though, back in '68, when there was lot of drugs around. It pissed me off, these zombies sitting around. A lot of people would come in that condition, which, I suppose, the music played to.

Phil: The band had a reputation for it.

Moe: Yeah, but I enjoyed it a lot better after that year and a half, two years when everybody was into drugs, when people started to come and see us straight. But it's funny, when you're playing onstage—everybody says this, and I'm sure you've heard it a hundred times, but you get a whole new "thing" of energy just from watching the people. You know I'd look out and I'd see someone just looking at me, looking, or enjoying the music, and I'd play a little harder. On that song especially, I'd think, "I'm gonna blow this guy's mind" [laughs]. It must have been strange to see. I regret that we have no films or anything of that, 'cause I don't know what we looked like playing.

Phil: I think Andy made a couple of films.

Moe: He did, but they were just of us sitting around in his Factory. I'd like to see what we looked like onstage.

Phil: *What was the stage presence of the band? Did they go up, stand there, and play the songs?*

Moe: We never jumped around, nobody ever jumped around at all. Sterling, in fact, was like a ridgepole. He didn't budge. His little foot would tap and that was it. Lou would move a little. He never danced like Mick Jagger, or moved that much, but if he was playing something, he'd get a little more movement than Sterling. But we were never a moving-type group. We didn't stand like dead-asses, but we didn't dance, either.

Phil: *So there were no little dramatic effects, or anything? Mostly standing there and playing the songs?*

Moe: Just the songs, yeah. In fact we were probably, at first, extremely sinister-looking. We all, through no mutual decision, always wore black. Maybe we were all in bad periods of our lives, or something. But we always wore dark blue or black clothes, and sunglasses. I always wore sunglasses, and so did everybody else. I'm sure everybody thinks that was our scheme. You know—we all wore black, and wore sunglasses so we'd look eerie and sinister. But it wasn't that at all. That's just the way we were anyway.

Phil: *Well, when those Betsy Johnson costumes came out, they seemed to be, not pretentious, but contrived in that sense.*

Moe: It was, in a way.

Phil: *. . . all black.*

Moe: Oh, no, we didn't all have black.

Phil: *What was it? Those are black and white pictures, and you can't really tell.*

Moe: Sterling had dark green, and John had black. He always wore black, and probably still does. And I had a cranberry-type color. And I forget what Lou had, if anything.

Phil: *How consistent was the band from night-to-night live?*

Moe: Semi. There were nights when I would get chills, we were so good. We were good. We were never rotten. Occasionally, Lou would improvise songs lyrically, to relieve tedium. You ever hear us live?

Phil: *No.*

Moe: You're kidding. Oh, that's a shame. All this devotion is based on records? That's sad.

M.C.: *All the live recordings are ones made by people in the audience; it seems like you never recorded live.*

Moe: No, that still pisses me off. I can't believe that none of those record companies had the sense to record us live. That's a shame.

Phil: *What was the extent of improvisation in some of the songs?*

Moe: A lot of our songs had a lot of improvisation, not everybody doing it, but maybe Sterl would play something else, or Lou would do something different, or I would. A lot of songs have to be tightly structured, like a slow ballad thing, you can't go nuts in that. Some songs were just a certain length—"Pale Blue Eyes" had a certain length; a few songs did. But most songs, you never knew when they would start or stop [laughs], there was a lot of improvisation, like "Heroin" of course, was never the same, really never the same. The basic part was, but the fast part and all that would be slightly different each time. And "Sister Ray," of course.

M.C.: *Well, the second time I went to see you there was a very slow "Sister Ray."*

Moe: We did that for a change of pace, just for fun. Sometimes we, not often, but a few times, we'd play "Heroin" real slow, or we'd play "Waiting for the Man" as a blues type song, rhythm and blues type song. You get sick of playing everything exactly the same every night.

Phil: *That song has been done so many different ways.*

Moe: Yeah, that's a good song. I like that song.

Phil: *Were there a lot of songs that were written and never recorded, but played live?*

Moe: Oh yeah! A lot, half of which I never remembered until I got a couple of tapes. "Mr. Rain" . . . oh, I can't even think of them now, but a lot! A lot of good ones too. Which is another sad idea.

M.C.: *What about "Sister Ray II," also known as "Sweet Rock and Roll?"*

Moe: Recorded in San Diego, once.

M.C.: *In 1971, Lester Bangs wrote in Creem about that concert. He quoted the words to one of the songs: "sweet rock and roll, it'll cleanse your soul." He wrote this song was slow, sweet, sad, rising and falling . . .*

Moe: I remember those lines.

M.C.: *And the story goes that the band heard the tape and loved it, but someone stole the tape. They had only played it once, and decided not to play it again. The tape was made at a Quicksilver Messenger Service party.*

Moe: It must have been improvised. I remember San Diego with Bo Diddley getting $500.000 for two nights. "Melody Laughter" was another one. We used to play it when Nico was with us. I think there weren't any actual lyrics, just warble. You know how she does. And that was another real interesting one. That would go anywhere from two minutes to forty-two. But it was real interesting. It used to drive me crazy, because it started off with a certain beat, and Lou would just do what he wanted, and the next thing you know, John would be doing what he wanted, and I had to stay at the same beat, and you're hearing this definite other beat. I used to close my eyes and count to myself. Really, it was like torture. "You've got to stop soon," I'd think. I'm sure that was real nice to sit and listen to, cause it was really interesting, very interesting. Cale would play the viola, put it down and pick up the bass, put it down, and if we had an organ or something he'd play that. It just went on and on.

M.C.: *There were some funny covers that I've been reading about you doing. Such as "Oh Carol."*

Moe: I don't ever remember playing any covers, except once we played "Roll Over Beethoven" at the Café Bizarre. That's the only cover I ever remember playing. Now we used to do, I think it was after Lou was out of the band, we used to do "Little Queenie," with Doug singing it, and maybe went into "Carol" from that, but it wasn't with Lou, I'm sure.

M.C.: *Then "Here Comes the Bride," for that wedding . . . [See "Mother's Mod Lament," page 5].*

Moe: Oh God. We didn't play "Here Comes the Bride," we just improvised something. That was funny.

M.C.: *There're some songs that don't turn up often on live tapes. "Oh, Sweet Nothing," for example. Do you remember if that was something you rarely played?*

Moe: No, that was in our repertoire; we played that. When I was looking through this list of tapes, I saw that that was the only recording of that song. I don't know why it is. We didn't play it every time we played, but every third time.

M.C.: *And also "The Murder Mystery." It's only on one tape, in the middle of "Sister Ray."*

Moe: I don't ever remember trying to play that live, although it's probably just the music.

M.C.: *It's just a part, the section about "Pick upon the parapet . . ." for about two minutes, and then it was back to "Sister Ray." So it's not the whole thing. Lou talks about it an interview, about how he'd sometimes go into it in the middle of "Sister Ray."*

Moe: We probably did it once or twice. I'm sure we didn't plan it, we probably just went into it.

M.C.: *So there were other songs you didn't do. Sterling said he thought that you didn't ever do "Lady Godiva's Operation."*

Moe: No, I don't think so, I don't ever remember doing it.

M.C.: *And also "I Heard Her Call My Name."*

Moe: Yeah, we used to do that. Not for the last year we were together, we weren't playing it, but we used to play it. When that stuff came out, the first album and *White Light,* we were also doing a lot of improvising. We'd maybe play two real songs, and then play one of these half-hour things with Nico banging on a piano or something. So, in the early days, we weren't really doing a set. But, we did play "I Heard Her Call My Name." Maybe not fifty times, but more than once or twice.

Phil: *How long did your concerts last?*

Moe: Oh, it varied. In some places it'd be a tight situation, where the guy would want everybody out, get another audience in, so you would only get a half-hour, or whatever. But like at the Tea Party, for instance, places like that, sometimes we'd play for forty-five minutes, sometimes an hour and a half. It really depended on our mood and the audience. Usually forty-five minutes to an hour.

M.C.: *How about the sets themselves, was there a set order?*

Moe: Not always, we'd change it almost every night. We'd all think about it, talk about it.

Phil: *Did you have it written out?*

Moe: Yeah, someone would write it down so we knew what was going on. Sterling, usually.

M.C.: *Do you remember a place called South Deerfield, Massachusetts, between Boston and New York?*

Moe: Yeah. Well, I don't remember playing there. I don't specifically remember the club or anything. I know we were there. But not specifically.

M.C.: *Of all places in the world, why would you play there?*

Moe: I don't know. I don't know what was there, or why we played there.

M.C.: *It was an old roller-skating rink.*

Moe: Yeah, yeah, yeah! Now I remember. That I remember. I don't know . . .

M.C.: *It was on an old highway, Route 5, right by Deerfield, historic old Deerfield.*

Moe: Wasn't it an old airplane hangar?

M.C.: *No, it was a roller rink, an old roller rink, and . . .*

Moe: Yeah, I remember that place.

M.C.: *It had a little stage that rose up . . .*

Moe: Very small stage.

M.C.: *Chairs on the sides.*

Moe: I don't know why we played there.

M.C.: *It was crazy . . .*

Moe: Maybe that's why.

M.C.: *It's farm country, there's no college.*

Moe: That's probably why. A guy asked us, and, "What the hell."

M.C.: *But it was a few times, that was what was strange.*

Moe: I think we got a really good reception the first time we played. We were kind of surprised, as I recall [laughter]. No, really, because it was out in the sticks, and who the hell's gonna come see us here? And the place was full, I'm quite sure the first night, and they really liked us. And it seemed as if 30% of them came because it was us, and the others just because, "Hey, there's a concert, let's get out of the house." And we won them over, which is nice.

M.C.: *You won over the hippies. The burgeoning hippie scene was just coming to the Greenfield area. People were just starting to do the mind dance [laughter].*

Moe: There sure was a lot of that.

M.C.: *You had two different nights, one for drinkers, one for not.*

Moe: Yeah, that's right, right. The more you say about it, the more I remember it.

Phil: *Had that been done any other time, when you had two different nights like that, that you remember?*

Moe: I wouldn't be surprised, because most places we played had the twenty-one drinking age. Then again, most of those places in those days didn't have drinking. Like the Boston Tea Party, they just had Cokes, and everybody came. None of them were bar-type scenes, they were just a place to go and lay around and watch the lights.

M.C.: *Yeah, "Chicks get fifty cents off" [laughter]. It was only two and a quarter.*

Moe: The prices then: wasn't that funny? When I see some of our posters, and a few of them have prices like three bucks. For us and someone else.

Phil: *One time you were billed with the MC5 in Boston. Do you remember that?*

Moe: Yeah, vaguely. Didn't they go around town with the speakers, was that them? Speakers on a car, announcing that, "The MC5 is gonna blow the Velvet Underground off the stage" or something. Someone did that once. I'm pretty sure it was them.

Phil: *That sounds similar to the description I heard of that concert, they were saying things before the show. And the Velvets said, "We don't want to have anything to do with this sort of attitude."*

Moe: Yeah, I've forgotten what they did, I don't know if they were breaking guitars, or what they were doing. It was this big Detroit thing. I guess they were gonna take Boston away from us. That was a weird night. They shouldn't have taken us on there. We blew them out of the place, of course.

Phil: *How extensive were your fans? How many people came to the shows?*

Moe: We'd always fill places. We never played a stadium, or anything like that. But we'd fill large clubs. Now it seems that they are coming back up, places to play. Another reason I want to move back East is that out here it's country and western. I got a letter from my brother a couple of weeks ago, with an article from the New York Times, and it mentioned a lot of clubs opening up. It listed ten, and told what they were like. It just sounded like what I want to do. I like to sit around, drink beers, and listen to music. That's what I enjoy doing. But you don't do that out here, or anywhere else like you do in New York. Boston's good too. But in the past few years there was just no place to play. Back then, every city had two or three Boston Tea Party-type places. And they'd be competing with each other. [To M.C.] Like you said, that silly little roller skating rink [The Woodrose Ballroom], you know.

M.C.: *I shouldn't have much more of this.*

Moe: [to husband, Steve] Don't pump these guys with beer. I don't think they're drinkers.

M.C.: *I'll also forget what I'm talking about. Going out and playing in front of people—you always liked that . . .*

Moe: Yeah, that's what I miss, playing in front of people, playing for an audience.

White Light/White Heat

Phil: *When was the second album done?*

Moe: 1967. That was the second one, White Light, with skull and cross-bones on the cover. The cover was Billy Name's tattoo. Andy Warhol's cohort.

Phil: There's a pretty wild roaring sound on this album.

Moe: That's the way we wanted it, the idea of the songs. Sterling and Cale had new sonic toys trying to blow each other off the track. On "Sister Ray" we blew the studio away, recording at one volume—live. We didn't think to work the mix, because, see, we didn't know what we were doing.

Phil: Where did the music to "The Gift" come from?

Moe: Oh yeah, "Booker T," we called it. Inspired by Booker T & The MG's' "Green Onions," anyway. It was something to relax us. Louie decided the words would go with it.

Phil: What production went into that album?

Moe: The second album was recorded in not an eight hour scene, but no two months. Tom Wilson was more interested in the blondes running through the studio. As witness, the forte song, "Sister Ray," where he forgot to turn on the damn mikes. Better than the first album but that part in there drives me crazy. In fact you mentioned in one of the articles you sent me, and it said, "Maureen beats the drums so hard, who cares if she missed a beat," or something like that. But, what happened in there—and I still want to hear it done right; I get so mad I could scream—is that, in that part Lou says, "Who is that knocking?" I was gonna tap on the drum rim. Tom Wilson produced this, and I said, "OK Tom, now when he says, 'Who is that knocking,' I'm gonna do this." So they put a microphone into the drumhole, got it all set up, and of course they didn't have it on, this one microphone, and would only turn it on when that part came. But, they didn't turn it on then either, so all of a sudden there's no drums. There's four beats, and then there's two, and then there's four, I think is what happens. And I could have killed myself, 'cause we did two takes of that as I recall, and it came out nice, it was really good, and here's this part that drops out the bottom. I was tapping on the rim, and it wasn't recorded. And of course everybody thinks that I stopped playing the drums [laughs], which infuriates me.

So that's the story of that. "I Heard Her Call My Name" was ruined in the mix—the energy. You can't hear anything but Lou. He was the mixer in there, so he, having a little ego-trip at the time, turned himself so far up that there's no rhythm, there's no nothing. And that was a good song, too. At that point, ten years ago, I was ignored simply because I didn't speak up—the drums weren't there on all these songs! I was ignored because I was the girl. On the albums, the sound came about because I was the girl in the group, and they didn't pay attention to my needs. It was Lou, and John, and Sterling saying, "I need more." Once, I got some new drums, that's all.

Music & Money

M.C.: *The other part for a band is having to take your music across the country and talk to these record company executives, people who are not really interested in music. Just the business part. Did the band put that on Sesnick?*

Moe: Yeah, we didn't deal with that at all; Louie wouldn't come near these people, and they didn't want to talk to me, of course [laughter]. Sesnick would handle those people.

M.C.: *So that seems to be a key part of it.*

Moe: Yeah, yeah. You can't deal with those people. It's a whole different world, you know.

Phil: *It's a matter of trust.*

Moe: It isn't even a matter of trust, I think. They're businessmen, forty-five, fifty-year-old businessmen—they don't know what you're talking about, and you don't know what they're talking about. You need someone who's a businessman, who can bullshit someone else, and all that crap.

Phil: *Someone you can put your trust in, you say, "You take care of it, we'll trust you with it."*

Moe: Well, how do you find out if you should really trust them?

Phil: *Right. There's a lot of stories about bands trusting their managers, and all the while the managers are stealing them blind. Horror stories.*

Moe: That happens. Constantly.

M.C.: *What in your contract did it say about artistic control? Could you write what you want, play what you want, record what you want?*

Moe: With the record company, you mean? Yeah, as far as I know. We never had trouble with them. We had trouble with radio stations. They wouldn't play our records, which was fine with us.

M.C.: *One of the times I saw you, Lou said something about, "This is a song that was banned in San Francisco."*

Moe: Yeah, "White Light," of all songs. And "Here She Comes Now," believe it or not.

M.C.: *The radio stations banned that?*

Moe: Yeah, they wouldn't play it.

M.C.: *How about in general with any other authorities, because I remember also Lou announcing "Heroin" rather nervously; he was looking around for cops?*

Moe: No, he was just joking. No, we never got stopped by the police or anything like that.

M.C.: *In introducing "Heroin," he said that, "This song is not in favor of it or against it, just about it."*

Moe: I've never been influenced myself. If someone I like sings about heroin, I'm not gonna go try it. So, I assumed at the time that no one else would either. I felt these people aren't gonna go out and try drugs because we're singing a song. But Lou, had a little period, or maybe Sesnick put it in his ear, I don't know, but he had a little period of thinking, "Gee, it's a good song, and I'm not gonna stop singing it, but let's make it clear," especially as in that place [Woodrose Ballroom] most of the audience was very young as I recall.

M.C.: *[looking at Moe's "All Tomorrow's Parties" 45]* *It's great to finally see one of the stock copies of these first two 45's.*

Moe: You never saw one?

M.C.: *Honestly, I know only one record collector who said they even saw one. You can't find people who have them.*

Phil: *How was it decided which songs would be released as singles?*

Moe: Commercially.

Phil: *Was that the record company, or you?*

Moe: Both. You couldn't really release "Heroin" as a single. A single is obviously an attempt to get commercial recognition, if you know what I mean. Especially back then. It's more albums now than it was then. For instance, they wouldn't play "Here She Comes Now," and they're certainly not going to play "Heroin," or "Venus in Furs." So you hit them with something that you figure is just a nice little song. But they still won't play it.

M.C.: *There were very few successful bands without singles back then.*

Moe: Yeah, and now they don't try at all for single material. In fact I'm pretty sure that most radio stations just have cassettes, and they just play the cuts from the album that seem to be most popular.

Phil: *Which is almost like playing singles.*

Moe: Yeah, right.

Phil: *They are only gonna play one, or two, or three songs. It's just a matter of the station deciding what the single is gonna be.*

Moe: It's funny how that came about. You would think the public, the buying public, would not stand for that, especially with the prices for albums now. And you can't buy any single you want, where you used to be able to buy almost any song you wanted on a single. And now, it's astounding. In fact, that's one reason I don't listen to new music, 'cause

I don't know what it is, and I'm not gonna pay eight bucks for something I'm not gonna like, so I don't buy it.

Phil: A lot of the band's singles—not all, but some—seem to have only been released to DJ's. Never commercially, never put into the stores.

Moe: Well, they wouldn't play them, and MGM didn't know what the hell they were doing.

Phil: So the story is, they would put out feelers to see if the DJ's would play it, and if they played it at all, then put it out commercially?

Moe: That was probably the record company's idea.

Phil: I've seen in catalogues, though, records that were planned, singles that never came out as stock copies. "Who Loves the Sun" I've seen all over as a mono/stereo DJ single, and yet in catalogues, like the big Phonolog guides, it's listed "Who Loves the Sun?" backed with "Oh, Sweet Nothing." I was always curious to find that, to see if it was edited from seven minutes, or if the whole thing was put on there. I've never seen it as a record, I've only seen it as a DJ copy.

VU Backstage

Phil: Were you social friends with the rest of the band off stage?

Moe: Yeah, I miss that too. We had a good time on the road, lots of fun. I was never that social. Most people would want to come and talk to Lou; and Sterling, being Sterling, would make more friends than I did. I would never say, "I'm the drummer, talk to me." If someone wanted to talk, that's fine. I never made any outside friends, except for the group.

Phil: Were you aware of the parting of the ways between Cale and Lou?

Moe: Slightly. There was friction. Why? I don't know.

Phil: I can see the conflict between Lou and John, being creative, sensitive types.

Moe: Yeah, yeah. I really don't know what happened with those two. I honestly don't know.

Phil: *Did you ever act as an intermediary between any of them?*

Moe: No.

Phil: *Stayed out of the way?*

Moe: Yeah, kind of. I'd say, "Hey, cut the shit." That was about it.

Phil: *Was everybody together personally?*

Moe: I don't think any of them were together at that time. Except me.

Phil: *Was splitting mutual?*

Moe: Yes. Lou said we could go with him or John. We went with Lou because he was the most influencial, he set the moods, he knew how he wanted it to sound.

Phil: *John referred to his influence as just being a bass player. Did he ever guide?*

Moe: We all had a say. We would talk about it. Lou would say, "Here's a song." We'd say, "Let's play with it." Now John, here he is over there with his viola, with all his classical training, and me with my three weeks and my Bo Diddley records. And putting those two together got a different sound, a whole different idea. But as the four together, as you know, we got a totally different sound, a completely different feel, especially then, with what was going on. I have visions of John, all in black—with a rhinestone choker—on the far side of the stage, with his black-blue hair, making feedback on the viola that went with the song. That was the topper.

Phil: *Was there ever a time when you felt, as a purpose of the band, to "break the barriers of rock n roll", to "kill rock n roll", open up new commercial outlets for certain things, change the world in any way?*

Moe: No, not me personally, anyway.

Phil: You can't speak for Lou on something like that?

Moe: No. I think our music sounded the way it did fifty, or maybe eighty percent, because of the songs, but also because of the people who were in the group. Now, playing the drums, I didn't learn to do a roll for five years [laughter]. I was lucky, because if I was Ginger Baker, the music would not have sounded the way it did. Because I'd have been going "tut-tut-tut-tut" all over the place, which would have changed the style of the songs, the mood of the songs. Since all I could do was beat them, that's what I did, and that made a certain style. Sterling has a certain style which he put into it, and Lou, and John, and Doug, while he was in the group. That's what I said before, to have those four who were so good together, who enjoyed each other, liked each other's styles, and enjoyed the music that they were playing, too, that's important, of course. You don't run across that a lot. To be in a group just to make money—I wouldn't. You might do it, but you sure wouldn't enjoy it.

M.C.: So the main thing for you was spirit, where it doesn't really matter so much if you know how to play, so much as to really want to give what you have, to express it that way?

Moe: In a way, yeah . . . yeah. But someone has to be able to play an instrument (laughs), like the Shaggs, now, for instance. They leave a lot to be desired. John, of course, had the most technical knowledge. Sterling has a lot of technical knowledge, because of picking it up from John, and also he used to play trumpet when he was younger, and I think learned a lot of music from that. But they'd talk about, "Oh, let's use the 7th, or the dominant 8th," or whatever. And I didn't know what the hell they were talking about. I wish I had listened and learned now, because I play guitar, and it's infuriating to not know. You know, I can't pick out chords from records, and I don't know what chords go together.

Phil: How was Doug found?

Moe: Sterling knew him from Boston. Hans [Onager, who worked with the band on the road] used to manage a band in Boston that Doug played in.

Phil: Was there a new sound because of Doug?

Moe: I don't think so.

The Velvet Underground

Phil: There is a specified air of secrecy, lack of information, on the third album.

Moe: That was MGM's doing, or maybe Sesnick's idea of attracting attention by being mysterious. But MGM wouldn't spend the money and then play mystery, they just had a problem not knowing what to do with it, where to put it, et cetera.

Phil: How long to record number three?

Moe: One week. Six hours at night. New York and maybe California. "Murder Mystery" is a bad mix, you can't separate the tracks. Now here's another example of ignoring the drummer because she's a girl. The cymbals I had were not the kind you're supposed to have to get the sound that you want, for that type of song. That was a Phil Spector-type song. You know, "boom, boom . . . whoosh." I had the type of cymbals that went "tsht," and there's this part, and everybody's waiting for this tremendous cymbal crash that's gonna last, and it just . . . poops out. Being an asshole, I just assumed, "Well that's the way they work," I'm thinking, "but how come they worked the other way on other albums?" But nobody else said, "Well, that's wrong," so, them knowing much more than me, I just stupidly assumed. I don't know what I assumed. I just didn't open my mouth. It was stupid. But that song can be much, much more powerful with the proper drum miking, the proper cymbals. Which I didn't know then. I had two cymbals. I was lucky to have them.

Phil: Was "Afterhours" written for you?

Moe: I'm quite sure! You would have to ask Lou, but he had me try it out before finishing it. I refused to sing it on stage live until someone asked for it in the audience, and sure enough, it was my debut. Very jumpy. I liked it—the hardcore fans loved it—especially after seeing me bash the drums with never a peep.

Phil: What do you think of the *Live at Max's Kansas City* version?

Moe: He sings better than I do.

M.C.: One record that is particularly odd is the one by the Carol Lou Trio, which is an EP, and it's just called "Afterhours," a very easygoing piano thing, and it's written by Lou Reed, it says, published by "Virpi." There's no date on it. Virpi was formed when the band was going, around '68, for the third LP?

Moe: Yeah. Does it claim on this label that Lou was playing on it or anything?

M.C.: Nope, it just says "writing credit: Lou Reed, published by Virpi."

Moe: That could just be a total mistake. And I know there are other songs called "Afterhours." Not that I've heard any of them, but I know there's one that's real old, called "Afterhours," and maybe that's what it is really.

M.C.: This is the type of thing that no one knows about, along with the Pickwick records. We can't find anyone who used to work there. They just threw these records out on the market, and didn't care about song-writing credits, or anything.

Moe: Right.

Phil: What happened to cause the split with the record label after the third album?

Moe: We weren't happy with them. Clive Davis at Columbia really wanted us. Sesnick did all the dealing, so I don't know why we went with Atlantic. But we weren't happy with MGM.

Live 1969, VU, Another View

Phil: There are rumors about songs that were recorded and just not released.

Moe: Yeah, that little "White Heat" EP. That was a whole album's worth of songs, which is another wacky business deal. MGM or whoever it was. It was in our contract to make a record every year or something, so you had to do it whether you wanted to or not. In that way they controlled us. But anyway, we recorded this for them, with no intention of releasing it—this was Sesnick's current scheme; I don't know why he didn't want to . . . maybe they weren't distributing the stuff. I don't know. But we recorded it, pretended we were trying. We did of course try to do it the best we could. But it never got released, and there are a lot of songs. We recorded that "Foggy Notion," and as I remember it, it was tremendous, because we had never recorded it before. I always wanted a copy of it and never had one, of course.

Phil: *When was that EP recorded?*

Moe: When we had Doug, 1969.

Phil: *So, before the 4th, and after the 3rd album?*

Moe: Yeah, between MGM and Atlantic. It was never intended for release, not by us; maybe Sesnick.

Phil: *Was it given to the record company?*

Moe: Probably. Don't they own it?

Phil: *They were paying for the studio time?*

Moe: Yes. That was the best session, with Gary Kelgren of the Record Plant, who died, drowned in his pool. Young guy, extremely helpful, a real nice guy, engineer, producer. We recorded in New York, six or eight days, tremendous. That was our best recording session, and we had no intention of releasing it, which was pretty absurd.

Phil: *What do you think of the other songs?*

Moe: Oh, I love it! It's nice to have them. That whole album is just gone with the wind.

M.C.: Most of that album might actually be on a tape that's been going around for a long time, unofficially called "22 Demos." It's got "She's My Best Friend," and a lot of stuff that shows up on Lou's solo albums.

Phil: "Andy's Chest," "The Ocean" . . .

Moe: Where do you hear about all of this stuff? You must have your ear to the ground!

M.C.: It would be nice if there were no more demos around so we wouldn't have to track them down [laughter].

Moe: Well we really didn't ever do much extra, you know. Pretty much what we did in the studio was what went on the album. Maybe a couple of songs, or a couple of tries that we didn't like. I don't really think there's that many songs floating around that we recorded with the idea of putting on an album, and then they didn't go. You know they never gave us carte blanche; we always tried to finish it up, and knew what songs we were gonna do when we were in there. The one I really regret not having is "Mr. Rain." Lou decided that it would actually rain when we played that song—because it did.

Phil: What kind of song was it?

Moe: Frantic, not improvised. A real bitch to play. Boy what a song that was. I had forgotten all about it, and someone mentioned it in an article or something, and I said, "Wow!" What a song that was.

Phil: Some people, especially at the time, considered the Velvets as Lou Reed's backup band.

Moe: No, I don't see that, because of what I was just saying before. We all put our own feelings and style into it.

Kate Messer: How do you like how those songs finally came out, on VU, and Another View?

Moe: I liked *VU* better than *Another View.* Sterling likes *Another View* better, which surprised me. His only complaint was that it had too many instrumentals. Then I read something where Lou said that he didn't like that idea too much either, but he could see where a fan would want to hear them even without vocals. It's true, and that's who the record is aimed at, people who have been fans already. But it's too clean, I just think the whole thing is too clean.

Kate: Both productions?

Moe: Yeah. And I was not happy at all with the mix of *Another View*. Not at all, I think they did a terrible job. Now Sterling suggested that maybe they didn't have the original four-tracks, that maybe they just had the master or something, and they couldn't do anything about the mix, but I don't know.

Kate: What did you think about the support that went along with them?

Moe: Very so-so. They did much better with the first one, but they still didn't do nearly what they could have.

M.C.: Those songs from '69 are from the Record Plant?

Moe: I'm quite sure they were, because I remember specifically looking in the control booth, and what's his name . . . Doug, was singing "She's My Best Friend," and I hated the ending, which I still do, I thought it was just tacky. Childish, you know, his vocal part. I remember that specifically, and they were all done at the Record Plant.

M.C.: How did the Live 1969 LP come out on Mercury?

Moe: They wanted to put it out . . . Well, this is a long story, and I don't remember very many of the details, but: I was working at the time, and the group was gone, none of us were together any more. And I got this call at work, and I think it was from Lou, saying they wanted to put this album out, but we all had to sign, giving our consent. And we had to sign for like, two hundred dollars, or something. I said, "No, no, I won't sign for two hundred dollars, what do you mean, two hundred dollars?" This was a long time ago, this is pretty old, '72 or something. Then some agent-type was calling me at work like mad. "Well, how about three?" So I said, "What, are you crazy? I broke my ass for seven years for three hundred dollars? Go to hell." Sterling and I held out for more. We said we're not signing for anything less than fifteen hundred, which even then was stupid—fifteen hundred dollars, which we foolishly signed for.

Phil: That was the first Velvet Underground record I ever heard, that live one, yeah.

Moe: It's the best one, I think.

Phil: I said, "I thought they were supposed to be really weird, this sounds really normal."

Moe: Yeah, ten years later it sounds normal.

Phil: Well, then I heard some real early stuff, and I said, "This is the weird stuff."

Enter the Yules; Exit Lou; Exit VU

Phil: Lou and Doug fought for control of the band?

Moe: Doug didn't understand Lou. He was young. Lou left because he was mad. Doug was a pest. I don't really know why; possibly lack of recognition. That would become frustrating, being on the verge of breakthrough. Six months to a year more, possibly, with the times catching up to us. In 1966, "Heroin," "Venus in Furs," "Black Angel's Death Song," were being heard by people used to the Beatles' "She loves you, yeah, yeah, yeah." By 1970 more catching-up was done. I wish we had quit after two years, instead of getting so close to being "heard" nationally.

I personally, during the last year of the first band, became generally depressed because there was all of this crap, and they couldn't get along, and also then we were getting a good following, and records were selling pretty nicely. After working for six or seven years, we would have liked a return of some kind. Your picture on the front of *Time*, or something (laughs). That was depressing, to have that stuff going on. It was useless and stupid.

Phil: How did Bill Yule become a member?

Moe: He was Doug's brother and a drummer. He was a senior in high school! The Max's Kansas City gig was in April or May through August. Lou's progression was varied. On *Loaded*, Lou was there from start to finish. March, April, May, June, July. I'm not on it. I wish I had been.

Phil: I wanted to talk about the end of the band. What was your life like then?

Moe: The band split up right after I had Kerry. I hadn't played for a while. She was born in June 1970, and the band split up in August. I hadn't played with them for two or three months before she was born. They were playing at Max's, and I went to see them there. I don't remember if Lou told me he was quitting or not. Still, today, it infuriates me that Lou left. I'm not mad at him; I feel that Sterling was the culprit in that situation, although, as I said, neither of them talked about it a lot. Lou talked to me about it, though in wacky terms—levitating in his bedroom and all this shit. I didn't know what he was talking about. I don't know if he just wanted to be on his own, or didn't want certain people around him. I'm not saying "certain people" because I don't want to say their names, but I don't know who. He never said to me, "Well here's the problem." Maybe he didn't really know, himself.

Phil: Sterling told me that Lou said, "I don't want to go out there, there's too many people that I know, that I don't want to see."

Moe: Yeah, that doesn't surprise me. Sesnick always handled Lou, not with kid gloves, but with—as you said, you just talked to Steve recently, and he talks as if he has the mental underlying affiliation with Lou. Ten years later, Lou's still sending him vibes through the *New York Daily News*. I always accepted his treatment of Lou, because Lou was special and different. He can't handle a lot of shit that I can handle, and that Sterling should be able to handle. Sterling, however, I guess it's because they were guys, I don't know, instead of saying, "Well, okay, that's Lou," he'd start digging, and there'd be all of this baby shit. Ego, I suppose. You have three guys competing in a group for the best riff, whatever. I never had that kind of problem like they had. Not fights or anything like that, just a lot of underlying shit. Which is extremely tedious, and used to infuriate me because there is no reason for it. Lou, being sort of a special person, I would think Sterl could bend a little to deal with things. Lou and I got along great, we never had any problems at all.

Phil: Maybe he was too close to Sterling.

Moe: I was closer to him than Sterling was. Lou and I used to share rooms, and be more social than Sterling. Sterling was not mean or hateful, but he'd never go out and eat with us. Well, not never, but nine times out of ten he wouldn't go. Maybe he was trying to protect himself in some way, I don't know.

As I said, it became extremely depressing to me the last year or so when I realized we really were good. Not just that Louie writes good songs, but the way the four of us could present them—it made for really good music. To have been lucky enough to find four people who went together well, that doesn't happen every day. I'm not going to bump into another Louie in Phoenix. It's a shame to have that go by.

But after that we picked up Walter [Powers] and practiced for a while and went out. We did nicely with them. I thought we sounded good. I think our major problem was that we didn't have any writing talent. Doug wrote some songs, but not like Lou. And Sterling started becoming disinterested, I guess. He didn't really talk about it; sometimes you don't know what his feelings are. Disinterest, dissatisfaction, I'm not sure which. But he started pooping out. We went down to Texas to play a job, and he just stayed there. Then we got Willie [Alexander], and continued for a while. We went to England, Europe—which was nice.

Phil: We talked about your audiences here. What about in Europe?

Moe: Tremendous. I'll tell you the truth though, it was kind of depressing on that trip.

Phil: The first time you went there was after Lou left . . .

Moe: It was after everybody left. It was me, Doug, Walter, and Willie.

Phil: That was the first time in Europe?

Moe: Yeah, I almost didn't go, as a matter of fact. I was working at that job I told you about. I was thinking I had to start taking care of my daughter, so I'd better start shaping up, so I thought that maybe I wouldn't go because it wasn't the Velvet Underground, really. And then I figured that maybe I wouldn't have another chance to see England. I always wanted to go to England, so okay. Now I liked the music the four of us—Willie, Doug, Walter and I—played. And I liked our renditions of Velvet Underground songs. But it wasn't the Velvets. I guess I thought I was cheating the people.

And after that, we came back, and . . . that was the end. After a few months we just said, "The hell with it." I went and got a job, a temporary job as a keypunch operator on Long Island. I do miss it tremendously. I miss having someone to play with. It's really a drag having no one to play with.

Maureen Tucker: Percussion

Being the first female drummer in the history of rock, does it surprise you that your influence has been mainly on male drummers?

Moe: Well, I guess most women still think drums aren't the thing to play. Although when we played in Tallahassee the other night [August 1987], the other band had a female drummer. There's been more guys than girls, but a lot of younger girls at these recent shows we've done say they like the Velvets, and they're 19, 20 years old.

Phil: Your drumming style, specifically, seems to crop up in a lot of places, on a lot of new records. Boom, boom, boom. Do you feel that that's sort of inevitable? Discovery of a sort of style—just reducing it to its barest elements. Do you think if you hadn't done it first it would have happened anyway?

Moe: Yeah, probably. Because I think music has, luckily, gotten a lot more basic. You know, for a while there it was just disco, and too much nonsense. That's just not rock and roll. Now it's gotten a lot more simple, back to more basic songs. If you wanna overpower the song, and do a roll every three bars, that's not the idea of the songs.

Phil: *How do you judge your own playing? Or analyze your style?*

Moe: Simple, by two ways. One, by a lack of technical knowledge, and two, by choice. My idea for how I wanted my drumming to sound was African drums—that's what I wanted my drumming to be like. Not in every song. In some songs you've got to have a little "tick-tick," but my idea was to have an African-type sound. And the best I could do at the time was turning the bass drum over, 'cause I couldn't find what I wanted. We looked around New York, in fact, once even up in Harlem, thinking, "Well, they might have a few, somewhere." But nobody knew where to get them.

Phil: *Looking for African drums?*

Moe: You know, a log, that kind of logs they have. But I never could find anything like that. I think for the music we were playing at the time, I really do feel that a Ginger Baker-type drummer, a regular drummer who wanted to show himself, you know, "Here's what I can do," would have ruined the songs. I really believe that. Now I purposely didn't learn to do all that stuff, because, boy, once you learn that, it's weird how hard it is to stop yourself from doing it. 'Cause there are certain places where, hey, you just feel that it's time for a roll, and boy, you've gotta hold yourself back. It's strange. In fact, on this tape I'm doing now [**Playin' Possum**, 1980], I can do more rolls, and things like that, because I'm sitting down. And on this tape I'm doing, I really have to keep telling myself, "Too much! Too much! You're doing too much [laughter]!" So I'm glad I never tried to learn how to do all that, because it would have changed a lot of the sound of the music.

M.C.: *What became of your other set of drums, the band drums?*

Moe: I have no idea. Sesnick had them at last account.

Phil: *Were they yours or the band's?*

Moe: No, they were mine. I didn't buy them—we used to buy all of our equipment just out of band money. But the guitars were theirs to keep, no matter who bought them.

Phil: *I've read accounts of you in concert playing standing up.*

Moe: Oh, yeah, I always did. The first job, I sat down, and from then on, I don't know why, until Lou was gone even, I stood up. I used to have a bass drum up this way, facing upwards. I had a special stand made. I got very clever and figured out how to invert a drum pedal so that it went up this way instead of going this way. Then we built this wooden box to lift it up higher, and I'd stand like this. The reason we did that was because I wanted to have sort of an African sound, and I couldn't find African drums, so the bass drum made a boomy low sound. Recently I saw that movie *The Rose,* and here's this guy he's got two of them, and he's got them up that way, and he's sitting down, but he's got these pedals that go up. I couldn't believe it. I said, "Look at that!"

Phil: So maybe someone was watching.

Moe: Yeah.

M.C.: So that was your idea right from the start, to turn the drums up, the bass drum?

Moe: Yes. At first, before I get the special stand, I sat on the floor. Yeah, I think I had a bass, a tom-tom, and a snare, and maybe I had one cymbal. It was almost a garbage can lid. It was such a mess. But I always stood up, I didn't sit down until the end, or towards the end.

Phil: Playing with mallets?

Moe: Yeah, mostly. I used to break the heads of the bass drum. I'd go "boom" and my arm would go right through it.

M.C.: The two times I saw you it was astounding—"How can she stand there and. . . ."

Moe: Weird, huh? Yeah, it was funny.

M.C.: You did this all night long.

Moe: I guess one thing that kept me going was that I didn't want to be the one to blow it. I wasn't gonna say, "Well, they'll say she's a girl, she can't do it." So I was determined, I wasn't gonna stop.

Phil: Another thing I've heard about you in concert is staring at Lou very intently while you were playing.

Moe: 'Cause I couldn't hear shit. I had to watch his mouth to see where he was in the song. I could never hear anything because he was next to me, and he'd be so loud. Sterling was playing rhythm, and the bass guitar was on the other side of him, so it was like a wall. In order to know what was going on I had to watch Lou's mouth to see where he was.

M.C.: Are there any drummers in particular that you'd say . . .

Moe: That I love? Charlie Watts. He influenced my idea towards drumming. I wasn't conscious of him influencing it, but he probably did. He stays away from the fancy shit, you know. He never overloads, he's just what you need. I love his drumming.

Phil: How about Ringo?

Moe: Ringo too. Ringo's the same way, he doesn't get crazy and overpower a song. I think the drummer should stay in the back. Not filling the song, and taking away from everyone else.

M.C.: One thing that was always impressive about the Velvets was that they cut right through the crap. Like, your role—being a woman, yeah, but being part of the band. How do you think about how things have come to be?

Moe: I think that I had a tremendous influence on the way things are now. Not consciously, I didn't try to, that's just the way I was. But having been a girl, and not the featured girl, like a singer, in a major group, I think had a tremendous influence on the way things are today. Like silly things—girls wearing pants to work. That sounds like a silly thing, but that's a major breakthrough when you've been wearing garter belts and skirts for thirty years!

Women in Music, Women in the World

Women in music, I think, are nowhere near where they should be. I think, still, women are tremendously held down, even if they don't realize it—by billboards, TV, everything. Really held down, told how to act. Not directly, but indirectly, by ads and movies, whatever. Kids my daughter's age. I'll be damned if she turns out to be some simpering asshole. I'll drown her.

I never said, "Well I'm a woman, and I'll do what I want." That wasn't my attitude. I just thought, "Well, I do my job, and if you don't like my pants, then fire me," which was the way it worked. I was fired once. This is a very funny story. I thought it was funny, anyway. I had this night job keypunching. You know what keypunching is?

Phil: Vaguely.

Moe: You type information onto an IBM card, which they then feed into a computer, and it gives the computer the information. It's typing, basically. To tell you the truth, I am really fast.

Phil: How fast?

Moe: A hundred and something a minute. Which is really fast on a keypunch machine. Anyway, I had this night job, and I was wearing my dungarees. A night job, in a bank, where there's no customers, no nothing. Six o'clock to twelve. So I'm wearing my dungarees. Clean, no holes. And I'm told by this supervisor, after about two nights, that we're not allowed to wear dungarees. I look out into the bunch of these other keypunch operators, and there's this two hundred and fifty-pounder, with a skirt that goes up to here, 'cause she's such a lard-ass that as she sits the whole skirt goes "whoosh" up to here. And there's these hips hanging over each side, and I said, "What do you think is more offensive, this or that?" And she said, "Well that's the rule, you'll have to," and I said, "Okay," and off I went. But that kind of shit: "You have to wear a skirt," what do you mean? Why—so someone can look at my knees? What are you talking about! I mean, my knees are ugly, you don't want to look at my knees. You want to see how many cards I'm putting out each hour, you know? What does a skirt have to do with keypunching?

So that kind of shit I think I had a tremendous influence on. I really do. Maybe just because a lot of younger people, kids, while they didn't necessarily consciously say, "Well Maureen did it, so I'm gonna do it," but I think me and some other people had a big influence in getting that kind of stuff eased off.

Phil: Is there anyone that preceded you in a similar role, that you know of?

Moe: Not that I know of. Maybe I'm full of shit, but I don't recall anyone just doing what they wanted to, judged on their own merits.

M.C.: To this day [1980] there doesn't seem to be many. Patti Smith is the only one that I can think of.

Moe: It's weird. I started to say that. Girls, just for some wacky reason, mostly because music is dominated by men, just feel, "Well, I can't play guitar." They don't think those words to themselves, but it comes across, and that's what you grow up thinking. And that's a shame. That's like telling all black people, "Well, you can't do this because you're black." Really, it's the same thing. Being a black woman must be astounding.

Phil: In the "New Wave," that's one thing that has changed somewhat. Some women do play bigger roles. But still, too often, they take pandering roles.

Moe: Yeah . . . yeah. I'd rather not do anything than do that. It's a shame, because Patti Smith—I've only heard her on TV once or twice, I haven't heard her albums, so I can't judge her music. But when I saw a picture of her in *Rolling Stone*, or something, she looked very much like Keith Richard. But, I thought, "Out of sight!", you know? Here's a woman just doing what she wants to do. Not trying to be cute, or curling her hair, or going through all of that shit. She's just doing and feeling what she wants to, and that's what you're supposed to do. This is our world, too. We live here.

Phil: It's still rare.

Moe: Yeah, I know. Oh, it's terrible. It will be a thousand years before women do, and say, and act the way they want to.

M.C.: Why do you think that is?

Moe: Society, the media. The media mostly, I guess.

Phil: *Did you get a lot of conscious, spoken feedback, shit, for being a woman in a man's rock-and-roll world?*

Moe: No, oddly enough, no. I think if I was the piano player, or the singer, it would have been "here's a girl singer" or "girl piano player." But playing the drums added maybe a hundred percent to the mystique, if that's the word. I remember a number of times looking out and seeing people just looking like they were thinking, "Holy shit! How the hell does she do that?" And I guess I always had that in the back of [my] mind that it wasn't gonna be me who had to stop the song. If they lasted twenty minutes, so was I gonna last twenty minutes. And maybe I did have a slight subconscious feeling about it all. If we would be unloading the van, I never shirked the duty because I was a girl. I picked up whatever I was able to. I couldn't pick up an amp, of course, but I carried the guitars, the things I could carry, and left the way open for them to carry the heavy things. But I never shirked, never made them think, "Well, shit, if there were four guys we could get this shit out of here faster, but there's only three." So that never came about. We never had any special ideas, or privileges. They'd watch their mouths a little bit around me, but that was it. When we'd get a hotel, there'd usually be two bedrooms and a living room. And Sterling would rush in, knock you down, step on your head, or whatever, to get the best bedroom, or the one with the TV. We'd just stand back, "Okay Sterl, take what you want." And then usually Lou and I would end up in a room together. And this one time, Hans was gonna be my roommate. I remember my quote was "no strangers," which meant that I didn't want Hans in my room, because I don't know him, and I wasn't wearing my pajamas in front of him [laughter]. So that was sort of the guide word for a month or two . . . "no strangers."

PART FOUR

Velvet Warriors

IGNACIO JULIÀ

FEEDBACK: THE LEGEND OF THE VELVET UNDERGROUND, THE FULLY REVISED VERSION (1986–1996)

Feedback: The Legend of the Velvet Underground is both a historical sketch of the Velvet Underground from a Catalonian viewpoint, by a man who has interviewed its former members on various occasions, and an oral history of the band as told by Sterling Morrison. The English translation of the original, which appeared in 1986, was famously problematic. The Morrison passages in that version were re-translations of taped interviews that Julià had first translated into Spanish. Understandably, a good portion of the flavor and sense of Morrison's words was lost. In this new version, Julià has gone back to the original tapes and transcribed them directly.

When in 1986 I was asked to write a documentary on the Velvet Underground for Catalonian public television, I immediately thought about the elusive Sterling Morrison. He accepted my offer to fly to Barcelona for the taping of the show. Many hours of interviews were recorded during that long week, which were used as the basis for the television program and my book *Feedback: La Leyenda de los Velvet Underground,* originally written in Spanish and later sold worldwide with an English companion translation.

Although Sterling liked the book, he was always uncomfortable with the way he sounded after being translated into Spanish and then back into

English. He said he sounded like one of his most hated targets, President Bush. So I always thought I owed him this, to get back to the original tapes (the longest interview he ever granted and a rich, colorful source of information) and redo it so his caustic, excellent conversational wit could be preserved forever.

I last saw him four weeks before he died. I had the chance to say good-bye to my friend, as the song goes, the most authentic person I have ever met during my twenty years in the rock business. "Life's an adventure. . . ," he once told me, and I know he lived it as fully as he possibly could. But I still cannot come to terms with the fact that Rocks isn't with us anymore. He'll always be my friend, and this is obviously dedicated to him.

"I'll be your mirror / Reflect what you are / In case you don't know"
—Lou Reed, "I'll Be Your Mirror"

"I wasn't holding my breath for this to happen. I could've never anticipated the acclaim we seem to be receiving of late. Why should I be better thought of down the road than I was at the time?"
—Sterling Morrison

1. A Louder Secret

The legend of the Velvet Underground fades away. It exists no more. It has been totally exposed to the light. Their secrets have been revealed and the myth has no more sustenance. The facts began to emerge as some of us began the search during the seventies. For more than a decade, all one could do to enjoy and try to fully understand this music was to listen with all five senses to the records released in my country, Spain, or imported long after their initial release. Some of them were even mutilated by censorship or simply ignored by record companies. We had very little in-depth information on the band or the solo careers of Lou Reed, John Cale and Nico. The mutilated, topical truth we did see, only served to enhance and reinforce the myth, the legend.

Sure, the New York band's recordings certainly spoke for themselves. They had an intense and urgent rhythm, their vision was sharp, their dominions vast. These few albums were intense enough to make us wonder how the persons behind them had reached such a powerful level, and try to imagine what strange thoughts had crossed their minds when creating pieces like "Heroin," "Sister Ray," "Pale Blue Eyes," "Foggy Notion," "Venus in Furs," "What Goes On" or "Sweet Jane." But who exactly were the Velvet Underground? In 1981, Mary Harron, writing for the British weekly *New Musical Express,* articulated a description I'm still unable to surpass:

> They were the first avant-garde rock band and the greatest. They were avant-garde in the true sense of exploring uncharted territory. Their songs not only sounded different but they expressed certain feelings, attitudes and kinds of experience that had never been heard in rock music before. They took the music as far out as it is possible without losing consciousness (which is what separates them from their sixties contemporaries, who did) and made so many new connections (combining poetry with trash, primitivism with sophistication, delicacy with violence) that they virtually laid the foundations for a new age in rock. They would influence later generations, but not their own. During the Velvets' own lifetime, from 1965 to 1971, they were simply notorious as the group who sang about heroin, transvestites and sadomasochism. Never stars, rarely interviewed, they were completely out of step with a rock culture dominated by West Coast psychedelia. They were cynics where that culture thought naiveté was a virtue, individualists where their generation wanted to melt blissfully into one, realists where the hippies thought reality was a curtain and if you all sat on the floor and held hands you could make the earth turn.

Aside from these historical circumstances, their songs had a depth beyond mere risqué subject matter and musical minimalism. Maybe this explains why they have fully survived the test of time. They kept their distance from the subjects they were studying, never became too involved in them. They watched with the cold blood of a surgeon, the deadpan irony of someone who's seen too much already. Their songs explored the harshness of a day-to-day existence in a large urban environment like New York City, scanned the strange underworld inhabited by the outsiders who walk the streets of any big city, existed on the poorly traced lines separating madness from sanity, good and bad, ups from downs. Their music reached levels of awesome intensity, depicted scenes of extreme abandon, but they could also sound as soft and vague as the drowsiness after an adrenaline fit. Their music could be truculent, loose and distressing, but always insinuated a rare beauty found only in ugliness and corruption, putting your hands inside the spiritual garbage can that is the subconscious. A flower crushed on the asphalt, choked by a putrid mixture of dirty water, gasoline fumes and dirt. The Velvet Underground.

If they taught us something that we didn't know—because their subjects were new for rock music, though not movies or novels—it could be the effortless relativity of all in life, that nothing is true and everything is permitted. That there is no good and evil, everything is good and bad at the same time. That euphoria and depression end up feeling suspiciously similar, and pain and pleasure could be two faces of a single coin. That everything is of very little transcendence because everything is too complex to be understood in its entirety. We are human beings, a deficient entity condemned to our freedom of choice, with no other escape than to partially disconnect from reality, to distance ourselves from it in order to survive. All the Velvet Underground's songs seem to tell you is: embrace reality and it will devour you, ignore it and you'll become an idiot. They declare: I've been up and down so many times that I just can't tell the difference. And they say it with the raw, compassionate sincerity of those who really have been around, seen a little of everything and gotten their eyelashes burnt.

Their poignant realism was spellbound by passion, and that's another reason why this music still bewitches new generations today. Phil Milstein, founder of the Velvet Underground Appreciation Society, once confessed that if he could relive any moment of the past, it would be the first time he heard *The Velvet Underground And Nico*. Even if that seems a little obsessive, I do understand his feelings. That amazing discovery changed Phil's life. This music made his existence less boring, less sad maybe, in a time—the seventies—still dominated by fat, disgusting rock stars. Now he was on to a secret the whole world wouldn't, couldn't share. That rarely praised music gave him the strength to overcome, or at least forget, his frustrations and vulnerability. It pushed him to be more himself. These weird records gave him company, because nobody can truly enjoy being alone, isolated. And Velvet fanatics seem to be solitary by nature, probably neurotic. Like myself?

"At the age when identity is a problem some people join rock and roll bands and perform for other people who share the same difficulties," wrote Lou Reed shortly after he left the group. "The age difference between performer and beholder in rock is not large. But, unfortunately, those in the fourth tier assume those on stage know something they don't. Which is not true. It simply requires a very secure ego to allow yourself to be loved for what you do rather than what you are. The singer has a soul but feels he isn't loved off stage. Or, perhaps worse, feels he shines only on stage and off is wilted, a shell as common as the garden gardenia. But we are all as common as snowflakes, aren't we?"

In 1966 not many would have said the Velvet Underground were common folks. They probably were, but looked more like dangerous degenerates. Their music was the inevitable degeneration of rhythm and blues and rock and roll. And as the future would show, also its regeneration. Aside from the originality of the subjects depicted in their lyrics, they were unique and fiercely peerless in their musical instincts. On a basic foundation that smartly disguised their rhythm and blues roots, a new structure was built, a framework of echoing textures and repetitive rhythms. It's like beholding a locomotive panting and throwing off sparks while accelerating its run slowly, or experiencing a sonic explosion rising upward until it culminates in a loud scream, a volcanic eruption. A truly mesmerizing frontal attack to the senses and the spirit.

Obviously, that phenomenal sonic charisma could be best experienced live. Try visualizing the scene. On one side stands a young Lou Reed nervously projecting his bastard interpretation of urban rock and roll, spitting his songs with infinite, deadpan disdain, playing an unpredictable, neurotic rhythmic game on the guitar. On the other side, John Cale and his denial of the classical discipline he had been subjected to, his challenging, crazy, experimental daydreaming. Between the two poles, balancing their antagonism, was Maureen Tucker and that astonishing, hypnotic reduction of drumming to its minimal essence. Adding an imaginative musicality, always ignoring common ground, was Sterling Morrison, a skilled and brilliant—though not always fully appreciated—guitarist that, in my opinion, should only be compared to the best of his generation. Caught in the fire between Lou and John, always maintaining the balance and adding precious details or simply superb chunks of rhythm guitar, Sterling represents that extra element that made the final mix bold but shiny.

They perfectly illustrate one of the most useful lessons from the sixties: rock and roll is at its best when cooked inside a creative team, not when devised as the fuel for a solo career. And as musicians they were surprisingly inventive. Take Cale's viola, more effective than a sitar or any of the other exotic instruments of the time. The guitars and amps were also treated in an unusual manner. Jonathan Richman, who boasts he saw them live a hundred times, remembers being fascinated by the sound of the Vox amplifiers and noticing how the sound changed gradually when they switched to Acoustic and then to Sunn amplifiers. It might sound like technical junk, but it helps understand the band's personality. Richman says the Vox amps had a darker sound, with more midrange, and were perfect to create feedback. The sound of the Vox fuzz boxes was also special, as shown in "Sister Ray" or "The Gift." He also admired Lou's Gretsch Country Gentleman guitar, improved by two extra pick-ups, a total of four. One was a pre-amp and the other a tremolo unit. That guitar could practically play itself: for every note fretted it could turn out 16, a primitive prototype of a guitar synthesizer. It was also converted to stereo, allowing a heavy sound in one channel and a clean sound in the other, broadening the sonic spectrum. With curiosity and a will to experiment, making mistakes and burning up more than a few electronic circuits, they were pushing the musical barriers of the time, expanding the way we listen and relate to rock.

But, above all, the Velvet Underground were inimitable, a group of charismatic talents both opposite and compatible. Everybody has covered their songs, but nobody has been able to match their sound. Their music inspired the late Lester Bangs to portray them with the same arrogant, heartfelt honesty they had shown in their work. "I belong to a generation for whom the Velvet Underground was our Beatles and Dylan combined," he wrote in *New York Rocker* magazine. "I don't care who did feed-back first, or if Lou Reed 'sang like Dylan.' Modern music begins with the Velvets, and the implications and influence of what they did seem to go on forever. 'Black Angel's Death Song' alone is still ahead of its time, and of course all the other stuff sounds right up to date over a decade later. Who else has created a body of work of which this can be said? Almost all the artists and albums since them which have mattered the most to me (us?) have been blatantly influenced by them: the Stooges, 'Sticky Fingers' and probably 'Exile' even, Roxy Music and Eno's work, Patti Smith, Richard Hell and the Voidoids, David Bowie if you like. The only thing I think would be a mistake in thanking them for this precious gift would be romanticizing them too much."

John Cale's exit cost the group strength, vision and internal discomfort, and though the energy was always maintained on stage, the records that came after Cale's departure show Lou Reed's artistic personality (and Cale's replacement Doug Yule's pop sensibilities) taking over. Their third LP, now seen as the first true "concept album," is an articulate narrative exploring the themes of falling from grace and redemption, subjects Lou as a writer extended into his solo career. When they recorded *Loaded*, officially their last album, the Velvets were much like any other rock band at the end of the sixties, though still with some significant differences. During their lifetime they were, as Sterling Morrison says, "a well kept secret." Twenty years later they still are, but perhaps a louder secret.

And now the cast of characters:

- Louis Allan Reed was born March 2, 1942, in Brooklyn, into a middle-class Jewish family. He spent his teenage years in Freeport, Long Island. As a child his parents had him take piano lessons, but Lou was more interested in collecting rock 45s, especially those by vocal groups and rockabilly artists. He underwent electroshock therapy as a result of his unstable behavior and love for rock and roll. At 14 he made his first record, *So Blue*, a single by The Shades. In 1960 he went to Syracuse University in upstate New York.

- John Cale was born December 5, 1940, in Crynant, Wales. He attended local schools until the age of 17. From 1960 to 1963 he studied music at Goldsmiths' College in London. Soon he became interested in electronic and avant-garde music, following the teachings of the British composer Humphrey Searle and the American artist John Cage. In 1963, with the help of Aaron Copland, he received a Leonard Bernstein scholarship to study with Greek-French composer Iannis Xenakis at the Berkshire Music Center at Tanglewood in Lenox, Massachusetts, but was expelled shortly thereafter. He moved to New York and joined drone-master LaMonte Young in The Dream Syndicate.

- Holmes Sterling Morrison was born August 29, 1942, in East Meadow, Long Island—about ten miles from where Lou grew up—to a middle-class Catholic family. He started playing the trumpet at the age of 7, but moved to the guitar at the age of 12. Inspired by Bo Diddley and Chuck Berry, he liked rock and roll alright but had a passion for black rhythm and blues. Morrison attended Syracuse University along with his childhood friend, Jim Tucker, Maureen's brother.

- Maureen Anne Margaret Tucker was born August 26, 1945, in New Jersey, to a middle-class Catholic family that moved to Long Island. After leaving school she worked as a computer operator, a job which did not prevent her from sitting in her room and playing the drums while listening to Bo Diddley and Olatunji records. She was in an all-girls band before being asked to replace the band's first drummer, Angus MacLise.

2. The Prehistory

In the early sixties, the future of the world and the serious troubles of mankind didn't seem to interest Sterling Morrison or Lou Reed. Let's say they were not the most exemplary students at Syracuse University. Sterling's higher education had begun at the University of Illinois, but he finished his second semester at New York's City College. His uncompromising attitude (good grades but unacceptable behavior) and his disdain for the ROTC, had precipitated the move. He attended City College for two weeks, but finding no place to live in New York, he moved on to Syracuse, where his friend Jim Tucker was.

Lou also had trouble with the ROTC. According to one story, he was suspended after pointing a pistol at an officer's head, which in military terms indicates a deep mental disturbance, or worse. Lou's room was right above Sterling's, so it's not surprising that music brought them together. Lou was attracted to the sounds coming from Sterling's record player, and asked to borrow a few records. Several days later, Sterling heard the sound of an electric guitar playing at full volume from the room above his. There were also other young musicians at the university: Felix Cavalieri, later of the Young Rascals, Mike Esposito of the Blues Magoos, and Garland Jeffreys, who would make his on-stage debut two years later at the Dom, backed by the Velvets, singing "Bright Lights, Big City."

Sterling and Lou began playing together, at first covering rhythm and blues hits by the likes of Ike and Tina Turner (according to Sterling, "It's Gonna Work Out Fine" was the first song they did together). They played in some bands whose exotic names (Moses and His Brothers, Pasha and the Prophets, L.A. and the El Dorados) changed every week so nobody would recognize this bunch of potential juvenile delinquents and they could still get gigs. There was alcohol and illegal substances thrown in, of course, and the hours were mostly spent at the bar. They shared a fascination for everything that smelled of delinquency, a loathing for almost anything and anybody.

After graduation, Lou returned to Freeport and accepted a job as a songwriter for Pickwick Records, a small company that specialized in cheap exploitation records. Pickwick would capitalize on any given fad, be it surf music or Mersey-beat. It was a quick and profitable business, since the records were sold for low prices in supermarkets. Lou was one of four writers in a room writing songs from nine to five. Once they finished some songs, they would go down to the recording studio and in a couple of hours would finish three or four records. That learning process would surely be of use for Lou's future in professional music.

In the meantime, since his dismissal from the conservatory, John Cale had joined LaMonte Young, his wife, Marion, and Tony Conrad in The Dream Syndicate. LaMonte was an avant-garde musician whose works consisted of extended, humming drones and conceptual conceits that had him talking to his piano or screaming at a plant until it would languish and die. The group constantly experimented, producing sounds based on the tension between scientific method and spiritual searching. Cale saw in Young an extension of the work he had done with John Cage, with whom he had participated in a groundbreaking 24-hour piano marathon. With Young, Cale could continue to develop his instincts, something often denied him during his classical training. "LaMonte was perhaps the best part of my education and my introduction to musical discipline," says Cale. His insatiable wish to continually experiment led him to use guitar strings on his viola and amplify it, a step towards the future sound of the Velvet Underground.

In the autumn of 1964 he moved into an apartment on Manhattan's lower East Side with Tony Conrad. Shortly thereafter, Conrad and an artist called Walter DeMaria asked him to join a pop group. A small record company needed a band to promote a song already recorded. The company was Pickwick and the song the work of a 22-year old Lou Reed. He had written this would-be hit after reading that ostrich feathers were going to be the season's fashion rage, and therefore "The Ostrich" could as well be the new dance craze ("Put your head on the floor and have somebody step on it," suggested the lyrics).

Encouraged by the chance to make some money, they decided to visit the Pickwick company on Coney Island and became The Primitives. With Lou as the singer, the group made a few promotional appearances at a school in New Jersey, a supermarket opening, a radio station and finally a TV show. The Primitives went no further, but there was clearly a spark between Lou and John. According to Tony Conrad, "John was really impressed with Lou because Lou had this unique ability to sing lyrics. He would go out there without anything in his head at all and just sing songs. Lyrics would just come out of his mouth. You didn't know where they came from but suddenly he was doing rock and roll."

Rock and roll music was Lou's passion, but he was having some personal problems. He was still living with his parents and was somehow failing at music, so John seized the opportunity to befriend him. Shortly thereafter, Lou left his parents' house and moved in with John, at 56 Ludlow Street in Manhattan. Tony Conrad had moved out and Lou took his place. This gave them the chance to get to know one other better and confront their musical ideas. Thanks to Hank Williams' songs and the rock records that Conrad used to listen to at all hours, John had developed an interest in this other music. Cale and Reed were both sophisticated talents, open to any kind of influence. They soon discovered that though they inhabited different musical worlds, they were intensely attracted to one another's ideas. Lou seemed to be very idealistic at the time, and completely possessed by rock and roll, even putting music ahead of his personal life. John was running away from his classical training, guided by a crazed, destructive instinct. It was a revelation to Lou, who lived his music very intensely and had an aggressive outlook, to find a collaborator for his personal obsessions.

Then one day in the winter of 1965, Lou encountered Sterling on the street—after not having seen him for a long time—and introduced his Syracuse friend to John. They went to Ludlow Street and discussed their common interests in music and drugs, deciding on the spot that they ought to be making music together. And gradually they began doing it.

With The Primitives, Lou and John had already seen that there were few chances for them to get into the commercial jungle. So they decided to ignore such goals and began to play the kind of music that really appealed to them, a sound that was truly theirs. They were casually joined by Angus MacLise, a poet and percussionist who lived in the same building and had also worked with LaMonte Young. From then on the apartment became a rehearsal space, a scene of nearly continuous musical activity. They recorded all sorts of crazy experiments that years later would help Lou develop his noise opus Metal Machine Music. Angus contributed his Eastern-flavored percussion and a mystic outlook on life. Years later, they would all remember this formative period as magical.

During this time, they met film maker Piero Heliczer. They appeared in his movies and played for the screenings. Also, in July 1965 they finally recorded their first serious demo with songs. The tape circulated and eventually made it to England. Cale was always going back and forth between London and New York and the records he brought back were listened to with more interest than any of the American bands. At one time they seriously considered moving to London, and they would probably have done it if they hadn't met Andy Warhol.

Up to this point, they had used different names for the band—The Falling Spikes or The Warlocks. One day, Tony Conrad found a book on the street and brought it to the apartment. It was called *The Velvet Underground* and purported to be "a documentary on the sexual corruption of our age." They were attracted by the sound of the words and the implied association with the underground film and art scene.

Alan Aronowitz, a New York music journalist who had written about the Beatles, the Stones and Dylan, heard about this unusual band playing at underground movie screenings, and, curious about their singer's claim to be "the fastest guitarist alive," he went to check them out at a screening. Aronowitz offered them a gig opening for a band he was associated with, the Myddle Class, at Summit High School in Summit, New Jersey. They would be paid the astounding sum of $75.

Angus MacLise, who was immersed in radical Oriental philosophy, had a problem with the gig: he strongly believed no payment should be accepted for art. Offended, he left the band. Desperate, Lou and Sterling remembered their old friend Jim Tucker and his sister Maureen. Besides needing a drummer, they needed an amplifier, and they knew that she had one. She was quickly recruited and they debuted as the Velvet Underground at the Summit gig, December 11, 1965. They played only three songs ("There She Goes Again," "Venus in Furs" and "Heroin") and two girls in the crowd fainted. Aronowitz saw potential in them, but also thought they needed some polishing and so he arranged a residency at the Cafe Bizarre in Greenwich Village, where he expected them to develop through long hours of working out, just as the Beatles had done in Hamburg.

This is where Gerard Malanga enters the picture. He was told about the band by Barbara Rubin, and when he went to check it out he encountered a strange sound that recalled that of a rock band, though the similarity seemed quite distant. The stage was practically at ground level, and so the band played close to the tables. Gerard waited some time before deciding to dance. He was hesitant, thinking the dancing would seem an intrusion. But when he began, Lou and John encouraged him. They wanted people to dance to their music, but with their intimidating sound they had few takers.

Of these early performances John recalls: "When we first put the Velvets together we formed a group around the guitar, bass, drums and my viola. We wanted the Velvet Underground to be a group with a dynamic symphonic flair. The idea was that Lou's lyrical and melodic ability could be combined with some of my musical ideas to create performances where we wouldn't just repeat ourselves. In the beginning, when Al Aronowitz was managing us and we were playing at the Bizarre, we practiced a lot and were pretty tight."

3. Seven Minutes of Noise

When I was a student at Syracuse, *Sterling Morrison tells me trying to fully remember,* I was just in my room one night late playing records with two friends—we had old blues records, Ray Charles, Lightning Hopkins and things—and suddenly there came a knock on the door. We thought it was the person in charge of the dormitory coming down to complain, because that's usually what happened. Instead it was the guy upstairs who turned out to be Lou, and he needed records because he had a campus radio show and he was running out of blues and that sort of thing. My roommate was a big collector, and I had my things too, so Lou borrowed some records. That's when we first met and we had made plans to have him see all we had, but he was kicked off the radio show before we ever did much of that. We lent him just a few albums. Lou was pretty guarded about himself, but he did let it be known that he was an English major and he liked to write poetry. He didn't say anything about playing music. Then one day the ROTC, which is a military training program that they have in colleges, had people out marching around the athletic field behind the dorm. And suddenly you could hear this real loud humming and buzzing upstairs, and it was somebody playing electric guitar at full volume. Then I knew that Lou was a guitar player too. And we just went from there.

Apparently, Syracuse was a very conservative university attended by young boys from rich families, the kids that would take over the business someday.

Syracuse is a very strange university, very bourgeois. The people that go there are there to be accountants and business administration. That's why Lou's parents sent him there, to see if they could make a good boy out of him. And it's an expensive school, it's a private school for fairly affluent parents. That does produce a certain percentage of pretty wild people: out of the whole university there might have been only one per cent that we considered the lunatic fringe, but it still was a hundred people maybe, and we had a great time, a lot of parties and music. Hellacious people, outstanding parties, outstanding lunatics, people whose families had a lot of money and were incorrigible crazies, great people. Oddly enough, Betsey Johnson, the fashion designer, was also at Syracuse the same time we were. Betsey was a cheerleader, she was not the lunatic fringe, she was very straight when she was there. We used to make fun of her for that, that she ran with the wrong crowd. She didn't want to roam with the crowd that was going to be kicked out of school, that was her main thing. We had bands, but we hardly ever played, nobody wanted to hire us. We had to keep changing the name so people didn't remember who we were.

We did black songs, rhythm and blues, that's what we liked. So when the Rolling Stones came over we liked them, but they were doing the things we'd always been doing, just covers of black songs . . . maybe better. We never treated these as religion, we weren't trying to do faithful renditions, we were just trying to do our version of it. We never tried to do faithful renditions of our material, let alone anybody else's. But even in the Velvet Underground, if we felt like it we would play "Little Queenie" or some old favorite from days of yore. In the early days with John I remember sitting around playing a lot of Smokey Robinson stuff, just for ourselves, "Tracks of My Tears" or whatever.

Sterling and Lou augmented their fun with the creative literary courses taught by Delmore Schwartz, a writer deeply influenced by James Joyce. Sadly misunderstood in his lifetime, Schwartz was only recognized after his death in 1966. His best-known work is a collection of short stories called In Dreams Begin Responsibilities.

Delmore was a teacher in the English department and he taught poetry and Joyce, and creative writing even for a time. But he was certifiably a paranoid schizophrenic and drunkard, so that made it very difficult for him to deal with students or to deal with anyone. And he just got crazier and crazier as time went on, partly because of a long business involving why he couldn't divorce his wife. He thought Nelson Rockefeller was mixed up in it and then he thought that Lou and I, and Maureen Tucker's brother and all these people, he thought we were all spies for Nelson Rockefeller and was afraid of us and hated us, which wasn't the way things started out. But Lou was closer to Delmore than I was, he was pretty hard to get close to when you think about it, but he was a good poet. No one needs me, or Lou, to say that. "European Son" is dedicated to him, it's just not on account of content although it does talk about a European son, so it's like the European Jew in exile in the United States, but that's not really why: Delmore despised rock and roll lyrics, he thought they were ridiculous and awful, and "European Son" has hardly any lyrics so that meant that was a song that Delmore might like. He didn't care about the music part of rock and roll, he just hated the lyrics, so we wrote a song that Delmore would like: twenty seconds of lyrics and seven minutes of noise. I think Delmore was a good poet, but I didn't treat him as my personal messiah the way Lou did. Lou really liked him. But Delmore was crazy, made worse by alcoholism, he was an incredible juicer.

But not all the teachers at Syracuse were like Schwartz. The atmosphere on campus was one of rigid morality.

College was a repressive place in the sixties, that's why people were trying to burn them down by 1965. Like in that movie *If*. The best way to improve the American university would be to first strafe it with machine guns and then set it on fire. It was incredible. They just told you what to do and you did it, or they threw you out on your ass, simple as that. In a way they're kind of getting back to that. I don't think Lou has no fond memories of Syracuse. He got his degree—it was like when they sent Lenin back to Russia in a boxcar—because they told him that if he kept his mouth shut and let nobody see him, just stayed out of sight, then he could show up, get his diploma and get out of there. He had offended a student who was in the Young Americans for Freedom, his father was a big corporation lawyer. They wanted Lou thrown out and the dean agreed, but when they finally did come in person to talk to the dean, this guy and his father were so obnoxious, they were so horrible, that the dean actually sided with Lou. So Lou did graduate, which was incredible. I was down in City College, that's where I was when I ran into him. I had seen him the previous summer, again by accident—Lightning Hopkins was playing in the Village, so naturally I made my pilgrimage and there was Lou. I saw him that summer and next time I saw him was in February of 65, he was with Cale. The two of them were doing nothing, I was doing nothing, so they said: well, why don't we just jam? I said, okay. So that was the Velvet Underground. And we kept doing it. Lou was living with his parents. I was living in the city, I was hip, not like people living in Freeport, Long Island, with their parents. That was ridiculous! John was living in Ludlow Street, so when we got together, Lou would drive in from Freeport and I would just take the subway down. We started playing maybe once a week, then twice a week, three times a week, and pretty soon every night we were at it. Then we all moved to the same place, to Grand Street, because Ludlow Street was basically unlivable, had no central heating, had a fireplace in each room, which is illegal in New York. The rent was something like $15 a month. It was just awful. We used to go out in the winter and find old crates and wooden pallets, and we would be out there tearing them up and taking them upstairs to make some fire in the fireplace. Without exaggeration—this sounds like these romanticized tales—we used to sit with rugs on our shoulders. It was so cold in that place!

A true bohemian image for three guys with higher educations. But there was no creative vision yet, no artistic pretensions.

This is not people practicing with a vision, mind you. We didn't say: we have a great idea and we're going to pursue it to great glory. That wasn't what we were doing. We were playing Smokey Robinson and related things, some of our little ideas too, but we were just playing for fun. If it's fun on that level, it's fun on any other level. This was music for its own sake. The nice thing about bands is that it's nice to play music with other people. I never wanted to be a solo artist. I kind of know why John does it, but I don't know which he actually prefers. John had lots of ideas, from LaMonte Young and everything. And things got strange musically. In Ludlow Street John wasn't playing any keyboards at all, cause he didn't have any, it was all viola and bass, and fooling around on guitar too. We all liked drones and I think you can hear the minimalist leanings of the band. The guitar players I like are Steve Cropper and people like that, very minimal. A few well chosen notes. A good guitar riff I always thought was worth more than a good guitar solo. There are songs, like "The Last Time" by the Stones, a great riff, beautiful. Having done that, they don't need to play slick solos or anything else. So we tried to put some thinking into that, what the song actually needs. Very few things exist just for instrumental breaks, unless it's like a warm up piece, but it wasn't like Canned Heat songs or like most electric blues in the sixties, two verses and then an extended solo so you could display instrumental virtuosity. We didn't have any to display so we weren't likely to do that. But I would say "European Son" just wanted to go off and be "European Son." We could have played a whole lot more and enjoyed greater success if we had delivered the hot solo at the right time. And also, one advantage with John was that he was always going back and forth to England and Wales to visit. Every six months or so he would take a trip and when he did he'd buy all these records, the things that appealed to him, which were pretty weird, so we were very tuned into the oddest music happening in England. We were very aware of the radical people, which we would not have been if it wasn't for John going there physically and bringing back these records. Lou and I also had a big stack of records, like Eric Burdon or Mick Jagger or Keith Richards, those guys were collectors. In a strange way we were collectors of European weirdness through Cale, and we had a big stack of rhythm and blues records, and a lot of doo-wop, before they got stolen in a succession of burglaries. Lou and I had three piles of 45s, right up to the ceiling, columns, tons of stuff.

Sterling talks about Little Richard, Bo Diddley, James Brown, T-Bone Walker, Lightning Hopkins. But, what were the group's musical priorities? What kind of musical background did each of them bring? What did they have in common musically and what separated them?

It was pretty hard to pry things out of Lou about his childhood, because of his odd relationship with his parents and that sort of thing, but it would come out in little pieces. His father was an accountant and always wanted him to work, like anybody else's. The first time he tried, the first day Lou made $50,000 worth of errors, so that was the end of Lou's accounting career. As far as I know, he was trained on piano apparently, because he can play piano some, but he didn't pursue it at all seriously. But we never got much keyboard playing out of Lou, he didn't compose on piano, he didn't write songs on piano. He might try the piano to get himself out of a tight spot, you can hear voicings better on piano sometimes than you can on guitar—Lou was a songwriter mostly just fiddling around on guitar. Then he had some teeny bands, the way we all did, but Lou went one step further than I did, a step further than almost anybody does, he actually made a record, that was going a long way from the small towns on Long Island. All records were made in New York City, which is a huge and scary place, and nobody knew exactly how you would make a record. Lou I think did it by dealing with someone who was a friend of his father, it has to be something engineered by adults, you didn't just go into New York with your guitar and say: record me. Not if you were a teenager from Long Island. There wasn't that much going on in rock and roll. Not everybody liked rock and roll music when it first started out, even among young people, but the people who really liked it decided they liked it so much that they would try to play it, and that was taking a big step. Everybody can sit around snapping their fingers, but who actually cares enough to try to do it? And then, who actually cares enough to try to make a record himself? Lou went that extra step. Is it a good record? No. But it exists. So that astounded me: not only had I found there was a guitar player upstairs, but also one who had made a record. John's background is a lot better documented, but John also didn't want to talk about it, and still doesn't. When we first met him he was rebelling against his formal training, it use to drive us crazy. In order to copyright a song you have to come up with a lead sheet, which is a notes and lyrics transcription. For Lou and me it was very difficult to do these things, we had to sit around trying to find out which notes they were.

John could do it instantly but refused, we could never get him to do the lead sheets. We'd say: John, it will only take you a minute, but he didn't want to hear about it. So when you asked John about his training, he didn't want to talk about it. I know he started piano at three and viola at five, and played on the B.B.C. when he was eight, he was considered a prodigy. John doesn't talk about that either, it doesn't make that much difference to him. But he always could really play. Again it was very difficult for us to even make him play keyboards, because he was too trained on keyboards and wanted to play instruments he wasn't trained on, like bass or anything else he could come up with, but keyboards, that was just too easy, he didn't like that. For my part, I started out on trumpet, for no apparent reason. If my parents had owned a piano, then I would have played piano and lived happily ever after as a keyboardist, because I like polyphonic music. I didn't like trumpet for that reason, it might help you think in terms of lines, linear melodies, but that's all you can do. It might even help minimal thinking: if on a trumpet, you can only do one thing in a given moment, what thing should it be? That might have led me kind of to the way I approach guitar. But as soon as I picked guitar I knew that was what I wanted to play. That's what you needed to play rock and roll, for one thing, but also I liked it. I liked being able to play various notes at once and that sort of thing. I was considered very good on trumpet, but then my teacher got drafted and so I didn't feel obligated to keep playing trumpet. My terrific teacher was drafted and I couldn't find anyone that I liked, and that was just an excuse for me to switch to guitar. That was never a popular decision at home, even if I bought my own instruments and amps and all that, it was always considered a colossal waste of time, and stupidity, and leading me to juvenile delinquency, but I was already there so I couldn't blame that on guitar playing.

John's neighbor, Angus MacLise, became their first drummer.

Angus was a poet and very self-conscious artist and world traveler. He spent years in India and Greece and traveled constantly. He died recently in Katmandu. From his travels, Angus was interested in various kinds of percussion and he had heard a whole lot of Eastern music. So when John, Lou and I were playing just casually, which was all it was, Angus liked to sit in playing all these percussion things he had picked up as souvenirs. We liked the way it sounded and we got used to it, so when we started to play behind films in the lower East Side Angus was there too. From the very beginning as the Velvet Underground we never did have standard percussion. We had one theory that said that all bands tend to sound alike because all the drumming is alike. We said our drumming is not going to be like everybody else's. Think about how much Keith Moon contributed to The Who's sound: his drumming style was different, he was very busy and very nervous, he wasn't like Ringo Starr. That really helped The Who, and our ideas about drumming helped us. Maureen Tucker was willing enough to part from the usual procedures, and that was good, and that's why she was the drummer after Angus. Angus quit, incidentally, because the moment that it became apparent that we could make money, he decided it wasn't art. For him art and money were two separate things. Angus would have stayed in the Velvet Underground forever provided that we never made a cent and kept starving to death at Ludlow Street. The amount of money that caused him to quit was $75, which was going to be split four ways. That was selling out for Angus! But we remained friends and he did in fact sit in with us one other time, when he discovered that he had made a mistake, that in fact you could be free and still be paid, you didn't have to make any compromises. If you don't compromise you don't get to play often, we never did these package tours, but you still could. He said then it wasn't what he thought, but I said: Yeah, but it's too late, Angus, unless Maureen quits, and she remains. That was a sad moment.

After various names for the band, a book found in the street caught their attention. That little exploitation book had a strong, attractive title. The Velvet Underground.

We didn't have a name for the band and so we'd make up a new one once a week. That goes back to Lou's practice at Syracuse: all the bands got such a bad reputation so quickly that people would say don't hire that band again, so we just changed the name of the band, and it turned out to be the same people and the same songs. We were continuing in that tradition, we didn't have a name and we didn't care about it. Angus saw the book, *The Velvet Underground,* and brought it down to Ludlow Street. We thought it was a good name because it had underground in it and we were playing for underground films, we considered ourselves part of the underground film community. We had no connections with rock and roll as far as we were concerned. Rock and roll consisted of Jay Dee and the Starlighters, guys who played the uptown clubs and who had matching suits. We didn't have any of those things, so we had no chance whatsoever of working on the Manhattan club scene. That was beyond us, we just couldn't do it any more than we could have gone to Las Vegas to play. There was this incredible gulf between what we were and what we could do—we hardly had any equipment—and what working rock and roll bands could do and did. So we said: We're not in rock and roll anymore, we're out of it, we're finished. We would just hang out with these film people and play back up music for their movies. That's how we knew Piero Heliczer, Jack Smith, Harry Smith and Jonas Mekas. The name didn't have anything to do with the leather and whips and all that stuff, but people thought it did. We did at the time have the song "Venus in Furs." That was completed before we met Andy, so that reinforced the associations with the book, that in fact we were trying to make some statement about being S&M. That was wholly accidental. The book itself is incredibly stupid, about wife swapping and swingers in the suburbs and all that. We always did like the name, I still like it.

4. Inevitable Plastic Explosion

At the Cafe Bizarre, a tourist trap in the Village, the Velvet Underground played Chuck Berry covers and some of their own music, songs that neither the manager nor the customers appreciated. They were getting fed up playing there for almost nothing; they began just before Christmas but decided they would be free by New Year's Eve. So when the manager threatened to throw them out if they played another weird thing like "The Black Angel's Death Song," they opened the next set with a furious version of it. They were fired.

That happened only a couple of days after they first met Andy Warhol through Gerard Malanga and Barbara Rubin. Paul Morrisey was looking for a band for Andy to promote, so they were invited to move to the Factory, the spacious attic at 231 West 47th St. which was both the artist's studio and a social gathering place. Warhol bought them some new amps and encouraged them to work on songs. The Factory was a big loft that Billy Linich (a.k.a. Billy Name) took care of. He was the only one living there and had covered the walls with silver foil. It was a forum open to all kinds of freaks, artists, dealers, celebrities, transvestites, drug addicts and other spongers. A never-ending party, that's the myth, with King Warhol hosting the guests surrounded by his freaky circle. Almost everybody, except for Warhol, was taking speed on a daily basis. The place was col-

orful, film cameras were rolling almost constantly, pop art being manu-
factured . . . while the Velvet Underground rehearsed in a corner.

Without realizing it they had entered a private universe, but they fit
perfectly in that new circle of constantly bubbling creativity. And Andy
needed them as much as they needed him—after leading pop art with his
serial paintings of icons of the American way of life and getting into film
making, he was making plans to meld all of his audiovisual ideas into a
multimedia extravaganza that would become known as the Exploding
Plastic Inevitable (E.P.I.). Andy always surrounded himself with young
bodies, unknown talents and aspiring celebrities. He vampirized them as
portrait subjects and collaborators, sucking their blood and ideas in a relationship beneficial to both parties. In those days the resident starlet was
the thin, slightly crazy Edie Sedgwick. And the big counselor was Paul
Morrisey, who helped with the financial end of things and also the film
making, which was a new adventure for the famed pop artist.

Warhol declared everything was fabulous and fun, which logically
decreased the value of his judgment. If the world was one immense
garbage can, an absurd piece of plastic, a cathode ray tube of gigantic proportions, that was alright. He was willing to enjoy it, even if the circumstances demanded that he himself become a piece of plastic to do so. The
banality of his attitude was perhaps surprising in an age of social revolt
and direct action against "the system," but his eloquent neutrality would
become meaningful with time, in a subtle and indirect manner maybe, but
effective nevertheless. The picturesque echoes of flower power and psy-
chedelia, Black Panthers and anti-Vietnam war demonstrations are pure
nostalgia today. But Warhol's work, its ambiguity and uncertainty, both
illuminates the sixties and reflects the present. With no loud opinions
about the portrayed subject, its essence has remained intact. It's no wonder the Velvet Underground found refuge and inspiration under his patron
figure.

"Andy told me that what we were doing with music was the same
thing he was doing with painting and movies and writing, i.e., not kidding
around," says Lou. "To my mind nobody in music was doing anything
that even approximated the real thing, with the exception of us. We were
doing a specific thing that was very, very real. It wasn't slick or a lie in any
conceivable way, which was the only way we could work with him.
Because the first thing I liked about Andy was that he was very real."

It was real, but was it fun? What did the Velvets do on New Year's
Eve, 1965? They met with Edie, her friend Donald Lyons, Andy and
Gerard to go see James Brown at the Apollo Theatre in Harlem (accord-

ing to Sterling: "We came storming in there for the midnight show and the comment of the ticket taker at the Apollo was: 'What is this? Bellevue recess?'"). From there they went to Danny Fields' apartment and watched Walter Cronkite on TV presenting some underground films. The show included excerpts from the Piero Heliczer film *Venus In Furs,* which featured the band playing "Heroin." Later they went to Lou and Sterling's apartment at 450 Grand Street, their new place after Ludlow Street. There was no heat and it was terribly cold, forcing everyone to leave their coats on. Andy was biting his nails and flipping through a magazine. John and Edie stared at each other with murderous looks. Nobody was willing to talk. It was a mixture of complicated people, and the resulting friction caused sparks which, in turn, were bound to cause an explosion. It was inevitable.

Lou Reed has said that the E.P.I. was not all Andy's idea, that the Velvets had played for film screenings before and doing it with Andy's movies was just a logical step. The strobe lights weren't his invention either, but a new thing anyone could have used. Indeed, the creativity in the Factory was collective, but it wouldn't have been the same without the catalyst Warhol provided. Andy, for instance, imposed upon the Velvets a certain German singer that he had casually discovered. It wasn't easy to convince them to accept Nico, and at first she pretended to use them as a backup group. While it was obvious that they weren't going to give up their musical character, the persuasive Andy talked Lou into writing a few songs for her, and even convinced them to be billed as The Velvet Underground and Nico. Nico would perform only her own songs, and the rest of the time would stand on stage doing nothing, acting as one of those passive beauties Andy found so fascinating.

The first proper work with the Velvets was a film, *The Velvet Underground and Nico: A Symphony of Sound,* that shows them rehearsing. The shooting was interrupted by the New York police, quite often attracted to the Factory by the noise and the stream of weird people coming and going at all hours.

In February 1966 they debuted at the film makers Cinémathèque on 41st Street as a part of Andy Warhol's *Up-Tight* show. The crazed lights, handled by Danny Williams, the choreographed convulsions of Gerard and Edie, the movies by Morrisey and Andy, and the highly electric, harsh sound of the Velvets, kept the audience in a huge thresher, stunned by a sensory overload that had them stuck to their seats. Some surely felt it was disgusting, but the audience was made up mostly of art critics, artists and snobs who were not ready to admit in public that they didn't understand what Warhol was trying to communicate. The truth is there was little to understand, it was all based on feeling.

Barbara Rubin had suggested the name *Up-Tight*, and of course the ever daring Andy found it irresistible. The songs played were "I'll Keep It with Mine" (a Dylan song that Nico insisted on singing, though the band intentionally played it so poorly that she eventually desisted), "Run, Run, Run," "Heroin" and others. "Venus in Furs" prompted the debut of Gerard Malanga's whip dance. The band was standing in front of the screen, which was split so two films could be shown at once. They played at full volume, and the swirling of lights and images built an atmosphere so hypnotic one felt petrified. *Up-Tight* then traveled to Rutgers University in New Jersey and the University of Michigan film festival in Ann Arbor. The memories of these first trips out of Manhattan are vague, but no one involved has forgotten Nico's driving, or the astounded reaction as the band played with their backs turned to the open-mouthed audience.

Morrisey and Warhol were looking for a place to settle with the show when *Up-Tight* was performed at Paraphernalia, an ultra-chic boutique featuring the fashion designs of Betsey Johnson, who would later marry John Cale. Brian Jones showed up, invited by Warhol. Shortly after, Morrisey found a place called The Dom on St. Marks Place. The lease was signed on the same day they were opening the show, in April of 1966. That afternoon, the Velvets moved their equipment in, and by 8 p.m. the place was full of people. Nobody wanted to miss the opening of the new show, the Exploding Plastic Inevitable, a multimedia event that substantially changed the way people perceived rock music.

"It was an audience event to me," explained scene maker and record company executive Danny Fields, "but it was also a musical event, because I preferred many times to close my eyes rather than see this psychedelic light-show travesty flashing on the group. To me it was the music. The great credit due to Andy is that he recognized it. He heard music when he first saw the Velvets. He thought that they were great. So, they were great before Andy. So, they were great during Andy, and afterwards, too. Andy might have created the E.P.I. but he didn't create the sound of the band. That was always there long before Andy found them. Lou's song-concepts were avant-garde and his lyrics were avant-garde, but I don't know if his melodies without John at that point would have been avant-garde. John really put a psychedelic air to it. I thought the Velvets were ahead of everybody. It's the only thing that ever, ever, ever swept me off my feet as music since early Mahler. They were a revolution."

The E.P.I. multiplied *Up-Tight*'s audiovisual effects and aggressive power. All the elements converged anarchically into one magnificent moment of hysteria, leaving nothing to the imagination, offering everything the senses could assimilate and more. It became a big success for Warhol, who had been thinking for some time about finding a public forum to exhibit his strange creatures. Everyone in the team was paid the same: during their stay at the Dom they made $100 nightly each, from Lou and Nico to Danny Williams, Ronnie Cutrone or Mary Woronov, Gerard's new dancing partner. They carried the money in brown paper bags, and saved enough for a recording session and their first trip to California.

They were about to begin recording, but Lou was getting bored with Nico and didn't want her to sing on the album at all. She insisted on singing like Dylan, which clearly bothered the rest of the group, and she flirted with Lou and John in an attempt to get what she wanted, playing the femme fatale of the song. But they were only amused at her attempts, having fun by disconnecting her microphone just before a show. The E.P.I. played at the Dom until the end of April. Meanwhile, they had begun recording what would be their first album in a small studio on Broadway, Cameo Parkway. With the sessions came further problems, as Nico had to be coaxed or coerced out of using what Sterling calls her "Germanic, Götterdämmerung" voice. Maureen Tucker, on the other hand, had developed a strongly personal style with her drums, adding much originality and edge to the band's sound. Once, when her drums were stolen, she went out with Lou and got a garbage can to play on.

At the Dom, there was a party every night. Invited by Barbara Rubin, Allen Ginsberg showed up onstage one night and sang "Hare Krishna." Barbara was very important for the show at the beginning, but she would be fired by Morrisey when she wasn't of use anymore. During their third week at the Dom they were offered the chance to go to Los Angeles for four weeks. As the owners of the Dom were not extending the lease, they accepted, thinking they would be able to go back to the Dom after California. The last show was on April 30. They didn't know it at the time, but they would never have such a perfect location again.

5. What Would You Like to Do?

It was our first club job as the Velvet Underground, *Sterling tells me about the Cafe Bizarre gigs.* My main memory is playing "Black Angel's Death Song" in order to get fired. We played it terrifically well, it was passionate. And it got the job done. One of the surprises about the Cafe Bizarre is that somebody actually did come down to hear us, it wasn't just random people off the street. Barbara Rubin was responsible for Andy and Gerard being there. Barbara knew us from the underground film involvement and liked the kind of music we played, so she came down to the Cafe Bizarre a few times. Andy at the time was looking for a band, he had the scheme cooked up to do a total show with live music. He needed a band, but he didn't know where to look to find one or even what kind of band he was looking for, since he never pretended to know anything about music. When he saw us he decided we were right, whatever he was looking for we were it, whatever it was we were. And Gerard came down with a whip. He wasn't involved in S&M or anything, he'd been given this whip as a present, so he came in with that and was dancing on the floor with it, with quite an effect on every-body else. What is going on? Who is that person? What is he doing? It was so strange that it made a lasting impression on us. We didn't think we were in the least bit weird, because we weren't—we were college students from New York and Wales—but these people certainly were, this character with the whip. I remember Donald Lyons sat in the front row with the *New York Times* and opened it up. I remember being there playing and thinking what I would like to do is stop playing, grab that guy's newspaper, grab him. . . . It was a very studied rudeness and it was hurting my feelings. I thought we were among weird people and creeps, that being Donald Lyons, who I really do like. I don't know what he was doing with the newspaper.

Probably reading the sports pages. After the show came the introductions, and the meeting between Lou and Andy. Twin souls.

We knew Andy by reputation. Didn't know anything about him in particular, except that he was this artist. That summarized his public image at the time, he was a pop artist. He had already started to make films, and at one of the underground film showings he contributed a piece or two, which you basically couldn't look at, you know, "Eat," "Kiss" or one of these things. So I didn't know anything about him, we weren't art groupies. But then he started talking about doing the show, and that did get our interest. It was kind of what we had been doing with underground films, except this time we could come out from behind the screen. We did and we didn't, because in the context of the show, with projections, you could hardly ever see us anyway. In the show we weren't trying to get the spotlight. It wasn't the Velvet Underground up front and then all the stuff behind just as backdrop. As a matter of fact we weren't in front. We were onstage and then in front of us were the dancers—Gerard, Mary, Ronnie Cutrone—and all their props. So if there's anything to look at, you might look at them, because they were much more active and mobile than we were, or you might wanna look at the background, films, lights and all the rest. The Velvet Underground were someplace, spread out, in among the equipment, with big piles of amplifiers. You could hide behind them if you felt like. So we didn't consider ourselves the center of attraction. If the show had a star, and it wasn't Andy, it would be Gerard or someone doing something spectacular. But we played the music. Danny Fields said it was always the music, but we didn't think so. I was reading something he said recently, he said he could close his eyes when the first album is played and he's at the show, because when he was at the show he used to close his eyes and just listen to the music. But we never thought we were the main thing.

How to describe the Factory, a place where so many hours were spent and so many ideas projected?

It was a fascinating place. Everyone who was talented or famous or rich or any of the above, sooner or later would come through the Factory and you would meet them. Dali, all the art people, all the money people, movie makers and movie stars. You would sit there, on that couch, and just say hello to whoever comes by. So we were there day and night for months, that's where we were practicing, it was a great place. The only thing we had to figure out was what parties to go to and in what order. The phone would ring and we would make a note. Where would we go to eat at night, that always took some thinking, we were a lot of people. Then to sort out the options as far as all these parties were concerned. It's not an exaggeration. Andy Warhol's been invited to more parties than any hundred people put together, you can't imagine how many things he gets invited to. And so the phone would ring and ring and ring: come do this, let's do that. That's all we did, meet famous people and go to parties. Where was our great striving for success? Well, it didn't manifest itself, we had it but . . . We worked on the songs, but the people were fascinating, talented and glib, like Ondine, a very witty conversationalist. We'd just come up from Ludlow Street, where no one visited us, with good reason.

Although the first album claims it's "produced by Andy Warhol," Andy rarely did anything by himself, preferring to watch others doing it for him. What was Warhol's essential contribution to the band?

Everybody seems to wonder what the Warhol contribution might have been. Does the first album sound different from *White Light/White Heat* because it reflects Andy Warhol's thinking? Was he in the studio saying "a little bit more treble on the guitars, fatten up the bass," and all those kinds of things? But that's not what happened. He's listed as the producer not in the sense that a record producer makes a record now, but more like a film producer who just puts up the money. We went into the studio with a combination of his money and our money, money that we'd just made at the live show at the Dom. He wasn't really with us in the studio much, but he would come down. If you ever hang around a recording studio it's boring for someone not connected with the music: hour after hour goes by without anything apparently happening, futzing around with microphone placement and endless soundchecks. Our sessions were a little bit zanier I guess. He would say what he liked, his main contribution was to give us confidence. We thought that Andy Warhol was very successful and very daring, so he ought to know what we ought to do—maybe Andy could be like our manager, tell us the right thing to do and then we could just go and do it, be successful the way he is, or famous or glamorous or something. But if you asked him a straight question like what should we do, he would do give you kind of a Socratic answer: "Well, what do you think you would like to do?" That was Andy's stock advice: think about what you're trying to do and then do it. One thing you'll have to admire about Andy is that he's not constrained by any idea of what will succeed or what won't, and what will impress the public and what won't. Film making for him should have been the most disastrous undertaking imaginable: he had an incredible reputation as a painter, even if it was a controversial reputation, and all of a sudden he announces he's going to make films, not knowing the first thing about films, not even knowing how to load cameras or which end to look into. He didn't care. All his early films were condemned by critics, justifiably, but he didn't care. So that kind of rubbed off on us, at least I hope it did. The thoughts that filled the heads of the Velvet Underground weren't: How can we become a pop success? What do we have to do to get 45s played on the radio? We never thought about that. The thing was: What it is that we do? What are we doing now that we like? What are we doing now that we don't like? What is it we think we can do that will be interesting to do? And thoughts like that, which Andy kept encouraging. It's s pretty grim business to day and night have to try to calculate the way to become a pop success. Well, perhaps we need better harmonies, let's work six months on harmony. Perhaps we need to restructure this song so it has a little hook in it. People who succeed in pop music accomplish something that takes some work. You have to somehow calculate what people want and then get yourself into a position where you're able to deliver it. That's hard to do. It's easier to be the Velvet Underground or to be Patti Smith or someone like that, only worry about your own art and forget about what the audience wants or would like to see you do. That's actually easier in an odd way than to try to sell out, to determine what the pop market is looking for and then somehow manufacture yourself into that kind of commodity. Michael Jackson looked in the mirror, did not liked what he saw, disappeared for two years then came back with a mannequin face and sold millions. I think Michael Jackson is the most radical example of repackaging for the pop market. He actually invented a body, he became a different creature, few people have gone that far, and it worked.

He says this without a trace of irony, as if confessing they never planned to pursue a successful career. They were also naive: they thought that success would find them with their first record if they stayed around Warhol. The E.P.I. was, of course, a blinding experience.

The Dom was an unused, huge hall with a nice high stage, nice high ceilings and a balcony, on St. Mark's Place. A wonderful location, perfect. When we opened the place, there was no East Village, so I would credit us with inventing the East Village and so we'll deserve all the blame for whatever it turned into. St. Mark's Place only had two hip things on it: a soda shop on 2nd Avenue, which has always been there, and Kadija designs, this African girl who made dresses, which was down towards 3rd Avenue. That was it, in between there was nothing, Polish grocery stores, nothing hip. Well, there was a prestigious jazz club downstairs. But after we operated there for a while things started to change. We never had a place after that, we needed a home base and the Dom was ideal, we had all our stuff in there and had continuity. We also got involved with politics within the Polish National Organization in America. The guy who ran the Dom wanted to take over the Polish Organization and then collectively we would do something with the whole building, that was the scheme, but he was opposed by various factions and it was a great mess. If these first shows were better, it's because it was easier to do them, we had the stuff there, had our people there, endless volunteers. Anybody who wanted to do anything could do it, maybe work the spotlights or dance. That's how Ronnie Cutrone started. Who were the dancers? People who could dance, that was all. No prior experience necessary. That's how we discovered Eric Emerson. It wasn't rehearsed, it was spontaneous. It was also a good outing for Andy. But once the papers started saying that something really strange was happening at St. Mark's Place, then all the mink coat people came down to see what it was. And we went to their parties and all, they had fabulous apartments and fabulous amounts of money. They were the people who bought us paintings and who were always looking for the next thing to do. If you are very rich there's not anything to do, the main problem is boredom, so if anything different happens these people would flock to it and see if it's really true. Unless it's something so dangerously different that they can't be seen at it—I don't think they patronized the radical punk movement, because they couldn't go to the clubs, which is good in a way.

Were the Velvet Underground punks?

In a way we were, perfect punks, delinquents anyway. We were described once as refugees from a motorcycle gang. I knew a lot of motorcycle people, I was gonna make a few runs at one time, they followed us pretty closely. We never let anybody endorse our records, but we saw a lot of the Angels. But the scariest thing I ever did—well, one of them—was when we were playing Cleveland and some guy from a black motorcycle gang talked me into going down to this bar that they would hang at. The name of the gang was the Sundowners. I was so happy to get out of there alive. I figured, what can happen to me in the company of these people? These guys were huge. But when we got to the bar I started wondering, if trouble starts how many people are gonna be killed in the first minute? It wasn't the safest place for a white, regardless of who he was hanging around with, it was black motorcycle gangs and other assorted criminals. That was strange.

Unfortunately, the Dom owners forgot their agreement while the Velvets were in California. [Albert Grossman had managed to take over the

It was stolen by criminals, criminals from the Albert Grossman organization. We had a volunteer box office person who was a Grossman spy. Albert Grossman, of course, was Bob Dylan's manager, and his organization a criminal syndicate. Albert Grossman is a criminal. Bob Dylan is, by extension, a criminal for having such representation. Grossman's business dealings caused one person to commit suicide in Chicago. He's been a rat since day one. But we didn't know Charlie Rothchild worked for Grossman. The Dom show wasn't that expensive, we were charging $3 at the door, and if you were a friend of ours then you got in for free, and anybody who made a big fuss about paying got in for free. We didn't set up the show to generate as much revenue as possible, we thought we'd have some, but anybody who knew anybody got in for free. Nobody can deny this. But rather than have the whole city getting in for free, we decided we'd put a stranger in the box office, so at least the people who wanted to get in for free had to put up some kind of fuss. And that was Charlie Rothchild. And also we figured he wouldn't steal the money, I don't know why we thought that. I don't know who brought him around. Certainly it wasn't me.

How were the two girls in the band acting in the middle of all this? What does he remember about Moe and Nico?

If I knew more about Nico I could say a lot about her. She was always very mysterious to us in the band: we were not widely traveled, we were not sophisticated, we were just suburban brats, except for John. John had traveled, but didn't have any money in particular. Nico was this glamorous European model and movie star, so we didn't know quite what to make of her, except that she could sing, and I always will insist on that. She was not there just simply to stand up and be beautiful, we didn't need that, we had beautiful people dancing. I suppose we all could have used more beauty, but we didn't need it in the band, we already had it in the show. But Nico could sing, she could sing the songs that we had her do, sang them well. She got her share of ridicule from the press with her deep Germanic voice, which I always tried to get her not to sing with. She could sing high and sweet if she wanted to. But she was not always around us, she had different friends and she was off shooting commercials, here in Spain or elsewhere. She was always apart from the band, she was an addition to the band. She might have been put there by Paul Morrissey, I hear these stories, but nobody was going to force her on us, we had to accept her. And Maureen was the sister of an old friend who also went to Syracuse and also was friends with Lou, and when Angus left we had no drummer. Maureen had been playing with an all-girls band in Long Island and they broke up, and so she just came in to do a little percussion and just fool around. It was very casual and since she was willing to do different things she stayed. Maureen's very smart, she was a scholarship winner. She got a tremendous amount of heat for being the girl in the Velvet Underground: if we were degenerates, what might she be? But nothing was further from the truth. Maureen is very conventional. She had a nice apartment, the best of the bunch really, over on University Place and 9th Street, a real good place. Her boyfriends were Olympic wrestlers and that sort of thing.

6. *Night of the Zombies*

It was Charlie Rothchild who arranged the West Coast trip. In early May, a group of 14 people flew to Los Angeles and stayed at the Castle, up on the Hollywood Hills, a mansion rock bands used to rent for $500 a week. The gigs would be from the 3rd to the 28th of that month.

The Mothers of Invention, who Lou despised deeply, supported the Velvets. At the first show, the crowd included several ambassadors from the California psychedelic scene, who came out of the show with mixed feelings. Members of the Byrds, John Phillips and Mama Cass, Jim Morrison and Ryan O'Neal were seen at the E.P.I. premiere. The second night, after their set, the performers left the stage with the guitars leaning against the speakers and the amps feeding back at full blast. That same night Gerard was arrested in the middle of the street for exhibiting his whip. On the third day the police shut the whole place down. The Velvets decided to stay in town and wait for the place to solve its problems and reopen. They were encouraged by the musicians' union to stay—they were told that if they waited until the stipulated date, they would have to be paid. They spent the free time finishing the first album at T.T.G. Studios. Once finished, they sent the tapes around to a few record companies. At Atlantic, drug and sexual references weren't well received, and Elektra thought that Cale should use a less strident instrument than the viola. Finally, Tom Wilson, who had produced Dylan and Simon and Garfunkel for Columbia, encouraged them to wait until he moved to MGM, promising them absolute freedom on Verve, an MGM subsidiary. Verve was a jazz label that wanted to add some progressive music to its roster.

The truth is that Warhol and the Velvets' reputation intimidated the flower children. And there were things happening at the Castle that could feed such fears. It was said they were a bunch of sadistic homosexuals, and the whip would only confirm that. For the calm Californians, this was nothing but a bunch of New York psychopaths. In L.A. they also met Steve Sesnick, who would later become their manager and play a decisive role in their career.

At the end of May, the E.P.I. played at the Fillmore in San Francisco. There was some tension between the band and Fillmore manager Bill Graham. The audience didn't understand or love them either. San Francisco was the hippie capital of the world at the time, and a bunch of malignant germs from New York were there to infect the California dream. Ronnie Cutrone remembers the Velvets' arrogant, negative attitude toward the California scene. While other bands sent out good vibrations proclaiming the beginning of a new era of love, peace, happiness and sexual liberation, the Velvets "came out and turned their backs to the audience. I remember one review said this is musical masturbation. The Velvets were into amphetamine. They wore total black, white face. They were totally electric, extremely loud."

In early June, Nico left for Ibiza; Lou got hepatitis and was hospitalized in New York; and Andy and Paul Morrisey were busy shooting Chelsea Girls. The rest of the somewhat depleted E.P.I. entourage set out for Chicago, where they had been booked at a club called Poor Richard's. To replace Lou, Angus MacLise came back temporarily, Maureen took over bass, Sterling kept the guitar and John had to sing and play keyboard. Andy sent Brigid Polk to represent him. The local journalists felt cheated by the absence of the two singers and Warhol, but the audience loved it and so the group was held over another week. One night, Angus showed up half an hour late and found the band playing without a drummer. He joined them onstage and, when the band finished the set, he kept playing while people were leaving, as if he was in a trance, stopping only when he had made up the thirty minutes he owed.

In July, Delmore Schwartz died, alone and forgotten, consumed by alcohol and paranoia. Gerard went to the funeral with Lou, and remembers Lou didn't say a word throughout the ceremony. In August the album was ready, but Verve showed no real interest in rushing it out. The Mothers of Invention wanted their album *Freak Out!* to be released first and get all the promotion. Their manager was always bugging the record company, and he succeeded in getting the Mothers' album out first. The Velvets had no one to take care of business matters, and they themselves despised hype and were naive about anything having to do with the business side of music.

The album was being delayed and the Dom no longer existed. The owners had rented it to Albert Grossman and now it was called the Balloon Farm. The Velvets were asked to perform there on opening night, and since they had nothing better to do they accepted. During the following weeks they would decide to do nothing until the album appeared.

At the beginning of September, the E.P.I. moved to Provincetown, Massachusetts, for two shows at the Chrysler Art Museum. Everyone began to feel the side effects of regularly taken amphetamines, and this time things went over the edge. The E.P.I. was taking on an out-of-control life of its own. Eric Emerson was arrested for stealing a whip and some belts in a leather shop, and the group had some problems with the manager of the motel where they were staying: when the toilet clogged, everyone started throwing shit out the windows. Emerson did not repent and stole a piece from the museum just to prove that he could do it. Morrisey had to return it without getting caught.

Nico was now on her own. She sang at the Balloon Farm, encouraged by Paul Morrisey who saw potential in her as a solo artist. Nobody from the band helped her for these first performances. In the autumn, John and Sterling reinforced their friendship by sharing an apartment, and a short time later Lou moved to the same street. From the end of October to mid-December the E.P.I. appeared at various cities in the Midwest, the West Coast and Canada. The record still wasn't out due to delays in manufacturing. Nico continued her solo act, accompanied by Tim Buckley, young Jackson Browne or Sterling, depending on the night.

When the record finally came out in March, the E.P.I. was slowly disintegrating. Verve gave minimal promotion to *The Velvet Underground and Nico* as the songs were thought to be too abrasive and explicit for radio airplay. It was abandoned to its fate with the vain hope that Warhol's name would sell it. The E.P.I. performed its last shows at places like the Rhode Island School of Design and the Architecture School at the University of Michigan, where between sets they were complimented by a young Jim Osterberg, later to become Iggy Pop. They attempted to revive the show at The Gymnasium in New York, but it didn't work. During the last series of shows, the audience had begun to integrate itself into the happening, to the point of getting onstage and dancing. The E.P.I. had become a simple social event. It was being assimilated, its virulence digested and neutralized.

Not even the New York stations were playing the album. In protest, the band punished their own town, refusing to play in New York from the spring of '67 until the final days at Max's in 1970. Andy, Paul, Gerard and

Eric were in Cannes presenting Chelsea Girls when Sesnick offered the Velvets a gig at the Boston Tea Party. Nico initially remained in New York at the Balloon Farm, but then changed her mind and showed up on the band's second night at the Tea Party. They refused to let her onstage. The ego problems, the tensions within the E.P.I. and some massive drug use were clearly starting to have their effect.

Ronnie Cutrone confirms that Lou always felt somewhat like the leader of the band, but that Cale's musical contribution was also vital: "You couldn't duplicate the group without John, even without Moe and her garbage cans, you just couldn't. They were willing to experiment in a time when everybody was getting very studio-produced. The Beatles had stopped touring and they were the only group that I know of who were out there trying new things and making mistakes that actually sounded great—all that feed-back was hit-and-miss. There was no way you could really plan feed-back, but it was working in the music and everybody was contributing to the basic sound."

In July they played for the last time as part of Warhol's entourage. It was a benefit performance at architect Philip Johnson's Glass House in Connecticut. They shared the bill with John Cage. They then decided they were firing Andy—when told, Warhol called Lou a rat. The band then agreed to adopt Sesnick as their permanent manager.

Lou Reed remembers: "One of the things you can learn from being at the Factory is if you want to do whatever you do, then you should work very, very hard. If you don't work very hard all the time, well then nothing will happen. And Andy works as hard as anybody I know. . . . Working with him was really fantastic. We worked until the show couldn't exist anymore because it was just so expensive."

During their collaboration with Warhol, they had passed on several opportunities to go to Europe where their music would probably have been better appreciated than in the U.S. In June 1966, Warhol had been invited to take the show to Paris, and there were negotiations with Brian Epstein, the Beatles' manager, who loved the Velvets' album. He wanted to buy into their music publishing company, Three Prong Music, and organize a European tour. On one occasion Lou and Brian rode in Epstein's limousine talking about the possibility of working together. Unfortunately, Epstein died and the chance was lost.

In the summer of 1967, while Warhol was in California, Gerard in Italy and Nico with Brian Jones at the Monterey Festival, the band entered Mayfair Recording Studios in New York to start work on their second album. It was the Summer of Love, but at Mayfair the mood was terrible.

The engineer warned the band that the volume meters were in the red almost constantly, but they ignored him. They just wanted to let everything out—all the tension and bad feelings—in a record that Sterling calls orgasmic. There were arguments when it came time to select songs, because each member wanted to include the song in which they were most prominent. At the end of the two days of sessions they decided to finish the recording with a long and tortuous half-improvised piece. To avoid further discussion, they agreed to record it once and keep it however it came out. As a consequence, each member tried their hardest to outdo the others since there would be no second chance. That's how "Sister Ray" came to life, a 17-minute monster sonic cathedral.

"We never changed our method from back on Ludlow Street," explains Sterling. "We would practice the beginning and the end of a song. As we never played it the same way twice it didn't matter if we practiced the middle. If there was anything weird there then we went over that. But the songs we practiced most—the truly polished pieces—we never recorded. We knew we could do them, so there was no more interest. We wanted to see if we could make something else work. Our best stuff, about 80% of it, was either radically reworked in the studio or written there."

They still lived in New York, but Boston became their second home, thanks to the shows at the Tea Party, where they were much better understood than in their own hometown. For the first time they had an audience that came to see and hear them and not the Warhol entourage. At the same time, Nico released her first solo album, *Chelsea Girl,* with instrumental and writing help from John, Sterling and Lou. One song, the mesmerizing "It Was a Pleasure Then," was in fact a full Velvets song. In January 1968, the second Velvet Underground album, *White Light/White Heat,* came out. Even with excellent reviews, it sold less than the first album. Both Cale and Sterling call the record a technical failure.

"It was just too cool, it was the coolest thing in the world at that moment," says Ronnie Cutrone. "Nobody knew what white light was. People thought it was acid. And white heat? Nobody understood that it was an amphetamine rush that made your toes hot and made your eyes go blind and see just clear white heat. I think the words, the imagery, the subtlety of the album cover confused a lot of people."

With their second record out, the Velvets felt very assured—to some they still had an arrogant attitude, to others they seemed paranoid and vulnerable—but they remained a cult band, ignored by the radio, proud of what they had done musically yet still troubled people living on the edge. 1968 was not a very pleasant year for the band. Sesnick got them gigs from time to time—in Texas, Canada and California. They made $600 one week and $2,500 the next, their only income due to poor record sales. The pressure of life on the road increased the differences between Lou and John—an opposition that was sometimes solved through violence. Lou was the lead singer and writer, but John had charisma to burn and a genuine musical talent that couldn't fully evolve within the band. In April he married Betsey Johnson, the fashion designer who sometimes dressed the band. In June they were recording in L.A. when they heard Valerie Solanas, a radical feminist, had shot Andy Warhol. Many realized then the never-ending party was finally over.

Finally in August, with no advance notice, Lou met with Sterling and Maureen at the Village's Cafe Riviera to announce that John was no longer part of the group. Morrison was outraged, but Lou threatened to dissolve the band, forcing him to choose between his friendship with John or the future of the Velvets. It was a "him or me" situation that he still has not forgiven.

"Lou and I eventually found the group too small for the both of us, and so I left," says Cale. He was in great creative shape and his absence would substantially change the band's sound, taking away its most aggressive, disruptive elements. The Velvets would never again be what they were at the beginning—the unlikely union of two polarized talents. Cale's last performance with the band was September 28 at the Boston Tea Party. Maureen missed him the most, him and the strange figure he formed onstage with his viola.

"The relationship between Lou and John was symbiotic in a certain way," confirmed Lynne Tillman. "They were very close. They loved each other, but they also hated each other. It was competitive musically." Nat Finkelstein, on the other hand, "never knew whether John Cale wanted to be Elvis Presley, Frankenstein's creature or the young Chopin." Probably, it could be added, he wanted to be the three of them rolled into one.

7. Spying on the Enemy

The first time we went to the West Coast was an amazing experience, *says Sterling*. It's the only way I could describe it. None of us had ever been out there and we knew it was a separate world, but we weren't quite sure just how separate it might be. We liked it a lot, but it was very intimidating also, because musically the West Coast was an organized force trying to dominate the pop scene. I remember we were in a rented car going back from the airport and when I turned on the radio the first song that came out was "Monday Monday." I thought: I don't know, maybe we're not ready for that sort of thing yet, to be taking these people on, right in their own backyard. So I was worried the whole time we were out there. But we were staying up in The Castle, John Philip Law's house, which was beautiful. We were not well received, I would say that. We got good reviews, kind of interesting reviews, and then once we got to San Francisco we were attacked because they had decided we were sent out there to destroy something that was innocent and pure. Ralph Gleason said that. Unlike the simple beauty of San Francisco music, here was some urban evil from New York trying to corrupt them. But they were already corrupt, anything with Bill Graham in it can't be very innocent. We got enough bad reviews; they didn't surprise us. Knowing that we were in Mamas and Papas country, we didn't expect to fare too well. But we liked California physically, it was beautiful. We were running around with Curt Von Meier, he had a beach house in Venice—we were out there for a while. He lent me a motorcycle which I tore around on for a long time. We had great places to stay and we liked it. For us, it was an astonishing adventure because we'd never been out there, and then we were able to do some scheming on our own after we knew what we were up against. We always liked going to the West Coast, and we were generally well received afterwards. The first appearance was the most controversial. After that, people said: this is a little bit different but we still like it.

While on the West Coast they had the chance to meet some of the Californian hippie bands. The Mothers of Invention were particularly hateful, Sterling despises them almost as much as he hates Dylan.

We played with the Dead a lot of times. And the Mothers of Invention. I always hated them and Frank Zappa. We were very naive as far as business and all that cut-throat crap, and Frank Zappa and his manager Herb Cohen's machinations were part of the reason the first album wasn't getting out. Zappa is horrible. Zappa is nothing. He's never written a song. I've never heard anybody cover a Frank Zappa song, hum one, sing one, whistle one, they don't exist, just album after album of heavy handed condescending crap. Does he really think he's the only person who could read music? It's ridiculous! Zappa is a triumph of self-pro-motion. He understands something about the audience, their desire for self abasement or something. Yeah, we did play with Zappa and shouldn't have, but we did. But a good psychedelic band, whatever that means, was Quicksilver. Steppenwolf were very good, but they were not psyche-delic. And I've always liked the Byrds, but never liked David Crosby much. I always thought he was a folkie and I don't like folk singers. But McGuinn was always on such a weird level that I liked them. If I had to admit there was such a thing as folk-rock, and I guess there was, then that's The Byrds. Very good band. And most of their problem was David Crosby, once they got rid of him, then I really liked them, like *Notorious Byrd Brothers,* that's my favorite album. Gram Parsons I never cared one way or the other, he's okay, but Crosby in that cape or whatever the hell he's wearing, get him out of here! On the other hand, I didn't think too much about Buffalo Springfield, it was soft and pretty and well performed. I met them at the Tropicana. I liked Dewey Martin, the drummer. I used to talk to him and Bruce Palmer. He was ordered out of the country, then crept back illegally and was thrown out the second time for drug problems.

After California, they went to Chicago—to a club called Poor Richard's—a city that saw one of The Velvet Underground's rarest incarnations.

We played the Poor Richard's concerts in the summer of '66, after we came back from California. As usual, we came back in disarray. Lou had hepatitis so he headed off to the hospital, and Nico had a modeling assignment and went to Spain. Andy decided he had something else to do also, and nobody felt like going to Chicago after the West Coast, but then it turned out that we had to do it for some reason. There had been some kind of agreement made so we had to go to Chicago—without Lou, without Andy, who still refused to go, and without Nico. We played for a week, with all different versions of the songs, with John on vocals, and we did lots of practicing just to make the songs work. It was fun. That was the first time that we ever played with people missing, and after that anybody could be missing and the shows would go on—John or Lou or anybody, it didn't matter. We had already demonstrated that we could do it. If John could sing, there was no demonstration of it before then. I figured he could, but he had such a strange voice, you could hardly sing harmony to it. He sang in Chicago, which did incredible things to Lou's paranoia. Without Andy, Nico or Lou, I thought this was doomed, that only idiots and drug addicts would do something like that. We had no Lou, we moved Maureen to bass and rhythm guitar. We got Angus MacLise, the original drummer, back to play drums. So here's this astonishing incarnation of the band. "Sister Ray" grew out of this one gig. How did we succeed? By the virtue of hard work, which the Velvet Underground had not been known to do. We had no choice. We had to rehearse all the songs, John had to practice singing. The solution was: John stays on keyboards completely. This all had to be determined on the spot. We didn't know what we were gonna do. How exactly are these songs to be played? But we came up with real good versions of them. We had to show up at eleven o'clock in the morning and rehearse the whole day. The times we ever did get together and think, we always did well. John and I had to figure out how to do all these songs. We had to do "Venus in Furs" and "Heroin" without the viola, that was a major problem. It was a pretty carefree summer gig. It also set the record in the Midwest as the hottest two weeks in history. Poor Richard's was the hottest place in the world. When I stood there on stage—all you could wear was t-shirts and there was no air conditioning—just tuning up there'd be a circle of sweat on the floor that ran off my elbows. That's before I started to play. If John wanted to do kind of real good bass stuff on the keyboard, like Ray Manzarek, then we did. Otherwise we had Maureen playing bass. On "All Tomorrow's Parties" Maureen played guitar, which she could do. She had played guitar in that all-girls band. She can play rhythm, no problem. And I had a variety of guitars. That was an interesting gig, but Lou meanwhile was languishing in the hospital with hepatitis. Did anybody call him from Chicago? No. Before we left and after we got back, did anybody go down there and visit him and wish him well? No. I don't like hospitals. If you are in a hospital that means you must be dying, so you don't wanna see me.

Some time later, they decided, out of arrogance not to play New York City. A weird decision for a band whose legend was tied to Manhattan.

About that time, our first album came out. We thought that if you made records you got played on the radio, that seemed to be a reasonable assumption. But when our record came out it wasn't played on the radio, except for listener sponsored radio—which was kind of radical—and then after a while they wouldn't play it because we refused to play a drug benefit. So then nobody was playing it in New York, even if it was being played on the West Coast. Then came the new FM stations, who had previously been all classical music and a little bit of jazz. And when New York opened their FM stations, naturally they opened them up without the Velvet Underground. FM rock and roll stations elsewhere did play us, New York did not. And they wouldn't accept advertising either, so that enraged us. We just took that attitude as typical of the place and that was it, we didn't play anymore, even if that was the largest market in the United States and our home base. We decided we were not going to play New York, so we didn't. This is my hometown! So we said: screw you! We played in Boston, we played in Philadelphia. We played a few private things that nobody could get to, but that was the extent of it for about three years. We played Lincoln Center once, Brooklyn Academy of Music and Stavros Niarchos show at Four Way. They paid us $3,500 to do that, sixties money, but I don't even remember playing at all, I was mostly standing there, faking it. Lincoln Center was nice, but it was something we believed in and wanted to do—it was Channel 13, which is national educational television, and in New York that was like the flagship station and they were celebrating their first year. It's the same station that had run a Warhol special two years before that. When all the fuss was being made, when the Fillmore East was open, we were the only band I know that never played the Fillmore East. There were two reasons for not playing it: it was in New York, that was one reason, and the other was Bill Graham, a big second reason. He used to call us up and scream and swear at us for not playing there. He'd call us and say: "You have to play there." We said: "No, hardly do we have to play the Fillmore East." Then he would start this obscene tirade about why we had to. We didn't have to, and we didn't. No kidding: I think we are the only band touring around in the sixties that didn't play the Fillmore East at least once. I've never even been in the place, I wouldn't go in it because of Graham. We meant business, we meant what we said. It wasn't a publicized thing, nobody read in the papers: The Velvet Underground refuses to play New York City. The people who knew us, knew why. It had an odd effect on my friends, because I would say we were doing pretty well, but they had no experience of it. They weren't hearing the records on the radio, they weren't hearing us play, so all they knew is that I would leave town and come back after a while. They really didn't know what the band was doing, unless they traveled out of New York, then they would find out we were making some headway. In '68 and '69 we had a pretty good reputation, maybe not in Europe, there were not many Europeans that knew about us, except in England and Germany. We never thought that it made sense to tour Europe, which we didn't consider a major market. That was pretty shallow thinking. We were interested in California and

Indiana, Ohio and Arizona, those were foreign countries as far as we were concerned. Who knows what those people did? You could speak to them, sort of, but that's about it.

To what extent was White Light/White Heat a technical failure?

White Light/White Heat was a real frustration, because we wanted to do something electronic and energetic. We had the energy and we had the electronics, what we didn't take into account was whether it could be recorded. If we went into a studio now and did *White Light/White Heat,* it would work, because they have the equipment—then they didn't, so there's incredible leakage from track to track. There were ways we could have done it, if we had all played individually, but we didn't like to, we liked to play simultaneously and used voice over live a lot of times. We didn't know the album was doomed until we actually mixed it down, because we would do the tracks and then you'd listen to them, track by track, and they sounded good, so you kept on going. The big surprise comes when you mix it down and then try to do a pressing. There's all this distortion and all sorts of fuzzing and compression and all this leakage, a lot of white noise. There was so much commotion in the tracks that even the gain had to be reduced for the stylus when they cut it. The quiet things are kind of okay, but the major electronic efforts—"I Heard Her Call My Name" and "Sister Ray"—are not. "Sister Ray" succeeds because I don't think anybody can perceive it in any way other than it is, but we intended it to be a lot cleaner and crisper, so even that was a disappointment. We were happy that something like that was on the record, but for the whole album we anticipated a much better sound, something that would just fly out at you, and that didn't happen. In fact all our efforts to make it happen were ironic, it made just the opposite happen: the louder we played in the studio, the quieter they had to do the mastering. Nobody was pleased with that, but there was nothing to be done. We didn't wanna discard everything, it wasn't that the studio time had been so expensive, we could have gone back and done the whole album over, but we wouldn't have gained anything. We just learned our lesson. But it was a good time for us in the band. The songs were great live. We liked the material, so in that sense it was a success. It's just our record-ed version didn't quite do what we wanted. Still though, as a record, it has its own little place in the rock pantheon. It did accomplish some-thing, maybe warned other groups: avoid these excesses. I'm not embarrassed by it, I just wish it could have come out a whole lot better. And I like the songs.

Without Nico, without Andy, the band went back to the original line up: Lou, John, Sterling and Moe. But John's days with the Velvet Underground were numbered.

Right after the album came out, we were having good times in the band, so that's why it was so strange that Lou wanted John out. I don't remember any reason really being given, it was some general statement that he couldn't stand playing with John anymore for umpteen inexpressible reasons. I always had my own weird interpretations. I don't recall Lou ever giving an exact reason for not wanting John there. John was playing great, so it had nothing to do with him falling down musically. His personal habits were commendable, he was running around with Betsey Johnson, was very well dressed and responsible, so he was doing fine, a true story of the successful rehabilitation of a classical musician. So I don't know, maybe Lou got jealous. I would attribute it to something like that. Not that John was easy to work with, but was Lou? Was I? Maureen was pretty easy, she decided that we were crazy and there wasn't room for one more, so she would just watch it work itself out, occasionally getting her sarcasm in there too—Maureen is sharp tongued. So just to say John was hard to work with, it wasn't that. I can remember one incident which was truly ridiculous. We were playing in a big place in Chicago, The Kinetic Circus, a beautiful place, fantastic. It had a big sound room that came down from the ceiling and they made multitrack tapes of every note played there. So we had good tapes of that place, but then it burned down in one of those Mafia fires. We were playing in this place, we were playing "Pale Blue Eyes," which is a quiet song, and I'm playing the solo, which is also quiet, and John is over here some place. And in the middle of the solo he steps on the button that kicks on my distorter, and it's a Vox distorter, so in this sweet little solo all of a sudden there's this blast of sound, distorted and three times louder than all the rest of it. John looks at me like I'm crazy, turns off the distorter and then kicks it! I just looked over at Lou and thought, well, okay, that's John. It was funny. If I had done that to him, he would have had a stroke. But there wasn't any greater or lesser friction in the band. I was in the Cale faction. John was my roommate on the road and as often as not in Manhattan. After he was kicked out of the band I was still hanging around with John. That whole business speaks very badly for me, because I should have quit or at least I should have called the bluff. This was Lou's scheme and he gets the blame for it, but I get the blame for complicity. I thought it was much easier to go along being the Velvet Underground than being nothing by siding with John. He wanted me to play on "Church of Anthrax" but we were out of town. I don't think I displayed good character in all of that, in fact I didn't. As Maureen would say, I was at my persuasive best, but I couldn't convince Lou. To me, all of it had a kind of unreal quality to it, it was like discussing your own funeral arrangements, you think it's never gonna happen.

Maybe it was because of musical differences, the easy excuse most bands give for unavoidable, explosive ego conflicts.

We had musical differences from the first minute we were in a room together, but that made the band good. If everybody has the same ideas all the time, then you have one idea, but if you have three ideas that fight for dominance, that's a dynamic process. That's what The Velvet Underground was. Even if we were selfish and stupid, the thing that you were trying to do, the ways in which it got resisted, made whatever came out of it something pretty good. So that was the way the band got to work, and that's why it did work, but it's an abrasive process, not simple. Also we didn't have a manager to tell us what to do, in fact nobody could tell us what to do, so we had to argue it out. Or test it out—a lot of things got tested on stage. If it was disastrous, then we didn't try it again. John that summer in fact was playing great. He was going out with Betsey, he was given all these snazzy clothes, fashion-wise he was ahead of everybody. Like that martial military uniform he wore on the *White Light/White Heat* promo shots. There was a project that failed, and Lou used that as a technical reason. We had just signed an endorsement with Acoustic, so we had terrific amps and equipment. But John decided he did not want their bass amp, which worked great. Instead, he wanted to buy a component amp, with some kind of phase linear amp, and we were paying for it. We had free stuff that we knew worked great, but we had to pay for this project. One of our problems on stage live was getting enough bottom, it was a problem for all bands then because the bass amp technology wasn't as good. But he said no. He took money out of the general coffers and got his phase linear amp. Then he got somebody to build him boxes—he had at least twelve acoustical suspension speakers, they were in sealed boxes. We didn't wanna know about all this. The only thing we knew were the checks, $1,000 here, $500 there. It cost us thousands to build this goddamn thing! The equipment managers were against it—who wanted to move it? So everybody was opposed to it. And then when it's done, it doesn't work. It didn't work well and John insisted on persisting to use it. He is stubborn, and he thought it could be perfected, he figured that ultimately it would work. That was one thing even I disapproved. I said fine, a good idea is a good idea only if it works, but this one didn't. So that was an irritation, but that's about the only quirky thing he did. Except he was leaning more maybe in an experimental direction, and Lou was maybe more in a pop direction. Lou always wanted to get there if he could, he only had to figure out how. It's tough to be a pop success.

8. On the Road

Doug Yule, a Bostonian who played in a local band called Glass Menagerie, took John Cale's place. The band knew him beforehand, as Sterling used to stay at the apartment where he lived when the Velvets played in Boston. Doug joined the band one Wednesday at Max's Kansas City. They rehearsed with their new bass player until Friday, and his first performance with the band was that weekend at La Cave in Cleveland, on October 2. From the 18th to the 20th of that same month they played the Avalon Ballroom in San Francisco. In November they started the recording sessions for the third album at T.T.G. Studios, now Sunset Highland Sound, on L.A.'s world famous Sunset Boulevard.

Yule fit in well with the band. Lou accepted him with no problems. They were playing at the Whiskey in L.A. while recording, and Doug had to sing a few songs because Lou's voice was quickly wasted. Lou confesses he probably demanded too much of a newcomer who probably didn't understand a word of what he was singing.

The Velvet Underground, their third album, was finished in a relaxed atmosphere of creativity. This time there were no manifestations of violence or wildness in the lyrics or the sound. Sterling was mainly silent after Cale's departure—the new songs didn't seem to inspire him as much as the previous ones. From the 12th to the 14th of December they were back at the Boston Tea Party, sharing the stage with the MC5.

At the beginning of 1969, the Velvets were a quite different band. As Danny Fields put it: "After the glamour died down it was Lou Reed and a back-up band. It was like any other rock group on the road." Anyone who had seen them in the E.P.I. was probably surprised at their basic, yet very personal rock and roll. They were not a weird creature any more, but one that pretended to act normally. Following the advice of Sesnick, they adopted a more subtle character and, in compensation for their change of attitude, they were boosted from Verve up to the MGM label. The record company also took charge of some of the touring expenses.

According to Maureen, this help was minimal and it was only thanks to live performances that they survived. On the other hand, in some places like St. Louis they got crowds of 2,000 people, even though the album wasn't available in stores. In any case, they still knew what they wanted on a musical level, and even with the lack of promotion and distribution, the audience reaction was very positive. "Their charisma was so strong that no matter what they did it was accepted," says Steve Sesnick.

The third record came out in March. The picture on the cover, a dark photo taken at the Factory, reflected the transformation: they're sitting on the legendary couch, Maureen and Doug looking at Lou, Sterling staring off elsewhere. Reviews were very good, noting the new sound—a kind of very special urban folk-rock—and the chance they had to be accepted by a wider audience. For the next six months they would play almost every weekend, returning to New York after each trip. They traveled through the South and the West including California, Oregon and Canada. Sometimes they spent whole weeks on the road, performing in small clubs like the End of Cole Avenue in Dallas or the Matrix in San Francisco, where the tapes that later became the double album *1969 Live* were recorded. They showed no interest in playing cities where they were unknown and their music would not be understood, so they only packed their bags when they were assured of a receptive audience.

The record company didn't know what to do with them; they were the first rock act that wasn't interested in quick cash. This attitude had its disadvantages, and some days they only had a couple of dollars apiece for food. The signs of demoralization began to show—it was painful to realize that the lack of record distribution was greatly limiting their chances of success. At the end of the year they started negotiations to leave MGM, with no hassles since they didn't sell enough records to keep the label's interest. Sesnick was also discussing the possibility of working with Atlantic Records' Ahmet Ertegun. During 1969 they had recorded demos for a fourth LP—the idea was to record new songs that they were convinced MGM wouldn't accept, then re-record them for their first Atlantic album.

The negotiations with Ertegun came to a good end at the beginning of 1970. He admired their music and independence, and set only one condition: no songs with strong emotions. As a consequence, "Heroin" was dropped from their live shows. The transition from one company to the other was quick. MGM still had the tapes for the fourth album and it has been speculated that those were the same tracks that would surface as the *V.U.* album 15 years later. But Sterling says the stuff on the fine *V.U.* collection is not the material from the lost album. They had recorded some songs on the West Coast and mailed the tapes to New York, but they never arrived and so the ghost album remains lost, probably forever.

In the spring of 1970 Maureen got pregnant and had to leave her place in the band. Around mid-June, the group finally forgave New York City and made their first official appearance in New York since the last days of the E.P.I. Sesnick arranged a ten week, Wednesdays to Sundays residency for them at Max's Kansas City. They were the first band to play at Max's, Mickey Ruskin's club-restaurant which was soon to become New York's hip musical hangout. Billy Yule, Doug's brother, took Maureen's spot on the drums.

Max's was a very popular club, and their old friends and new followers gathered upstairs for their sets. The band felt at home. Meanwhile, they began recording *Loaded,* putting to tape the basic, soulful rock and roll the band had been conjuring with as much enthusiasm and confidence as the experiments of the early days. Maureen went to visit them at the studio and also at Max's. She doesn't remember perceiving anything to indicate that the end was near. As Sterling tells it, Lou was in one of his paranoid periods. He slept very few hours and pretended that Sesnick protected him from people of the past whom he didn't want to see.

Doug had entered the band with no ambitions—Lou often presented him on stage as his brother—but was impelled by Sesnick to take center stage and control the group, guiding what might be their last chance at pop success. Sterling, who was finishing his studies and had already inquired about teaching positions at various universities, was colder than usual to Lou. He didn't feel like taking part in the band's affairs. And Lou, under pressure from his parents, who had never completely lost control over their son, ended up just getting tired. He hated playing at Max's because Sesnick was pressuring them to be more dynamic and friendly onstage. He had never before done something he didn't believe in, and felt he was doing it now.

That made him sick: "I'm not a machine that gets up there and parrots off these songs. And I was giving out interviews at the time saying yes, I wanted the group to be a dance band, I wanted to do that, but there was a large part of me that wanted to do something else. I was talking as if I were programmed. That part of me that wanted to do something else wasn't allowed to express itself, in fact was being canceled out. And it turned out that that was the part that made up ninety percent of Lou. But the last night I was there, when Brigid Polk made her tape, that was the only night I really enjoyed myself."

Sterling wasn't of much help. He had quit smoking and taking drugs, and had organized his life. Performing at night and working on the album increased the already existing pressures. They all felt weary from this routine: Lou seemed puzzled by Doug and Sesnick's ideas about trying to make a hit record, and the three of them spent long hours discussing songs, recording different versions. On the other hand, Sesnick was continuously pushing Lou to be less laconic on stage, something that was contrary to his moody personality.

The music business in general was suffering some remarkable changes. Places with medium capacity like the Boston Tea Party and the Avalon Ballroom were closing down, and the Velvets found themselves having to choose between playing small clubs that couldn't afford to pay them the necessary amount or getting into bigger places and being forced to adopt a large stage show, something they had already left behind after Warhol. They could have come up with a bigger, more spectacular version of the E.P.I. and taken it around the country, but they had no financing and didn't like the idea of theatrical rock shows.

"The ambiance at Max's during the Velvets gig was one of intimacy," says Danny Fields. "As it turned out as soon as the gig was over the next day they broke up and you realized that was it, because you knew Lou wasn't coming back. Suddenly there was no one left. For us it was always Lou Reed. But I think that must have been the general feeling as well because he was the one. It didn't end when Andy or Nico or John left. It ended when he left."

Two days after their last Max's set, Sesnick told Sterling Lou had left. Maureen had had a premonition when they rehearsed with Doug in 1968. Her feminine intuition and the way Lou accepted Doug into the band, always telling him that he was a fine musician, made her fear the worst: "I sensed it somehow, and I said to myself, 'Holy shit! Take it easy, Lou, you're going to blow up this guy's head and we're going to have problems.'"

Without the presence of their engine, the Velvets kept playing for a while. Yule recruited a Boston bass player named Walter Powers and began touring with the intention of promoting *Loaded*, which came out in September on Cotillion, a subsidiary of Atlantic. In spite of the tensions surrounding the recording and the dispute over the final mix, which according to Lou was ruined by Yule and Sesnick, the critics praised *Loaded*. The ironies of life: without Lou, and with an album much different from the original concept of the band, the Velvets were finally accepted. To Lou, back with his parents, this was obviously deeply painful.

Sterling quit a year later, when the University of Texas answered his job inquiries. The band was performing in Austin, and he called and was told he was hired. He didn't mention it until the band got to the airport, but the next Monday he was working as a teacher. While he was starting his first classes and trying to assimilate his past (something he had to do in order to inspire his students to discover the pleasures of literature), Doug Yule hired Willie Alexander in Boston to replace him. With this bastard line-up the band toured Europe for the first time, with only Moe as an original member. Yule would go as far as recording a solo album, *Squeeze,* credited to the band. Its release in 1973 was a postmortem insult to a band that never accepted short cuts and never bowed to external advice or commercial pressure.

"It was a process of elimination from the start," Lou clarifies. "First no more Andy, then no more Nico, then no more John, then no more Velvet Underground."

9. Sweet Rock'n'roll

Doug Yule was a friend of ours from Boston, *Sterling tells me*. He wasn't exactly a friend, we just knew him. Our road manager at the time, Hans Onsager, had invested money unsuccessfully in a band that Doug was in, so when John was out we needed somebody that we kind of knew. I kind of knew Doug because he stayed at a place I used to stay at fairly often, and so we just said let's do it. Ideally a band should never change members, you shouldn't have to worry about such things. We never had auditions, but just said: Dougie, we know you can play so let's go if you want. He said yeah, and we did. Doug can play, he's a good guy. The only problem with Doug was . . . he was not John.

The change definitely upset the balance—or [the] creatively positive lack of it—within the band. Indeed Yule was not Cale. He was just another young rock musician able to do the job. His first work with the Velvets, the third album, lacks the madness and raw feel of the first two records.

Was the third album a stunned reaction to the second? Since electronic madness had done us in on the second album, should we forsake electronics on the third and go back to something that we could manage?

An odd incident preceded the third album in that all our electronic gizmos, that were stored and carried around in ammunition boxes, were stolen at the airport when we were on our way to the West Coast to do the album, so all our electronic bag of tricks had evaporated. Rather than try to replace them we thought about what we could do without them. We never made fixed plans about what we would do in the studio. We knew we were going to play some songs in the studio, we didn't know which they would be, and there was never any way to tell. We would do what we felt like doing on a particular night. I think our mood overall when we were doing the third album was subdued for some reason or other, maybe because of the Cale thing. We were just subdued—I was—and so we made that kind of record, even if not by design, that's the way it came out. We could have been fired up and ready to do something crazy, but we never were, just night after night we were sort of in that same mood.

Without Cale, playing live was also a different experience. The band did not lose all its power, as the bootlegs from that period show, but the confrontation between the two heads was gone. The sound was still fierce, but now the monster was running in one direction.

It was another kind of experience. It was easier in that there was only music to worry about. It was portable, it was lonelier. But then we discovered that a lot of the people we knew and liked were, for some reason or other, in the places that we played. There would always be somebody that would cheer us up, more in California or Texas than in Columbus, Ohio. Somebody unpredictably would be there. I had started to have fun playing I guess around the summer of '67, around the *White Light/White Heat* summer, and through '68. With no John, I had less fun after that. It was still enjoyable, but not quite the same. The first year playing with The Velvet Underground was not fun, because the music was so weird and so ill received. It's very hard to play for people that have no advance idea of what to expect—and then when they hear it, they don't like it. This kind of wears on you, that's why I wasn't too eager to go play, why bother? The Dom shows were fun, but getting out on the road wasn't. Whatever fun we had was among ourselves, in the entourage, the musical experience was not fun, not in the sense that the audience is sustaining you with love and affection. We were totally sealed in ourselves, we played the songs because we were playing for ourselves. We wanted to hear them, they didn't. They didn't

know us, because they hadn't heard anything. They were attracted by
Warhol's name or by the idea that we were something avant-garde from
New York. It was strange. But once people started to know what we
were doing, and came deliberately to hear it, then we started getting
interested in the audience per se, someone not to play at but to play to,
or for.

*These small clubs, usually in remote parts of the country, led the Velvets
into a phase of total dedication to a basic and dynamic rock'n'roll represented officially in the Live 1969 double album. Sterling still dislikes
that set, which was released without his approval in 1974. According to
him, it was a trick pulled by Lou to cover the commercial failure of his
solo record Berlin. To make the point stronger, he mentions what he
recalls as the best show ever by the band.*

I didn't like *1969 Live* because all the tracks are from small clubs. That
gives you a very good idea of what we sounded like in a small club, but
it's very subdued, there's no rough edges because the volumes are turned
way down. Part of that was our problem, all we had was big amps, real
big. Those things would put out a lot of sound. Terrific power amps,
wonderful, I wish I had mine now, I'd use it for my hi-fi. The Boston
Tea Party was a pretty good sized club, our favorite size, something that
would hold about 1,200. We could play there for real, but in small
clubs it was all subdued. On the *1969 Live* album at least you get to
hear a lot of songs clearly, but I wish some of the stuff had been recorded at the bigger clubs we played on that tour. We played Austin, Texas,
and I know terrific recordings were made of that but they never
appeared. That stuff was well, well recorded, and it was a good show.
We also did a four track tape when we played with Quicksilver. We did
the show and then went to a party, and Lou and I and John Cipollina
were sitting on this couch. I'm sitting there and I heard Quicksilver—
that had played first—and it was fabulous. So then I hear us tuning up
and I said to Lou: Well, I think I'm getting out of here! I didn't want us
sounding terrible compared to Quicksilver, and I figured we had to
sound terrible compared to them, because I'd just heard how great they
had sounded. Cipollina is a real good guitar player. After tuning, we
started with "Waiting for the Man" and it didn't sound so bad, so I
stuck around. Then came "Sweet Rock and Roll." That was the first
time Lester Bangs heard us, before he was a critic. He was talking the
rest of his life about "Sweet Rock and Roll," which was never recorded

and never played again. We wanted that tape, it sounded so great, so there was no point in recording it. I suppose we did it a time or two after that, but it was nothing compared to this first one. I remember the chords and some words: "Sweet rock'n'roll is good to your soul . . .". We used that as a preamble to "Sister Ray," it kind of just goes along and then hits the chords, which were very heavy. It was good. It was heavy, serious. Cale played keyboard on "Sweet Rock and Roll," and that was really what carried it. Good keyboards.

The recording sessions for Loaded were the backdrop for the denounced conspiracy that ended Lou's involvement with the Velvets. Playing at Max's and recording at the same time wasn't good for the band. It intensified the problems and accelerated the end.

Lou says Sesnick was on his case to do this and that. Lou may have felt that we'd done too much to wind up just sort of playing in a club in Manhattan, which I felt too. I would have been willing at any moment to say: Let's stop doing it, let's not play here at Max's. It was a problem for us: exactly how do you play live. You have to play clubs or else you play these big amphitheaters where you need laser lights and smoke bombs, stuff we didn't care about. But Lou never told me he was leaving or he had left, I heard that from Sesnick. What I could see in the cards was that if all of a sudden I'd decided out of the blue to finish my degree, I must not have thought there was much in the way of a musical future. I was pretty bored and depressed. We were gonna do the *Loaded* album and then fool around at Max's. I was against it. I really didn't particularly want to do it, it was hell on me having to play and go to school. We weren't being paid anything in particular, how could we be? The place wouldn't fit anybody much. I liked Mickey Ruskin, so I liked being able to do it for Mickey: our first official date back in Manhattan in three and a half years, for a person we truly do like. But I knew it was gonna hurt Lou's voice, which it did, making it impossible for him to sing on half of the songs on the album. That's not desirable, that's stupid, no excuse for it. Just things like that. I'm sure I said something, like this is stupid, and probably got the reply from Sesnick, something like "don't be negative, just go read your books and mind your own business." I said alright, but it was stupid. The album came out okay, as far as production it's the best, but it would have been better if it had real good Lou vocals on all the tracks. The *1969 Live* album at least indicates what he could do, vocally that's better than anything on

Loaded. Max's was my clubhouse—a place to hang out—and not well suited for the band, as usual. It was small, we were playing too loud for the size of the place. I didn't like that, but I liked the fact it was so easy. We weren't used to playing in New York, but I was actually playing music without the big hassle of being on the road. I used to come back and forth to Max's by bicycle and leave it locked up in the office. Also I was in summer school, in City College, and that reminded me of when we had just started out, I was at City College then and playing in the Village. But there wasn't any particular weirdness, and if there was it wasn't on account of me. I was too busy with other things to get involved, I didn't even hang around between shows. I had to read books in the dressing room, I was reading all these Victorian novels. And I didn't have anything to say to Lou, I was mad at him for something. I was there and when it came time to play I'd come down from wherever I was, play and then go back.

The Max's gigs were documented on Live At Max's Kansas City, the first officially released bootleg.

We signed a two record deal with Atlantic, so we delivered them *Loaded,* which is a very good album. Jerry Wexler liked it, King Curtis, everybody liked it. I liked it, Lou liked it while we were making it, track by track we were very happy with what was happening. That record won us the Edison award in 71, that thing in Amsterdam, as best rock and roll album. Anyway, we had the album made and then we were horrified about the fact that they weren't making it available. It was getting airplay and still not in the stores. We were so furious with Ahmet that, when he said we should go out on the road, we told him to start the promotion and distribution first, then we will tour. He said: "No, you play and I'll do this." It was chicken and the egg. So we went skiing and did that the whole winter, that's where that picture from the Alpine comes from. We played a little bit on weekends in return for money and free board and room and free lift passes. That was a real good time. Meanwhile Ahmet is in New York raging. And we were mad too, we had this great album that was going no place because it wasn't being pushed or distributed. Worse than MGM, which we never would have thought possible. Comes time to make the second album, so we tell Ahmet we don't like what happened with *Loaded* and we're not gonna record a second album. We were just not gonna do it. So Ahmet comes back a week or two later and he says he's bought this tape—from Brigid

Polk, for $2,000—of one of our performances at Max's. I said: "Hell no, it's something done on a cassette recorder!" He claimed he was going to release that tape as our second album unless we got all our asses in the studio and made one. I never thought he would do, so we said that if he was crazy enough to release a cassette tape as an album he should go ahead. And he released it! That record should only be understood as an attempt by Ahmet Ertegun to punish us. Atlantic did not release it because it was good, they released it because they wanted to screw us for not wanting to go back to the studio. That constituted the second album and we avoided breach of contract, which was the club that Ahmet was holding over our heads. But that's never an album I've taken pride in, if I want to hear rotten sounding tapes there's enough of those around. Generally I thought we played really well at Max's—when I was playing, I was playing. It was a great relief to be doing that instead of reading Victorian novels.

As they say, record companies mean business . . .

All the fun and all the energy was in one place in the late seventies. It was good, it was great. There might have been some self destructiveness in the movement, but I think mostly they were screwed by the record companies. When we signed to Atlantic, we asked Ahmet Ertegun, who's had everybody under contract to Atlantic and all its subsidiary labels, who was his favorite. "Iron Butterfly," he said. "'In-A-Gadda-Da-Vida.' Ten and a half million units!" I said: "Get me out of here, why am I talking to this man?" Ahmet Ertegun had Aretha Franklin, the most incredible soul artist that ever was, but he said Iron Butterfly, ten and a half million. That's it, that's all you need to know about record companies. Even some-one like Ahmet, who signed all these black people, is like that. I thought he had somewhere some feeling for blues and rhythm and blues, but he had stronger feelings for the bottom line: cash. What the hell is Iron Butterfly even doing on Atlantic? That was the mystery to me.

Two days after leaving the band, Lou suggested to Sterling they start a new band from scratch, the two of them, without Yule or Sesnick. It would be interesting to see what that new start would have brought, but it never happened.

Lou suggested after he left that he and I pick it up and start all over with a different manager, get back to the way it was at the beginning.

But the way it was at the beginning wasn't going to include Cale, we weren't going that far back apparently. I don't know why I didn't do it, an interesting decision. I was pretty sour on pop music in general at the time, and I was mad at Lou for who knows what, but I hadn't been very friendly to him for the preceding couple of months. And Lou at the time accepted responsibility for that, he said it was his fault because he was on these crazy diets. I don't know, I just didn't. I had already thought that perhaps we had accomplished enough—to start all over would be like rolling the rock up hill again. One of the lines I used to Lou, I guess I was trying to tell him not to leave, was that even if we did do it, that it would take us three years to get back to the point that we were at the minute we were talking. And there was no certainty that we would do it anyway. I had kind of decided to go back to school, get away, I was pretty disillusioned. And I might have been right, it took Lou a long, long time to get back anywhere near where the band was. More than three years, all the way to *Transformer*. Since we didn't get very much airplay—we were usually banned from the radio—and we got no record company promotion, The Velvet Underground was a well kept secret, even in the U.S. All they could write about us was in the magazines, and not the musical magazines. We'd be in the society gossip pages, or we would pop up in the weirdest places. Do you know *The New Yorker* and how snobbish that is? Their column "Talk of the Town"? They once had this story about Gian-Carlo Menotti trying to raise money so the Velvet Underground could go to the Spoleto festival, that jazz and contemporary music festival in Italy. And they went on and on about what sinister creatures the Velvet Underground were, based on what they knew from what they heard about New York. We were a secret, we had a little crowd of friends, our little circle in New York, and we were happy there. I didn't care if we went to Ohio, I didn't wanna tour the world, I didn't even wanna tour the States. I was content to sit in Manhattan amusing myself with some very amusing people. Was I lazy? Paul Morrisey said that we were lazy or crazy or whatever, that he never could understand why we just didn't seem to want to do anything. But we did do things, we wrote songs and what-not. We never wanted to go on promotional tours. To promote what? Records that nobody's heard? So it just took a while for people to hear us. No record company made our records available, at least have them in the stores. That was not done well. We said: "Don't push them, just distribute them." When we were going around with *Loaded,* record store people were screaming that it was not available. They couldn't get them. I guess they had their reasons. We never wanted a big promotion out of the record company—I hate that kind of hyping, lying stupidity, the way they market these records. Everybody gets marketed that way, it's embarrassing. Just put the records in the stores and let word of mouth take care of the sales, but they didn't even do that.

10. Trapped in the Present

I have to make the most of the time left. Tomorrow Sterling is flying back to Houston and from there driving to Austin, Texas. He's going back home. The ten days spent in Barcelona have flown away, but we have had enough time to get to the bottom line about the Velvet Underground, almost always of Sterling's own will. Whether we were in the shady atmosphere of a club, the television studio where he overdubbed guitar on a Cale performance of "Waiting for the Man," having breakfast at his downtown hotel or in a rented car en route to Cadaques, the small beach town where Salvador Dali lived, he was always willing to tell me anything I wanted to know about the band. And I never stopped asking questions. For instance, what was the band's main contribution to the history and evolution of rock?

That's a hard question. Somebody credited us with officially introducing S&M into rock music, but that kind of happened peripherally, it was not a central contribution. I think we kind of showed that you could influence pop music by not exactly being in pop music. Maybe our main contribution was that . . . that even if we were operating outside of it, on the fringes, we were still able to affect what happened at the remotest points. I don't think we affected Herman's Hermits, but anything that's peripheral like that I guess takes a long time to have some kind of ripple effect into the middle. We are more influential now than when we were playing, because when we were playing not that many people got to hear us. I think the Velvet Underground encourages people to do what they feel like doing, use whatever instruments they feel like using, play whatever songs they feel like playing. And also, as I've said, the music it's not preachy, and that makes it bearable over the years. And it's not topical, there's nothing newsy about it. "I'm Sticking with You" has some vague references to Vietnam, but that's all pretty remote. When we mentioned Vietnam we didn't mention anything about get in or get out, win, lose or surrender—just as usual it was just a statement of fact, this is what's going on. So maybe some people would learn from the songwriting that you could just describe what you think, what you feel, what you perceive, and maybe it could be interesting. Some of our songs are pretty goofy, but some of it is intended to be funny. Musically you maybe could listen to the kind of minimal arrangement and over-dubbing, minimal use of studio effects—that might be admirable. If we went into a studio now I don't know precisely what we would do. We would have 32 tracks to begin with, we don't have 32 tracks worth of ideas—we probably do, but it wouldn't be Velvet Underground music in the end. It'd be something else. We might have these celestial harmonies, all sorts of overdubs, it would be a lot different. How many tracks do you need to do something like "Femme fatale"? We probably could have recorded that on one track, everybody close to the mike and play-ing at the same time. Certainly on four tracks. A lot of the early Beatles stuff was done on four track, and it sounds good, it's straight stuff. That would be all I could say about that. The people who are influenced might really have more to say.

The rights to some of the songs, legally credited to Lou, have been regained by Cale and Morrison. According to Sterling, the name of their publishing company, Three Prong Music, shows that there were three minds at work. Why didn't he, an English literature student, contribute to the lyrics?

I always did contribute to lyrics, but since Lou was singing them he pre-ferred to sing his own than somebody else's, that's all. I made consider-able modifications on a lot of stuff, and John had ideas for lyrics too. But basically, you know how Lou operates, if you gave him fixed lyrics, he's gonna depart from them anyway, he doesn't usually sing a song the same way twice, he's always changing them, just to fool around with them. I never cared about lyrics that much, given a choice I care about the music. I certainly wasn't gonna try to say anything important. But we had some good songs, accidental lyrics, they're not trying to say any-thing profound so maybe that's why they're good. If you could just say the obvious, then you've said a whole lot. If you could actually express what people think but don't say, that would be an amazing accomplish-ment. You don't have to get into these incredible, conceptual bags, and try to teach people anything. I don't want to teach people anything ever, in music. If you can remind them of what they've been thinking all along, that'll be great.

But your songs did make statements about things . . .

But always obliquely. If you take the radical ones, something like "Venus in Furs" doesn't tell you to do anything. Go through all the Velvet Underground songs and try to find a song that tells you to do something, that's instructional, that implies you ought to do this, this is the way you want to be, this is what you should do. There aren't any. We never did any preaching, which is wonderful, that's why I still like the band, that's why I wanted to be in there. No, really, think about it! Something like "Venus in Furs," it's just there. And if you find something attractive in the lyrics then you might be led to pursue some course of action, which none of us ever did, we were not S&M and bondage freaks. Nevertheless, it's just there. There's nothing in the song saying do this or don't do this, the lyrics just describe states, behaviors. Maybe that's why our music is still palatable now, because it wasn't telling you to go to San Francisco and put flowers in your hair, and it wasn't telling you not to go. We don't have any songs that say anything about the flower power movement. If that's what you wanna do, then go and do it. We don't have any songs saying that you ought to live in New York City or not live there. This is good, I think. The closest that we ever came to preaching is "Heroin," but that's such a nihilistic statement. It's against everything that would make people prefer drugs as an alternative, and it's also against drugs. Drugs are not portrayed very favorably in "Heroin." That's total nihilism: you can't help, not you guys, not you girls, and not you drugs either, everything can take a walk. But this little catalog of evils—"dead bodies piled in mounds, people making crazy sounds"—I asked Lou to take that out of there. It seems to be a topical reference, sounded kind of sensitive, and I don't like that. But basically the song is just a rejection. It was very controversial, very. Not only for what it said but the sound of it, the viola and all that.

Rock and roll and politics are worlds apart, he strongly believes.

Rock'n'roll should have no social consciousness, whatever. It should go on by itself and let everything else happen. Folk singers cared about the starving in Africa—I care about the starving in Africa, but it has nothing whatsoever to do with rock'n'roll music. If I want to contribute money then I would just do it, you don't need songs about the evils of apartheid in South Africa. That's not what rock'n'roll is concerned with, it shouldn't be, I don't think it ought to be. Specific little issues, who cares about them? If you care about them, you shouldn't write songs about them. Rock and roll is supposed to be fun, it's not supposed to be thoughtful. So that's my objection to all that sort of thing.

How could he sum up his attitude while in the band?

I was interested in the present. The present moment only. Not the future, not the past. I wasn't working towards any particular goal and I was not nostalgic about what show was great last year. I was just locked in the present. I was worried about tonight, if we were gonna play, that's what I was worried about. Whether anybody records it or not I don't care, because after the show I'm worrying about tomorrow night. Is my amp performing well? What's wrong with these guitar strings I'm using? I used to change my strings every set, twice every night. I got a lot of complaints about that from my road manager, he said I was wasting money, but I wasn't, I just couldn't have my strings break. This general logistical stuff, that's all. But I wouldn't worry about how was the tour going, that involves too much past and future projection. When I was on stage I'd be very aware about how the song was going—is it dying or am I imagining it? Strange feelings you get when you play anyway. The best nights are nights when you feel you can drop out without affecting the band, that what you do doesn't really matter, the song is going by itself, it has its own momentum. Those are the best nights, you can relax and do what you feel like doing. The worst nights are the nights when you feel like the juggler in a circus, you have all that stuff up in the air and if your concentration wavers for a moment, the whole thing is gonna collapse. It just takes this incredible amount of will to make it happen, those are disastrous nights. That is really painful, Sisyphus rolling the rock. You feel if you pause for a second everything is gonna stop. That's a bad feeling, didn't happen to us too often. It's completely metaphysical, it happens to athletic teams, anything that's a communal endeavor. Some nights it just doesn't get off the ground, you can always play competently or workmanlike, but something is missing. But the good nights, it doesn't really have anything to do with audience's enthusiasm, that's not what makes it good or bad. Sometimes just . . . go! And you just hang on for the ride. That's great. Those are the nights where you can really do something, turn it loose and see where it goes. And you do what you want. Amen.

Watching him talk, emptying one beer after another, launching ideas
into the air just to shoot them down when the story illustrating them
loses his interest, I ask myself where's his self-effacing reputation. He
seems self-conscious, but he's also talkative.

As Paul McCartney said of John Lennon, he wasn't Saint John, he could
be a pain in the ass. Who would doubt it? People get down on Paul
cause he's always saying bad things about John Lennon. Do you think
John Lennon was necessarily a sweetheart? They say he was a raging
drunk, which I don't know at first hand. Do you think Jim Morrison
was a sweetheart? Every time I met him he was naked, drunk or both.
Or Lou Reed? Or me? The thing that made me pleasant in the days of
the band was that I didn't talk to anybody, so you weren't subjected to
my nastiness. I didn't talk to strangers, if I was sitting at a table with a
group of people and some people I didn't know, I wouldn't bother to
say anything until they left. I didn't say mean things, I didn't say nice
things, I just said no things. And then, within my own group, I was
caustic and critical. I don't want anybody to think I was perfect and
Lou was so hard to deal with: I was a pain in the ass. Perfectionism
means incredible pain. I was always willing to be critical, and I was
always critical of myself. After a performance, if anybody said I was
great, I would characteristically start saying that it wasn't that good. So
the first thing you would hear from me was not how wonderful you did
on this song or how great your singing was, but what happened there?
Or why that happened? I know that got to Lou, but that wasn't why I
was doing it. I was compulsive I guess, a bad trait. I know because Lou
complained about it at one point back in the later days of the band,
complained that he seldom got any praise out of me, that I only told
him his voice sounded like it needed an operation or something. It wasn't
always that way, but that's bad. Lou and I play real well together, and
with John too. One of the things that people who observed the band
live always remarked on was the communication on stage among people
who were not looking at each other but doing whatever. We could hear
each other real well and paid attention. That's one of the things we
could really do. Jazz musicians do, you can't do any kind of improvisa-
tional music if people aren't listening, if all you pay attention to is what
you're doing. Then you have the opposite side of the coin, I listened real
well so I heard things and could say: Well, what's the matter with you?
Why can't you do this? If I thought I played badly, it didn't matter if the
audience tore the house down with joy, I was unhappy because I

thought I had played like shit. And I figured out that if those people were smarter, if they knew how the stuff ought to sound like, then they would realize I played badly. So I suffered as much from my own criticism as Lou and John did. John would just dismiss it, but Lou would listen and get irritated.

Both Lou Reed and John Cale have led careers marked by controversy and erratic sales, plus the expectations of an audience spoiled by the legend, the myth. Reed made a strong reputation for himself doing the best (Berlin, Coney Island Baby, Street Hassle, The Blue Mask) with the worst, but he could always surprise audiences with a memorable performance on stage. Cale, on the other hand, has been an idiosyncratic musician and producer, the author of great works (Paris 1919, Fear, Sabotage, Music for a New Society) that range from punk to classical. He's also made a living out of the crazy genius routine, playing shows of almost suicidal status. Piano tuners around the world still fear him.

I still want John to make some serious accomplishments in classical music. I would like to see him employ his training in the way it was originally directed, which he is doing apparently with *The Falklands Suite*. Anybody can play three chord rock 'n' roll, but John has a way to make three chord rock'n'roll into something else, because he is so sharp as a musician. But I would like to see him just sit down and do serious music, which he does, like in *Paris 1919*. But he should be writing chamber music and all the rest of it, however weird he wants to and for whatever ridiculous assortment of instruments. Lou always wanted a pop success, whereas John didn't exactly, he wanted a musical success and be happy with music and actually doing something original and different. Lou always wanted a pop success and I think it's always eluded him. His reputation is very high but it's not based on any particular song that he has done by himself, there's no Lou Reed song popular as a Beatles song. In fact I'd say his career mostly depended on Velvet Underground stuff, it's not the things he's done solo that have impressed people but the stuff we all did together. If there's any falling off in the quality in Lou Reed material it might be because of the fact that it's Lou Reed and not him, John, Moe and me. It's hard to do things by yourself. You hire people to play and they pretty much do what you tell them. You get all the credit but you never get criticism, these people aren't gonna tell you what to do. I've sat around in hotels with Lou and his band people, and they just sort of hang on whatever he is doing, there's no possibility of criticism. The road manager is not going to say anything, or he'll be fired too. So Lou is insulated from any kind of objectivity. You look at all those Lou Reed picture books and what do you see? Do you see Lou Reed marching a straight course from the Velvet Underground to the present? No. You see this creature transformed every six months into something else. Now it has blonde hair, now it has painted nails, now this and that. Not because Lou feels like being that creature, Lou likes to look like Lou and, as far back as I've known him, that is a person with nice curly hair, usually wears sunglasses, dresses neatly. That's Lou, and then there's these other aberrations, Lou trying to adapt himself to some market or other. Did it work? Did it speed things up or slow them down? I don't know, I can't say. But certainly nobody is gonna tell him not to do it. If he had showed up like that in the Velvet Underground he would have been subjected to ridicule. What the hell is that? Or why did you bleach your hair? What would have happened if John suddenly bleached his hair or shaved a swastika in his hair? This is ridiculous, this shouldn't be happening. So that was sort of my impression, at the time. I know underneath there someplace is Lou, but Jesus! He obviously decided that whatever he was going to do he was going to make it happen, that he had to succeed in music. I always felt I didn't care if I didn't, I'd do something else. Wisely perhaps. Lou is never particularly happy. I don't know what he needs to be happy, but I think he needs people to deal with him honestly, which I don't believe he has. If he talked to me I would tell him what I think. I do genuinely like him, that's why I'm so mad at him. If I didn't like him I would be much less angry. People I don't like I just don't care about.

The only Lou Reed album Sterling admits having owned is Transformer. And he remembers fully why he did not enjoy the metal versions of Velvet Underground songs that formed the successful Rock'n'roll Animal, the album that introduced "Sweet Jane" and "Heroin" to a wider audience.

They all sound the same, and I'm not saying this because I'm not playing on it. Listen to the guitar players, there is not one change in the tone or intensity on any track. Track to track is identical. This to me is death. This is very poor. This sort of ruthlessness will make me change tones or pick ups, I'd pull the switches arbitrarily. If I was getting a terrific sound I would remember where it is and go some other places or do something else. But not these guys. They had one sound and it goes from the start of the album to the finish.

While we are saying good-bye and having the first of our last beers, he looks directly into my eyes and tells me I shouldn't make Lou the bad guy in this story. Among other reasons, simply because he wasn't. But we'll never know, maybe he would have enjoyed the part.

One last thing, would he play again?

School has been a considerable distraction, but that's over, it's finished now. I'm gonna finish or they finish with me, so one way or the other. But to answer the question, if I told you tonight it was my ambition to return to music, that demands the question: If I wanna go back to music today, why didn't I go back ten years ago? Or, why did I leave in the first place? That's what I'm gonna ask myself, even if I think it will be fabulous. If it was so great, why did I leave? Then I would have to start thinking about the reasons that impelled me to leave. It wasn't that I thought I couldn't do anything, as I've said Lou wanted me and him to start again. How could I come around to that kind of conclusion? That's why I avoided playing, it's disquieting, hearing live music upsets me, agitates me, so I try not to hear too much of it, or I do. But I do like doing it.

M.C. KOSTEK

WE HAVE A LITTLE SURPRISE FOR YOU . . . (1990)

In 1990, a long wished-for VU reunion took place in a small town outside of Paris, raising hopes that were briefly fulfilled by the Velvets' 1993 European tour. Cale and Reed were on hand for the opening of a Warhol exhibition, which included a section on the Velvet Underground, and to play some songs from *Songs for Drella,* their recent collaboration in memory of Warhol. After the fifth song, Reed introduced Tucker and Morrison, and for a historic moment the Velvets were once more. They played only one song: "Heroin." Here are three fans' accounts.

"Three hours ago this was not possible. Now I'm overcome by emotion."
—*John Cale*

"Shit, that was great!"

—*Moe Tucker*

"That was extraordinary! To have those drums behind me, that viola on one side, and that guitar on the other again, you have no idea how powerful that felt."

—*Lou Reed*

"Not bad! Was I in tune?"

—*Sterling Morrison*

After some bad times (the passing of Andy, Nico, Ondine, Jack Smith), the past two years have brought a bounty of good things: Lou's *New York* and tours, Moe's *Life In Exile,* John's *Words for the Dying,* the *Drella* concerts, video and album—all culminating in the celebration/reunion in France on 15 June 1990.

This reunion happened about the only way possible. No million dollar offer, no howling, adoring mob at CBGBs, no worldwide Rock Awards banquet could have made this come to pass. In the end, it was the graceful magic of Paris followed by the charm and perfect beauty of Jouy-en-Josas, the small French town 20 miles southwest of Paris (5 miles from Versailles) where the Cartier Foundation is located (along with, it must be noted, the large sums of money it took to bring about the exhibition), that helped melt the hard feelings of twenty years. The band came to realize the intense love and appreciation shown by all those at Cartier and those 2500 folks present at the event, and did decide, at the last minute, to play. Once again, Europe shows a greater appreciation for American artists than does America. This is a long-time tradition with US jazz artists. I saw a little French TV in Paris. One show was a French version of *Wheel of Fortune,* and the one puzzleboard I saw was of a "Personality": Charlie Mingus. Both contestants missed, probably because they were shocked at the use of the informal "Charlie." On the Pop channel, it did take just five minutes after I first arrived in Paris to see a clip of, yes, believe it, Jerry Lewis, but this was followed by a full frontal nudity clip from *Last Tango in Paris* (at 4 PM). One of the commercials shown was a Levis jean ad that is set in New York, New Year's Eve, 1958. A young woman is pondering on just how to get the attention of the young star who's popped out of the limo: Eddie Cochran. The Levis do the trick, and it's a gala New Year. I wonder where Eddie Cochran comes out in the national "Q" recognizability tests they give US audiences? Above or below Charles Mingus? We all have been buffeted, these last few years, into a solid realization of how difficult it is just to drag our tired old bodies around this large globe for 40 or 50 years, and how harder yet it is to cut against the commercial grain in pursuit of an artistic vision. The great thing about this Paris celebration was that it happened while most of the principals were available to smell the roses. Present at the show was this crew: Lou, John, Moe, Sterling, Ari (Nico's son), Sylvia Reed, Risè Cale, Moe's daughter Kerry, Martha ("Mersh") Morrison, Billy Name, Fred McDarrah, Nat Finkelstein, and Ultra Violet.

Sometimes things are perfect. This setting was perfect: rolling green French hillsides, a perfectly warm summer day, Andy's prints in one building, a great Velvet Underground/EPI installation of rare photos, posters, records, films, etc., in another (a World War I cement bunker!), a respectful European media blitz, and throngs of calmly rabid fans. (The exhibition did pull a few punches in terms of making the EPI easier on the casual observer: only 20 minute excerpts of the *EPI* and *A Symphony of Sound* films were shown, and although original plans called for a true EPI room, with movies, exploding lights and a wild tape from an actual November 1966 EPI show, the room was toned down to lights and the first album playing. The original EPI remains too intense in 1990!)

This day, Friday, June 15th, changed much. As of the preceding week, no one was going to play. As of Thursday, John and Lou would perform some *Drella* songs. And as of Friday morning, Lou, and John and Moe were talking about doing "Pale Blue Eyes" after the *Drella* songs. Lou and Sterling sat by each other at the brunch, and chatted in a friendly fashion. But still, 30 minutes before the set, when the car came to drive Sterling from the Chateau brunch to the stage area, Sterling was not going to play. "Please hurry, Mr. Morrison. You must not be late to play," said the driver.

Sterling threw up his hands as if Frank Zappa had appeared: "I'm not playing! I'm not playing!" he called, backing away from the car. It was only at the stage, where he was given a guitar from the opening band Pulnoc, that he consented to play. Lou asked Moe how her muscles were, if she was up to playing "Heroin" instead of "Pale Blues Eyes." Everything fell together, in the same casual manner the band originally fell together.

John and Lou played five songs from *Drella*. They were both a bit nervous, with the wind blowing their music about, but did a fine job. Before they played, Sterling appeared briefly at the back of the stage for a quick guitar sound check. Still, it was a truly eerie moment of surprise at the end of the *Drella* set when Lou said, "We have a little surprise for you. I'd like to introduce Sterling Morrison. And Maureen Tucker." The crowd roared as both came up, and the band moved slowly, carefully into "Heroin." However randomly their musical affairs fall into or out of place, there is nothing random about their playing. Even after 22 years, these four people make marvelous music together. No rehearsal, no warm-up. Just "Heroin." Time stops rushing on its run. The crowd holds its breath. Birds chirp gayly in the forest behind the stage (you'll hear them in tapes of the event), the people in the villas across the street peer out at the stage, the sun shines sweetly; the entire scene is peaceful, tranquil, frozen in its perfect setting. Moe pushes the beat, starting the fast breaks a bit more quickly than on the record, and Lou misses a few of the lines, but overall, it is amazing. John's viola flies with powerful style and force, and Lou and Sterling's guitars bang together perfectly. Heaven ends, time begins again, and Lou motions them all out for a bow. Sterling waves his hands in classic W.C. Fields "It was nothing" style.

Afterward, Lou wipes his eyes. Moe bubbles. John is quite moved. Sterling wears a satisfied look he hasn't had for years, and says he was hoping they could have done two hours worth of "What Goes On," and really done some playing. Says Lou, "That was one of the most amazing experiences I've ever had in my few years on Earth! That was extraordinary! I moved up into the pocket between you, John and Sterl, and . . . holy shit!" Says Moe, "Who needs practice? We played that song quite a bit back then, you know." That night, and for the next two nights, all four go to dinner together. There's no telling what will come of this, once they're back in the US, and the spell of Paris wears off. John and Lou are talking about playing some *Drella* concerts in the US and Europe, and that's a change. There was even talk of getting together to play in a club in Paris that night, although nothing came of that. All we know is that for one glorious day, Paris truly shone as the city of light, the highest common denominator of human behavior on the planet, and gave the Velvet Underground their just due. The band responded in kind, and perhaps at last felt at peace with their coming of age in the world.

CHRIS CARTER
SOME STERLING MO(E)MENTS:
THE VELVET UNDERGROUND REUNION (1990)

There is no bass. The drums are pounding, huge, thunderous and monolithic. The twin guitars stutter and burn, cut and slash, jagged and raw.

And in-between, under and over this runaway train of rhythm, the harsh, dissonant scream of an amplified viola pulls you deeper into the maelstrom of feedback crossfire. And all the while the singer's world-weary vocals are spat out like punches, sharp, filled with bitterness and invective: "I . . . don't know . . . just where I'm going."

The song is "Heroin," soundtrack to a thousand narcotic dreams and nightmares. The four people on stage: Lou Reed, John Cale, Sterling Morrison, and Maureen (Moe) Tucker, are the legendary Velvet Underground. The power and cathartic beauty of this music and their mesmeric vision is undimmed by the ravages of time, success, excess or obscurity. All the puny pretenders to the throne are trampled underfoot in the rush to see the genuine article in full flight effortlessly stoop to conquer.

But this is not some dark basement filled with noise and the blinding lights of Andy Warhol's 1966 EPI multi-media extravaganza that blitzed New York City. This isn't even *Live 1969* or *Max's Kansas City* either. Or any of Lou Reed's weird and wonderful solo personas on any of his innumerable tours. No, what we are witnessing here is history in the making, a further chapter in the incredible story that is the Velvet Underground, ... the Velvet Underground Reunion!

Yes, that's right, official. But only for one song—ten minutes of the purest music I'll ever witness—and then gone again. Poof! Looking back on it, it seems incredible. The famous "reunion that will never be," according to Lou on many occasions, actually did occur.

The place? Jouy-en-Josas, a small village set in beautiful countryside about 30 kilometers west of Paris. More precisely, on a stage set up in the spacious grounds of an imposing castle/chateau—the home of a prestigious institution that supports contemporary arts, the Cartier Foundation.

The time? June 15th, 1990, approximately 4:30 PM (10:30 AM on the east coast of the US, to give perspective). The event? Nothing less than the grand opening of Cartier's Andy Warhol Exposition, a celebration of everything Warholian. The whole shebang cost thousands and took months to set up, and is in liaison with the Grey Art Gallery and Study Center and the Museum of Modern Art, both New York cultural institutions. We're talking serious money here, folks, and some heavy intellectual connotations (despite all the connotations . . .), and not yer average rock'n'roll scene at all.

Cartier should be congratulated for having the style and verve to pull off something as spectacular as this, for if you can stomach the brain-squishing contradictions of the ultimate New York style/sleaze kings rubbing shoulders with an artistic and cultural elite (just as, in fact, the original Factory scene was), then your sensory equipment would've gone into over-load when you got a good look at the scope and size of this whole extravaganza.

For a start, the exhibition is going to run three months—until August 20—to paying customers from all over the world. On this particular day entry was by invitation only. My ticket to enter came via my good friend Bruno Blum, a French music journalist who has met and interviewed Lou and other characters in the VU story on quite a few occasions. It was Cartier who decided to break new ground and stage an entire segment of this Warhol show on the Velvets and recognize the importance of their work with Andy. To do this, Cartier had enlisted the assistance of numerous organizations, among them the ever-reliable and accurate-to-a-fault Velvet Underground Appreciation Society, and also paid the expenses of the bandmembers and associates to come to Paris. Not to play, you understand. That possibility existed only in the diseased minds of terminal VU junkies like myself who never got to see the original band and whose mental video facilities have been stuck on 'pause' ever since that particular moment when we were first inoculated with the VU virus (still no known cure, by the way!). Nevertheless, Cartier, in their infinite wisdom, decreed that the band should be present for this tribute, as that alone would be quite fitting, and also create quite a stir among the assorted music and art biz types who would flock to see these living legends and then pass on the news via their own lines of communication (I have never seen so many TV cameras, videos and cassette recorders present at one gig; it seemed as if every person in the 700-odd audience had some means of assuring that this slice of rock history wouldn't be doomed to slide into oblivion as have so many early VU moments).

The exposition? It included various Warhol works housed in a small cluster of separate buildings: paintings, art work, drawings, photographs, videos, films, etc.; a treasure trove of Warholia. The programme for the day included a brunch held in the large chateau on the hill, which spilled outside onto the grounds, where the star players in this junket disported themselves on legendary French cuisine, rare wines and the approbation of a culture only too ready to sing their praises today, but who, in the sixties, might well have reacted differently. The brunch was beautiful. Dozens of uniformed waiters rushed hither and thither, at the whim of patrons from (it seemed) all walks of life. Duchesses and film producers rubbed shoulders with the Czech rock band Pulnoc (in traditionally scruffy rock clothes) and a few scruffy rock media types (Vive la Egalité! At least un peu Egalité!).

After food and wine, Pulnoc came out to play. Their story is an interesting one. They are the descendents of the 60's Czech band, The Plastic People of The Universe. In 1968, Václav Havel brought a copy of *White Light/White Heat* back to Prague from a trip to the USA. This album, and the VU, caught the ears of the Czech dissidents in a big way. In the wildness of songs such as "I Heard Her Call My Name," they heard the freedom they were longing for. Tape copies of the album spread throughout the leaders of the various movements. The band became the focus of the Czech revolutionary movement. The Communist regime cracked down fiercely. Anyone with a Velvets album, or tape, or lyrics, or caught singing a VU song did hard prison time. Many members of the Plastic People did time in jail. Thus Pulnoc was an inspired choice to open, as they are a living example of the world-wide influence of the band. They do great cover versions of Velvets songs. Lou says if you close your eyes while watching them play live, you would swear you were listening to the Velvets themselves. They played an impressive set, although I could only pay them partial attention, given the enormous variety of things to do and the sensory overload which accompanies twenty-odd years of VU addictions suddenly given limitless possibilities for overdose. Too much was happening!

For instance, in the World War I bunker down the hill from the stage is the VU/EPI exhibition. On my left is Ari Boulogne, about 25, Nico's son. He is immortalized, inside the bunker, in Andy's film of the Velvets playing in the Factory: *The Velvet Underground: A Symphony of Sound.* This features 20 minutes of the original band murdering an improv piece they called "Melody Laughter" (see *Live 1966* for details). Their weapons are a combination of funky r'n'b guitar, Cale's awesome and wondrous "Thunder Machine," (a wicked hell-noisemaker consisting of amplified bedsprings!), and Nico on 3rd guitar (playing it with a drumstick). Ari runs in and out of camera frame. There is no bass. A video copy of this film is on display here, which is, I believe, its first screening outside the USA, where it has been shown very rarely. Do you get the idea of what fabulous goodies were on display here? We're talking rare! EPI posters never seen since that particular night's happening 24 years ago! Photos developed for the first time for this show! The *Aspen* magazine with "Loop!" Sealed mono Banana albums! The back cover layout for *White Light!* The press kit for the third LP! We're talking live VU! Many Holy Grails! I have to return the next day, dazed, to try to take in all the exhibition.

Lou and John did a soundcheck that morning, so it is definite they will play. They will do some songs from the album, *Songs for Drella*, Pulnoc finish their set, and the crowd, who had been scattered all over the grounds, has suddenly gravitated to stage front. In everyone's mind is the immortal question, "Will the VU play?" From where I'm standing, front stage left, I can see hubbub of people clustered backstage: Lou, and wife Sylvia, John, Moe, hmm, no sign of Sterling . . . are you sure he's actually here? Hasn't he actually been on stage only twice since 1971 (he left the band after Lou and before Moe), and that just for a couple of songs during Cale encores in Austin, Texas? Would I recognize him anyway? Behind the row of high-class, suited bouncer-security and the road crews are various members of the entourage. Ultra Violet and Billy Name, among others. Bruno, great chap that he is, circulates backstage and emerges with proof of Sterling's presence: he's gotten my paperback copy of the trashy *Velvet Underground* book signed by Lou, John, Moe and Mr. Morrison, with bonus signatures from Ari (for Nico), and Ultra Violet (for Andy).

After what seems like an eternity for the audience (no one wanted to be the one to shatter the delicate chemistry with any undue noise, such as breathing), two figures walk out on stage. Lou and John do a brief tune-up. Lou looks cool healthy, together; John is angular more than ever, eccentric, in a wildly slit suitcoat. The concert begins quietly, Cale coaxing washes of sound from his keyboards while Lou strokes fizzles and sparks from his small but beefy headless guitar. The first song is "Style It Takes," which well sums up Andy, the VU and this whole venture. Somehow I can't imagine this all taking place in England, which is strange, considering the number of bands who cite the VU as their strongest influence and the fact that, of the 4000 names on the VUAS mailing list, very many of them are English. However, I saw only five English people the entire day; two of them were myself, a good friend I had taken with me. Another was erstwhile fan Tim Mitchell, whose review of the BAM *Drella* show appears elsewhere in these pages. The fourth was journalist Nick Kent, and the fifth was Simon Pettifar, a fan, and Black Spring Press publisher of Nick Cave writings as well as (let's-hope-one-day) Sterling Morrison's recollections on the VU days, *The Velvet Underground Diet*. Now almost all the Americans I noticed were guests of Cartier, but it is quite a steeper $tep to Paris from the US than from the UK. But say, there's Bill Bentley from Warner Brothers Records, who used to be in the Bizarros with Sterling in Austin in the 70's; he paid his own way. And there's Toronto's Rob Bowman with his gal Sue—he's compiling the 3 CD set of Lou's solo career for BMG/RCA—they paid their own fares. And there were loads of other VU fans from all over Europe: Spain, Germany, Italy, Greece, Sweden, The Netherlands, Belgium, who made the effort. And of course the Czechs.

After "Style," (which was similar in sound and feel to the LP version), they slip into "Slip Away (A Warning)." The poignancy of hearing Lou sing, "Still there's no more Billy Name and Ondine is not the same," while Billy himself is standing just thirty feet away is actually heightened by the fact that he is here when so many others are not (Andy and Nico, most notably). I was introduced to Billy earlier at the brunch, and I marvelled that this bearded and jovial man-mountain is in fact the same man as the thin, emaciated figure I am familiar with from Factory photographs. When you meet living legends, you have to be prepared to face the fact that the person today is certainly not the same one idolized for the last twenty years in a freeze-frame mental sculpture, nor the person he himself will have usually been at great pains to project. No, the real person is someone else, perhaps unknown to both the myth and the myth-maker. Certain it is that the beautiful sadness of this moment in time was for its brief recapturing of an entire subculture, gone, forever gone. The power of the Velvets is such that they could still transcend their environment, ridiculous or sublime, and take you back to that mythic time when it was new, exciting and dangerous. In other words, they could still walk it as they talk it with their dignity still intact. The King of Pop Art is dead and the Knights of the Ultra Violet Factory are holding a requiem. Hold your tongue and refrain from comment—your life is in here too, somewhere! After "Slip Away" comes "Nobody But You," Lou's loveliest melody from *Drella*, and a bona-fide hit if radio bothered to listen to it. Lou and John do a haunting and delicate version of it here, the punch line delivered with particular venom, as on the previous song. Whom is he directing this vehemence at? The audience? The paparazzi? Himself? The Factory hangers-on? Whomever, Lou is in particularly fine voice today, as he summons reserves of emotion and poetic bile not much in evidence until recently. Perhaps he too is genuinely moved by the immensity of the moment. Lou and John play together with an intuitive and scintillating brilliance. They look at one another as they play. They begin "Forever Changed," and it turns into a long version with a rhythmic blitz of instrumental savagery in the middle, bracketed by Cale's sonorously aristocratic vocals and those pinched, enigmatic cheekbones, ever the wayward iconoclast. Suddenly the song is snuffed out in a howl of feedback, and they are doing "Hello It's Me," soft, almost acoustic, immeasurably sad. What are they thinking as they play it? Who knows, but somehow they pull it off without being sentimental. And then it's over. The audience response to each song has been belated and muted, perhaps intimidated by the size of the occasion and the heavy cultural tag hanging in the breeze. I should say here that the weather is warm and sunny, and I can't help noticing the contradiction between what my eyes are seeing and what my ears are hearing. All around is lush greenery. Except for the music, there is only the sounds of the French countryside: birds chirruping, a slight breeze ruffling the leaves on the trees, and an occasional airplane. To the left is the boundary of the Foundation's acreage, with private houses on the other side of the road. Some nameless French villager is having a bonfire in his back garden and the smoke and pleasant fumes drift across the stage, adding a bizarre element of rural tranquility to this epitome of urban noise and confusion.

As the last echoes of moderate applause fade, Lou turns to look backstage, then moves back to the mike. He looks at this feet for an instant, then says, in his shaky, almost inaudible voice, "We have a little surprise for you." A moment of stunned, incredulous silence, and then, "I'd like to introduce Sterling Morrison." A gaunt, extremely tall and obviously nervous person enters stage left, to a smattering of applause. The audience can hardly believe what is taking place. I am frozen, rooted to the spot, all other thoughts are secondary to the next few minutes. "And Maureen Tucker." Moe gets a more immediate and bigger cheer, the crowd coming alive and realizing that this is actually going to happen, and that it's now okay to make a bit of noise. After all, this is a rock 'n' roll concert, isn't it? Yes, but with a difference!

It would not be an exaggeration to say that at this point you could have heard the proverbial pin drop. The four on stage are briefly tuning up. It's an incredible sight: Cale, stage left, holding his viola, Lou commanding centre stage, and Sterling, fiddling with an unfamiliar guitar (courtesy of Pulnoc) standing to his right. Behind them is Moe, resplendent in shades, and the only band member to sport them. The tuning stops, there is a moment of magical silence, Lou looks at John and nods. I catch my breath and swallow hard. This is it.

A gentle melody ensues, the first few notes of what can be thought of as their theme tune. Lou is at the mike, and the first few words ring out: "I . . . don't know . . . just where I'm going . . ." Now the crowd is suddenly alive, roaring, cheering this anthem to the perverse, this paean to confusion and isolation, this song of splintered splendor. Lou spits and snarls the words as if the intervening 22 years since these same four people shared the same stage had never existed. The tempo quickens and the rhythm kicks into higher gear. The volume swells and the wail of the viola begins. And then it goes on . . . and on . . . and on . . . getting louder, more intense, more violent with each chorus. And then there's the floating, dreamy drug haze bits in-between, where you can feel each shiver and sigh. There is this magnificent background booming of Tucker's metronome beat, now a monstrous shudder, now a delicate flutter, a heart-beat. Lou's chopping out the rhythm with great swatches of guitar noise, and Sterling is adding his accompaniment of fleshing out the chords and overlaying a more intricate welter of notes. But among these legends today it is Cale who stands tallest, who most impresses, with the sheer volume and frenzy of the viola over-shadowing everything else on display here, even beating the famous record-ed version on the first album for sheer unmitigated ferocity. Towards the end he turns and bends forward over his amp, and bends the wailing screech up into sustained white noise feedback, his fingers maniacally caressing the viola's neck while the right hand saws savagely at the strings with the bow. This is incredible, and it goes on for ten minutes, before dying away to a gentle whisper and then into silence.

There is a moment of transcendence before the audience erupts, and part of me is blindly hoping that there would be more. But even the Velvets would not have been able to top or sustain that level of musical and emotional intensity, and they wisely call it a day right there. The applause goes on for a while, and then Marie-Claude Beaud, Cartier Curator/Organizer comes out to thank all the band members, and Andy, and suddenly it is all over. Let us remember them this way.

Backstage members of Pulnoc look dazed and happy beyond all words. What a year for them! They win their freedom after 45 years, and on, for some of them, their first trip outside of Czechoslovakia, they see the Velvet Underground play. The Cartier suited security have dispersed, and lesser mortals like myself can wander back to say hello. Lou, Moe and John are nowhere to be seen, only Sterling is standing around. He looks a bit lost, but bemused amongst this rock'n'roll circus. He's on his own, so I go up to him and congratulate him for making a lot of people very very happy. I tell him I can finally say I saw the original Velvet Underground line-up live, after 21 years of waiting. His response was a little terse and nervous: "Was my guitar in tune?" I assured him it was, though to be sure it wouldn't have mattered if it wasn't. They all were there, living, breath-ing, being. For that alone, many of us are grateful. I'm sure the spirits of Andy and Nico and all the other casualties of this incredible story without end looked down and smiled. There was no bass.

IGNACIO JULIÀ

THE VELVET UNDERGROUND RESURRECTION (1990)

Impossible is a word that has been definitely eliminated from my vocabu-lary. Impossible was, for those who knew the dark parts of the band's his-tory, a VU reunion. Even if there was a small ember of hope inside the VU cult, what with Moe working with Lou lately, and *Songs for 'Drella* bringing Lou together with, to most people's surprise, his estranged musical brother John Cale, any reconciliation with Sterling Morrison seemed impossible. They were separated by two decades of incommunication, regrets, remorse, frustration, and suffocated rage. A friend of Lou's since their teens, Sterling is one of the few people who never accepted his game, and who said things straight to his face, as anyone who's read one of Sterling's interviews knows. He landed in Paris with no comment on *New York* or *Songs for 'Drella*.

Sterling looked nervous the morning of the opening, not ready for a meeting and less for a surrender. Twenty years out of the music business, first as a University grad student/teacher, and now as a tugboat captain, has made him a confirmed skeptic, although a skeptic who shades his bitterness thanks to his vitality of character.

The chances were minimum, but it happened. We went to Paris hearing that the opening for the Andy Warhol System, an exhibition with a section dedicated to the band, would have no live music. When we got to the Foundation grounds—a huge park in a small town, the idyllic setting for the exhibition was inundated by the sounds of a viola and an electric guitar. Lou and John's sound check was taking place on a small open stage. Walking through the bunker, where they have set up a Velvet Underground tribute—a space transformed into a Platonian cavern invaded by photographs, records, posters, books, videos, magazines, films, instruments, memorabilia, hommages to the band by various French artists—was already a tremendous shock for the senses, a shock only heightened by meeting the real protagonists: the four original members of the band, Factory photographers Billy Name, Fred McDarrah and Nat Finkelstein, and Ultra Violet.

It was about four in the afternoon, after a magnificent brunch on the French countryside, that John and Lou got on stage in front of an elite crowd of about 1000. They played "Style It Takes," "Nobody But You," "Slip Away," in semi-improvised versions, the two veterans balancing their hurried sound check and nervousness with 25 years of musicianship and the magic of what happens when they play together. During "Forever Changed," the sheer force of John's playing helped Lou's guitar take off with electric fluidity, and in the finale of "Hello It's Me," the song that puts them directly in front of Andy's ghost, Lou's voice was showing obvious emotion. And then, the unexpected happened. Sterling, who during brunch had talked to his old friend for the first time in many years, had agreed to put on a guitar. And Lou, who had just announced a "little surprise," introduced them: Sterling and Maureen Tucker. The first chords of "Heroin" began. Then the unmistakable drums of Moe (basic, off-beat, magnificent). Then the hissing viola of John. The answer from the audience was one difficult to forget. The sound coming from the speakers was miraculously identical to the one stored in our memories. On stage we had four people nearly a half century old, separated by an old betrayal—the expulsion of Cale—and the passing of time, high on the affection and respect shown by Cartier and the crowd, and the euphoria of reconciliation, but let lightning strike me if they did not sound like the Velvet Underground and Nico, live at the Dom at St. Marks Place, 1966. The intensity, the message, the transcendence, the effect were the same: devastating, incredible, but real. The Velvet Underground resurrected for 10 intense minutes, as real and penetrating as their legend would have us believe.

With the applause and goodbye, the spell was broken. The imperturbable Lou Reed couldn't contain his tears. Feeling surrounded again by this special sound was too much for him. John looked overwhelmed, Sterling and Moe were beaming. That night they had dinner together, and the night after that, and the night after that. They visited the Louvre Museum together. From now on, everything's possible, even if I don't have any hopes for a future project together. In fact, I don't want it. When a band lives inside such a powerful myth, it's best to leave things as they are. A lot of people will remember the beginning of this decade because of the falling of the Berlin Wall. I will know that other walls tumbled down.

Sterling Morrison succumbed to lymphoma on August 30, 1995, after nine months of difficult treatments. By all accounts he handled his illness with characteristic grace. The three articles that follow are memorials by some who knew him.

SAL MERCURI

IN MEMORY OF STERLING MORRISON (1995)

The last time I saw Sterling Morrison, we didn't get a chance to speak. It was backstage after Moe's show at Tramp's in N.Y.C., October 8, 1994. It was a great homecoming for Moe and Sterling. The place was packed. The crowd was dotted with some N.Y./V.U. celebs—Victor Bockris, Sylvia Reed, Luna's Dean Wareham. Sterling's wife, Martha, was there with their young son. It was a great show and a great night.

Anyone who's ever met Sterling knows how tough it is *not* to talk with him. Apart from playing guitar, talking had to be the thing Sterling did best. I remember immediately after the groundbreaking performance with John Cale and Lou Reed at NYU December 5, 1992, Sterling lingered on stage with Victor Bockris, chatting. I approached him, a bit nervously and offered my 'Banana' lp for an autograph, making the usual fan chit-chat. As he handed the signed record back to me and I thanked him and turned to go, he said, *'Hey, you know some guy bought one of those with Andy's signature on it for $15 bucks a couple of years ago.'* I muttered something about that fellow's good fortune and once again turned to go. But Sterling still wanted to talk, and talk he did—*'I wasn't playing loudly enough,'* *'John had the advantage because I was sitting'*—and on and on until I felt I had to pull myself away. Not because I didn't want to stay and talk all night long, but because I felt he was just being nice and was waiting for me to go. I realized later that I could've stayed all night and Sterling would have regaled me with his conversation until dawn.

Six months later, after a triumphant set at the London Forum, I once again found myself in the enviable position of being backstage and floating on air as I thanked each member of the Velvet Underground for a magical night. I reminded Sterling of our meeting at NYU and he recalled it fondly, not the meeting but the concert, I'm sure. He was sitting and stood to shake my hand so that we could formally be reintroduced to each other.

Now that we were friends from way back, Sterling proceeded to tell me all these great stories—how his book would reveal all the dirty, backroom dealings of the VU, how he'd tried to intercede on behalf of Victor Bockris and tried to sway Lou into letting Bockris be his biographer, noting prophetically that with or without Lou's cooperation, the tale would be told. On and on he went and once again, I was the one who said good night first.

People who saw Sterling playing in Moe's band these past few years, invariably commented on how great he looked, and he did. A tall and deceptively youthful 50-something, Sterling emitted the aura of a new kid on the block—reserved, a little tentative, shunning the spotlight. This was part of his abundant charm. No Rock Star posturings or ego. He got onstage and played guitar in his characteristically subdued yet distinctive style. Fans have often wondered who played what in the Velvet Underground. The reunion tour of 1993 demonstrated that Sterling's brilliant guitar was at the center of such classics as 'Pale Blue Eyes' and 'Waiting for My Man.' If there's one thing that Sterling never got right, it was volume. Fans would yell 'Crank it up, Sterl!!' and he didn't. Preferring instead to blend in with the rest of the band.

Last spring, I heard that he was ill, very ill. His family had asked that details of his illness not be revealed. So, life went on. Moe toured Europe without him. Ignacio Juliá visited him at home in N.Y. in August and told me that although the disease had taken a great toll on Sterling's appearance and sapped him of his strength, he was expected to make a full recovery. Plans for a reprise of the landmark Kiss/Eat shows with Moe and John Cale in Lille, France, in October went forward. Tickets were printed.

I won't say that Sterling and I were friends because we didn't know each other well at all. We had an open date to quaff a few beers at the White Horse Tavern in the West Village which unfortunately went unfulfilled. I will say emphatically, however, that I've never met a man, nevermind a Rock-n-Roll icon, who could so easily be a friend.

Holmes Sterling Morrison left a few things unfinished. He left Martha, two children, and many, many fans who will miss him more than the music and lyrics can say.

DOUG YULE

STERLING MEMORIES (1996)

Sometime in the mid-eighties, the phone rings in the wood shop where I am working. It's *Sterling*. I can sense a certain discomfort in his voice but he is cheerful, spending only a moment on hi-how-are-yous. He invites me to join him, *Maureen* and *John* in a lawsuit to try to collect past royalties from the record company and *Lou*. I agree to become part of the group again for this purpose. This brief exchange is the last time I will talk to *Sterling*. The next [time] either one of us makes any attempt to contact the other, it is me, trying to reach him after hearing that he is sick. His phone rings busy every time. He is off at a hospital, receiving treatment. Finally, when someone does answer, it is *Martha, Sterling*'s wife. He is unable to come to the phone. I talk to *Martha,* and then to *Maureen.* A few days later, *Sterling* dies and with him goes the part of me that always assumed I would see him again, that we would play music together one more time and argue about whatever came up.

Sterling was the one who put the bug in *Sesnick*'s head that eventually pulled me into the group. He was the one who wanted me to join the reunion twenty five plus years later to play the bass. He was a very fair if somewhat cantankerous character that I loved more than I knew.

Lou used to call *Sterling Stella*, sometimes lengthening it to *Stella Stardette*. The name was chosen, I think, to zero in on *Sterling*'s reluctant need for recognition and the intent, while joking on the surface, was to control and diminish. *Sterling* never complained about it, never bitched about being kidded. He had a prodigious memory and an ability to analyze a situation while he was in it, and he always argued from a rational perspective, rarely an emotional one. I remember him in bits and pieces, little still-life moments frozen among the long dreary grayness of life on the road.

* * *

Sterling is sitting on the bed, cross-legged, leaning slightly forward with his forearms resting on his knees. The local alternate press is crowded around him, leaning in to catch every word. His eyes sparkle and he wears a sardonic smile; he's in his element. He answers each question as it comes, a note of incredulity lurking constantly in his voice as if to say, I can't believe you people have been fooled by all this bullshit. It is the central issue in his relationship with the leadership of the Velvets. I'm sitting on my bed with the young woman I picked up and shared a bed with but never touched, a rarity on the road but it does happen. I watch Sterling performing the act we have come to call "holding forth". He loves it. He thrives. When Lou or Sesnick is with him, he retreats, becoming quieter and more cautious. Even with them present he will dart forward into the conversation occasionally to correct some inconsistency or misstated fact. Rarely does he get center stage, the place he most wants to be.

* * *

We are sitting in the dressing room at the Whiskey in LA. Steven is lecturing on whatever subject he feels will be listened to. Lou, Maureen and I are listening, each making preparations for the show. Sterling sits in one corner, head down, intent on his fingers as he plays his sunburst Gibson 330, apparently oblivious to whatever Sesnick is peddling. In a tactic worn thin from so much use, Steven responds to a remark from one of us that "that's true on one level, but on a higher one, it's not . . .". Without lifting his head or stopping his fingers, Sterling says, "you've got so many levels, Steven, you should have been a carpenter." In and out, just like that; a verbal jab just to let us know he's not allowing any bullshit just because he seems to be otherwise occupied. This is the night we will come face to face with a dark skinned, soft featured guitar player after the first show who will tell us he loved the music and the energy. After he had gone we look at each other and realize it was Jimmy Hendrix and we didn't know what to say. The Velvets were always musically inventive but socially unskilled.

* * *

In LA, I discover a little boutique with handmade shirt in trendy, flowered prints. Sesnick comes up with some money and I buy two of them. One is a plain cream colored crepe thing with a squared off collar. When I show it around to the rest of the group, it turns out that Sterling has been into the shop and bought the exact same shirt, only one size bigger. From then on, we consult before each show to see who will wear the shirt that night. The last thing we want is to appear as look-alikes. One hot night in Philadelphia or Baltimore, it is Sterling's turn and he wears the crepe shirt in a show where the stage temperature reaches 100 degrees. Sweat rolls off of all of us. At the end of the set, standing in the dressing room, Sterling holds out his hands, laughing in disbelief. The shirt, dripping wet, has shrunk while he played and the cuffs which used to reach beyond his wrist, now barely clear his elbows.

* * *

Sterling is standing in the airport in Houston, I think it was Houston. Next to him is an empty suitcase, a fact at that moment known only to himself. He stops the progress of the group towards the gate with the announcement that he will not be returning to New York with us, he is going to Austin in a few days to begin a fellowship there, to return to school and complete his education. We are stunned. I am stunned. How could you do this with no warning, this is like a knife in the back. Why did you wait till now to tell us. Why did you bring your suitcase if you're not going? He explains, "I always said I would go back to school," as if this is reason enough for deserting. He wears an embarrassed smile, his head bobs about like a rear deck ornament in a full dress chevy. He looks like a six foot tall child caught with his hands full of forbidden cookies. This is the last time I will ever see Sterling. I will not know until he dies twenty five years later that he acquired a degree in Medieval Studies and picked up a tugboat captain's license. This last time together, he is once again in the position that more than anything else has defined his life, or at least the part of it that I have known; torn between the obligations he lives within and the path his heart wants to follow.

LOU REED
STERLING MORRISON: VELVET WARRIOR (1995)

Sterling said the cancer was like leaves in the fall, a perfect Morrison description; he loved the English language. When I asked if he had a guitar to play, he said yes, he did, but he had watched seven—he'd counted—seven layers of skin peel from his body, and that had made guitar playing and quite a few other things painful. This eye for detail was very much Sterling. In fact, it saved my life once. We were playing in an airplane hangar in Los Angeles in 1966. This was two years after we'd got out of college, where we'd first met, student friends and musician buddies. I was standing near a microphone when I heard Sterl call gently but firmly, "Don't move." I turned my head just in time to see smoke, one of my guitar strings vaporized by the ungrounded microphone it had just touched. I would have been ashes.

I arrived at his house by train from the city with depressing thoughts in my head and not one decent suggestion. I was struck by how big he was. Perhaps that was accentuated by the extreme gauntness of his once-muscular physique. He was bald with nothing but skin over bone. But his eyes. His eyes were as alert and clear as any eyes I've seen in this world. Not once did he complain. We spoke of music and old band mates. We talked baseball. We never spoke of what was going on.

Maureen, old friend and Velvet drummer, and Sterling's wife, Martha, had gone downstairs. Sterl lay in bed, seeming to drift off, and I wondered if I should leave. I walked to the side of the bed to say goodbye when he suddenly stuck his hand out. "Help me up," he said. He was strong despite the illness, but then he'd always been the strongest one. When he had played his passionate solos, I had always seen him as a mythic Irish hero, flames shooting from his nostrils. We sat like that, him upright in bed, me sitting with my back to an open window, holding his hand. And all the questions I had were answered and all the past differences resolved. And in the extraordinary moments when men transcend their bodies and words are spoken at their own peril, in these moments that move beyond speech and picture, in these moments that only an artist can capture, I saw my friend Sterling: Sterl, the great guitar-playing, tug-boat-captaining,

Ph.D.-ing professor, raconteur supreme, argumentative, funny, brilliant; Sterl as the architect of this monumental effort, possessor of astonishing bravery and dignity. The warrior heart of the Velvet Underground.

I missed the train back to New York and sat on the cement pavement waiting for another. I very badly wanted a cigarette and a drink. My God, I thought, We'll never play guitar together again. No more Nico. No more Andy. No more Sterl.

On the day of the Mass, I was in Cleveland playing rock-and-roll, my answer to every crisis. As the chords to "Sweet Jane" swelled up, I hoped somehow my friend heard them and got a laugh. After all, he was the first one who heard the song the night I wrote it, more than 25 years ago, in the summer, before the leaves fell in the fall.

Discography

The Velvet Underground discography is a work in progress as bootlegs, demos, various promotional items, and collections continue to surface. The band produced four studio albums—*The Velvet Underground and Nico, White Light/White Heat, The Velvet Underground,* and *Loaded,* followed by the release of two live albums—*Live at Max's Kansas City* and *Live 1969*—after the band broke up; and then 1993's *Live MCMXCIII* (Sire 9 45464-2), recorded during the reunion tour. But records of all sorts have been released in various countries over the years. Fortunately, the Velvet Underground Appreciation Society (VUAS) folks collect, catalog, and make available all manner of rarities. This discography appeared in *The Best of What Goes On #1 & 2* in 1986. Although somewhat dated, it is filled with useful information. It is also an extremely helpful orientation to the extensive VUAS catalog, which is available by faxing M.C. Kostek at (561) 283-6195, or by writing to the VUAS, 5721 SE Laguna Avenue, Stuart, Florida 34997. The most ambitious additions since 1986 are *The Velvet Underground: What Goes On*— a three-CD collection from Australia's Raven Records (RVCD-28) that includes a historical essay by Clinton Walker as well as interviews, mono and alternate mixes, and various "curios"—and *The Velvet Underground: Peel Slowly and See,* the excellent 1995 five-CD collection from Polydor (31452 7887-2).—A.Z.

M.C. KOSTEK AND PHIL MILSTEIN
THE VELVET UNDERGROUND:
A CRITICAL DISC/FILMOGRAPHY, 1957–1986

For an album largely recorded in three days, mixed (for mono) in another, released by a record company that had no idea whatinhell was going on, and wrapped in a mysterious package that gave scant clue as to what lay within, behold! Not only does *The Velvet Underground & Nico* survive, it thrives! Come with us now on an odd, complicated journey . . .

The Velvet Underground & Nico

The Players: Tucker, Reed, Morrison, Cale, Nico

USA: Verve 5008 (mono).

V6/5008 (stereo)—March 1967 (Also on cassette and 8-track)

Polygram 825 290 (reissue)—March 1985

UK: Verve M/VLP (mono), S/VLP (stereo) 9184—Oct. 1967.

Polydor 2315 056 (reissue)—Aug. 1971

GET THE MONO; SEE THE DISAPPEARED ACTOR

Get at least a tape of it. Sterling Morrison says the lp was recorded for and mixed in mono. The "stereo" is artificially created. So the true mono is a great (and about the only) place to hear the Velvets as a rock & roll band.

Also, the original issue of the album carries the disappeared actor. Originally, the big photo of the band was framed on top and sides in superimposed light show fashion by the upper torso of one of the actors from the *Chelsea Girls* film.

According to Sterling Morrison, "This guy, Eric Emerson, needed some money at the time. Seeing how no one asked him about putting his picture on the jacket, he asked Verve for a lot of money. Verve got scared and airbrushed it out."

Indeed. In Beatle Butcher Cover-up fashion, they slapped big black and white "Velvet Underground and Nico" stickers over the whole dang photo on the copies they had left, and airbrushed Eric into a hazy light show blob for the rest of time. This incident not only left a dark aura around the band on the back cover, it damaged whatever chance the record had for a quick blast off into some sort of commercial acceptance.

UK Original: Back on Front

The original UK version did not open up, had the back of the US cover as its front, and info from the US gatefold on the back. Follow? Deleted 1971.

No True UK Banana Anywhere, Anytime

When UK Polydor re-issued the lp in 1971, they put a limited amount in imported peelable US covers. From then on, they've put out a printed, non-peel banana.

Only Japan Has a Peel

No more "Peel slowly and see." Hard times have about eliminated the pink banana from modern society. Just about every current version everywhere of the first lp comes with a rather crudely-printed banana. In the US, the album has gone in and out of print. Verve had a printed banana cover with a gatefold in print until Polydor bought the MGM/Verve catalog in the late 70s. In 1981 it joined the low budget ranks with budget-line packaging: no gatefold; song titles and info printed on the back, with the lp title slapped on front.

In March of 1985, Polygram followed up the *VU* release by reissuing the three Verve lps as budget $5.98 items. As they couldn't remix the original tapes (the original plan), they used the best copies of the original tapes they could find (from Japan, natch) and remastered 'em to clean the sound. Trouble is, *tooclean* is the word. In general, they've boosted the voices and toned down the wild sounds that engulf the original vinyl. Thus the insane, barrel-house piano Cale pounds in ATP is now not as prominent as Nico's vocal. Nor does the screaming viola supercharge BADS with eerie glee—it too has been turned down. The avowed purpose of these reissues was again to make them available while making them sound up-to-date. 'Tis a great thing to see them in stores again, but these are not the same records. In short, the VUAS scoreboard:

First lp—Nope. 80's aural distortion.
WL/WH—O.K. Some of this sounds better cleaned.
Third lp—Maybe. The remastering didn't change much.

They changed little else except someone had the unnecessary thought to print "Special Low Price" right smack on the covers of the lps and cassettes.

The only people doing the banana justice these days are the Japanese. Their current edition features a superb pressing, Japanese/English lyrics (with many humorous mistakes, of course, in trying to decipher Lou's streettalk), the original gatefold, and yes, a banana you can peel (even if it is a rather flimsy plastic banana—the thought was there). The only things they lack are the original mono mix, and Eric Emerson.

GREEN BANANAS? NAY!

We've heard tell there were two German versions way back then. One peeled as in the USA. The other peeled to reveal . . . a blue banana. We've also heard tell of a green banana under the peel. One of our readers swore there was, and our previous discography thus said there was. Meanwhile, we asked A. Warhol and S. Morrison. They said, "No. No blue or green bananas." So okay, enough! Until we lay some of our own eyes on one of those thangs, we hereby declare: *All Bananas Are Pink! Pink! Pink!*

MORE FOREIGN ODDITIES

In 1979, Italy and Germany issued a version of the lp with no-peel bananas, no gatefold and only song titles and band members' names on the back.

As a companion to their compilation lp *Andy Warhol's Velvet Underground,* German MGM issued a 45 of "I'm Waiting" b/w "There She" in a pic sleeve featuring the coke bottle and lips from the lp.

In 1978, Arista UK made a nice 12" of Lou's "Street Hassle" by popping "Waiting" and "Venus" on the flip. In 1982, Polydor UK made some other tracks from the 1st lp sound great with a 12" ep of "H"/ "Venus"/ "Run"/ and "Waiting." They messed up tho, with a post-Cale photo on the front.

A. WARHOL: PRODUCER?

Andy Warhol is credited with producing this album. Even says so right on the spine. Sounds/looks fab, but Andy produced this in much the same fashion as the films he was associated with at the time: he arranged places, dates, people, and loosely supervised production. Most of the producing was done by the band themselves, with the important exception of Tom Wilson. Tom was a most hip producer (Dylan, Zappa, Animals) who did the great things with "Venus," "ATP," "Sun. Morn," "Waiting" and "H." *Uptight* reported Wilson produced a "Longer, poppier" 45 of "Sunday Morning." Not so. The 45 is the same as on the album.

Mexico put out the first lp in '84 with a different cover (late 70's blue Lou blowing smoke) in another Polydor series—"30 Anos De Musica

Rock-Salvat" (saved?). Thing is, they put a group photo with Doug Yule on the back cover.

Mexico: Polydor 822 308-1—1984

IN A TEN-LP BOX? ON DGG?

Even with all these odd turns in the *VU & Nico* story, perhaps the oddest company the album has ever kept is in this big fat box.

Story goes, according to the record importer Blue Angel's catalog, that a few years back (probably bored) managers at Deutsche Grammophon (generally regarded as the world's greatest record company) were looking through back issues of *Sounds* (a European music mag), and noticed that many of *Sounds'* strongly recommended albums had lapsed into ungettibility. 'Zounds,' we imagined them crying, 'we haff zose darn tapes in the basement!' And lo they were, and were made again into records and filled a box full as *The Sounds Set*:

Phil Spector's Christmas Album
Doctors of Madness
King Crimson / Earthbound
Eno / Here Come the Warm Jets
Savage Rose / Travelin'
Tony Williams Lifetime / Turn It Over
Julie Driscoll / Julie Driscoll
Slade / Whatever Happened to Slade
The Who / Live at Leeds
and The Velvet Underground & Nico

I don't think the peel peels. DGG 2675229

Side 1: Sunday Morning, I'm Waiting For The Man, Femme Fatale, Venus In Furs, Run Run Run, All Tomorrow's Parties

Side 2: Heroin, There She Goes Again, I'll Be Your Mirror, The Black Angel's Death Song, European Son

White Light/White Heat

The Players: Reed, Tucker, Cale, Morrison

USA: Verve 5046 (mono), V6/5046 (stereo)—Dec. 1967

MGM M3F/4950 (reissue)—1974

Polygram 825 290 (reissue)—March 1985

UK: Verve S/LP 4021—1967

UK: MGM 235 3024 (reissue)—1971

The dark, mysterious aura of the Velvet Underground was forever cemented in place with the release of this baby. From the sleek menace of the cover to the roaring drug wars inside, this album still challenges, still kicks, still thrills. While this record hasn't had the marketing adventures of the first, it's had a few variations.

BLACK SKULLS, BOOTLEG NON-SKULLS

Both the original US and UK versions carried the black-on-black skulls. After a few years, though, things got odd. Credits on the back popped on and off. We haven't been able to detect any pattern or rationale in the different ways that "Cover Concept: Andy Warhol," "There She Comes Now (sic)," and "Lou Reed: Lead Guitar" (as opposed to "Lou Reed: Guitar") are there or not there together or separately. There are even copies of the lp that leave "The Velvet Underground" off the spine. We've also found copies with both "mono" and "stereo" printed on the label (turned out the things were mono, but guess Verve wasn't quite sure). And we've also found two copies with the cover pasted upside down.

In North America things went black around 1972. The tatoo went away, and the label went from blue to black. Some say this was Verve's own low-budget doings, while others say this was the low-budget doings of bootleggers who were simply putting out the album on their own. Meanwhile in 1974, MGM sort of rereleased it as part of their *Archtypes* series. Same music, incongruous cover. By 1977, definately illegitimate copies arrived. They pack no skull, and have fuzzy printing. Good vinyl, tho'.

Meanwhile, in England in 1971, Andy's black on black was replaced by . . . toy soldiers (we've never heard a reason why). And the current copies of the lp carry a blurry photo of the original dumb soldier photo.

Our Japanese friends kept the skull alive on their copies, and cheers to Polygram for getting the skull on their reissues.

MONO OR STEREO?

Despite massive bleed-through, the stereo mix generally separates the band. It's gtr/drums (left) gtr/organ (right) mostly. The mono mix makes for a *big* pile of noise on the loud tracks. Too piled up, in our opinion.

There's too much going on in the band to jam everyone onto one track. So in reverse from the first lp, the mono *WL/WH* sounds phony. After being hammered by the mono, I sighed with relief when I went back to the widescreen roar of the stereo. Also with the mono, "The Gift" can't be split between the narration and the instrumental "Booker T." We all need to hear just "Booker T" every now and then. Go to the mono *WL/WH* only when you're ready for an intense experience.

GOOD REMASTERING WORK

The new version does sound better. For the most part. Some of you may well miss the black forcefield the original carries. However, the incredible distortion has been helped in the process. Things are clearer and thus even more powerful. The distortion is still there but doesn't interfere, doesn't sit on top of the instruments—it's as if it's on a separate track. Aside from all that, they've mixed down the narration on "The Gift," a good move.

Side 1: White Light/White Heat, The Gift, Lady Godiva's Operation, Here She Comes Now

Side 2: I Heard Her Call My Name, Sister Ray

The Velvet Underground

The Players: Reed, D. Yule, Morrison, Tucker

USA: MGM SE-4617—March 1969

Polygram 815 454 (reissue)—March 1985

UK: MGM CS 8108—May 1969

Polydor 2353 022 (reissue)—1971

After the sonic slaughter of *WL/WH*, this third album came out perversely "removed." "We did the third album deliberately as anti-production," says Sterling. "It sounds like it was done in a closet—it's flat, and that's the way we wanted it. The songs are all very quiet and it's kind of insane. I like the album." Indeed. It is a hell of a statement to blast the VU meters on one album, then record the next "in a closet." (It should be noted that factors contributing to the decision to record simply and quietly were the absence of both wildman Cale, and all of Sterling and Lou's amp-blasting equipment, which had been stolen at the airport.)

In any case, it seems that engineer Val Valentin made a regular, normal, clean mix of the tapes, but Lou came along to create the "closet" mix that came out as the album in America.

For some reason, the original UK release not only cut the photo of Lou sideways (where it was cut up and down in the US), but was the Val Valentin (V.V.) mix. The US mix soon replaced the Valentin mix, and the 1971 reissue cut the photo the up & down way.

THIRD OUT OF THE CLOSET

Somehow, a German vision of the V.V. mix popped up in the early 80's, and Japan had it as well. As Polygram got their master tape for the three reissues from Japan, it's our good fortune that this different mix is finally available in the USA. So what? So guitars! Drumbeats! Bass lines! Vocal inflections! Subtle nuances! Whole new effects! After 15 years, the Velvet Underground's third album is finally out of the closet.

DIFFERENT MIXES, DIFFERENT "KINDA LOVE"

There's a night and day difference in the mixes. I can't think of another rock album where the mix is so important. We now have a new perspective to listen to and judge the 3rd lp, an album that has been neglected due in large part to the muffled mix.

So let's check out this new sound: The most obvious change is the different take of "Some Kinda Love." I'd guess this one wasn't used due to Lou's singing—he's hoarse and congested (remember those times during *Loaded* and at Max's in 1970 when his voice gave out and he couldn't sing). However, his condition doesn't detract from the tune; rather it gives it a more intimate feel. The other big change is the song's instrumentation. The US version has one guitar, in counter point to a cowbell. This new version has two guitars, one ringing in each channel. Their conversation and presence pushes the song along. One of the unending talents of this band was the way Sterling and Lou could buzzsaw eternal rhythms and jangle asphalt jungle leads. In this version we can hear that, in a faster, wilder atmosphere than the US.

Overall the Valentin version is brighter, snappier, funkier, more colorful, more exciting and interesting. Everything sounds better. And there are other differences: "Beginning to See the Light" begins with a joyous screech of electric guitar; Moe's bass drum is boosted to become a very important part of "I'm Set Free;" "What Goes On" is shifted to a guitar/organ duet/duel; and "Murder Mystery's" guitar, organ and drums swirl back and forth, heightening the challenge, the fun, and the mystery of the song. So hurray for whomever. Now we have two valued and contrasting versions of this mighty fine record.

THE TRADITIONAL COVER CHANGES

The UK cover has lighter photos—you can see more of the radiator, chair and wall behind the band on the front. It's lighter to the point that Polydor UK adds their own black circle around the band. So on the US, there's the band, and black airbrushing around them. On the British, there's now the band, the US airbrushed black and a second painted black ring. Tow black auras for our heroes. The black cover is lighter as well. We can see much more of the fern branch in the corner. No added black aura, though.

The current German issue repeats the cover photo on the back, doing away with the goofy-looking Lou cut-in-two shot.

THE TRADITIONAL CREDIT CONVOLUTIONS

On the US edition it goes, "Photos: Billy Name. Art direction: Dick Smith." On the UK it says, "Photos and Convolutions: Billy Name." And so does the 1985 US reissue. Why? Dunno. And you'll note the German copy dispenses altogether with production credits. And how about this: the French reissue offers "Beginning" twice at the start of side 2.

HOW LONG DOES "WHAT GOES ON" GO ON, AND WHO LIED ABOUT "JESUS"?

The back cover of the US lp lists "What Goes On" with a 4:52 running time, while the label says it goes 3:35. Well, "Some Kinda Love" follows, and it also has a 3:35 time and we bet that's the mix-up cuz "WGO" surely is 4:52. Except on the 45 which fades after chorus #2 and clocks in at a snappy 2:40. Remember now, AM radio and its *hit* singles ruled the pop world in 1969. "Underground" FM radio was little-known, and certainly unknown to MGM. OK, so they threw "WGO" at the AM wall, what the hey. The funny thing is "Jesus," on the flip, is listed as being 2:55 on the 45 when it's actually the same length as on the lp—3:24. This leads us to suppose some canny MGM wag lied, and listed the song at 2:55, knowing no AM station wanted any 45 more than 3 minutes long inside their building. This is funny considering that "Jesus" has probably yet to be played on any AM station anywhere. If someone did this seriously to keep it in the airplay ballgame, that's funny. If Lou or someone did it as a pure joke, that's funny too. Only thing that's unfunny is if this was simply another of MGM's dumb mistakes. Boo. Let's hold the "Jesus"-on-the-AM-radio thought awhile, shall we?

So be sure to get yourself a copy of this new/old mix. Best pressing is from Japan, as you already knew. They even toss in a lyric sheet.

Side 1: Candy Says, What Goes On, Some Kinda Love, Pale Blue Eyes, Jesus

Side 2: Beginning To See The Light, I'm Set Free, That's The Story of My Life, The Murder Mystery, Afterhours

Loaded

The Players: Reed, Morrison, D. Yule, B. Yule (drumming while Moe was with child)

USA: Cotillion SD 9034—Sept. 1970

UK: Atlantic 40113—1970

After all the fighting within the band over the arrangements and mix, the finished result has remained untampered with. It's still in print! Always has been! With even the same catalog number for 15 years now! So why do I see regular copies at record collector shows going for $8 and up? Atlantic's even put the dang thing in the budget line now.

ONLY TWO CURVEBALLS

The German reissue sports a back cover photo of Doug, Moe, Walter Powers and Willie Alexander. And we've also been told the UK cassette has side 1 where side 2 should be and vice versa. And that's about it. Think how different the VU story might have been had they been on a real label from the start . . .

Side 1: Who Loves The Sun, Sweet Jane, Rock & Roll, Cool It Down, New Age

Side 2: Head Held High, Lonesome Cowboy Bill, I Found A Reason, Train Round The Bend, Oh! Sweet Nuthin'

Live at Max's Kansas City

The Players: Morrison, Reed, D. Yule, B. Yule (Moe too pregnant)

USA: Cotillion SD 9500—May 1972

UK: Atlantic K 30022—1972

The first "legal bootleg" documents the band's final night (Lou left after this performance). Beyond that, the lp has had, like *Loaded,* a quiet history. Culled from Warhol pal Brigid Polk's little cassette player, it came out as a $3.98 list budget album in the days of the $6.98 giants. Stayed in print, too, although the list is up to a now budget-line $6.98.

Mono? Stereo? Blank?

Oddest thing about this record is that some labels say mono, some say stereo, and others take no position and are blank as to the aural content. Some even have stereo printed on the label and a big "MONO" stamped over it. No matter. Sound-wise, it's all tinny cassette-style mono from Brigid's little recorder.

"Sunday Morning" gets credited to Lou and John instead of Lou alone as on the first lp. Yes, that is Jim Carroll mumbling for Pernods between songs. Double Pernods.

Japan Again

Even though this is one of the easiest (and least expensive) VU lps to find, you can fill out your Japanese VU set with one of these. It seems wonderfully silly for them to turn their high-tech vinyl standards toward this audio wretch. They've also included a lyric sheet, complete with Lou's between-song chats.

Side 1: Waiting, Jane, Cowboy Bill, Beginning

Side 2: Mirror, Pale, Sun Morn, New Age, Femme, Afterhours

Live 1969

The Players: Reed, Tucker, Morrison, D. Yule, and perhaps Cale

USA: Mercury SRM 2-7504—April 1974

Mercury/Polygram SRM 2-7504 (reissue)—March 1985

Who? Where? When?

This album popped right up in 1974 when it was commonly thought (by me anyway) that the Velvet vaults were shut forever. But here came two discs full ("103 minutes of music" as it said as a selling point on the cover— the band was not a hot item in 1974) with lots of good sound and fine music. I have no complaints except . . . something's a bit indefinite here . . .

"1969 is something of an arbitrary date," says Lou of the package. You'll notice no personnel, no dates, nor places are named. And the centerfold photo has a big black spot where Nico used to sit, and Cale is shaded into haze. What's up?

We suppose this was done to avoid any legal problems as Mercury tried very hard to roll this collection into a simple concept of this being the VU, 1969, live.

Thing is, it really sounds like Cale's organ rolling around "WGO" on here. Considering the lack of info on the album, it really means these tapes could really be from anywhere, anytime. Now if it is Cale on "WGO," that would make that track from 1968. There are other keyboards on here, but none so Calean. This isn't a big problem in the scope of world problems, but it is damned aggravating not to know if we're hearing the original four in action or what.

OKAY, WHERE?

Most of *1969* was recorded in a private club in Dallas named End Of Cole Ave. Which it was. The most likely spot for any 1968 tracks with Cale would be The Matrix, in San Francisco.

Beyond all that, this album has had little variation. US Mercury put out a 'Highlights' 8-track when the album was released, with about half of the songs. In 1983, Italy put out *Live Success, Vol. I & II,* as two albums that add up to *1969.* It stayed in print pretty well with Mercury, lasting through a few label changes. Polygram bought the Mercury label, and reissued the album in 1985 without the gatefold.

Side 1: Waiting, Lisa Says, WGO, Jane

Side 2: We're Gonna Have a Real Good Time Together, Femme, New Age, Rock & Roll, Beginning

Side 3: Ocean, Pale, H

Side 4: Some Kinda, Over You, Sweet Bonnie Brown/It's Just Too Much, WL/WH, Mirror

Squeeze

The Players: D. Yule, Ian Paice

UK only: Polydor 2383 180—Feb. 1973

DOUG YULE & NO MOE

A cheaply smutty cover and no band credits make this a shamefully deceptive package. Issued only in the UK (good enough), this features one

D. Yule writing, arranging, producing and playing everything. Except drums, which were somehow bapped by Ian Paice. Yes, the Deep Purple machine head. Sterling was long gone to Austin, leaving just Moe as a real member.

Poor Moe. Too pregnant for *Loaded* and Max's, she was even squoze off *Squeeze*. Of course missing this Doug Yule solo affair is not the same as missing *Loaded,* but it's sad it happened. A bit unclear as well. Best we can ascertain Doug wanted her, but manager Steve Sesnick did not, and somehow positioned Moe out.

Beyond that, there's little to note. It has remained in print all this time with no 45s.

Side 1: Little Jack, Crash, Caroline, Mean Old Man, Dopey Joe, Wordless

Side 2: She'll Make You Cry, Friends, Send No Letter, Jack & Jane, Louise

VU

The Players: Morrison, Tucker, Reed, D. Yule, Cale

USA: Polygram 823 299—Feb. 1985 (cassette also)

Biggest VU noises in recent years came from this album of cleaned up demos. This album began when someone mentioned to Lou what a good thing it would be to remaster/clean up the VU lps. The time was right as a new company, Polygram, had just taken over Polydor, who had owned the old Verve/MGM catalog. Lou said yes; Polygram was interested; and work began. This was, either the original tapes couldn't be found, or the tapes were damaged and could not be reworked. The good thing was that as they looked for the lp tapes, they found a number of unreleased demo tapes. They decided to clean them up, and you know the fine results. Most of the demos had been available for a while (mostly on tapes made from Sterling's noisy acetates) but it certainly is fine to hear them in pure form.

There were some surprises: "Lisa Says," and "I Can't Stand It" hadn't been out before. Also, the original lineup for the album not only had slightly different mixes on some tracks, but also included "Ferryboat Bill" instead of "Ocean." The reason was that "Ocean's" master tape was lost, and the rough reference mix could only be EQ'd to sound better. However, artistic form prevailed over technical merits, and "Ocean" replaced "Bill," even after many advance release cassettes had been sent out with "Bill" and the different mixes. See VU Demo Sessions on page

286 for further info. This isn't the 'Great Lost VU Album' per se (there is no such thing), but rather about as good an album of these sundry tapes as could be fashioned.

Side 1: (all tracks with D. Yule unless noted) I Can't Stand It (recorded 1969), Stephanie Says (March 1968, with Cale), She's My Best Friend (1969), Lisa Says (1969), Ocean (1969)

Side 2: Foggy Notion (1969), Inside Your Heart (March 1968 with Cale), One Of These Days (1969), I'm Sticking With You (1969)

The Music Factory

USA: MGM—1968 (promo only) (2 lps)

The only sort of official VU interview ever distributed by MGM was part of this "Music Factory" series. MGM produced these for the "underground" FM radio of the day. On them, a very laid-back Tom Wilson would chat with MGM's musical guests, and play hip MGM cuts. On this one, Lou and John chatted about playing many odd instruments, and John speaks at length on using sound vibrations to cut brain tissue, create weather and regulate people's moods.

Also on here is an ad for Nico's *Chelsea Girl* lp. Songs played are by Tim Hardin, the Mothers, as well as "The Fairest of the Seasons" by Nico, and the VU's "Mirror."

The album is very rare, with probably only a few hundred made. See the Boston-area *Forced Exposure* fanzine for a complete transcription in their summer '85 #7/8 issue.

Spinning at a Faster Speed

VELVET UNDERGROUND 45s

The record companies, for the most part, picked the 45s. Thus these are an odd mix of the bizarre and the could-a-been-hit-ifs . . . The hardest thing to find out about the 45s is which ones were actually released to the public. Often times labels will release a 45 as a promo first. If it doesn't generate interest/airplay, end of story. Thus most of the USA 45s can only be found as dj copies. The first two did come out as regular stock copies, and there's not even many of those about (only ones we've found were at Moe's house).

"All Tomorrow's Parties"/ "I'll Be Your Mirror"

USA: Verve 10427—1966 (mono only)

"Mirror" is cut to 2:16. This first release came in a beautiful promo-only picture sleeve. Gaze at it in the back of *Uptight*.
"Sunday Morning"/ "Femme Fatale"

USA: Verve 10466—1966 (mono only)

Uptight says "Sunday is a longer, poppier version." Wrong. It's the same as on the lp. It peaked at 103 on the *Cash Box* singles chart. These first two 45s came out before the album.
"White Light/White Heat"/ "Here She Comes Now"

USA: Verve 10560—1968 (mono only) (promo only?)
"Here She Comes Now"/ "I Heard Her Call My Name"

USA: Verve 10560—1968 (mono only) (promo only?)

UK: Verve SVLP 9184—1968 (mono only)
"What Goes On"/ "Jesus"

USA: MGM 14057—1969 (mono only) (promo only?)

This was also released in the UK. See the section on the 3rd album for details on the discrepancy between the times listed on the lp and the 45.
"Who Loves The Sun"/ "Oh! Sweet Nuthin'"

USA: Cotillion 44107—1971

We've only seen promo copies of this. They have "Sun" stereo on one side, mono on the other. However, one of our readers writes he has a stock copy of "Sun" with "Nuthin'" on the flip, and the "Nuthin'" is an uncut 7:23. Which prompts him to say it "stands as one of the most artistically uncompromising 45s ever."

LATER FOREIGN 45s
"Waiting"/ "Run"/ "Candy"

UK: MGM—1971 (stereo)
"Waiting"/ "Candy"/ "WL/WH"

Holland: MGM—1971 (picture sleeve)
"Head Held"/ "Train Round"

France: (?) (pic slv of *Loaded* cover drawing with "Train Round The Bond" (*sic*) printed on top.
"Sweet Jane"/ "Rock & Roll"

Germany: 1974 (pic slv of *Loaded* cover again)
"Who Loves The Sun"/ "Sweet Jane"

UK: Atlantic—1971
"Sweet Jane"/ "Rock & Roll"

UK: Atlantic K 10339—1972
"Waiting"/ "Run"

Germany: MGM 2006 310—1973 (?) (pic)

This 45 comes billed on the sleeve and record as "Lou Reed & The Velvet Underground." The sleeve is a glitter rock style item, with Lou in solo eye makeup days. On the back it pictures "The Latest LP," the silver swirl with round pic of Lou in the middle (1975/6 reissue).

TWELVE INCHERS
"Street Hassle" Flipside

UK: Arista ARIST 12198—1978 ("Waiting," "Venus") (out)

Polydor 12"

UK: Polydor POPSX 603—1982 ("H," "Venus," "Waiting," "Run")

Good package. Only slip-up is a Yule photo on front of these Cale-days tracks.

VU Promo 12"

USA: Polygram PRO 349-1—1985 ("Foggy," [edit], "I Can't Stand It") (promo only)

ENTER THE COMPILATIONS

Velvet Underground

USA only: MGM GAS 131—1972 (?) (out of print)

GAS was MGM's Golden Archive Series, in which some of their dormant (i.e. unselling) back catalog was reshaped into, voila, a Big Series of Collections with Similar Covers. Ironically, the series cover theme was repeated photos of the artists in the style popularized by . . . tada! Andy Warhol. And like most Big Collections with Similar Covers, this one seemed to jump straight into the cut-out bin. This was the first VU compilation, and though, to look over the company they kept on the MGM roster (Wayne Newton, Billie Holiday, Cowsills, Ian & Sylvia) is to see how lost the band was on that label.

Beyond that, this is a tolerable grouping of songs from the first three albums. A bit tame perhaps:

Side 1: Candy, Sun. Morn., Femme, WL/WH, Jesus
Side 2: H, Beginning, Here She, Afterhours

Lou Reed and the Velvet Underground

USA only: PRIDE/MGM PRD-0022—1973 (out of print)

As Lou crashed the charts with "Wild Side" in 1973, the VU vaults creaked open again and . . . top billing! Thus VU repack #2, and the first with Lou's name up top (although some promo copies of *Loaded* came with a "featuring LOU REED" sticker). On the first printing, the label is subtitled "That's The Story Of My Life." Nice touch.

Pride was MGM's budget line quickie label. Once a group got popular, as the Small Faces and Grateful Dead did, Pride would buy some of their old tapes and toss 'em out (nearly directly into the cut-out bin) in trashy slap-dash packages. What is this four-way swan doing on a VU lp cover? At least these compilers weren't afraid of the *WL* lp, as we get four from there, including "Sister Ray."

The 1973 Italian issue of the album had a different cover and Waiting instead of Story.

Side 1: That's The Story, Ray, Godiva
Side 2: H, Sun Morn, ATP, There She, WL/WH, Femme

Andy Warhol's Velvet Underground Featuring Nico

Germany: METRO 2683 006 (2 lps)—1973

UK: MGM 2683 006 SELECT—1973

Nice set in its songs & sound, but quite indistinct and fanciful in its liner notes. The uncredited notes try to justify the Warhol top bill by stating that Andy "opened his own club, The Velvet Underground," which was "the first to be truly psychedelic," with diversions that were both "chromosonic" and "cosmotronic" (?). The notes go on to say how Andy wanted "very loud, very heavy music," and thus formed his own group. "And so the Velvet Underground was born." Of course, "the many demands on his time meant that he did not remain an active member for long, but his instigation of it had predestined its future and he left an indelible mark on its style."

Lots of other facts on the album are fuzzy as well. Nowhere does it say where it was made, and the liner notes are badly translated from German. Nico is called "an edition" (addition?), there are a few typos, and the notes end with this curious sentence: "[this album] is an important historical document tracing the development of a group which has both witnessed the insection [?] of the wilder underground and participated in its evolution." HMMM . . .
   Side 1: Waiting, Candy, Run, WL/WH, ATP
   Side 2: Sun Morn, I Heard Her, Femme, H, Here She, There She
   Side 3: Ray, Venus
   Side 4: Euro Son, Pale, BADS, Beginning

Superstarshine Vol. 20

Holland: Metro/Polydor Special 2356097—early 70s
   Side 1: Waiting, Sun Morn, BADS, Here She, There She, WL, Lady
   Side 2: Fairest of Seasons, Winter Song, Lenny Bruce (these three by Nico), Beginning, Candy, Afterhours

Pop History Vol 19

Germany: Polydor 2626 019 (2 lps)—early 70s

This is the infamous 'Once Upon a Time' series with the lobster bomber cover. Nico's songs mixed in with VU.

Side 1: Lady, Eulogy to Lenny Bruce, WGO, Winter Song

Side 2: Some Kind of, Gift, Chelsea Girls, Set Free

Side 3: Murder Mystery, Little Sister, Mirror, Wrap your Troubles in Dreams

Side 4: Fairest of Seasons, Afterhours, It was a Pleasure Then, Story of My Life

Pop History #12

UK: Polydor 2612 021—?

Lou Reed and the Velvet Underground

Germany: MGM 2315 258 SUPER—1976

Side 1: Waiting, Ray, Lady

Side 2: Who Loves Sun, ATP, There She, WL, Femme

The Velvet Underground

UK only: MGM 2354 033 SPECIAL—1976 (?)

These VU compilations almost always were part of some large series of lps. These series usually had a unifying theme, such as Pop Innovators, or People Who Took Drugs Every Second. This album was part of the "Special Price Series."

Side 1: WL, WGO, Venus, That's The Story, Here She, Beginning, Jesus

Side 2: Run, Some Kinda, The Gift, I'm Set Free, I Heard Her

The Story of . . . Velvet Underground

Germany: Polydor 2664 405 (2 lps)—1978

This is a reissue of the 1973 'Warhol' set. It's part of another Big Series which includes Jimi Hendrix, the Rubettes and the Spotniks. Even so, this is a better than usual package. There are long liner notes (in German, so I'm only making educated guesses about them) that seem basically ok (Andy doesn't get credit for starting it all). Only mistakes I can see are that they captioned Sterling's photo with Cale's name, and they named Doug Yule's photo Sterling. Also, all the songs are listed on the back cover as being recorded and published in 1969, though even the liner notes know better.

Of special note: I showed this album to Sterling a few years back, and he chuckled and beamed proudly at the notes on the cover that call the VU "eine Banddie vor nichts haltmachte." He waved the record around to get his family's attention. "See, see?" he called happily. "'A band that knew no bounds . . .'"

The Velvet Underground & Lou Reed

Italy: Superstar SU 1012—1980 (?)

Another "series" lp. This Italian "Superstar" line does feature swell color photos in a 12-page booklet, and as I write this, the album has popped up for about 5 bux in some US record shops. The pictures alone make this a good deal, but we also get Lou quoted about lots of things (Zappa and Dylan are two), as well as VU history, Lou history (in Italian, so I don't know exactly what they are saying), and a good bit of discography.
> *Side 1:* Ray, Venus
> *Side 2:* Euro Son, Pale, BADS, Beginning

Rock #38: The Velvet Underground

Spain: Polydor 28 61 301—1982

Another series lp here, with big blowup of the Eric Emerson photo on the front. Best thing about this package is that it doesn't fool around: "Ray" kicks off side 1, and "Euro Son" leads on 2.
> *Side 1:* Ray, Venus
> *Side 2:* Euro Son, Pale, BADS, Beginning

VU TRACKS ON SAMPLERS & COLLECTIONS

Entwicklung der Pop Music, Vol. 2

Germany: DGG 2536016—1969 (?)

DGG working with some of the Polydor stable: Hendrix, Cream and the VU ("Waiting").

Pop Giants

UK: Polydor 2482 260—1972 (?)

Strange. The jacket says "Heroin performed by Lou Reed," but it's actually the VU. Fades out halfway as well.

Underground

Germany: Polydor 184 190/1—1972 (?) 2 lps

This seems to have been released in conjunction with *Der Stern* magazine in Germany, as their name's all over the album. It's Cream, Hendrix, Arthur Brown cuts until side 3, which is given over entirely to the VU: Waiting, Sun. Morning, Head, Here She, Euro Son. Side 4 opens with cuts from their first three lps.

The Mothers vs. the Velvets

Germany: Polydor—1972 (?)

Sorry, that's all we know about this record. Heard of it being on a collector's list. We've made the scientific guess that this album is the same grouping of tracks as the VU/Mothers lp from the *Underground* set.

Rock of the USA

UK: MGM—1975

"Waiting" is on here.

All You Need Is Love

UK: Theatre Projects Records/Polydor 9199 995 (cassette 7299Ä995)—1975

This was a tie-in with a British TV series. Even though the nasty and ubiquitous "Waiting" was never mentioned on the program, it's one of the twenty tracks on the album. Right between "Apache" by the Shadows and Neil Sedaka's deadly remake of "Breaking Up Is Hard To Do."

Polygram In-store Sampler

USA: Polygram SA-057—1985 (promo only)

Some of the best company the VU's ever kept—Van Morrison, Richard Thompson—makes this 6-song EP very fine indeed. There's two songs each, and the VU tunes are "Foggy" and "Stephanie."

Baby Boomer Classics—Twelve Electrifying Hits of the 60's

USA: JCI Records—1985

There's about twelve records in this 'Baby Boomer' series. Most are regular pop hits, but this one (#12 we believe) carries "ATP."

Lou Reed: Before the Beginning

Jades 45

USA: Time 1002—1957 (out of print)

"Lewis" Reed is credited with writing "Leave Her For Me." The Jades, one of Lou's high school combos, were first the Shades, then changed to the Jades and released this record. Lots of confusion about that.

"Leave Her" is semi-satirical teen anguish: "Take away the rosebuds, but leave her for me" is the tone. A spoken middle and massed Jordanaires-type chorus echoes the heavy sentiment of this respectible doo-wop shaded 45.

Can't pick Lou out singing or playing on here, though.

"So Blue," written by another Jade, comes with a honking sax, more Jordanaire vocals, and unlike side other, I can guess that's Lou chopping out some guitar chords. Pretty good song too.

LOU'S REED'S PICKWICK/DESIGN YEAR—1964

Lou: "We'd go down to the studio for an hour or two and cut three or four albums really quickly . . ."

1964: Lou Reed graduates from Syracuse University. Goes back home on Long Island. Gets a job songwriting for Pickwick Records. Commuted daily to this job in New York City. He's 22.

In many ways, this is the craziest part of the entire crazy Velvet Underground story. No work Lou has done is so trivial, so pre-fabricated, so tossed off (*Legendary Hearts* and "Disco Mystic" notwithstanding). Yet that year at Pickwick may have taught Lou some important things, and helped bring out talents and traits that stay with him to this day. And no period in his recorded life is so vague, so unknown. Nowhere is there much explanation of what went on at Pickwick. None of the records give any true info, the bootlegs only guess, and the VU/Lou books are quite sketchy (*Uptight* only mentions the Primitives 45). So let's try to look a little deeper . . .

Pickwick Records was (they went under in 1982) the USA's #1 low budget record scamp operation. They specialized in reissues, rack jobbing and exploitation lps. They'd 'exploit' musical trends by taking whatever was hot, and putting out ersatz lps that would resemble the hot thing in cover and music, but would be made by studio musicians. For the surf beat, for example, they'd have a surfboard on the cover, and some basic surf sounding beats on the album. Completely phony, completely capitalist.

So what a crazy atmosphere for a 22-year-old rock and roll lover to work, really work. "Writing songs." Lou: "There were four of us literally locked in a room, writing songs. They would say, 'Write ten California songs, ten Detroit songs.'" After studying Latin poetry and working with Delmore Schwartz at Syracuse, this cynical exploitative reduction of his beloved rock & roll to hack formulas must have clearly made Lou fully aware of how the Music Machine works, and how songwriters are not always inspired by pure love of life.

What a negative, nutty situation! Grinding out cheap imitation songs to cash in on whatever was hot. And for what audience? Have any of you ever seriously bought one of these albums really thinking Beats=Beatles? This was pop trash in its lowest, most unhip form. And only some of it was bad enough to be good in a camp way. All Pickwick cared about was selling records. So no one really cared what was said, what went down on tape. So there was no reason to be profound, but there was plenty of room to be wacky, as who'd care? With no writing credits on the album, not even Lou's parents would know if he wrote anything depraved.

Thus the peverse dichotomy: two-bit, disdainful situation of fast buck hackwork/yet with Lou fueled by inspirations of sources (and who knows what else) and free to work without any ego fears or such.

And out they came: Cycle Annie, The Ostrich, Sneaky Pete, You're Driving Me Insane, Tiger In My Tank. All written and recorded in 1964. We can hear Lou for sure singing, yelping nothing-matters vocals. All the tracks share the same rough, "party" sound. Lou may be twanging guitar as well, but there's no telling. We know only a few things for certain about these tracks, and the road gets tricky ahead, so let's look at the facts:

DEFINITE LOU INVOLVEMENT

Soundsville

USA: DESIGN DLP 187—1964 or 65 (mono or stereo)

Design was Pickwick's label for such phony business. The cover tells the theme of the album: songs from all around the hit capitols of the world! England! New York! Detroit! Hot Rod! Big grab bag of all that was happening then. Thus what was probably the same group of Pickwick troupers was given many different names. Lou's songs hail from England (as the Roughnecks, "You're Driving Me Insane,") Hot Rod (Beachnuts, "I've Got a Tiger In My Tank") and Motorcycle (Beachnuts again, "Cycle Annie").

Tricky thing here is, besides the obvious vocals, we don't know what Lou does on any of these Pickwick tracks. There are several schools of thought on this. One of which says Lou wrote and plays on the whole *Soundsville* album. Could be. What do you think?

Out of Sight

USA: Design DLP 269—1967 or 1968

We're guessing 67/8 here, as the cover has gone hippie lettering. Here Design has gathered some bad tracks by big names (such as Paul Revere, Joe Tex, Lou Rawls and Vic Dana) and filled out the lp with a few of their own. "Cycle Annie" returns, along with two other *Soundsville* cuts.

PRIMITIVES 45

"The Ostrich"/ "Sneaky Pete"—Pickwick 1001—1964

These were the tracks Pickwick thought could actually make some noise on their own. They put them out as a 45, and had Lou put together a backing band for about six appearances in the NYC area. Thus did Lou, John, Tony Conrad and Walter DeMaria dabble in the live pop life.

The 45 gives us the only credits of the Pickwick days. Both songs are credited to the writing team of Vance-Sims-Reed-Phillips.
"Insane"/ "Cycle Annie" 45

USA (?): Obnoxious Records/Skydog SMAC-001—1976 (out of print)

This 45 came out right before the *White Heat* ep. Good cover, but the sound of these Pickwick ditties is inferior to other boots and tapes. They also go so far as to give Lou sole writing credit. It's hard to say where this record comes from as it does carry a French address, writing ("Velours Souterrain", get it?), even a Paris phone number. However, many bootleggers throw in misinformation such as that to confuse. Until we hear differently, we say it's a USA job.
Side 1: Insane (Roughnecks)
Side 2: Cycle (Beachnuts)

White Heat EP

USA (?): no label or number—1976 (out of print)

"All composed by L.H.Reed" (*sic*) this anonymous record reads. But there's lots of clues on the well-done pic sleeve—Lou in sunglasses in front of band and U-Haul; frontside is NYC skyline with pin-ups, the band, Warhol, etc. scattered across town. Best of all these VU demos sound mighty fine.

Side 1: Foggy

Side 2: Inside Your Heart, Sticking, Ferryboat Bill

Primitive: Pre-Velvets

USA: no label or number—1976 (out of print)

Here came more of the Reed Pickwick years, all notated as to which group and even on which record the cuts originated. The sleeve also thanks "Lenny the K" (let's guess Lenny Kaye) and CIA rep Constantine Radulavitch," the estimable VU collector and chronicler who hasn't been heard from in a long time and who should please please contact us.

The sound here is fine. For the cover they chose the mysterious "Beats" photo (the one on the left of the *Beats!!!!The Merseyside Sound!* Pickwick scam lp). That has probably spread the notion that it's Lou and/or John in there. We say no to that, based on complete denials from Sterling and Moe, as well as what our eyes say. No Lou, no John.

Side 1: Ostrich (Primitives), Cycle Annie (Beachnuts)

Side 2: Sneaky Pete (Primitives), Insane (Roughnecks)

All three of these 45s are nice to see, and did fill a need in the late 70's. However, the songs are available elsewhere on easier to obtain lps and tapes.

History of Syracuse Music, Vol VII

USA: ECEIP PSLP 1013—1975

One of a series of lps of dubious legality that chronicled the Syracuse scene. "Cycle Annie" is here.

History of Syracuse Music, Vol X–XI

USA: ECEIP PSLP 1016/1017—1978 (?) (2 lps)

Good area, good school, but eleven albums worth? Lou is here in the shape of "You're Driving Me Insane." Of added interest is the portion of a press conference on here with John and Yoko. The occasion was an art show of their work in 1975. However, they don't talk about Lou, or the VU. They do mention Jesus, though.

Robertha Williams 45

"Tell Mamma Not to Cry"/ "Maybe Tomorrow"

USA: Uptown 707—1964 (?)

Songwriting credit for both sides of this most likely Pickwick offshoot label goes: Vance-Sims-Reed-Phillips. That's the great Primitives songwriting crew. So Lou's involved to that extent. Anything more, however, is unknown.

"Maybe Tomorrow" also showed up on a low-budget lp. It's the same track as the 45, except credited to another person. Yes, the lp is titled *Irma Thomas-Maxine Brown-Ronnie Dickerson*. It's Grand Prix KS-426 (a Pickwick label). And Ronnie is credited with "Maybe Tomorrow." 1968 or so.

"Tell Mamma" is an okay Shangri-La type tune of teen torment (she's running off with a teen tough, but Tell Mamma it'll be ok . . . somehow). "Maybe Tomorrow" is similar, Spector-echoing females opining that "Maybe Tomorrow I'll find that special one."

"Love Can Make You Cry"

Just to keep everything confusing, we'd like to point out that another of the songs credited to Ronnie Dickerson on this album is titled "Love Can Make You Cry." There's no credits at all on the lp, but in an interview in Holland, Lou said he once wrote a song titled "Love Can Make You Cry." Make of this what you will.

POSSIBLE LOU INVOLVEMENT

Soundsville

Some folks say many of the other tracks on the lp are good and/or goofy enough to have been largely written and/or influenced by Lou. Why, "I've Got A Tiger In My Tank" is on the Primitives boot ep, even though we can't be sure Lou's on the track.

Anyway, these Pickwick albums were released around the same time as *Soundsville,* and Lou may be lurking within:

Jan & Dean and the Satellites (Design DLP-181)—1964

Tubby Chess and His Candy Stripe Twisters Do the Twist (Grand Prix 187)—1964

Swingin' Teen Sounds of Ronnie Dove & Terry Phillips (Design DLP 186)—1964. Yes, the same Terry Phillips of Primitives fame.

Surfsiders Sing the Beach Boys Songbook (Design DLP 208)—1966 (?)

REED/CALE BEATLEMANIA?

Some of the planet's dumbest and worst ever albums came to pass when the Beatles landed. Their cash explosion seemed to inspire every quick-buck "artist" into a frenzy to follow the fabs and release albums that (1) Englishly sang of "gulls" (girls), (2) had harmonies that sang "oooooh" lots, (3) had some sort of long-haired creatures on the cover, and (4) printed at least three of these words on the cover—"beat," "beetle," and "Mersey," "Liverpool," "England," and "Mania." Yeah, yeah, yeah. These records took at least a week to be recorded and released, and must have sold dozens in some of the USA's finer drug stores. This is the setting for the *Beats* and *Merseybeats* lps, and the rumor that Reed and maybe Cale decorate the covers and embellish the awful sounds within. These are the possibilities:

Beats!!!! The Merseyside Sound
(Design DLP 170)—1964
Beat-a-mania *(Design DLP 172)—1964*
The Liverpool Beats *(Rondo)—1965*
Billy Pepper & the Pepperpots/ "Merseymania" *(UK: Allegro All 731)—*
1965 (?)

The Beatles were so big they inspired *two* quickie lps from Design. Let's look first at *Beats!!!!*

This is the record that started all the talk about Lou/John being on the cover etc. It's complicated as *The Liverpool Beats* is the same record as *Beats!!!!* Apparently Rondo leased the record from Design and put it out in a similar package a year later. Or maybe Rondo is another Pickwick label. In any case, these are the infamous cover photos, one of which turned up on the Primitives ep bootleg, implying Lou/John involvement, or a sly sense of humor on the bootlegger's part. Okay, that ep photo maybe could be perhaps Reed or Cale. But in proper context, no, doubtful. You see, The Rondo lp took one photo from *Beats!!!!* album and blew it up big on the cover (the one of them pensively sitting). To be fair, it's not the exact same photo; it's the same pose, but it's a second before or after the *Beats!!!!* shot. In this shot the chap in the upper left does look a bit like our pal John . . . although some say it's Lou.

However, the *Beats!!!!* cover offers more photos, and it's clear that it's neither Cale nor Reed on there. Clear to us anyway. Check it out yourself. See what the guy you thought was Lou/John looks like in the other photos. We showed this to Sterling (who had never heard the rumor). He scoffed heartily at the entire notion. So there we are—no hard evidence of involvement. Maybe they're in the grooves, but they're not on the cover.

The second "Beatle" album on Design, *Beat-a-mania*, has screaming teens on the cover. None of them look like John, Lou, Nico or Moe. The music is the same type of trite trash as on *Beats!!!!*—imitation harmonies, clumsy chord changes and inane subject matter.

Even England itself suffered the release of *Beat-a-mania,* in the guise of Billy Pepper and the Pepperpots. *Merseymania* is the title, with the same screaming teens cover. The liner notes, surprise to say, praise the 'Pots as being good. To think this was a year or two before *Sgt. Pepper* itself unleashes ironies that boggle all my brain.

NON-PICKWICK POSSIBLE LOU INVOLVEMENTS

Here's a number of 45s Lou's rumored to have worked on:

Spongey & the Dolls 45s

"Looks Like Love"/ "Really Really Really Really Really Really Love"

USA: Bridgeport 2001—1964 (?)

One of our readers says that Lou told him he played on this record, and co-wrote one or two of the sides (the story's gotten fuzzy by the time it reached us). That's all we know.

This is another big sound/low budget woman group production, with chimes and teen love springing eternal. The title of the flip, "Really (6 times) Love" gives a good idea how that song goes.

Felix & the Escorts 45

"Saved"/ "The Syracuse"

USA: Jag—1964 (?)

Bomp #12 reported Lou offered "technical advice" to these lads, who featured Felix (later of the Rascals) Cavaliere and Mike (soon to be a Blues Magoo) Esposito. "Saved" can also be found on the *Syracuse Hits* lp.

All Night Workers 45

"Don't Put All Your Eggs In One Basket"/ "Why Don't You Smile Now?"

USA: Round Sound 1—1965 (?)

Lloyd Baskin (later of Seatrain), Peter Stampfel (Fugs, Holy Modal Rounders), and Mike Esposito (Blues Magoos) were the main men in the Workers, and Syracuse pals of Lou. Thus they did the b-side ditty written by Lou and John along with Vance and Phillips from Pickwick. Vance also is listed as "Musical Director" on the label. "Eggs" was a bit of a regional hit in a few regions. "Smile" is given a good garage job. Is Round Sound another Pickwick branch label? Could be. Rumors persist that Lou and/or John play on this.

Pre-VU: Nico, Cale, VU

Donnie Burks 45

"Why Don't You Smile Now?"/ "Satisfaction Guaranteed"

USA: Decca 32134—1965

One more early odd record worth mentioning. Terry Phillips at it again, producing both sides. Mr. Burkes may be a Syracuse chum of Lou's. In any case, another creditable job on "Smile." No reports of Lou/John being on here.

Carol Lou Trio EP

USA: Juke One Stopper JB-2013—1970? (out of print)

Into the music biz twi-light zone we go here. Juke One Stopper is most likely another low budget Pickwick label, and the Carol Lou Trio a studio concoction like the Archies or Beachnuts. The A-side of this easy-listening record is a couple of ditties as innocuous as their titles: "Soft Summer Breeze" and "Canadian Sunset." They're described on the label as "piano instrumentals," and right they are.

Side 2 is the puzzler: the song there is titled "Afterhours," and credited to "Lou Reed," and published by Virpi, the VU publishing company for the 3rd and *Loaded* lps. Virpi? Says Sterling, "Moe and I are Virgos. Everyone else—John, Lou and Doug are Pisces. Thus Vir-Pi. Not that we were particularly astrologically-minded . . ." OK, thus it must be guessed that it is somehow our pal Lou credited with writing this song. This "Afterhours" is a very light melody played sparingly by piano, bass and very quiet drums, and has no resemblance to the VU's "Afterhours." A few bars into the song, the Trio leaves the original melody behind and moves on to a long workout of "Begin The Beguine" for some reason. So what is this thing?

We have a few possibilities. Lou may have written this limpid tune in his Pickwick days, and here it is, a "Cycle Annie" for MOR stations. Even stranger are the implications in it being the Carol LOU Trio, as if this is some sort of schizo perversion Lou has hit us with—a Metal Machine Music the other way. Or mayhaps someone was having a laff by tying Lou to this dreck. Or punishing him. Sterling insists Virpi does not publish this "Afterhours." As for us, best thing we can think of is that it's a simple clerical error—someone mixed up writing credits on two songs with the same title. Dull, yes, but the most likely story. This "Afterhours" comes in the *Everything . . .* box and the *Afterhours Tapes* (natch).

Nico 45

"I'm not saying"/ "The Last Mile"

UK only: *Immediate* 003—1965

UK only: NEMS/*Immediate* 003—1982

UK: bootleg reissue—1982 (inside *Everything . . .* box)

USA: *Compleat* 672007/*The Immediate Singles Story* lp—1985

Nico's first record is a two-sided example of 1965 musical styles and times. The third release on Rolling Stones manager Andrew Oldham's very hip pop label, "I'm Not Saying" is a breezy version of a Gordon Lightfoot tune. It must be noted that Gordon still had credibility as a folk singer and writer of songs such as "Bay of Fundy" and "Early Morning Rain." This was a hip, commercial choice for Nico. Unfortunately, they put her into a Judy Collins-type Pretty Folksinger mode, and added cloying strings. It was no hit, and is still no fun to hear today.

"The Last Mile," however, is the true Nico emerging. Jimmy Page and Oldham cooked up an "Eve of Destruction" style song of strum and doom. Page is listed as the producer and arranger of "Last Mile," as well as the producer of "Saying." However, the 1982 legit reissue says he also arranged, while the original lists one David Whittaker as arranger of the

strings of syrup. "Saying" also appeared on *The Immediate Story* (IMME-
DIATE/VIRGIN V2165) in June, 1980.

JOHN CALE PRE-VU RECORDINGS

Aside from the rumors of Cale working with Lou on Various Pickwick
tracks, there's not too many recordings Cale worked on before the VU. In
the summer of 1985 I chatted briefly with John. He was evasive about the
question of if he had worked on records before the VU ("Yes, and I have
them all," he said quickly, then changed the subject). However, he did deny
at length his most widely-reported appearance on a pre-VU project. He said
he was not on the *Theatre of Eternal Music* LaMonte lp (USA: Shandar 83
510)—(reported to be limited to 98 copies and sold for $1950. Each. In
1963.). John says he's not on any LaMonte lp, but is "on a year and a half
of daily recorded rehearsals." Although Cale says he's not on the lp, this
description of the album, written by Bruno Blum and Chris Carter in the
4/79 issue of *Best* (#129, France), probably gives some idea of what they
were rehearsing: "Indian-conceived hypnotic music with an incredibly
weird one-sided album with 39 minutes on the one side that offers a unique
and perfect sound that is to change only as you move around the room."

John is very mad that one and a half years of rehearsals, his "devoted
inspiration," remain locked up in Young's studio. He went on to say
LaMonte was losing his funding, and the building he works in was being
sold. "They'll have to look for work," said John with a wry grin. If Young
is in cash crisis, he may be forced to release some of the tapes.

Sunday Servants 45

"I'm Putting You On"/ "Who Do You Love?"

USA: World Pacific WP 77825—1964 (?)

Yes, it is said Reed and Cale play on this. For a fact, however, it says on
the label that J. Cale is writer/producer of "I'm Putting You On" (fitting
enough title). "Who Do You Love" is a Snuff Garrett production. We
haven't heard the record. We opine it's actually J.J. Cale who's on the
World Pacific lp *Leathercoated Minds* from this same period. Snuff
Garrett produced that too.

Larry & Tommy 45

"Yo-Yo"/?

UK: Polydor—1968 (?)

"Yo-Yo" is listed as being written and produced in New York by J. Cale. He's not mentioned on the other side. We haven't heard this one either, but one of our English readers says "Yo-Yo" is light pop with enough odd twists to be our Cale. But "the record's not worth the vinyl it's pressed on."

Earliest VU

EAST VILLAGE OTHER—ELECTRIC NEWSPAPER—HIROSHIMA DAY

USA only: ESP 1034—1966 (out of print)

USA (?): bootleg (no label)—1980

This is a historical hippie/yippie New York City collision of the "USA vs. Underground," in which poets (Sanders, Kupferberg, Weaver), some odd musicians (jazzman Marion Brown, Holy Modal Rounder Steve Weber), scenemakers (Gerald Malanga, Ingrid Superstar, A. Warhol) and our heroes, the EPI-era VU, appear in an aural happening. This all was their reaction to the insanity of the 1966 Vietnam world, recorded simultaneously with the inane pomp of Luci Johnson's wedding day. The date was August 6, the anniversary of the A-Bomb drop on Hiroshima.

Don't Be Misled

All this is carefully spelled out on the cover of the original ESP release. Don't be misled by modern-day naughty bootleggers who have made copies of the album and coyly slapped only "Noise by the Velvet Underground" on the cover and the label. Boo to that, cos there's only about 87 seconds of partially audible VU "noise" improvised on here.

Good Idea Gone Bad

This "Electric Newspaper" was a good idea. However the ABC broadcast of the Luci's wedding is as loud as the performers, and tends to distract and overwhelm. The VU's "noise" comes before (and during) Gerald and Ingrid's "Gossip," about matters such as Steve Reeves' masculinity, and not after, as listed on the ESP cover.

Don't Buy This Record

The boot goes for $10+, and the ESP original can be twice that. Don't buy this if you want to hear the VU play; it's a hardly memorable minute and a half. Get this only if you want to hear some of the atmosphere the band was working in at this time. "Noise" itself is best heard on the *Etc.* boot or the *Afterhours* tapes.

INDEX

USA only: flexi-disc—1967 (out of print)

This comes from *Index*, a book "by Andy," about his exploding multi-media world. There are lots of striking photos, people askew, dynamic designs. Attached inside came this cardboard disc, about the size of a 45. Printed on it is a sunglassed, mum Lou, and the clear grooves run round and round his head. The other side is blank. Tear it out, put it on the phonograph and hear a party at the Factory. The first VU lp plays in the background while Nico and Lou take a tour of the forthcoming *Index*. Nico comes across most prominently: "I think the rest of the world is like us . . . What about the empty pages? Why don't they remain empty? . . . . It's a very sentimental book. We're not really that sentimental. Or we're not supposed to be . . ."

And when everyone is informed that they are making the very sounds that will fill the record in the book *right then,* they take it in stride. There is a pause. Nico says, "Coffee," and a short time later breaks into the chorus of the Beatles' "Good Morning" from the just-erupted *Sgt. Pepper.* A brief foray into Andy's *1967* world. Available on *Etc.* and the *Afterhours Tapes.*

"LOOP"

USA only: flexi-disc from Dec. 1966 *Aspen Magazine* (out of print)

Aspen was a self-consciously arty, experimental magazine that came in a box. The editors and purveyors would fill this "first 3D magazine" with sundry items. There could be newspapers, pictures, seeds, postcards, records, flip books, etc. It was expensive ($4 an issue, which would spill out to more than $10 today) and didn't last too long. Andy designed issue #3. *Aspen* used "guest editors;" Marshall McLuhan did #4. Andy made the *Aspen* box into a Fab detergent box, and inside were some of the shooting moments of the mid-60s growing pop-up explosion. Lou essayed in "Life Among the Poobahs" on his dear love for rock & roll, with its "reaching for the moment," and how this beauty was being missed and scorned by the intelligentsia of the day.

A flexi-disc also came in the box. One side was Peter Walker ("musical director for Timothy Leary's LSD religious celebrations") and "White Wind," a "love raga."

Side two was quite different. "Loop" is credited to the Velvet Underground, and written by John Cale. On the label it says "guitar and feedback," and "first half of a 15-minute recording made with two monaural tape recorders, final groove left purposefully open."

"Loop" begins with just droning guitar(s) or bass repeating in a tape loop. Enter a ringing guitar noise that builds in intensity, begins to feedback and screech, then fades out, and we're back to the original hum. The pattern begins again, climaxes, etc. Lou says that he, Angus, and John were often making such tapes back in '65, before there was any band. "Loop" is most likely one of those, and would seem to be entirely Cale's doing.

In 1966 Velvet Underground released their first three records: the subversively pretty 45s of "Mirror" and "Sunday Morning," and a precursor to *Metal Machine Music*, "Loop." Nice contrast. Nice start.

And So On and the *Afterhours Tapes* carry the entire "Loop."

VU Demo Sessions

July 1965

The Players: Reed, Cale, Morrison, MacLise

The earliest tape of VU songs was made in New York City (as all the demos were) to test the waters of reaction. They sent copies out to several people in England, one of whom was Miles Copeland, future IRS Records and Police mentor. Alas, no copy of the tape has since surfaced.

Songs included: H, Venus, Wrap Your Troubles in Dreams, BADS, and something Sterling only remembers being known as "Never Get Emotionally Involved With Man, Woman, Beast or Child."

Fall/Winter 1966

The Players: Morrison, Cale, Reed

Recorded in a cold NYC loft on a slow running Wollensak tape recorder ("All those tapes should have been sped up," says Sterling), these demos have the quiet, informal atmosphere of the Dylan/Band Basement Tapes. With no percussion (Moe still had a day job), calm guitars and occasional bass or viola, this is a foreshadowing of the third album.

By far the most interesting tracks are the two versions of "Here She Comes Now." In the first, quavering guitar, bass and viola provide a floating backdrop while Lou seems to be singing anything in his head. However, the next take suddenly has most of the lp words.

The rest of the songs are of minor interest. "Sheltered Life" has two versions, and again the second has much better lyrics. Too much kazoo though, in both versions of this ironic tune of someone with "small town ways" who hasn't seen the wide-open action of the big city.

"It's All Right: The Way That You Live." Again, the words aren't ready. Some lines are set, others end in mumbles. This is the bare bones of a slow tune that has possibilities, but needs work.

"I'm Not Too Sorry" features a mysterious sound, a sliding guitar that keeps curling notes. That's Sterling with a foot pedal Vox gave him. Meanwhile, Lou's ". . not sorry that you're gone/I don't think I'm sorry cause I found a new one." That sort of song. Some slashing chords punch things up.

These demos have appeared on many tapes and boots, but the only source that has them at the right speed are the *Afterhours Tapes*.

Winter 1966 demos: Here She Comes Now, It's All Right The Way You Live, I'm Not Too Sorry, Sheltered Life.

FEBRUARY 1968

The Players: Reed, Morrison, Tucker, Cale

Sterling says these were done at RCA Studios, Moe says Atlantic. In any case, we're coming into more familiar territory, thanks to the VU lp. "Stephanie Says." Sterling says in a letter he wrote about the VU album, "Cale plays bass, celeste and the very romantic viola line. We could do songs like this any time we felt like it, and this is a good representative of the type."

"Inside Your Heart." Again, Sterling: "A relic from the days when we were a 'fun' bunch who liked each other's company." This is an ok song, but is more notable for the odd vocal parts. Lou added several frivolous parts to his lead vocal, and Lou, John and Sterling were to add the doo-doo backing vocals. However, instead of singing only at the proper moments, they all chatted away, thinking their extraneous noises would be mixed out ("I can talk to myself," says Lou happily). However, for some reason, the track was left in, and we hear all the cutting up.

Sterling again: "I like the song per se, but the glimpse it affords of the band 'at work' is more interesting (especially since the talking is uncontrived and has survived only by accident)." Both of these tracks are on *VU*.

1968 demos: Stephanie Says, Inside Your Heart.

RECORD PLANT 1969

The Players: D. Yule, Reed, Morrison, Tucker

We haven't been able to find out where most of these tracks were recorded. They most likely do hail from either the Record Plant or a makeshift studio at MGM. In any case, these recordings are the closest thing to the 'Lost Album.' Whereas the band chose not to pursue all the previous demos, these tracks were locked away by MGM when the band moved to Atlantic. MGM still had the band under contract when these were made, and thus owned, sat on and forgot about the tapes. Only through tapes and bootlegs have these been in circulation (made from acetates, which is why all the recordings sound so hissy). As VU has made many of these tracks familiar to all, we'll spend time mostly on the still-unreleased songs.

The quoted comments here will be Sterling's. "Foggy Notion," "She's My Best Friend," "Andy's Chest" ("not pretentious like the *Transformer* version"), "I Can't Stand It," "Ocean," and "I'm Stickin' With You" ("very pleasant . . . unfolds musically like a poker hand—you don't show all you got until the end. The direct link to *Loaded* and thus appropriately the last cut on the album") all were recorded in June, 1969 at the Record Plant. "One Of These Days" hails from Sept. 1969, and "Lisa Says" ("monotonous and incomplete") was done in Oct., 1969.

Although we can't find an exact date for "Move Right In," we're guessing it hails from this 1969 time zone. Main reason being there's no trace of Cale in this nice little Grateful Dead-style shuffle instrumental (although the bursts of bass do drown out everything else, we gotta think Cale would've twisted things around more).

"Rock & Roll" is a rough version in the same manner of the *Loaded* track. It's basically the same, but plodding and ordinary.

"Ferryboat Bill" is a mighty silly ditty ("and your wife has married a midget's son/and that's the long and short of it" is about the short and long of the song.) This is dumb fun, with some good guitar, but that's about it. There's a much livelier version on a live 1969 Tea Party tape.

Seeing as "Lisa Says" and "Can't Stand It" weren't in circulation before *VU*, it stands to reason there are other songs hiding unheard. We've heard tell of another "Ocean" (Morrison: "in the can at Atlantic with me on slide guitar. It's pretty good as I recall"), "Real Good Time Together," "Ride Into The Sun," and something known as "Coney Island Steeplechase." Polygram may include some or all of these in a future release.

Baddest missing tape is a VU version of "Sad Song." Sterling remembers it as being "the best of all these, by far. It was done in a similar arrangement as on *Berlin*, but much better." The people at Polygram have thus far looked in vain for "Sad Song." There's also supposed to be a song called "Lonesome Cowboys" to go with a Warhol film of the same title. This is said to be different from "Lonesome Cowboy Bill."

The 1969 Record Plant demos: One Of These Days, Lisa Says, Foggy Notion, Ferryboat Bill, I'm Stickin' With You, Andy's Chest, Rock & Roll, She's My Best Friend, Ocean, and most likely, Move Right In.

Underground Undergrounds: VU Boots

ENTER THE BOOTLEGS

Evil Mothers

Holland?: Skydog LP 003—1974 (out of print)

Holland?: no label (reissue)—1983

This was the first VU bootleg, issued over ten years ago. It was great then, but has been outdated by other albums (mainly *Live at Max's*). Since the Dutch (?) reissue usually comes with a $20 price tag, get this only if you must have *everything* VU.

Side 1: (everything live at Max's 1970 unless noted) I'm Set Free, Walk & Talk It, Lonesome Cowboy Bill, Ostrich (Primitives), Waiting

Side 2: New Age, Sneaky Pete (Primitives), WL, Jane

Etc.

Australia: Plastic Inevitable First-1—1979

Good sound, good selections, good cover, good price, good liner notes (even if writer C. Walker has only a 'foggy notion' about the demos). This is the best record of this odd stuff (although the newly-circulating *Afterhours Tapes* are even more comprehensive). The original issue of *Etc.* came with swell hand silk-screened covers.

Side 1: (All Pickwick pre-VU Lou except where noted.) Cycle Annie, Ostrich, Sneaky Pete, Insane, Conversations (the *Index* flexi-disc)

Side 2: (All VU demos except where noted) Foggy, Inside Your Heart, I'm Sticking, Ferryboat Bill, Noise (from the *East Village Other* lp)

Live Paris 29-1-72 Reed/Cale/Nico

Italy: 782 Records (also issued with no label or number)—1980 (?)

This concert was a fine, subtle ending note to the Velvet Underground. It was the last time these three played on the same stage, and next to the last time Reed and Cale performed together (Lou played some songs with John at a gig of Cale's at the Ocean Club, NYC, 1976). More than that, Lou and John actually rehearsed and worked out some canny versions of some great VU songs. They also performed some of the best of their solo songs of the time. Perhaps the fact that the concert was broadcast on French TV spurred them on—where is the video tape?

The Bataclan is a small nightclub in Paris. The quiet, acoustic nature of the music (guitar, piano, viola) helps this relatively poor recording sound fine. The bootleg cover is a simple affair, with merely the names, date and some titles typed out. Nico probably doesn't appear until "Femme." Of special interest is the bouncy ditty John sings about "The Biggest, Loudest, Hairiest Group of All," which seems to be a bittersweet, thumbnail sketch of the VU's insanely wearying ups and downs.

Side 1: (first 4 songs: Lou—vocals ac. guitar; John—piano, viola, ac. guitar) Waiting, Berlin ("my Barbara Streisand song," says Lou), BADS (This slower version comes billed on *And So On* and the *Afterhours Tape* as having "clearly audible lyrics." That's true, but it's hard to tell if Lou truncates and scrambles some of the lines here due to artistic license or artistic nerves), Wild Child, Empty Bottles (a Cale song sung by Jennifer Warnes on her Cale-produced lp)

Side 2: H (terrific version, with Reed singing and on ac. guitar; Cale on viola), Ghost Story (Cale alone, on ac. guitar as he is on the next song), The Biggest, Loudest, Hairiest Group of All, Femme (Nico sings these last three; here with Lou and maybe John on backing guitar and vocals), ATP (sounds like just one guitar), Janitor of Lunacy (Nico alone, on harmonium)

1966

USA: no label 104025—June 1981 (out of print)

Long building pounding ringing moaning cranking diddling wigging pulling lazing noodling whipping zipping . . . a fascinating, unique document of the original five on a long EPI jam jaunt, November 4, 1966, in Columbus, Ohio. Good cover, good sound. No recognizable 'songs' as such (although Sterling throws in some hot "S. Ray" licks).

This was recorded by a Cincinnati area record shop owner who put it out in 1981. He was going to reissue it (hence the "Available Again Soon" ad in *WGO* #3) as well as put out the rest of the tape when, a short time after #3 came out in 1982, he reportedly died. In mid-1985, a 1966 tape of the band doing seven songs turned up. That may be from this night.

And So On

Australia: Plastic Inevitable Second-1—1982

This follows *Etc.* in being well-crafted, well-packaged, essential VU historical chronicles. This one packs good, informative liner notes (a rarity with boots) done by our own Phil man and a fine-sounding group of VU curios '66–'72:

Side 1: Guess I'm Falling In Love (live '67), The Way That You Live ('66 demo), Pale (live '70), One Of These Days (1970 demo), radio ad for 3rd lp

Side 2: BADS (Lou & John live Paris 1972), I'm Not Too Sorry (1966 demo), Stephanie Says (1968 demo), Loop (1966 *Aspen* flexi-disc)

Everything You've Ever Heard About . . .

UK: VU Records VU-333—1982

Close. Not quite everything. But a lot. Too bad this big, expensive, now generally unavailable box is inexpertly pieced together. This one should have been *it—the* definitive Velvet collection of rarities. Dopey-looking banana on the front too (well, at least they tried).

There are two versions. The deluxe ($35–50) comes with a "Souvenir Discography" xeroxed booklet of pretty good recent US and UK VU articles circa '77–80, a peelable banana on the front, and a replica of Nico's first 45 ("I'm Not Sayin'"/"The Last Mile"). Ironically, the 45 was being reissued at the same time legally, by Virgin, some 17 years after it came out. Some of these boxes have red cover lettering, some white.

The plebian, casual fan who only has $15–30 gets just the three lps in the box. The first record is a good history, from the Carol Lou Trio through all of the Pickwick tracks. Several of these tracks aren't readily available elsewhere.

Side 3 has the different version of "Some Kinda" from the different mix of the 3rd lp. There's a "WL" which is probably the 45 version. There's no real difference, except it's in overload mono. "Rock & Roll" is the 1969 studio demo that hasn't been around much before.

After the 1969 demo version of "Ocean," is a song listed as "Fever In My Pocket," which is really "Guess I'm Falling In Love." This cut hails from an April 1967, New York live date. A few years ago, John was on a New York radio show. He chatted, played some of his favorites, as well as this live track. Good sound on this, well described by Cale as "crunchy, get-out-of-my-way bam-bam."

"Foggy Notion" is listed as being on side 3, but is nowhere on here.

Side 4 is all demos. Side 5 is all live at Max's. The sound is ok, but boxy, in the manner of all the Max's tapes. Lou introduces "Candy Says" as "my favorite song." "Some Kinda" gets an extended break, lots of high note riffing. "Cool It Down" is done as a funky walk.

Side 6 Sound pretty muddy. This is a rehearsal for the long stand at Max's and probably recorded 26 July, 1970. "I'm Free (?)" is built around a blues guitar run that is ironically quite similar to the Who's "I'm Free" from their 1967 *Tommy*. Lou sings it, as he does "I Found A Reason." Best thing about all these Max's tapes is hearing Lou sing many of the songs he hadn't on record. "Walk & Talk It" is straightforward. "Head Held High" is worked on a lot. They stop at the building drum break and go over it with, we presume, Billy Yule. Doug finishes the side singing "I'm Set Free." Sides 5 and 6 should have been edited down to one side.

Side 1: Afterhours (Carol Lou Trio), Leave Her For Me (Jades), So Blue (Jades), Why Don't You Smile Now (All-Night Workers), Ostrich (Primitives), Sneaky Pete (Primitives), Cycle Annie (Beachnuts)

Side 2: I've Got A Tiger In My Tank (Beachnuts), You're Driving Me Insane (Roughnecks), *Index* record, Noise (from East Village lp)

Side 3: Some Kinda (alt. version), WL/WH (mono 45), Rock & Roll (demo), Ocean (demo)

Side 4: Inside Your Heart (demo), I'm Sticking With You (demo), Ferryboat Bill (demo), Guess I'm Falling In Love (live 1967)

Side 5: (all live at Max's 08/23/70) Candy, Some Kinda, Cool It Down, Who Loves The Sun

Side 6: (all Max's rehearsal 07/26/70) I'm Free, I Found A Reason, Walk & Head, I'm Free

Black Side of the Street

Europe?: Incredible Record Makers (no #)—1983

Large quantities of this album supposedly burned right up in a 1983 NYC record shop fire. This threw the price of unburnt copies toward the skies ($20+). Be careful if you're tempted to part with a large sum to own one of these. This is an interesting but so-so sounding affair that's sloppily put together:

Side 1: Ray (the lp claims this is the VU at the Bottom Line in 1970. This may be from Bottom Line, but it's not the VU. Rather, it's Lou on his own, so it must be from '72 on. This is a good version, but mastered too damn fast), Foggy (VU demo).

Side 2: I'm Set Free (VU Philly '70), Pale (same), H (Lou & John rehearsing for the '72 Paris show. It's great to hear John's viola shadings on this, but now the record sounds too slow!), Waiting (Lou live with Patti Smith Group at CBGB's 05/04/77. Badly recorded, this is a straight-forward run through. It's funny to hear an excited Patti singing "baby I'm your man" as Lou sings "I'm waiting for my man," through the first chorus. Sounds slow too.)

Live '68

Australia: Lurid 101—1983

This is quite all right. The sound is so-so, but the album captures solid highlights of cassette tapes from Cleveland's La Cave Club.

1968 was the year of Cale's exit, so the album has performances with both Cale (April '68, "H") and Doug Yule (from Oct. '68, which the liner notes say was his first gig with the band). The album is also on the *Afterhours Tapes*.

Side 1: WGO, Move Right In, Can't Stand It
Side 2: Foggy (10 *hot* minutes worth), H

Orange Disaster

USA?: Clean Sound CS 1005—1984

Best thing about this lp is the cover. It features the lettering from the VU paperback, and the photo from the back of the VU lp. The contents are rare, and sound is rough, but that's forgivable given the sources (acetates, old tapes, soundtracks):

Side 1: (all VU demos) She's My Best Friend, Andy's Chest, Move Right In, Sheltered Life, Here She (2 takes)
Side 2: Walk & Talk It ('70 rehearsal), H, Venus (these two from the 1966 EPI Chicago film), Jesus, Story of My Life (these two come from LA Cave, Cleve. 10/02/68)

Metal Machine Sound (Lou/VU)

UK: XL 116—1985

This is one of the more imaginative boots, as it traces the MM sound through Lou's career. Great color cover of Lou's clear guitar leaning on an amp. The only thing really wrong with the record is the sound, which is generally so-so.

Side 1: S. Jane (Lou, sounds like *Take No Prisoners* days, with the sax), Hedy Soundtrack excerpts, Ray (VU from a 3/69 Tea Party date).
Side 2: I Wanna Be Black (prob. same gig as 'Jane'), Temporary Thing

(Lou 22/11/76), "Metal Machine Improv" (Lou, Den Haag 5/4/77; coda to Charley's Girl).

Screen Test—Falling in Love with the Falling Spikes

UK: Shining Star DOM 001—1985 (mono)

This recent British boot is a fair collection of sundry VU tracks lately unearthed. We again turn to John Balance for a report:

"1st track (*Hedy* excerpt) is excellent and they get steadily worse. Bass rumbles and screeches. 4/10 quality except for 1st which is 8/10. Black and blue cover, horrible non-descript design. White label. *Vol. II* planned."

Side 1: 'The 14 Year Old Girl' (from *Hedy*), Oh! Sweet Nuthin' (VU live Phil., Jan 2, 1970)

Side 2: 'Vamp' (the odd bit from the beginning of the April 17, 1970 Springfield, Mass. concert), 'The Gerard Malanga Story' (long VU instrumental passage from *Chelsea Girls* film)

Live at the Boston Tea Party

UK: Velvet 1—1985

"This is a speeded-up recording on record. Unplayable on one side and bad quality. Lo-fi recording anyway," writes John Balance (Psychic TV, Coil) of this recent boot. All tracks hail from a 10 Jan. 1969 Tea Party gig:

Side 1: WGO, Can't Stand It, Candy, Beginning, WL, Pale

Side 2: Ray, H, Move Right In (vocal), I'm Set Free, Run, Waiting

Crushed Velvet

Velvets Rule

Yo! Wait a minute! We've actually seen these records on people's want lists. Good luck getting them, cos unless Tim Yocannon's ready to part with them, he'll remain the only person in the world to have these two records. Why? Because Tim went and had his '22 Demos' tape made into two acetate albums (see *WGO* #3 for details). With covers too. Course if Tim's played them more than five or ten times, the acetates (which come from a few generations removed of tapes made from scratchy acetates to begin with) won't sound so hot, as acetates aren't made to be played very much anyway. No, these lps are one-of-a-kind jobs that display the Do It Yerself ethic we yell a lot about in the VUAS halls and alcoves.

With video recorders now in the generally affordable $300–500 range, folks all over the world are beginning to seek filmed images of the Velvets. And they, along with BBC producers and video tape compilers are finding much the same thing: very little. Despite the fact that the VU worked in the eye of the media hurricane, and they were filmed quite often, practically nothing is available. Sad to say, most all of these films and tv performances remain unseen by your dilligent *WGO* writers. We've heard several of the soundtracks, but will have to rely on other sources (such as the books *Uptight* and *Rock On Film*) for info on the films. Let us hope we can get some of the missing celluloid out of the closet soon.

"ANONYMOUS" BACKING FOR "UNDERGROUND" FILMS

Spring–Summer 1965

The Players: Cale, Reed, Morrison, MacLise.

These films were the catalyst for the formation of the Velvet Underground. The chance to play "free-form" accompaniment to films and some of the first mixed-media "happenings" (presented by Angus and Piero Heliczer) gave these four adventurous people rhyme and reason to experiment, to combine the power and excitement of rock and roll with the experiments and fire of the musical "avante garde." Heliczer taped some of these performances to play at later screenings. It would be *very* informative and enjoyable to hear those tapes today.

Some of Piero's films they played for were *Christmas on Forth* and *The New Jerusalem.*

CBS-TV; filmed Nov. 1965; shown 31 Dec. 1965.

No one we know has seen this since it was first broadcast. *Uptight* mentions the band, Edie Sedgewick, Andy Warhol and Gerald Malanga going to the Apollo Theatre to see James Brown, then going to Danny Field's apartment to watch the show.

CBS wanted to do a story on the new US "underground" films, so they sent a camera crew to film Piero Heliczer directing *Venus in Furs*. The VU can be heard playing "H" and "Venus" off camera. Jim Condon, writing in *What Goes On* #3, says Heliczer played saxophone on this performance, and used the sound portion from the broadcast in the film. Walter Cronkite supposedly narrated for CBS. See *WGO* #3 for film listings for Nico and Angus.

Venus in Furs

Piero Heliczer dir; starring Lou Reed, John Cale, Angus MacLise, Barbara Rubin; filmed fall 1965. Music by the Velvet Underground.
And that's what we know.

Hedy the Shoplifter

70 min., B&W, Andy Warhol prod & dir; starring Maria Montez, Mary Woronov, Jack Smith; filmed Nov. 1965. First shown 3 Mar. 1966. Music by Lou Reed and John Cale.

One of our readers says there's a soundtrack lp to this film. Even gives a label, ESP, and a catalog number, 1036. But many many others have cried, "No No No! No album exists of Lou and John screeching and droning guitars behind this campy half-spoken, half-sung improvised version of actress Hedy Lamar's real life shoplifting arrest, trial and conviction!" Since no one else even thinks they ever even heard of an lp from this, we'll have to file this under the 'Non-Existant' label until proof shows up.

The excerpt of music from the film on the *Afterhours Tapes* reveals some loud guitars pounding piano improvising long mood pieces for the film. There are no recognizable songs, but rather some hellacious songs, as well as some interesting quiet passages. This is perhaps the best place to get an idea of what those earliest 1965 performances accompanying the Heliczer films (among others) sounded like. Even the grainy sound (you can hear the celluloid being pulled over the exciter bulb on the projector) adds to the realistic atmosphere.

'Sunday Morning' Film

$2\frac{1}{2}$ min, color; starring Lou Reed, John Cale, Sterling Morrison, Rosalind Stephenson. Filmed fall 1965 (?).

This is a home movie shot by a friend. It shows the lads fooling about on a piano. Stills from it appeared in the July/Aug 1980 *New York Rocker*.

Psychiatrists Convention EPI Show

Jonas Mekas dir; filmed 8 Jan. 1966, Delmonico's Hotel, NYC.

Does this sound made up or what? But *Uptight* says it's so, and this was even the first EPI with choreography by Andy. Bring it on!

The Velvet Underground & Nico: A Symphony of Sound

70 min., B&W, Warhol dir & prod; with Mary Woronov, General Malanga; music by the Velvet Underground; filmed Jan. 1966.

This is reportedly a film of the VU and Nico practicing at the Factory, making waves so large the police arrive to calm the storm. Might be worth seeing.

WNET—New York City

Feb. 1966, "USA Artists" Program.

That week's USA Artist was Andy Warhol. The VU/EPI segment went like this:

Andy: "I'm sponsoring a new band. It's called the Velvet Underground. Since I don't really believe in painting anymore, I thought it would be a nice way of combining music, art and films all together. The whole thing's being auditioned tomorrow at nine o'clock. If it works out, it might be very glamorous." Interviewer: "What sort of thing do you intend to do with the band?"

Andy: "Well it would be the biggest discotheque in the world, and it will have 21 screens, and three or four bands." (Sounds as if the liner note writer for the *Andy Warhol's VU* lp got most of his "info" from this odd chat.)

Enter this "new band," on film. Pounding, beating drums, skittering, wailing electric violin. Lost in the din, a human voice cries, "I am tired/I am weary/I could sleep for a thousand years." Guitars bang and the noise subsides. Then more. More wailing, more crying sounds of metal and screeching feedback, as the voice can hardly be heard, saying something about heroin.

I can't imagine what the good liberals gathered around their Public Television sets thought of this. Hellish caterwauling; most likely. But this sonic explosion is pure joyous noise, and a great dose of the instant havoc the EPI VU caused.

More Milk Yvette

Warhol dir; with Mario Montez; music by the Velvet Underground; 1966.

One day we'll find out more about this.

The Chelsea Girls

210 min., color/B&W, Warhol dir & prod; with Ondine, Brigid Polk, Mary Woronov, Nico, Eric Emerson, International Velvet, Ingrid Superstar; filmed summer 1966; first shown 15 Sept. 1966.

Rock on Film: "Nico doesn't sing here, but instrumental noodling by the V.U. (playing just out of camera range) is heard toward the conclusion of Warhol's mostly improvised epic of the 60s New York Bohemia."

The band was recorded live especially for the sequence in the twelfth reel (remember this is a 210-min. movie) in which there is a long shot of Nico's weeping face. The so-called "noodling" actually contains some striking and beautiful guitar work by John and Lou. In the 25-minute segment heard on *Afterhours Tape* #18, they do some excellent ambient backing of Ondine's "Pope" character that would make Eno proud. There is some twisted rock riffing that needs visuals, but a good quality tape of all this would be a top treat.

We guess the "Gerald Malanga Story" is in here somewhere . . .

Live at the Balloon Farm

Oct. 1966.

Uptight says someone filmed a gig at this NYC nutspot. Maybe it will come out on the 20th anniversary of the event . . .

Andy Warhol's Exploding Plastic Inevitable

30 min., B&W/color, Ronald Nameth dir.; documentary.

June 1966: Lou in hospital with hepatitis; EPI booked June 21–26 in Chicago at a former church-turned-nightclub called Poor Richard's; Nico & Andy also absent (although Ingrid Superstar went over well pretending to be Andy). So Angus returns as a temporary fill-in on percussion, Maureen moves to bass, and John and Sterling take on the vocals. Despite/because of reviews that fired words such as ". . . menace . . . perversion . . . brutalized . . . horror . . . helpless . . . madhouse . . . flowers of evil in full bloom" at the reader (sounds a bit appealing, no?), and the odd line-up, the week went very well. They were held over for another, and the group did the Chicago media scene: Studs Terkel, Playboy, radio shows.

Adding to the irony of all this, local artist Ron Nameth filmed the "EPI" footage at this time. Thus, the oddest VU ever is preserved in the film (although only about 10 seconds of the band is shown). More interesting is the music: "H" + "Venus." Cale's deep rich voice gives an unsettling neutral tone to "H," underscored by the fact that the band plays it all at the same tempo. No breaks, no rushing on their run. Angus was playing tablas (Indian drums) on here, which adds to the trance effect. "Deader off than dead," sings John at one point. "Venus" has a similar lugubrious, eerie power. The film cuts "Venus" off abruptly, and so it goes on the *Afterhours* tape. The lp versions of "It Was A Pleasure Then," "Euro Son" and "Mirror" are also used in the film.

See *WGO #3* for more on this film.

Upbeat TV Show

Cleveland, Ohio, July 15, 1967.

This was a rock type show that featured live bands. Pretty wild stuff for 60s TV (it was a shock to even *see* an electric guitar on TV, never mind hearing one twang live). All Sterling recalls was that it was live, real good, and they chose (in perfect VU complete commercial disdain fashion) to play "Guess I'm Falling In Love."

"* * * *"

1500 min., Warhol prod & dir; with Viva, Ondine, Nico, Brigid Polk, Pat Close, Taylor Mead, Edie Sedgewick, Alan Midgette; 1967.

Rock on Film: "Warhol extravaganza shown in its entirety on only one occasion, with occasional music by the V.U." Sounds like they weren't at the screening either.

"It Was A Pleasure Then" from Nico's first album, *Chelsea Girl,* was written for and first performed in this film. The *Chelsea Girl* cover supposedly is similar to the visual style of * * * *.

Diaries, Notes and Sketches

Jonas Mekas dir.; with Warhol, the VU, Nico, Gerald Malanga; 1970.

Is the VU appearance in here from the 1966 Psychiatrists Convention gig he filmed? Or different material?

Dynamite Chicken

76 min., color, Ernest Pintoff prod & dir; with Richard Pryor, Paul

Krasner, John Lennon, Lenny Bruce, Yoko Ono, Muddy Waters Blues Band, Velvet Underground, Ace Trucking Company; 1971.

Not a bad line-up. Alas, as is traditional with the too-good-to-be-true setups, this one is bogus, a slap-dash quickie "mixed media collage" mess of old, short footage of the musicians mixed in with satiric comedy material by Pryor and the Ace Trucking Co. As for the Velvets, they're not in it; only one of their songs is in the film. This thing is so bad, that our reporter couldn't remember which one.

Paris TV Concert

29 Jan., 1972.

We've heard this concert was originally telecast on French TV in its entirety. However, no video tape is in general circulation. We've also heard that a half hour version was shown later. That would explain why this particular audio tape is only 25 minutes long (see Bootleg section for complete details). Two French announcers speak in three places. The tape goes like this: (announcers), Berlin, (announcers), Waiting, H, (announcers), Ghost Stories (truncated), Femme.

Rock & Roll High School

93 min., color, Allan Arkush dir., featuring Mary Waronov. Again.

About 48 seconds of "Rock & Roll" (*Loaded* version) are located in the movie. Early ads for the film named the VU in the list of soundtrack performers, but "Rock & Roll" is not on the soundtrack album (unlike Todd Rundgren's "A Dream Goes On Forever," which is on the lp but not in the movie).

We're sure they'll be many additions/corrections in the next version of this discography, for example; how about the Warhol film *"Vinyl"* in which the VU are said to take turns tying each other up? There's said to be other "acting" appearances in Warhol films as well.

Afterhozurs Tapes

#1 VU: *Third LP—Alt. Mixes, Oddities; Live in Philadelphia, 1970* (pt. 2)

#2 *Cover Versions and Tributes (Vol 1)*

#3 *Velvet Underground Live—Boston Tea Party (Jan. 10, 1969)*

#4 *John Cale Live in Boston (Oct. 19, 1982)* plus other assorted live Cale recordings

#5 *VU Live—La Cave, Cleveland (Oct. 2, 1968)* plus misc. covers; Nico sings "New York, New York"

#6 *Reed/Cale/Nico at Bataclan* (Jan. 29, 1972) plus assorted solo stuff (mostly Cale & Reed, some Nico)

#7 *Velvet Underground Live—Second Fret, Phila. (Early 1970)*

#8 *Nico Live at CBGB (NYC, March 1979)* plus "I'll Keep It With Mine"; Nico's very first single

#9 *Rare Early VU Recordings*

#10 *Velvet Underground Live Bootlegs—'1966', 'Live' 68*

#11 *Lou Reed Live Chronology (Vol. 1)*

#12 *Soundtrack Extracts*

#13 *White Light, Banana Album—Mono Mixes*

#14 *Mixed Bag of Rarities*

#15 *Metal Machine Music—Plus Assorted Oddities*

#16 *Interview Excerpts*

#17 *Velvet Underground—Live And Lowdown*

#18 *Miscellaneous Rarities*

#19 *Cover Versions And Tributes (Vol 2)*

This set of tapes is the single most important event in VU recording history since Lou left that night at Max's. Nineteen 90 minute tapes, well-produced, recorded, and annotated. Herein lie almost all of 27 years of recorded mysteries by Lou Reed, John Cale, Moe Tucker, Nico, and Sterling Morrison and their various associates. It's here: pre-VU, VU, post-VU; live, studio, mono, stereo, outtakes, demos, ads, interviews, soundtracks, covers, goofs, dialogue. From Lou's first record in 1957 through rare Warhol film soundtracks, to the band's last gig in 1973, to REM doing "There She Goes" in 1984, there's 98% of all the rarities. History, music, great nights, bad nights, it's all there. We've never seen a better, more complete archive for any band.

Quibbles? Just a few. Part of me likes the way the tapes are put together; most concentrate on one subject, and a few odd tracks fill the time at the end. Thus Lou's Pickwick cuts are on the same tape as *Metal Machine Music*. Spanning Reed's career like that reminds us constantly that indeed the same person wrote "Cycle Annie" and "MMM". Now I know these juxtapositions came about because fitting history into neat 90 minute segments is uneasy work.

However, another part of me wishes things were arranged more chronologically. For reference sake, that would be easier indeed.

But's that not too bad. The liner notes are 99% correct, the sound beats *all* the bootlegs (the important boots themselves are preserved here), and previous sources. Only the *VU* lp has an edge in sound quality of some of the demos on one of the tapes, and even there it must be noted that the *Afterhours* project came out before *VU* did, and some people prefer the rough demo sound to the "clean" *VU* production.

This set is a great thing. A huge, previously uncharted history is at our fingertips. Also, most of the tapes come with unlisted surprises. Some have music on the end of a side, some interview snippets.

#1 *VU 3rd LP (Alt. Mix)*, *Oddities*, *Live in Philadelphia (Part 2)*

#1 begins with the great original mix of lp the third, and is mostly filled out with solid, previously unheard live sounds.

The third lp's all here except for "Murder Mystery." The liner notes say it's left out as it seems to be the same mix as before, but it's not (see the notes on the 3rd lp).

Beyond that, Doug Yule sings a pretty good version of "I'm Set Free;" there's a simmering combo of "Ray" and the only live bit of "Murder Mystery" that's yet surfaced.

Side 1: 3rd VU lp (alt. mix) (except for Murder, ep ad for 3rd lp, I'm Set Free (live at Max's, summer 1976; VG sound), Afterhours (infamous Carol Lou Trio).

Side 2: Ray/Murder (LaCave, 28 Jan. 1969; G+ sound; here's a very controlled Ray that never explodes, but moves with menacing strength, and moves Lou into about 34 lines of Murder Mystery—variations on the "sick upon the carpet/nuns on the seawall" section), WGO, Cool It, SJane (live, Main Point, Phil., May 1970, G+ sound; all three of these songs suffer from spotty performances by both band and tape. The recording centers on the rhythm guitar almost exclusively, and all else suffers).

#2 *Cover Versions and Tributes (Vol. 1)*

There are only a few cuts on here that are flat. Most are quite good, and/or historic.

Side 1: DAVID BOWIE/Waiting, BIG STAR/Femme, TRACEY THORNE/Femme, CRAWDADDYS/There She, JEFF SCOTT and JOSEF MARC/Mirror, CABARET VOLTAIRE/Here She, EATER/Thinkin' of the USA, DR MIX & THE REMIX/SRay, PLAIN JANE & THE JOKE/WGO, PETER C. JOHNSON/Pale, DICTATORS/Two Tub Man, TANT STRUL/Afterhours (Swedish), THIRD RAIL/SJane.

Side 2: FLEETWOOD MAC/Gypsy, DETROIT/R&Roll, RACHEL SWEET/New Age, EARTHQUAKE/Head Held, WAYNE COUNTY/Max's Kansas City 1977, ALL NIGHT WORKERS/Why Don't You Smile Now, DONNIE BURKES/Why Don't You Smile Now, HALF JAPANESE/Foggy-Farmer John, PATTI SMITH GROUP/Real Good Time Together, LESTER BANGS/Let It Blurt, HALF JAPANESE/I Can't Stand It, THRILL/Hangin' Round, GEFILTE JOE & THE FISH/Walk on the Kosher Side, AFRIKA CORPS/Juvenile Delinquent, PATTI PRAVO/Wild Side (Italian), HARVEY GOLD/Close Watch, BAUHAUS/Rosegarden Funeral of Sores.

#3 LIVE—BOSTON TEA PARTY, 10 JAN '69

The Players: Morrison, Tucker, Reed, D. Yule

This is a mighty fine tape of the band cruising through a set in one of their favorite spots—Boston's Tea Party. It's early 1969, and all the songs sound fresh, especially the five from the soon-to-be-released third album. It's true as it says on the tape that the sound is a G+, "not wide dynamic range, but instruments and vocals are very clear and distinct."

Side 1: H (solid version), Move Right In (with words; done at a faster tempo with added riff in the middle that adds power and direction), I'm Set Free (Lou sings), Run (good long version with loud ostrich guitar), Waiting, Can't Stand It (more wails from the ostrich).

Side 2: Candy (slow; Yule sings), Beginning (raucous version, sung by Lou), WL, Pale, Ray (good Yule keyboards; more guitar rave ups).

#5 VU LIVE—LA CAVE, CLEVELAND (OCT. 2 1968)
PLUS MISC. COVERS; NICO SINGS "NEW YORK, NEW YORK"

Herein lies the tape from which the compilers of the *Live '68* boot took "WGO" and "Foggy." The *Live '68* folks also equalized the tape, and gave the record a sharp, loud edge. The drums and bass kick hard on it. On here, however, is a muddy sound that traps the bass drums and vocals. Not bad, but the record sounds awfully good.

We also get some covers of interest, including the most likely first ones (pop versions somehow by a Dutch band in 1967), Roky Erickson doing an EPI-style H, and yes, Nico, live, "New York, New York." Why? Dunno.

Side 1: WGO, Waiting (slow, bluesy version; band yells chorus in rowdy good spirits), Pale (featuring an ad-libbed section about how sister Jane went "round the world, came back shot full of holes," and "me, I never had no home," and how the church changed Miss Sarah "into a piece of ice," and "back on the street again . . . my partner right by my side/the meanest damn band in all the land." The final verse is quite Dylanesque in both imagery and delivery. It concerns the angel and devil "comin' down on the ceiling in my room." The devil looked like "the mad monk from Afghanistan . . . you should have seen the mother when he came down/I certainly couldn't get out of there too soon."

We know these improvised lyrics were products of the moment and never meant to be scrutinized, but they do allow a telling view of Lou at work).

Side 2: Venus (speedier, with some tape break-up), Beginning, Ray (this also is done at a faster tempo; this is a good, driving, raving rendition that always threatens to go over the edge. They slow to an "oom pa pa" section before ripping up again, faster than before).

Covers: RIATS/Sun Morn, Run (These first VU covers—1967!—aren't too bad. "Sun" is punctuated by a poppy cow bell and piano, while "Run" is a teen handclap version guided by a swell cheesy organ. They even get most of the words right.) SLITS/That's The Story (great, disjointed version), ROKY ERICKSON/H (cool chuggingbashin' version that harkens back to the 1966 EPI film version), NICO/NY, NY. (This live version comes from a 1982 NYC mixed-media presentation. Nico croons her breathy style at a chatty crowd.)

5 VU Live—La Cave, Cleveland (Oct. 2, '68) plus misc. covers; Nico sings "New York New York"

SIDE ONE
*What Goes On**
I'm Waiting for the Man
Pale Blue Eyes (with false start, so Lou's mic level can be turned up)
Foggy Notion
Heroin
Jesus

SIDE TWO
Venus in Furs
Beginning to See the Light
Sister Ray
RIATS: Sunday Morning, Run Run Run. *Dutch group; two sides of a '67 single—the first ever VU covers?*
SLITS: That's The Story Of My Life. *Eng., late '70s or early '80s.*
ROKY ERICKSON: Heroin. *Recorded in New Orleans, '82; bit of breaking up near beginning is on original.*
NICO: New York New York. *From soundtrack to a film, shown in NY, '82; beginning is cut off on original.*

---

*probably identical recordings to those on *Live '68* boot; cf. tape 10, page 306.

#6 Reed/Cale/Nico at Bataclan (Jan. 29, '72), plus assorted rare solo stuff—mostly Cale and Reed, some Nico

Side 1: same as bootleg lp; plus CALE/ "Sylvia Said" (flip of "Man Who Couldn't Afford To Orgy" 45).

Side 2: REED/ "Wild Side" (bleeped 12" release from the *No Prisoners* lp; the bleeps make for surreal listening), NICO/ "Saeta" (live, BBC Radio, Sept. 1981), CALE/ "Mercenaries" (non-lp 45 studio version), CALE/ "Rosegarden Funeral of Sores" (non-lp b-side of "Mercenaries"), REED/ "Oye Colorado" (duet with Genya Raven from her 1978 *Urban Desire* lp), CALE/ "Temper" (*Academy In Peril* outtake), REED/ "Berlin" (8-track version, with some 30 seconds of extra piano), CALE/ "Coral Moon" (substituted on some copies of *Helen of Troy* for "Leaving It Up To You"), REED / "Hexorcist World Premiere" (inane break-in record that uses a bit of "Wild Side").

#7 Velvet Underground Live—Second Fret, Phila.
(Early 1970)

The sound is all average quality. What really makes this tape interesting is the variety of performances. Culled from several tapes, there are different lyrics and different versions of some songs, as well as the only live "Oh! Sweet Nuthin'" that's surfaced.

Side 1: (first four songs are from Jan. 2, 1970) WL/WH (the main question about this tape is that several of the songs sound a bit slow. Either there was a slow tape somewhere in this cassette's history, or the band is pretty drunk. Could be either). SJane (slower, with much ad-libbing about fun and frustration), Over You (before this Lou says he'd like to do his Billie Holiday impersonation; he also introduces "Over" as being "from the opposite side of the tracks"). Foggy (the rest of the songs save Ray are from mid-1970), Some Kinda, New Age (more different lyrics).

Side 2: Candy (Doug sings; slow, no drums), Head Held, Train Round (muted version with several loud/soft shifts that lead directly into:) Oh! Sweet Nuthin', Ray (3 Jan '70) (after some odd Jeff Beck squeaks, they begin Ray in a hot tempo, then slow to a peaceful interlude. They build again, but not with amphetamine hurry, but in a celebratory fashion, whooping and yelling "Sister Ray" quite happily. They build more speed, and end with a snap. The band's never sounded so happy). Waiting (excellent, long bluesy, version of the VU song that's been done more than any other. And almost the same pounding way! It still sounds good even after all the overuse, but this version shows it's a versatile tune).

See tape #1 for the rest of the Phil. recordings.

#9 RARE EARLY VU RECORDINGS

Sound: fair to good. Many early odds 'n sods on here. All of the demos in circulation are scooped up into one spot, which is damn handy. The other side carries many odd tracks of '66 and '67 vintage. The most important thing here is the first appearance of corrected speed versions of the six 1966 demos. Until now, they haven't been heard at anything but the original draggy speed. The perpetrators have even left the snippets of the original versions for reference. See the Demo section for full details on all the demos, page 286.

Side 1: It's All Right The Way That You Live (1966), One Of These Days (1970, two versions), I'm Not Too Sorry (1966), Stephanie Says (1968), Inside Your Heart (1968), Move Right In (1969), Rock And Roll (1969), Ocean (1969), She's My Best Friend (1969), I'm Sticking With You (1969), Ferryboat Bill (1969), Foggy Notion (1969).

Side 2: Andy's Chest (1969), Sheltered Life (1966, two versions), Guess I'm Falling In Love (live, NYC, 1967), H, Venus (these two from the EPI film), Noise (from *East Village Other* lp), Loop (*Aspen* mag flexidisc), Index (from the Warhol book), Venus, H (both from WNET-TV, 1966).

#10 VU BOOTLEGS—"1966," LIVE '68

These are two of the most interesting VU boots (see their listings for details), and while the '68 item seems still to be available in the States, the 1966 lp has been long gone for years. These two lps are perhaps the finest VU boots, and are essential listening, page 289.

See Bootleg section for track listings.

#12 SOUNDTRACK EXTRACTS

Sound: fair to good. Refer to Film/Soundtrack section for details.

Side 1: Music from *Hedy* (VU), *Caged Heat* (Cale, 1974).

Side 2: more *Caged Heat*, Lou's dialogue from *One Trick Pony* (1980), Lou's monologues from *Jimi Hendrix* (1973), Cale, *Who Am I This Time* (1982), Reed dialogue and some of "Little Sister" from *Get Crazy* (1983).

#13 VU MONO MIXES—WL/WH, 1ST LP

Sound: excellent, with only some surface noise to bother. We've written about the mono pros and cons in the album section. As mono versions of these albums are quite scarce, this tape is the easy way to hear them.

Side 1: WL/WH lp, plus run.
Side 2: Rest of 1st lp.

#14 MIXED BAG OF RARITIES

Sound: G- to E.

This mixed bag roams through history from the 1957 Jades 45 to a 1982 track from Moe's Paris 1942 band.

Side 1: NICO / "No One Is There," "Frozen Warnings," "Janitor Of Lunacy," "Secret Side" (live BBC 1971; these make up the Desolation Angel ep boot, except these are at the right speed), VU / "ATP" (mono 45, edited to 2:55), ANGUS MACLISE ET AL / "The Joyous Lake" (*Aspen* mag flexidisc), TERRY PHILIPS / "Wild One," "You," "This Rose" (more Pickwick-era noise that Lou may be on), CALE-NICO / "The Jeweler" (live 1975; Nico in minor role), NICO / "Secret Side" (live, BBC-TV 1971).

Side 2: REED / "I'm Stickin' With You" (live 1979, teaching it to his band), REED / "I'm So Free," "I Can't Stand It," "Walk And Talk It" (solo acoustic demos ca. 1971), VEVLET UNDERGROUND / "Somebody To Love" (Australian band of the same name doing the Airplane tune around 1969), 'OCCUPANTS' / "Lady Godiva's Op." (tape-distorted version of the studio track), VU / "Afterhours" (live in the UK 1971; Moe sings to a very yakky crowd), MARIE & LES GARCONS / "Attitudes" (Cale prod. 45 ca. 1978), SPONGEY & THE DOLLS / "Looks Like Love," "Really Really Really Really Really Really Love" (Lou on here? ca. 1964), MAUREEN TUCKER / "I'm Sticking With You" (the 1974 version done with J. Richman. This and the next track come from a 1982 radio interview in Phoenix), PARIS 1942 / "She Cracked," JADES / "So Blue," "Leave Her For Me," BEACHNUTS / "I've Got A Tiger In My Tank," BEAT-A-MANIA / "In A Little While" (Pickwick; Lou?), REED / "Little Sister" (from the *Get Crazy* soundtrack).

#15 METAL MACHINE MUSIC PLUS ASSORTED ODDITIES

Sound: mostly excellent.

Side 1: REED / "Metal Machine Music," sides A and B, LOU at Pickwick / "The Ostrich," "Sneaky Pete," "Cycle Annie," "You're Driving Me Insane," PATTI SMITH GROUP / "My Generation" (with Cale on bass, live 1976).

Side 2: REED / "Metal Machine Music" sides C and D, REED / "MMM" at 16 rpm (3 min worth; sounds like normal feedback), MAUREEN TUCKER / "Around And Around," "Will You Still Love Me Tomorrow?" (her 1981 *Trash* 45), ROBERTHA WILLIAMS / "Tell Mamma Not To Cry," "Maybe Tomorrow" (Lou co-wrote both these Pickwick items).

Sound: good to excellent. Great range here: Lou talking stoned 1969 hippie, Cale curtly intoning wild musical concepts, Nico's agreeable . . . vagueness . . . , Sterling's proud pragmatism, Maureen's true love of music, and the days of old. Willie Alexander and Walter Powers are also heard from, speaking on the post-Lou VU days. Doug Yule also speaks with Lou in the 1969 Boston radio chat. The only thing missing is the outrageous Lou. He gets fiesty in a few spots, but unloads little of his infamous verbal scorn.

A good measure of the VU personas, public and private, can be found in these 90 minutes.

Side 1: CALE / BBC, 1981, REED / early 70's, REED / NYC radio, 1979, TUCKER/Phoenix Radio, 1982, REED/SFX cassette mag, 1982, MORRISON/1980, VU (Reed & Yule)/1969, ALEXANDER & POWERS/1981, REED/NYC radio, 1972, REED/mid-70's.

Side 2: NICO/Seattle radio, 70's?, REED/RCA open-ended interview lp, 1982, CALE/interview excerpts from the *Hear Fear* lp, 1974, TUCKER,/1980, VU (Cale & Reed) / "all the important segments" from the MGM promo lp *The Music Factory,* 1969, CALE/NYC radio 1979, REED/phone call from Dutch radio station, 1982, REED/1980, NICO/BBC TV, 1967 or 68.

#17 Velvet Underground—Live and Lowdown

Sound: G+ to VG+. *Live And Lowdown* is a great tape. Culled from several VU concert tapes from 1969 to what may have been the last gig in 1973, every cut is worthwhile. Highlight of this tape full of highlights is a hellacious 35 minutes from the Tea Party in 1969. This is the hottest playing we've ever heard from the band!

Side 1: Run (1969, at a festival in New Hampshire. Much hot guitar. The liner notes wonder if this was their only outside concert, but they actually did a few.), Candy, Ferryboat Bill (Boston 1969; Bill gets an extended finish with SRay style organ fills. The basic riff is repeated with enough energy and variety to give this version power way beyond the demo version.), WGO (1969, New Hampshire), BADS, H (Cale and Reed in 1972 rehearsing these two numbers for the Bataclan show), It's Just Too Much—'Oh Mickey' (these hail from a 1970 rehearsal at Max's; 'Too Much' is a Chuck Berry–type rave-up toss-off. 'Mickey' is an impromptu ode to club-owner Mickey Ruskin and his club.), Little Jack (Wales, 1972. Heavily based on the "Pinball Wizard" riff, this up-tempo tune at least is lively and much better than the cut on the *Squeeze* lp.)

Side 2: WGO, H, Ray (Tea Party, 1969. The liner notes note the recordist was a "guitar freak" who made the tape from Lou's guitar amp. Thus we hear little of the vocals, and much of Lou's screaming guitar, and these three great songs become almost instrumentals. And two wailing guitars, drums and organ fly and zoom with verve, grace and speed. This is the live post-Cale VU at its best.), Oh Jim (1970. Western Mass. A muffled, short version of this elusive Reed song.), Let It Shine (Boston, November 1973; you could fool Dead Heads with this one, as it sounds like *American Beauty* Dead.).

#18 MISCELLANEOUS RARITIES

Sound: G to E. Most of this is post-VU, but there are some rare 60's VU tracks here.

Side 1: NICO / "Chelsea Girls" (BBC TV 1967 or 68; great live performance), REED / "My Name Is Mok" (from 1983 animated film *Rock And Rule*), NICO / "Waiting" (live 1982 with Bauhaus), CALE / "Guts" (live NYC 1976, with M. Ronson, D. Byrne and A. Lanier), KISS / "A World Without Heroes" (Lou co-wrote, 1981), NILS LOFGREN / "I'll Cry Tomorrow" (Lou co-wrote, 1979), NEURONIUM / "Vuelo Quimico" (Nico reads poetry by herself and Poe in this long 1978 trance track), KEVIN AYERS / "Irreversible Neural Damage" (Nico co-sings, 1974), SURFSIDERS / "When I Grow Up To Be A Man," "Help Me Rhonda" (1964 Pickwick tracks that Lou may play on; terrible programming here, with twenty minutes of dream-like music jarred by this ersatz surf trash).

Side 2: CALE / "Waiting" (live NYC with Reed, the last time these two have played together, 1976), VU (music from *Chelsea Girls* soundtrack—see VU Films section for more), CALE / 'Shopping for a Piano' (1983 Holland, music and street chat), REED / "Wild Side" (1983 Italian TV; Lou sings live over the original backing track), CALE / "Fear is a Man's Best Friend" (live, from a Roxy Music bootleg; Roxy backing? At least Manzanera), CALE/Radio ID, Jupiter, Florida, CALE / "Amsterdam," "Antarctica Starts Here," "Chorale" (live 1983, solo Holland).

#19 COVER VERSIONS AND TRIBUTES (VOL. 2)

Sound: mostly excellent. Another pile of covers and related items. Some of it is notable musically. All is notable historically. Highlights: The Cars absolutely twisting "Here She" and maybe "Head Held" into a dopey "original;" bad sound but cool version of "Waiting" by the last Yardbirds in 1968; Really Red's fine Nico tribute; the indefatigable Half Japanese ripping through "Euro. Son;" NRBQ pulling "WL" out of their "magic box" and not liking it much; two good versions of "Why Don't You Smile Now"; and a very pretty "Perfect Day" by the British Electric Foundation.

Side 1: JIMMY CASTOR BUNCH/Wild Side, ED ROBICHAUD/R&Roll, CARS/ 'Come Back Down,' DOWNLINERS SECT/Why Don't You Smile Now, SLITS/No More Rock & Roll For You (some Ray in here), SCOOTERS/ Hygene (French SJane), FRED SMALL/Walk On The Supply Side (Wild Side parody), YARDBIRDS/Waiting, REAL KIDS/Do The Boob, REALLY RED/Nico, HALF JAPANESE/My Generation-R & Roll, Euro. Son, KENNE HIGHLAND/ I'm Waiting For Maureen Tucker, All Pep Lester's Parties, GIZMOS/I'm A Regular Dude, KIDS/Foggy, NRBQ/WL.

Side 2: GENYA RAVAN/Darling I Need You, GREAT IMPOSTERS/Waiting, JOHN THE POSTMAN/Louie Louie-SRay, CRAWDADDYS/Why Don't You Smile Now, NURSES/I Heard Her, BIG BALLS AND THE GREAT WHITE IDIOT/ WL, PETER LAUGHNER/Pale, JOHN JACOBS, JINGLEHEIMER & SCHMIDT/Wild Side parody, ART/Ugly People With Fancy Hairdos, FEELIES/Run, BLUE SWEDE/R & Roll, PATTI SMITH GROUP/Pale-Louie, Louie, BRITISH ELECTRIC FOUNDATION/Perfect Day, DAVID BOWIE/WL.

Selected Bibliography

Books

Bangs, Lester. 1988. *Psychotic Reactions and Carburetor Dung.* New York: Vintage Books.

Bockris, Victor, and Gerard Malanga. 1983. *Uptight: The Velvet Underground Story.* London: Omnibus Press.

Bockris, Victor. 1994. *Transformer: The Lou Reed Story.* New York: Simon and Schuster.

Burroughs, William. 1966. *Naked Lunch.* New York: Grove Press. ©1959.

Clapton, Diana. 1987. *Lou Reed & the Velvet Underground.* London: Bobcat Books.

Doggett, Peter. 1992. *Growing Up in Public.* New York: Omnibus Press.

Heylin, Clinton. 1993. *From the Velvets to the Voidoids: A Pre-Punk History for a Post-Punk World.* New York: Penguin.

Kostek, M.C. 1992. *The Velvet Underground Handbook.* London: Black Spring Press.

Reed, Lou. 1982. *Velvet Underground: Lyrics.* Milan: Arcana Editrice.

Schwartz, Delmore. 1967. *Summer Knowledge: Selected Poems (1938–1958).* New York: New Directions.

———. 1978. *In Dreams Begin Responsibilities and Other Stories.* New York: New Directions.

Selby Jr., Hubert. 1957. *Last Exit to Brooklyn.* New York: Grove Press.

Thompson, Dave. 1989. *Beyond the Velvet Underground*. London: Omnibus Press.

Trevena, Nigel. 1973. *Lou Reed and the Velvets*. London: Bantam Books.

Violet, Ultra. 1988. *Famous for 15 Minutes: My Years with Andy Warhol*. San Diego: Harcourt, Brace, Jovanovich.

Warhol, Andy, and Pat Hackett. 1980. *Popism: The Warhol 60s*. San Diego: Harcourt, Brace, Jovanovich.

West, Mike. 1982. *The Velvet Underground and Lou Reed*. Manchester, U.K.: Babylon Books.

Witts, Richard. 1993. *Nico: The Life and Lies of an Icon*. London: Virgin Books.

Magazines

Cohen, Scott. "Velvet Madman." *Spin* (May 1990). Re Cale.

Coley, Byron. Interview with Maureen Tucker. *New York Rocker*, 30.

Fevret, Christian. Interviews with Reed, Cale, Tucker, Morrison. *New Musical Express* (October 6–13, 1990).

Flanagan, Bill. "White Light/White Heat." *Musician* (April 1989). Re Reed and Cale.

———. "Bonfire of the Strawmen." *Musician* (April 1989). Re Reed

Harron, Mary. "The Lost History of the Velvet Underground: An Interview with Sterling Morrison." *New Musical Express* (April 25, 1981).

———. Interview with Cale. *Punk*, 11.

Holdship, Bill. "'Some kinda love . . .' 20 Years of the Velvet Underground." *Creem* (November 1987). Includes interviews with Reed, Cale (Roy Trakin), Nico, LaMonte Young (John Neilson), Morrison, Tucker, Yule (Thomas Anderson).

Isler, Scott. "Bloodied but Unbowed." *Musician* (April 1989). Re Cale.

Kaye, Lennie. "The Velvet Underground." *Zigzag*, 16.

Kemp, Mark. "Fifteen Minutes with You." *Option* (July–August 1990). Re Cale and Reed.

Kostek, M.C. *What Goes On*, 1–5. Velvet Underground fanzine.

Lake, Steve. "Velvet Underground: Opening Doors of Perception." *Melody Maker* (May 25, 1974).

Mercuri, Sal. *The Velvet Underground*, vols. 1–5.

Pearlman, Sandy. "Velvet Underground." *Crawdaddy!* (June 1968).

Reed, Lou. "Interview with Václav Havel." *Musician* (October 1990).

———. "From the Bandstand." *Aspen Magazine* 1 (no. 3).

Savage, Jon. "Waiting for My Band." *Village Voice* (July 27, 1993).

Williams, Richard. "It's a Shame that Nobody Listens." *Melody Maker* (October 25, 1969).

Contributors' Notes

Lester Bangs was one of the most prolific and idiosyncratic of rock critics. He wrote of himself: "In the five years he worked (at *Creem* 1971–76) as head staff writer and in various editorial capacities, he defined a style of critical-journalism based on the sound and language of rock 'n' roll which ended up influencing a whole generation of younger writers and perhaps musicians as well." A representative collection of his essays has been published under the title *Psychotic Reactions and Carburetor Dung*.

Tim Bradstock is a Velvet Underground collector from New Zealand.

Chris Carter lives in London. He is still at work on his magnum opus, a twenty-seven-page poem about the Velvet Underground entitled "Utopia/Distopia."

David Fricke is a senior editor at *Rolling Stone* and author of the historical essay included with the Polydor box set *The Velvet Underground: Peel Slowly and See*.

Donna Gaines is a sociologist, journalist, and the author of *Teenage Wasteland: Suburbia's Dead End Kids*. She teaches sociology at Barnard College of Columbia University and writes for the *Village Voice, Spin, Rolling Stone,* and *Newsday*. Dr. Gaines lives and works in New York City.

Ignacio Julià was born in Barcelona, Spain, on Andy Warhol's birthday, August 6, 1956. He saw his writing published for the first time in 1977 in underground magazines. In 1985 he founded Spain's foremost all–rock and roll magazine, *Ruta 66*, which is still printed monthly. He's also written books (in Spanish) on Bruce Springsteen, Neil Young, and John Lennon, as well as the authorized Sonic Youth biography *I Dreamed of Noise* (in English). He lives in Barcelona with his wife, Lola, and two daughters.

M.C. Kostek saw the Velvets in 1968 and was inspired enough to help Phil Milstein start the Velvet Underground Appreciation Society in Amherst, Massachusetts, in 1977. M.C. took over the VUAS in 1983 when Phil retired and runs it out of his Stuart, Florida, bungalow. He publishes the VU fanzine *What Goes On* and has written a discography, *The Velvet Underground Handbook*.

Wayne McGuire was an aspiring visionary essayist in the Boston area in 1968 when he decided to send an unsolicited article to *Crawdaddy!* to set them straight on the Velvet Underground, the Boston sound, and the meaning of life.

Sal Mercuri's Fierce Pup Productions published *The Velvet Underground* fanzine, volumes one through five, and *'69 on the Road: A Velvet Underground Photo-Essay by Doug Yule*.

Katherine Messer played guitar in and served as musical director for Maureen Tucker's band from 1985 to 1988, effectively resuscitating Tucker's musical career. She lives in Austin and writes for the *Austin Chronicle*.

Philip Milstein was a cofounder of the Velvet Underground Appreciation Society and continues his association in the capacity of "editor demeritus" of *What Goes On*. He writes for the Beastie Boys fanzine *Grand Royal*.

Jeff Schwartz is a doctoral candidate in American culture studies at Bowling Green State University and is a professional musician. His writing has appeared in *Popular Music, Postmodern Culture,* and *Transformations,* and his web page is at http://www.bgsu.edu/~jeffs/main.html. Projects in preparation include a biography of Albert Ayler and a dissertation on Amiri Baraka, Archie Shepp, free jazz, and Black nationalism.

Paul Williams founded the first U.S. rock and roll magazine, *Crawdaddy!,* in February 1966 at the age of seventeen. He has gone on to write more than twenty books, including *Bob Dylan, Performing Artist* Vols. I and II, *Only Apparently Real: The World of Philip K. Dick,* and *Rock and Roll: The 100 Best Singles*. In 1993 he revived *Crawdaddy!* as a quarterly newsletter for music lovers who want to discuss the stuff outside the influence of the music business (write Box 231155, Encinitas, CA 92023 for info on the new *Crawdaddy!*).

Ellen Willis directs the cultural reporting and criticism concentration in the Department of Journalism at New York University. She is the author of two collections of cultural and political criticism, *Beginning to See the Light: Sex, Hope and Rock & Roll* and *No More Nice Girls:*

Countercultural Essays, and has been a columnist and longtime contributor to the *Village Voice.* Her articles have appeared in such publications as *The New Yorker,* the *Nation,* the *New York Times Book Review, Mirabella,* and *Dissent.*

Permissions

"Syndromes Pop at Delmonico's," by Grace Glueck, from the *New York Times*, January 14, 1966. Copyright © 1966 by the New York Times Co. Reprinted by permission of the New York Times Co.

"Mother's Mod Lament: 'Not the Wedding We Had Planned,'" by Linda LaMarre, from *The Detroit News*, November 21, 1966. Reprinted by permission of the Detroit News.

"Beginning to See the Dark," by M.C. Kostek, from *What Goes On* #1 (1978). Reprinted by permission.

"Notes from the Velvet Underground," by Philip Milstein, from *What Goes On* #3 (1983). Reprinted by permission of M.C. Kostek.

"I'm Beginning to See the Light," by Paul Williams. Copyright © 1969 by Paul Williams; first published in *Planet*, May 15, 1969. Reprinted by permission of Paul Williams.

"Velvet Underground Appreciation Society, Peking Languages Institute Chapter," by Tim Bradstock, from *What Goes On* #3 (1983). Reprinted by permission of M.C. Kostek.

"The Boston Sound/The Velvet Underground and Mel Lyman," by Wayne McGuire, copyright © 1968 by Crawdaddy Magazine Inc. (First published in *Crawdaddy!* August 1968.) Reprinted by permission of Paul Williams.

"Angus MacLise and the Origin of the Velvet Underground," by Jim Condon, from *What Goes On* #3 (1983). Reprinted by permission of M.C. Kostek.

Index